MrExcel LIBRARY

PowerPivot for the Data Analyst: Microsoft® Excel 2010

Bill Jelen

800 East 96th Street,
Indianapolis, Indiana 46240
USA

Contents at a Glance

PowerPivot for the Data Analyst: Microsoft® Excel 2010

Library of Congress Cataloging-in-Publication Data

Jelen, Bill.
  PowerPivot for the data analyst : Microsoft Excel 2010 / Bill Jelen.
      p. cm.
  Includes index.
  ISBN-13: 978-0-7897-4315-2
  ISBN-10: 0-7897-4315-9
  1. Microsoft Excel (Computer file) 2. Business intelligence—Computer programs. 3. Business—Computer programs. I. Title.
  HF5548.4.M523J4544 2010
  005.54—dc22

                                                                  2010017037

ISBN-13: 978-0-7897-4315-2
ISBN-10: 0-7897-4315-9

Printed in the United States of America

First Printing: May 2010

Trademarks

Warning and Disclaimer

Bulk Sales

Que Publishing offers excellent discounts on this book when ordered in quantity for bulk purchases or special sales. For more information, please contact

U.S. Corporate and Government Sales
1-800-382-3419
corpsales@pearsontechgroup.com

For sales outside of the United States, please contact

International Sales
1-317-428-3341
international@pearsontechgroup.com

Associate Publisher
Greg Wiegand

Aquistions Editor
Loretta Yates

Development Editor
Sondra Scott

Technical Editor
Bob Umlas

Managing Editor
Sandra Schroeder

Project Editor
Mandie Frank

Copy Editor
Keith Cline

Indexer
Tim Wright

Proofreader
Leslie Joseph

Production
Jake McFarland

Designer
Anne Jones

Contents

Dedication

To Mark Hauser, for trusting me to be a data analyst. We would have thought we were in heaven if we had PowerPivot way back then.

About the Author

Bill Jelen, Excel MVP and the host of MrExcel.com, has been using spreadsheets since 1985, and he launched the MrExcel.com website in 1998. Bill was a regular guest on Call for Help with Leo Laporte and has produced more than 1,200 episodes of his daily video podcast, Learn Excel from MrExcel. He is the author of 30 books about Microsoft Excel and writes the monthly Excel column for *Strategic Finance* magazine. You will most frequently find Bill taking his show on the road, doing half-day Power Excel seminars wherever he can find a room full of accountants or Excellers. Before founding MrExcel.com, Jelen spent 12 years in the trenches working as a financial analyst for finance, marketing, accounting, and operations departments of a $500 million public company. He lives near Akron, Ohio, with his wife, Mary, Ellen and his sons, Josh and Zeke.

Acknowledgments

Rob Collie moved to Cleveland, Ohio, in 2009. Rob is one of the project managers on the PowerPivot team. If you've ever lived in Cleveland, you understand the words "snow belt" and "lake effect snow." Sitting on the southern coast of Lake Erie, Cleveland is one of five places in the world to experience lake effect snow. There is a section of Cleveland, on the leeward side of Lake Erie where the snowfall triples. As well as Clevelanders understand Mr. Jingaling, we've lived with the words "expect 2 inches of snow overnight, 8 inches in the snow belt." Of course, Rob relocated to the heart of the snow belt and is probably cursing Cleveland as I write this. However, for me, being the guy writing the first book about PowerPivot, having Rob, one of the most knowledgeable guys about PowerPivot, move into practically my backyard was an amazing coincidence. Thanks to Rob for many lunches where he talked about the vision and the reasoning behind PowerPivot. Did I mention Rob spent several years as a project manager on the Excel team? When my head was spinning with DAX formulas, we could always go back to the comfortable territory of why Excel does something bizarre. Thanks to Rob and Jocelyn for happening to end up in Cleveland during the writing of this book.

Thanks to David Gainer for laying the groundwork for Excel 2010 and for sending that e-mail saying that Rob was moving to Cleveland.

On the SQL Server Analysis team, Donald Farmer, Howie Dickerman, and Amir Netz have been tremendously helpful.

Thanks to Dan Bricklin and Bob Frankston for inventing the computer spreadsheet. Thanks to Mitch Kapor for Lotus 1-2-3.

Here are a few new names to thank: Bob Frankston's brother, Charles Frankston, went to work for another Cambridge start-up. In 1985, Charles, along with Rob Firmin, Stan Kugell, Christopher Herot, Arye Gittleman, John Levine, Louise Cousins, and Peter Pathe, developed some software called Javelin. In 1985, Javelin and Microsoft Excel 1.0 were nominated for InfoWorld's Product of the Year. In a close battle, Javelin won. The concepts debuted in Javelin went on to be used in Lotus Improv and went on to be used in Excel pivot tables. Now—the Microsoft Excel team has expanded pivot tables way beyond the capabilities of Javelin and Improv. But, as the PowerPivot team takes Pivot Tables to unimaginable heights, the original Javelin team deserves a tip o' the cap.

Like everyone else who uses computers to make a living, I owe a debt of gratitude to these three pioneers.

I've learned that when writing five books, there is not much time for anything else. Thanks to Tracy Syrstad, Barb Jelen, Schar Oswald, and Scott Pierson for keeping MrExcel running while I wrote. As always, thanks to the hundreds of people answering 30,000 Excel questions a year at the MrExcel message board. Thanks to Wei Jiang and Jake Hildebrand for their programming expertise.

At Pearson, Loretta Yates is an awesome acquisitions editor. If you have ever written a book for any other publisher, you are missing out by not working with Loretta Yates. Bob Umlas is the smartest Excel guy that I know, and I am thrilled to have him as the technical editor for this book.

Finally, thanks to Josh Jelen, Zeke Jelen, and Mary Ellen Jelen. In particular, it was Mary Ellen who realized that things had to change if I were going to get the books done on time.

We Want to Hear from You!

As the reader of this book, you are our most important critic and commentator. We value your opinion and want to know what we're doing right, what we could do better, what areas you'd like to see us publish in, and any other words of wisdom you're willing to pass our way.

As an associate publisher for Que Publishing, I welcome your comments. You can email or write me directly to let me know what you did or didn't like about this book—as well as what we can do to make our books better.

Please note that I cannot help you with technical problems related to the topic of this book. We do have a User Services group, however, where I will forward specific technical questions related to the book.

When you write, please be sure to include this book's title and author as well as your name, email address, and phone number. I will carefully review your comments and share them with the author and editors who worked on the book.

Email:
feedback@quepublishing.com

Mail.
Greg Wiegand
Associate Publisher
Que Publishing
800 East 96th Street
Indianapolis, IN 46240 USA

Reader Services

Visit our website and register this book at www.informit.com/title/9780789743152 for convenient access to any updates, downloads, or errata that might be available for this book.

Introduction

I am a PowerPivot FanBoy.

I remember the exact moment that this happened. Once a year, Microsoft invites all of their MVPs to Redmond, Washington, for the MVP Summit. The event consists of two days of executive keynotes and two useful days spent with the project managers of your individual technology. I always go to the MVP Summit, looking forward to spending time with the Excel project managers. During those two days, you go from meeting to meeting on the Redmond campus, hearing about various plans for the next version of Excel.

On Wednesday of the 2009 Summit, the noon meeting was not in the usual building 33 that houses the Excel team. As I walked into that room in another building, I noticed something strange. The left side of the room was filled with people I knew: the Excel MVPs. They are people whom you know of if you read Excel books or if you've asked a few questions at the MrExcel.com message board: Curt Frye, Bob Umlas, Richard Schollar, Smitty, Greg Truby. The right side of the room was full of a bunch of people whom I had never seen before. They were eyeing us suspiciously, and we were wondering what the heck they were doing in our meeting.

The speaker that day was Donald Farmer. Scottish. Hair longer than JWalk's. He comes walking in, carrying a desktop PC under his arm. Read that again. He came walking in with a desktop PC. Who shows up to a presentation carrying a desktop PC? Donald set up the PC in the front of the room, plugged it into the projector, and proceeded to start a demo about something called Project Gemini.

"There's Row 20 Million"

Donald Farmer had carried in a 64-bit windows machine with 8GB of RAM. By Christmas of 2009, you could walk into Best Buy and buy such a machine, but I had never seen a machine with more than 3GB of RAM in early 2009.

Donald sets up a scenario. He had two data sets:

- Data set 1 was every DVD rental transaction at a fictitious chain of video stores.
- Data set 2 was box office data that he had downloaded from the Internet.

Donald fires up something that looks basically like Excel and shows us data set 1. He grabs the vertical scrollbar on the right side of the data and starts to scroll. Like a hot knife through butter, the PC responded snappily and Donald says, "There's row 20 million."

It literally did not sink in with me.

Donald continued...

"There's row 40 million."

"There's row 60 million."

"There's row 100 million."

I am thinking to myself that it is 2009 and seeing row 1 million in Excel was exciting at the 2006 Summit, but really why is this guy wasting our time showing us that Excel now has a million rows?

Wait. Did. He. Just. Say. 100. Million? I looked at the screen and tried to focus on how many digits were in the row count at the bottom of the screen.

Donald went on to sort 100 million rows. He used the AutoFilter drop-downs to filter 100 million rows.

Here is a guy who carried in a desktop PC and had a 100 million row data set in something that looked like Excel. I decided I better close my Outlook and pay attention.

"The PivotTable Field List Has Fields from Both Tables"

Donald proceeds to build a pivot table from the 100 million rows of data. This seems only natural. What else would you do with 100 million rows of data? Just about any time that I get a data set, my first inclination is to build a pivot table, so making a pivot table makes perfect sense.

There is something weird with the pivot table field list, however. It is listing fields from both table 1 and table 2. Donald is only using data from table 1, though. He adds one of the new slicer filters that we had just learned about the day before.

Then, Donald suggested that we compare rentals by genre with box office receipts by genre.

For all of the Excel people reading this book, a very easy quiz. To mash up the data from Sheet1 with Sheet2 what tried and true method will you have to use?

a. `=VLOOKUP()` functions

b. `=INDEX()` functions

c. Cut and paste

d. `=VABRACADABRA()` function, preferably while waving a magic wand

Of course, the answer is a. A nice set of VLOOKUPs will get the data from one sheet onto another sheet. Although, I cringed, 100 million VLOOKUPs are going to take a long time.

Except Donald didn't knock out a VLOOKUP function.

All he did was clicked a field from table 2 in the pivot table field list. This was an early version of the product and a ToolTip popped up saying "We've inferred a relationship between table 1 and table 2". The box office data was now summarized in the same pivot table as the DVD rental information.

> **NOTE** According to Rob Collie, "stuff that looks good in a demo may not actually work well when real people try to use the product." Microsoft ended up backing off from the automatic relationship detection in favor of giving people some control over setting up a relationship. It is still very easy to do, easier than setting up a VLOOKUP.

Now, I Love VLOOKUPs

To me, there are two kinds of people in the world.

- People who can do a VLOOKUP with their eyes closed
- Everyone else

If you've happened to catch one of my live Power Excel seminars, I usually talk about how I used to be a manager of financial analysis. When we needed to hire financial analysts, the person in Human Resources would ask about what requirements I wanted on the job posting notice. I usually had a single requirement: "Can do VLOOKUPs in their sleep." As long as someone could do VLOOKUPs, everything else would fall into place.

I don't want to sound harsh, but it comes down to this; if you can do VLOOKUPs, you are employable. If you can't do VLOOKUPs, well, you might be employable, just not by *me*.

When Donald Farmer clicked a box next to field from Sheet 2 and Excel produced a pivot table from two worksheets without having anyone enter a VLOOKUP function, that was a game-changer.

Suddenly, hundreds of millions of people who (a) know how to use a mouse and (b) don't know how to do a VLOOKUP are suddenly able to perform jaw-dropping business intelligence analyses. They all might actually be employable, by *me*.

"How Much Will This Cost? Well, the Client Is Free"

It was crazy talk.

Microsoft was demonstrating the greatest invention in a decade and they were giving it away for free.

It wasn't unprecedented. Lotus used to sell Lotus Improv for $199, and Microsoft borrowed all of that technology and gave it away on the Excel data menu back in 1993. Of course, it would have been a blatant rip-off if they would have put "Improv" on Data menu in Excel 5, so they changed the name to something called a "pivot table."

Pivot tables were the greatest computing invention since VisiCalc, and Microsoft bundled that for free with their Excel product.

I was watching the greatest computing invention since pivot tables, and now Microsoft was planning on bundling it for free with Excel 2010.

This Book Was Pitched Eight Hours Later

Based on the two facts: (a) 100 million rows in Excel and (b) a pivot table from multiple worksheets without a VLOOKUP, I knew that I wanted to write a book about this new product. Loretta Yates from Que was in town for the MVP Summit, and I had tentative approval for this new book less than eight hours after I saw the product.

There Could Be Five Titles for This Book

Any one of these mega-benefits would make PowerPivot worthy of a book:

■ *100 Million Rows: Miracle Product Allows Unlimited Rows in Microsoft Excel!*

■ *VLOOKUPs Shrugged: Why You Don't Need VLOOKUPs Any More*

■ *ATOM & CSV: The Marriage of Disparate Data*

■ *L.Y. Actuals & C.Y. Budget: How Named Sets Enabled the Obvious But Previously Impossible Pivot Table Report*

■ *Calculated Fields: Designed by an Intern? How DAX is Empowering Real Calculations in Pivot Tables*

This sixth title might not appeal to the Excel audience, but would make a great whitepaper:

■ *Store It Columnwise, Stupid! How to achieve world-class data compression*

At that first meeting with Donald Farmer, only the first two points really sunk in with me. (1) They had busted through the one million row limit in Excel. (2) You could join Sheet1 and Sheet2 without VLOOKUP.

There are other benefits to PowerPivot that I did not begin to understand until I was working on these books, including the following:

- PowerPivot can consume data from many places and present them all in the same workbook. You can have low-tech data like flat text files. You can have data coming from SQL Server. You can have data from Excel. Data from Access. RSS feeds.

- All pivot tables are lousy at handling asymmetric reports. If you try to show last year's sales and this year's budget in the same pivot report, you are going to have to endure having last year's budget and this year's actuals in the report, too. This means you will manually be hiding some columns and replacing the built-in total column with your own column. The Excel team fixed this in Excel 2010, but only for people reporting from OLAP data sets. Here is the funny thing about PowerPivot: It makes regular Excel data into OLAP data sets. Saying that you want to use PowerPivot just to enable asymmetric reporting is like saying that you want to use a $100 million laser to heat up your coffee. It is a huge underutilization of a $100 million laser. But...the fact is that the laser will heat up coffee, and you've frankly been living without a microwave since 1993 when the first pivot table hit Excel. So, if you have a need to report last year's actuals next to this year's budget, well, PowerPivot is going to enable this for you.

- Calculated fields in pivot tables were always sort of quirky. They would work for simple things. When you see how the new DAX formula language enables you to do really powerful things with calculated measures in PowerPivot, you will realize that calculated fields can't hold a candle to these new calculations.

Any one of those benefits should be enough to get the Excel data analyst to want to upgrade to Excel 2010. Put all of the benefits into a single product, and price that product at the price of $Free and there will be a lot of Excel people who should be drooling.

Who *Are* Those Other People in the Room?

There are at least three audiences who are watching PowerPivot with great interest:

- **There is us. You know us:** You. Me. Excel people. We do everything in Excel. We think that Microsoft Word is a useless add-in for people who can't manage to use Edit, Fill, Justify. We are the front lines of the decision-making process.

- **There are SQL Server people:** They are the people who are sitting on top of 100 million rows of transactional data. They are the people who get us the nice and tidy one million row summaries of the transactional data. (Between you and me, if they embrace PowerPivot and just let us get to that 100 million rows of transactional data, we can actually run a few different iterations before we figure out what data we actually need.)

■ **There are SharePoint people:** SharePoint people keep talking about having "one version of the truth" and it is stored in SharePoint. The SharePoint people like PowerPivot because if you and I design a cool report in PowerPivot, we can publish it to SharePoint and that helps to justify why the company needs SharePoint.

I have to tell you, it is a little bit uncomfortable being in the same room with all these people because frankly, our relationship had been a little adversarial over the years.

PowerPivot is in a sweet spot between these three groups.

The SQL Server people will actually have less requests from the Excel people. Get us the data and we will slice and dice it.

The SQL Server people feel like they have more control because they get to make sure that the original link to the data is to data that they bless. Also, the relationships in PowerPivot help to make sure that the Excel people don't screw up the data.

The Excel people can iterate over various attempts at producing reports without having to go back to the SQL Server people in IT. It gets expensive buying a dozen chocolate Krispy Cream donuts every time you need a new report from the IT department.

For the Excel people, if the SharePoint people will host our reports, we've secretly offloaded the need to refresh the report every night because the SharePoint people can schedule a nightly refresh. That means that we can spend a week at the beach without having to dial in every morning to run the reports.

For the SharePoint people, you can see which reports are being accessed and by whom. Those Excel people create a boatload of reports and there are probably two or three that are actually used by the big important people in the company. With SharePoint, you can see which reports are actually getting traffic and thus know which reports you should (a) make sure don't go down, and (b) know which reports are good candidates for turning into other systems.

This Book Is For The Excel People

I have configured exactly one SharePoint server in my lifetime, and that was with a lot of hand holding from a write-up by Vidas Matelis on the Web. I've installed SQL Server three times, and only two of those installations were successful. (I still can't figure out what I did wrong with the third installation.)

If you are a SharePoint person or a SQL Server person, I don't have a clue about the things you are talking about. I know that you both have an interest in PowerPivot, and I hope that Rob Collie or someone writes a book for you. My goal is to get those Excel people up to speed with PowerPivot. I realize that the three groups of people can have a great symbiotic relationship with PowerPivot. I hope to deliver the Excel masses to your door, clamoring for access to your SQL Server data and your SharePoint servers.

How This Book Is Organized

I am writing this book for the Excel audience (the 500 million people who use Excel day in and day out). All but one chapter will be focused on using the PowerPivot client inside of Excel 2010.

The first two chapters gets PowerPivot installed and show you what is possible with PowerPivot.

Chapter 3 takes a look at the upsides and downsides to using PowerPivot.

Chapters 4 through 6 cover how to get your data into PowerPivot, how to define relationships, and how to work with data before it becomes a pivot table.

Chapters 7 through 9 deal with the process of creating and using pivot tables with PowerPivot.

Chapters 10 and 11 deal with the really powerful ways to use Data Analysis Expression (DAX) measures.

Chapters 12 and 13 cover how to format your PowerPivot reports.

Chapter 14 identifies the benefits of using the server version of PowerPivot.

The appendix offers a list of additional resources.

Conventions Used in This Book

The special conventions used throughout this book are designed to help you get the most from the book as well as Excel 2010.

Text Conventions

Different typefaces are used to convey various things throughout the book. They include those shown in Table I.1.

Table I.1	Typeface Conventions
Typeface	**Description**
Monospace	Screen messages and web addresses appear in monospace.
Italic	New terminology appears in this *italic*.
Bold	References to text you should type appear in **bold**.

Tab names on the Ribbon, dialog box names, and dialog box elements are capitalized in this book (for example, Add Formatting Rule dialog, Home tab).

In this book, key combinations are represented with a plus sign. If the action you need to take is to press the Ctrl key and the T key simultaneously, the text tells you to press Ctrl+T.

There were not many changes from Excel 97 to Excel 2000 to Excel 2002 to Excel 2003. Most people upgrading to Excel 2010 will be coming from one of these versions of Excel. I collectively refer to these versions as "Legacy versions of Excel."

Special Elements

Throughout this book, you'll find tips, notes, cautions, cross-references, and case studies. These elements provide a variety of information, ranging from warnings you shouldn't miss to ancillary information that will enrich your Excel experience but isn't required reading.

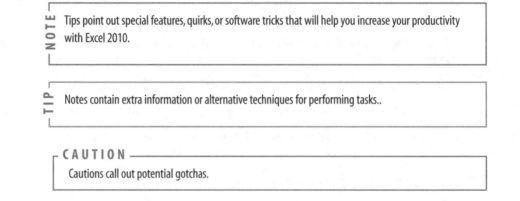

> **NOTE**
> Tips point out special features, quirks, or software tricks that will help you increase your productivity with Excel 2010.

> **TIP**
> Notes contain extra information or alternative techniques for performing tasks..

> ┌ **C A U T I O N** ──────────
> Cautions call out potential gotchas.

In most chapters, a YouTube video demo will be available for one topic.

Cross References

→ **See** Chapter 9, "Cool Tricks New with PowerPivot," for more information.

CASE STUDY: OTHER ELEMENTS

Case studies are set off in boxes such as this one:

Case studies walk you through the steps to complete a task.

Sidebars

Historical glimpses and other information that is not critical to your understanding appear as sidebars. I imagine that if the Cliff Claven character from *Cheers* knew a lot about Excel, these would be the kinds of things he would write.

Downloading and Installing PowerPivot

This chapter walks you through the installation of PowerPivot and introduces you to the various elements within PowerPivot.

System Requirements

To install PowerPivot, you need a Windows version of Excel 2010, in either the 32-bit or the 64-bit variety.

PowerPivot will not work with legacy versions of Excel. Microsoft embeds the PowerPivot database inside of the Microsoft Excel workbook. This required new application programming interfaces (APIs) that were built in to Excel 2010 and were not available in Excel 2007 or earlier. It seems unlikely that Microsoft would ever retrofit Excel 2007 to work with PowerPivot.

It is possible to install 32-bit Excel 2010 side by side with legacy versions of Excel. So, if you have some need to keep a legacy version of Excel, you can run Excel 2010 on the same machine.

PowerPivot has not been developed for Excel for the Macintosh. Currently, it is a Windows-only product.

32 Bit or 64 Bit?

Two client downloads are available for PowerPivot, a 32-bit version and a 64-bit version.

If you are not sure which version of Office you have, open Excel and go to File, Help. On the right side of the Excel backstage view, you will see a line that says: Version 14.0. If that line ends with (64 bit), = you have the 64-bit version of Office and you will need the 64-bit version of PowerPivot. Or, you can use RegEdit to check HKEY_LOCAL_MACHINE\Software\Microsoft\Office\14.0\

> **TIP**
>
> The download that you choose must match your version of Office 2010. Even if you have a 64-bit machine, you must match the version of PowerPivot with the version of Office.

Outlook. Look for a Registry key called Bitness. A value of x86 indicates that you have 32-bit Office installed. x64 indicates that you have 64-bit Office installed.

If you have not yet purchased Office 2010, you need to evaluate the advantages and disadvantages of the 64-bit version of Office:

Table 1.1   Advantages and Disadvantages of 64-bit Office Find Assistant

Advantage	Disadvantage
64-bit versions of Office can handle larger size Excel files. The 32-bit office can only load 2GB of Excel data into memory.	Many Excel add-ins are written as 32-bit applications. Any ActiveX controls or COM Add-ins that were written for the 32-bit environment will not work in the 64-bit environment. You will have to obtain new controls and hope that the add-in vendor will eventually provide support for 64-bit applications. As an example, the Easy-XL from MrExcel add-in is a 32-bit COM add-in. The plan is to start offering support for a 64-bit edition by mid-2011. There is not support for reading from Access databases using the Jet database engine, so VBA code using Jet to connect will have to be rewritten for ACE.
Enhanced security protection through Hardware Data Execution Prevention.	64-bit Office can not co-exist with any prior versions of Excel. You will have to uninstall all previous versions of Office and Office Viewers.
	64-bit Windows does not offer support for MMX graphics. This might mean that some graphics-intensive operations might run slower on 64 bit.
	VBA macros that made use of the Windows API via a `Declare` statement must be rewritten to be compatible with 64-bit Office. This is often not a huge deal, but it requires the person who wrote the VBA to still be around to make the change. Often, a series of VBA macros are written by one employee, and then they continue use after the employee leaves the company.
	You cannot mix 32-bit and 64-bit Office on the same computer. Because there was not a 64-bit version of Office 2007, if you hope to have Office 2010 run side by side with Office 2007, then you are forced to go with the 32-bit installation. It is possible to run 32-bit Office on a 64-bit machine. This is called Windows 32 on Windows 64 mode (WOW64). If you are upgrading an old version of Office, you will be forced into 32-bit mode.

If you have any macros or make use of any add-ins, you should seriously consider the 32-bit installation. Microsoft is recommending that enterprise editions of Office get installed as 32-bit.

> **CAUTION**
>
> If you insert the Office 2010 retail DVD in your computer and do an install from the root directory, they will default to 32-bit. If you want to get the 64-bit version of Office 2010, you must unload every shred of 32-bit Office, including any viewers and compatibility packs and then install from the x64 folder on the DVD.

Not Excel Starter Edition

If you bought a new PC, there is a good chance that it came with Word Starter Edition and Excel Starter Edition. I apologize for Microsoft's shortsightedness in naming their products, but this is not Excel. It is a new name for Microsoft Works. It works fine for small spreadsheets, but it does not support PowerPivot.

Not Excel Web Apps

Although the new Excel Web App is really cool and can render a view of a workbook with PowerPivot data stored in it, you cannot edit this workbook in Excel Web Apps. The PowerPivot database is stored inside the workbook as a blob (binary large object), and the Excel Web App "sees" this database as an external database.

Installing PowerPivot

PowerPivot is not on the Office DVD. You have to download PowerPivot from http://www.powerpivot.com.

Make sure that all of your Office programs are closed, and then run the installer. In a few minutes, the PowerPivot install will finish.

When you first launch Microsoft Excel 2010, a brief notice will display as Microsoft registers the PowerPivot add-in. After that first time, Excel should silently load PowerPivot and you won't notice any delay when launching Excel.

The Many PowerPivot Tabs

In the Excel 2010 Ribbon, you will see one PowerPivot tab to the right of the View tab. The PowerPivot tab is shown in Figures 1.1 and 1.2.

The PowerPivot tab that appears in the Excel Ribbon contains an odd mix of icons. Some of these icons are duplicated in the PowerPivot application. A few of the icons make sense here:

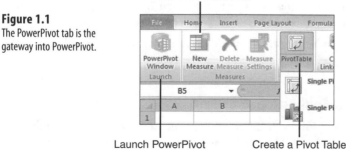

Figure 1.1
The PowerPivot tab is the gateway into PowerPivot.

Build DAX Measures

Launch PowerPivot   Create a Pivot Table

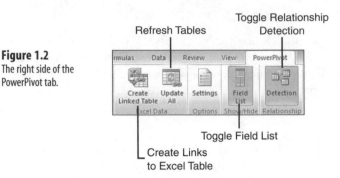

Figure 1.2
The right side of the
PowerPivot tab.

- **PowerPivot Window:** Use this icon to actually get to the PowerPivot grid.
- **New Measures:** After you have a pivot table, you can use the Data Analysis Expression (DAX) formula language to create a new calculated field. In PowerPivot, these calculated fields are called *measures*, and they run circles around regular calculated fields.

  → **See** Chapter 10, "Using DAX for Aggregate Functions" and Chapter 11, "Using DAX for Date Magic," for details on creating DAX measures.

- **Create Linked Table:** There are two ways to get Excel data into PowerPivot. One way is copy and paste, and the paste portion of that is handled in the PowerPivot application. The other way is linking to a real Excel table, and it makes sense that you would need this icon in Excel.

  → For information on linking to an Excel table, **see** Chapter 4, "Getting Your Data into PowerPivot."

- **Toggle Field List:** That PowerPivot Field List is not really the PivotTable Field List. The PowerPivot team hides the online analytical processing (OLAP) version of the Field List and presents a more-friendly PowerPivot Field List. You can toggle the real PivotTable Field List back on using the Field List icon on the PivotTable Tools Options tab. Figure 1.3 shows the two field lists side by side. You can see that the PowerPivot Field List offers a more intelligent way to define slicers. However, it is missing the Defer Layout Update button and the drop-down to rearrange the fields and drop zones. You will also see that the PivotTable Field List on the right is a bizarre OLAP version of the PivotTable Field List.
- **Detection:** This icon toggles on or off automatic detection of relationships between tables.

Ribbon Tabs in the PowerPivot Application

When you click the PowerPivot Window icon on the left side of the PowerPivot Ribbon, you are in the PowerPivot application. This application has four ribbon tabs and a tiny Quick Access toolbar.

- **File tab:** Offers Save, Save As, Publish, and Close

Figure 1.3
The PowerPivot Field List is a fake version of the PivotTable Field List.

Rearrange dropdown

- **Home tab:** Offers tools for getting data into PowerPivot, tools for creating a pivot table, and then tools for formatting, sorting, and filtering data in the PowerPivot grid
- **Design tab:** Offers tools for managing relationships
- **Linked Table tab:** Offers tools for managing the links back to your Excel workbook
- **Quick Access toolbar:** Offers an icon to return to Excel and an icon for saving the workbook

Using the File Tab

Everything on the File tab will take you back to Excel. Using Save As will return to the Excel application and launch the Save As dialog. Using Publish will attempt to republish the workbook to either SharePoint or your Windows Live SkyDrive. Using Close will return to Microsoft Excel.

Figure 1.4 shows the File tab.

Figure 1.4
This short file tab mostly leads back to Excel.

Using the Home Tab

The left side of the Home tab is all about getting data into PowerPivot as shown in Figure 1.5. You can paste data from the Clipboard either as a new table, to append to a table, or to replace an existing table. You can also import external data from a database, from a SharePoint report, from an ATOM feed, or from a text file.

→ Read more about each method in Chapter 4.

Figure 1.5
The left side of the Home tab gets your data into PowerPivot.

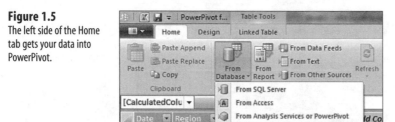

As shown in Figure 1.6, the right side of the Home tab deals with looking at your data in the PowerPivot window.

> **NOTE** I really don't know why these tools are here. The filters that you apply here do not carry through to the pivot table. I am not sure why anyone would really be formatting your data in the PowerPivot window. The whole point of PowerPivot is to make pivot tables. There isn't anyway to actually print this data from PowerPivot, so it seems useless to have ways to format it.

→ **See** Chapter 6, "Using Data Sheet View," for information on the data grid and the PowerPivot window. Chapter 6 also touches on these tools briefly before talking about adding calculated columns.

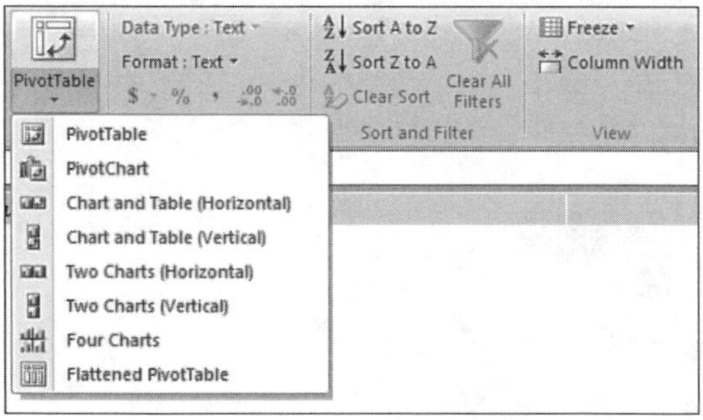

Figure 1.6
The right side of the PowerPivot Home tab offers tools for working with your data in the PowerPivot window.

Using the Design Tab

The Design tab in PowerPivot allows you to add new columns and create relationships between tables. Well, you can actually add new columns just by clicking in the Add Column column in the grid. But, if you need to add a column to the left of an existing column, the Add Column icon will let you do that. (Figure 1.7)

→ To read more about creating relationships, **see** Chapter 5, "Creating and Managing Relationships." To read more about creating columns, **see** Chapter 6, "Using Data Sheet View."

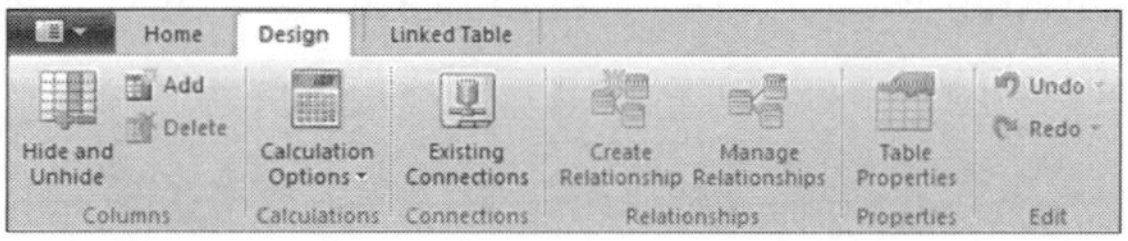

Figure 1.7
The Design tab allows you to add columns and create relationships between tables.

Using the Linked Table Tab

This tab is available only when you have linked an Excel table to PowerPivot. (Figure 1.8) You can use these icons to refresh the link to the table and control if the update mode is automatic or manual.

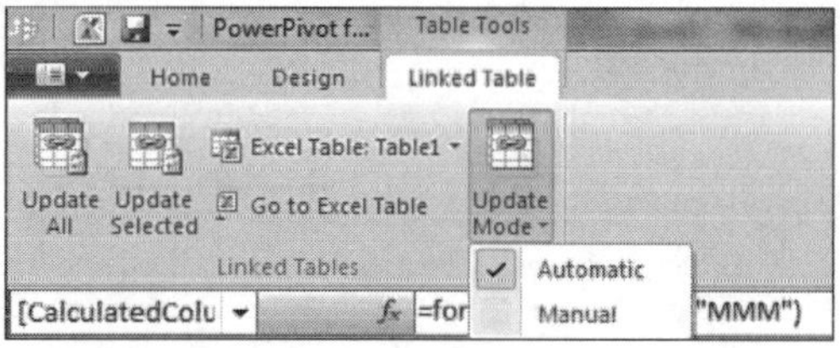

Figure 1.8
The Linked Table tab offers a way to refresh linked Excel tables.

Using the Quick Access Toolbar

There is not a lot of customization available on the Quick Access toolbar. If you open the drop-down at the right side of the toolbar, you can choose to show or hide two icons, show the toolbar below the ribbon, or choose to minimize the ribbon (see Figure 1.9).

Figure 1.9
The Quick Access toolbar offers only two icons.

Uninstalling PowerPivot

You actually have many choices if you need to get rid of PowerPivot:

- If you want to free up room in the ribbon, you can hide the tab. Use File, Options, Customize Ribbon. Clear PowerPivot from the right list box.

- To temporarily disable PowerPivot, go to File, Options, Add-Ins. At the bottom of the Excel Options dialog, select Com Add-Ins from the Manage drop-down and click Go. You can then clear the PowerPivot for Excel check box and click OK.

- To completely uninstall PowerPivot, close Office and use the Programs and Features icon in the Control Panel.

> **NOTE** The official name of PowerPivot is Microsoft SQL Server PowerPivot for Excel, so look for the item in the "M" section of installed programs.

Next Steps

In Chapter 2, you create your first PowerPivot pivot table.

The Promise of PowerPivot

This chapter walks you through one process of building a PowerPivot report. You will learn how simple it is to merge data from two sources in a single PowerPivot pivot table.

You can download these data sets from http://www. MrExcel.com/powerpivotbookdata.html.

Before trying these steps in this chapter, make sure that you have installed the PowerPivot client in Excel 2010 as described in Chapter 1, "Downloading and Installing PowerPivot."

Preparing Your Data for PowerPivot

If you are using your own data in PowerPivot, you need to ensure that your data is formatted appropriately. PowerPivot can deal with many different types of data. But unfortunately, people and software vendors do a lot of weird stuff with their data.

One of my favorite large data sets comes from a cash register vendor. They produce these large 1.8 million row data sets as flat text files and send them to my client every day.

In Figure 2.1, you can see the top of the data set. Row 1 contains the words "Run for:" and the date. Row 2 is blank. Row 3 has headings. Row 4 has underscores. Seriously? Underscores? Who are those really for?

PowerPivot cannot deal with three of those first four rows. PowerPivot can deal with the field headings, but the Run For, the blank row, and the underscores have to go. This either means a request sent to the software vendor or a daily trip through Notepad to delete those rows.

If you want PowerPivot to treat a column as a date column, then 100% of the values in that column

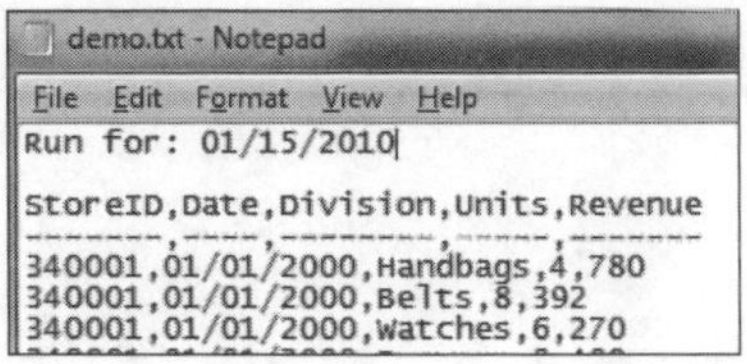

Figure 2.1
PowerPivot has no problem with 1.8 million rows, but it can't deal with the extra rows at the top.

```
demo.txt - Notepad
File  Edit  Format  View  Help
Run for: 01/15/2010

StoreID,Date,Division,Units,Revenue
-------,----,--------,-----,-------
340001,01/01/2000,Handbags,4,780
340001,01/01/2000,Belts,8,392
340001,01/01/2000,Watches,6,270
```

have to be dates. This same vendor loves to use dates of **/**/**** for new items that are not yet in inventory.

The point is that any date is going to have strange characteristics that you will have to deal with. Work the IT department or your vendor to get the data cleaned up for PowerPivot.

In Figure 2.2, removing three headings solves the problem.

Figure 2.2
One row of headings, followed by data records.

```
demo.txt - Notepad
File  Edit  Format  View  Help
StoreID,Date,Division,Units,Revenue
340001,01/01/2000,Handbags,4,780
340001,01/01/2000,Belts,8,392
340001,01/01/2000,Watches,6,270
340001,01/01/2000,Eyewear,8,400
```

If your data is in Excel, you want to follow the same format. One row of headings followed by data rows. No blank columns. No blank rows. Make sure that any date columns are 100% filled with dates.

In the text file, there is only a store number. It would be nice to add store name, region, and so on. In Figure 2.3, a small 150-row data set provides information about each store.

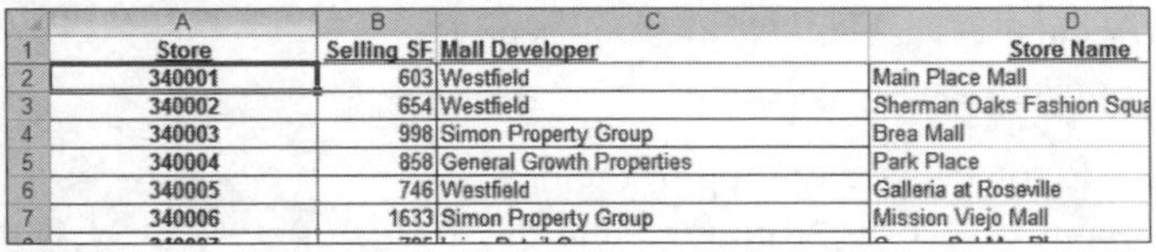

Figure 2.3
Identifying information for each store.

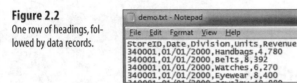

	A	B	C	D
1	Store	Selling SF	Mall Developer	Store Name
2	340001	603	Westfield	Main Place Mall
3	340002	654	Westfield	Sherman Oaks Fashion Squa
4	340003	998	Simon Property Group	Brea Mall
5	340004	858	General Growth Properties	Park Place
6	340005	746	Westfield	Galleria at Roseville
7	340006	1633	Simon Property Group	Mission Viejo Mall

Getting Your Data into PowerPivot

In this example, you will be importing two different data sets into PowerPivot. You will be importing the text file. For the Excel data about the stores, you can either copy and paste into PowerPivot, or define a table and link it to PowerPivot. For this example, a simple copy and paste will work.

→ **See** Chapter 4, "Getting Your Data into PowerPivot," for details on using the linked table method.

Decide on a Sequence for Importing

You should import the main transaction table first. In this case, the main transaction table is the 1.8 million row file with sales information. After that file is imported, you can import the lookup table information.

You should follow this sequence for two reasons:

■ In the PowerPivot Field List, the tables are presented in the order that they were imported. You will want your main table at the top of the list when building pivot tables.

■ The PowerPivot relationship detection logic expects the main table to be first.

So, for this example, you will be loading the text file first, and then pasting the stores data into PowerPivot.

Import a Text File

To import the 1.8 million row file into PowerPivot, follow these steps:

1. Select the PowerPivot tab in Excel 2010.

2. Select the PowerPivot Window icon. A new PowerPivot application window will appear. PowerPivot offers two ribbon tabs: Home and Design. The left side of the Home tab is shown in Figure 2.4.

Figure 2.4
The Home tab of the PowerPivot application.

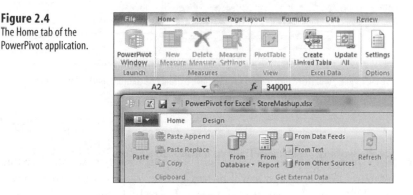

3. You want to import your main table first. This will be the large CSV file shown in Figure 2.2. From the Get External Data group, select From Text. PowerPivot shows the Table Import Wizard (see Figure 2.5).

4. Because your first row of the file contains headers, select the Use First Row as Column Headers check box.

5. Click the Browse button and locate your text file. PowerPivot will pause for a second and fetch the first 50 rows of data from the text file to provide a data preview, as shown in Figure 2.6.

6. If there are any columns that you don't need to import, clear them.

Figure 2.5
Preparing to import a
text file.

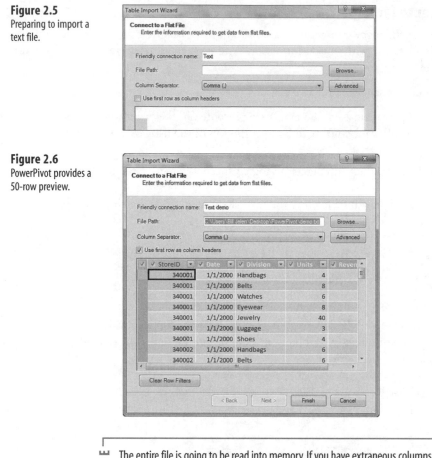

Figure 2.6
PowerPivot provides a
50-row preview.

> **NOTE** The entire file is going to be read into memory. If you have extraneous columns, particular columns with long text values, you can save memory by clearing them.

7. Note that there are filter drop-downs for each field. You can actually sort and filter this 1.8 million row data set here, although it will be slower than in a few steps from now. If you open a filter field, PowerPivot will scan the entire file to build the list of filters, as shown in Figure 2.7. You can choose to exclude certain values from the import.

8. Click Finish and PowerPivot will begin loading the file into memory. The wizard will show how many rows have been fetched so far (see Figure 2.8). Loading data can take a long time. If you would need to interrupt the import, the Stop Import button is available at the bottom of the wizard.

9. When the file is imported, the wizard confirms how many rows have been imported, as shown in Figure 2.9. Click Close to return to the PowerPivot window.

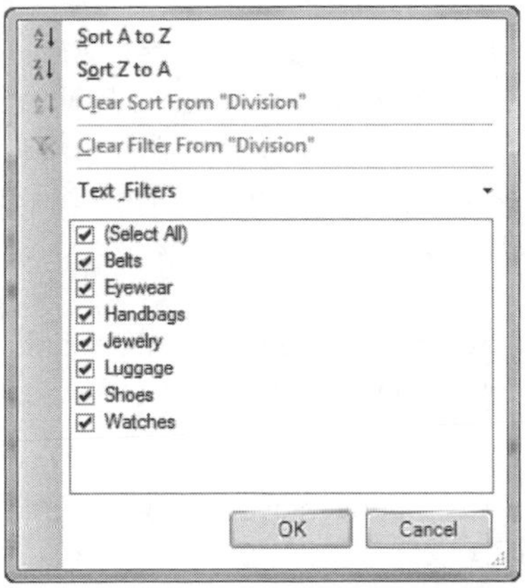

Figure 2.7
To conserve file size, you can choose to exclude certain divisions from the import.

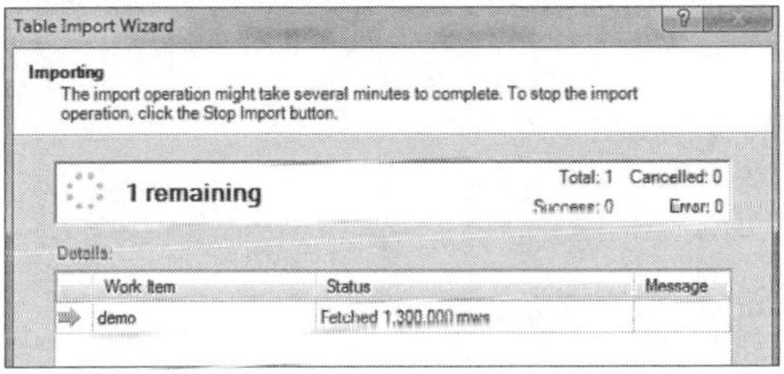

	Sort A to Z
	Sort Z to A
	Clear Sort From "Division"
	Clear Filter From "Division"

Text Filters ▾

☑ (Select All)
☑ Belts
☑ Eyewear
☑ Handbags
☑ Jewelry
☑ Luggage
☑ Shoes
☑ Watches

[OK] [Cancel]

Figure 2.8
PowerPivot provides an update on how the import is progressing.

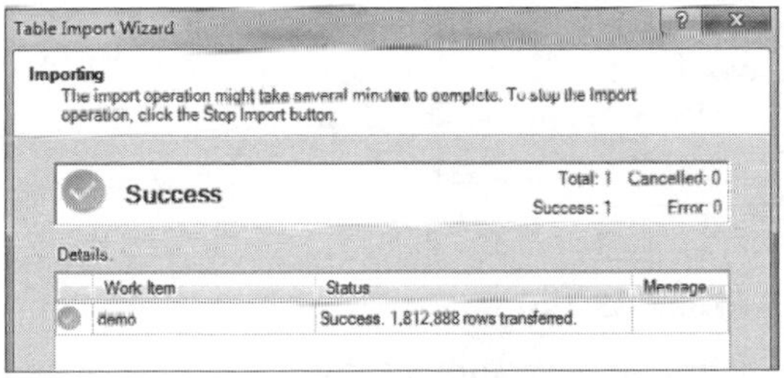

Table Import Wizard

Importing
The import operation might take several minutes to complete. To stop the import operation, click the Stop Import button.

⟳ **1 remaining**   Total: 1   Cancelled: 0
Success: 0   Error: 0

Details:

Work Item	Status	Message
demo	Fetched 1,300,000 rows	

Figure 2.9
These 1.8 million rows are now stored in your Excel file.

Table Import Wizard

Importing
The import operation might take several minutes to complete. To stop the import operation, click the Stop Import button.

✓ **Success**   Total: 1   Cancelled: 0
Success: 1   Error: 0

Details:

Work Item	Status	Message
demo	Success. 1,812,888 rows transferred.	

10. The 1.8 million row data set is shown in the PowerPivot Window. Go ahead. Grab the vertical scrollbar and scroll through the records. You can also sort, change the number format, or filter (see Figure 2.10).

 To see a demo of importing data, search for PowerPivot Data Analyst 1 at YouTube.

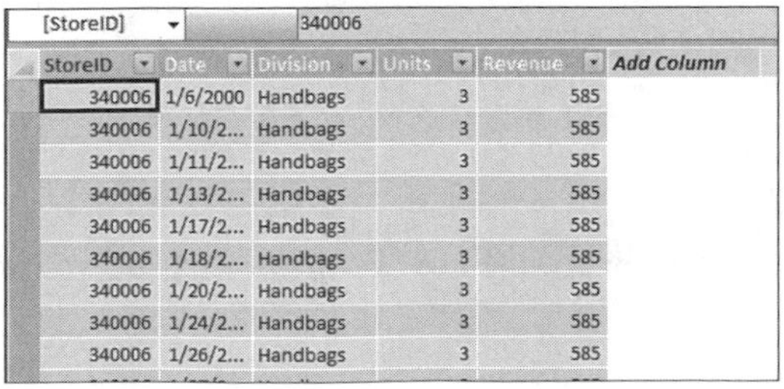

Figure 2.10
1.8 million records are in a grid that feels a lot like Excel.

[StoreID] ▾   340006

StoreID	Date	Division	Units	Revenue	Add Column
340006	1/6/2000	Handbags	3	585	
340006	1/10/2...	Handbags	3	585	
340006	1/11/2...	Handbags	3	585	
340006	1/13/2...	Handbags	3	585	
340006	1/17/2...	Handbags	3	585	
340006	1/18/2...	Handbags	3	585	
340006	1/20/2...	Handbags	3	585	
340006	1/24/2...	Handbags	3	585	
340006	1/26/2...	Handbags	3	585	

> **N O T E** Note that although this feels like Excel, it is not Excel. You cannot edit an individual cell. If you add a calculation in what amounts to cell F1, that calculation will automatically get copied to all rows. If you format the revenue in one cell, all of the cells in that column will get formatted. You can change column widths by dragging the border between the column names just like in Excel.

The filters in PowerPivot are not as powerful as the new filters introduced in Excel 2007. In particular, the date columns do not show a hierarchical filter where you can choose a year or month.

If you right-click a column heading, a menu appears where you can rename, freeze, copy, hide, unhide the columns (see Figure 2.11).

Bottom line: You have 1.8 million records that you can sort, filter, and later, pivot. This is going to be cool.

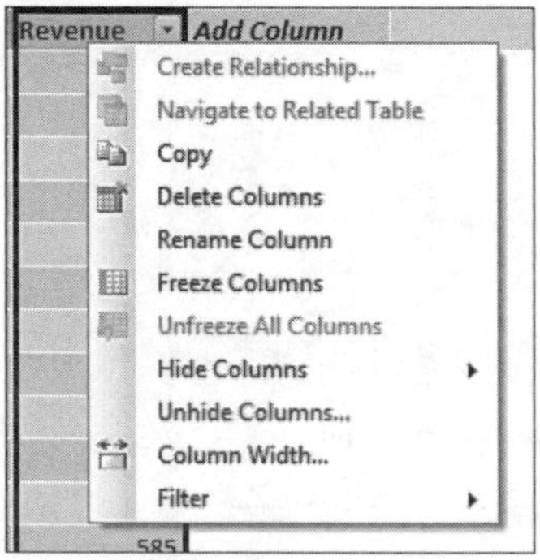

Figure 2.11
Right-click a column to rename it.

Add Excel Data by Copying and Pasting

Next, you want to add your store information to PowerPivot. As mentioned previously, you could either link to the Excel data or copy and paste. For this example, a simple copy and paste will work.

→ **See** Chapter 4 for more information on linking.

To return to the Excel workbook from PowerPivot, you can press Alt+1 or click the tiny Excel icon at the top left of the PowerPivot window (see Figure 2.12).

1. Open your Stores table in Excel.
2. Select the data with Ctrl+*.
3. Copy it with Ctrl+C.
4. Click the PowerPivot Window icon. PowerPivot returns and you see your 1.8 million row data set.

Figure 2.12
Use this icon to return to
your Excel workbook.

5. Click the Paste icon on the left side of the PowerPivot Home tab. You will see a Paste Preview window.

6. Give the new table a better name than Table. Perhaps StoreInfo (see Figure 2.13). Click OK.

Figure 2.13
Give the pasted table a
name.

Store	Selling SF	Mall Developer	Store Name
340001	603	Westfield	Main Place Mall
340002	654	Westfield	Sherman Oaks F
340003	998	Simon Property G...	Brea Mall
340004	858	General Growth ...	Park Place
340005	746	Westfield	Galleria at Rosev
340006	1633	Simon Property G...	Mission Viejo Mal
340007	725	Irvine Retail Group	Corona Del Mar .
340008	535	Westfield	San Francisco C.
340009	1190	The Macerich Co...	Kierland Common
340010	1070	The Macerich Co...	Scottsdale Fashi.
340011	708	Westfield	Valley Fair
340012	1000	Bellevue Square ...	Bellevue Square
340013	971	General Growth ...	Perimeter Mall

You will now see the store information in a new StoreInfo tab at the bottom of the screen. Notice that there are now two worksheet tabs in PowerPivot, as shown in Figure 2.14.

Define Relationships

Normally, in regular Excel you would be creating VLOOKUPs to match the two tables. It is far easier in PowerPivot. Follow these steps:

Figure 2.14
You now have two unrelated tables in the PowerPivot window.

Demo tab

StoreInfo

1. You will be linking from one column in your main table to a column in another table. To simplify the relationship process, navigate to your main table and select a cell in the column from which you will be linking.

2. Click the Design tab in the PowerPivot Ribbon.

3. Select Create Relationship. The Create Relationship dialog appears. By default, the selected table and column will appear in the first two fields, as shown in Figure 2.15.

4. If you skipped step 1 and the correct table is not shown in the Table drop-down, then select Demo from the Table drop-down.

Create Relationship

Figure 2.15
Define a relationship between tables. By selecting the key column before starting, 2 of the 4 fields are populated.

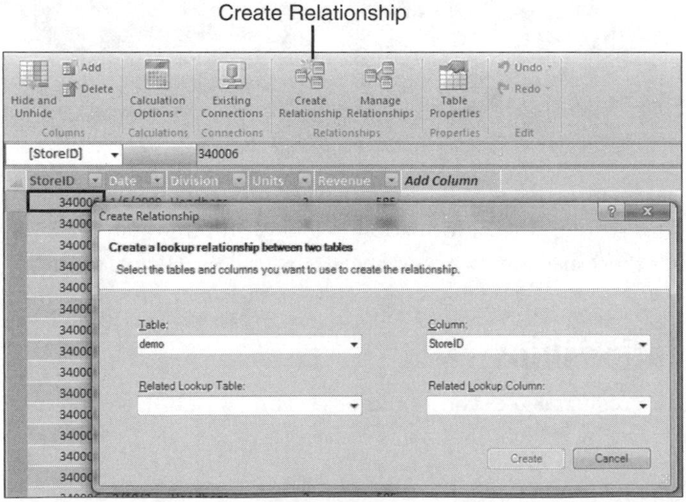

5. If you did not select the correct column in step 1, open the Column drop-down. Select StoreID.

6. Open the Related Lookup table drop-down. Select StoreInfo.

7. Open the Related Lookup Column drop-down and select Store (see Figure 2.16).

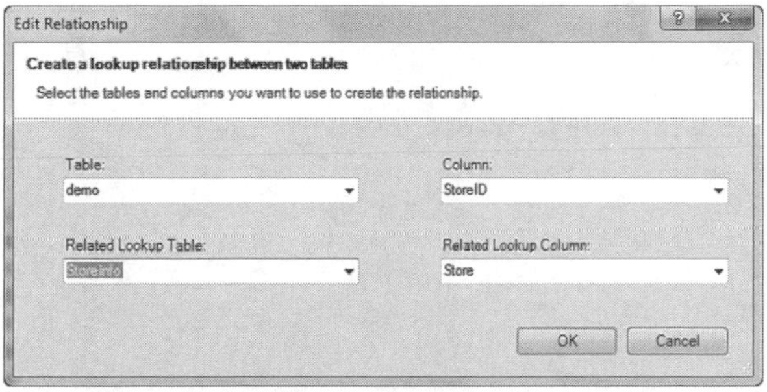

Figure 2.16
This simple dialog replaces the VLOOKUP.

8. Click Create. You've now created a relationship between the two tables.

Add Calculated Columns Using DAX

One downside to pivot tables created from PowerPivot data is that they cannot automatically group daily data up to years. Before building the pivot table, let's use the Data Analysis Expression (DAX) formula language to add a new calculated column to the Demo table.

Follow these steps to add a Year field to the Demo table:

1. Click the Demo worksheet tab at the bottom of the PowerPivot Window.

2. The column to the right of Revenue has a heading of Add Column. Click in the first cell of this blank column.

3. Click the fx icon to the left of the formula bar. The Insert Function dialog appears with categories for All, Date & Time, Math & Trig, Statistical, Text, Logical, and Filter. Select Date & Time from the drop-down. You will instantly notice that this is not the same list of functions in Excel. Five of the first six functions that appear in the window are exotic and new (see Figure 2.17).

4. Luckily, some familiar old functions are in the list as well. Scroll down and select the YEAR function. Click the first date in the Date column. PowerPivot proposes a formula of =year(demo[Date]. Type the closing parentheses and press Enter. Excel will fill in the column with the year associated with the date, as shown in Figure 2.18.

5. Right-click the column and select Rename Column. Type a name, such as Year.

6. Repeat the process to add a Month column using a formula of =Month(demo[Date]). Figure 2.19 shows the table after adding two columns.

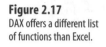

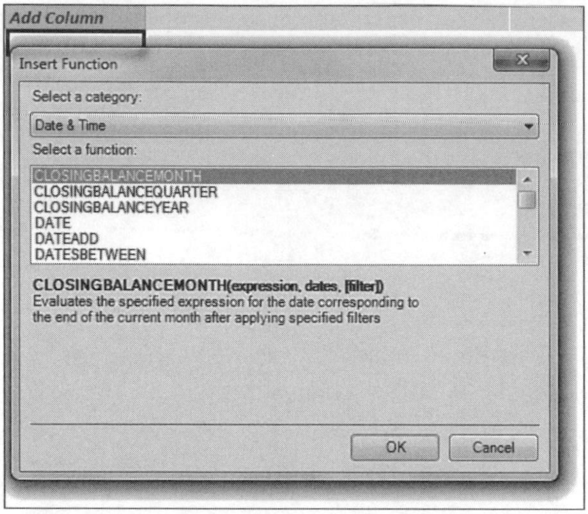

Figure 2.17
DAX offers a different list
of functions than Excel.

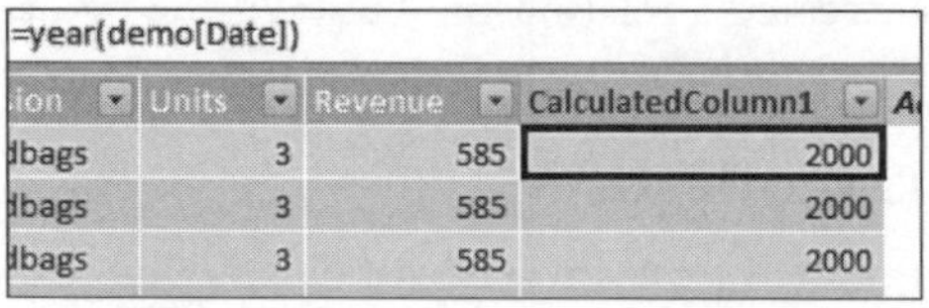

Figure 2.18
A new calculated column
is added. You will want to
rename this.

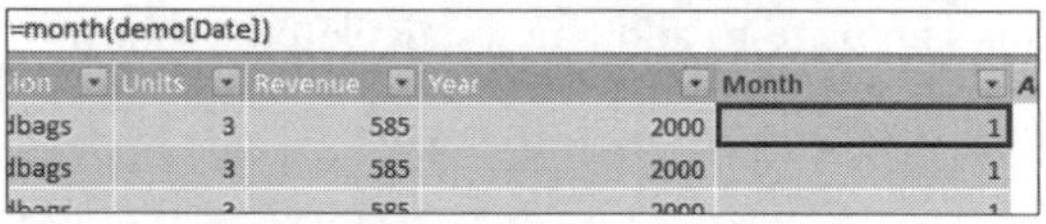

Figure 2.19
You now have years and
months.

TIP

The language used to create that column is called DAX. There are two types of calculations that you can do with DAX. Figure 2.19 shows a DAX calculation in the data grid. A more powerful type of DAX calculation is adding a DAX Measure to a pivot table.

→ **See** Chapter 10, "Using DAX for Aggregate Functions" and Chapter 11, "Using DAX for Date Magic," for more information on DAX.

There are many more columns that you might think of adding, but let's move on to using the pivot table.

Build a Pivot Table

One of the advantages of PowerPivot is that multiple pivot tables can share the same data and slicers. Open the PivotTable drop-down on the Home tab of the PowerPivot Ribbon.

As shown in Figure 2.20, you have choices for a single pivot table, a single chart, a chart and a table, two charts, four charts, and so on.

→ To read more about layouts with multiple elements, **see** Chapter 7, "Building Pivot Tables."

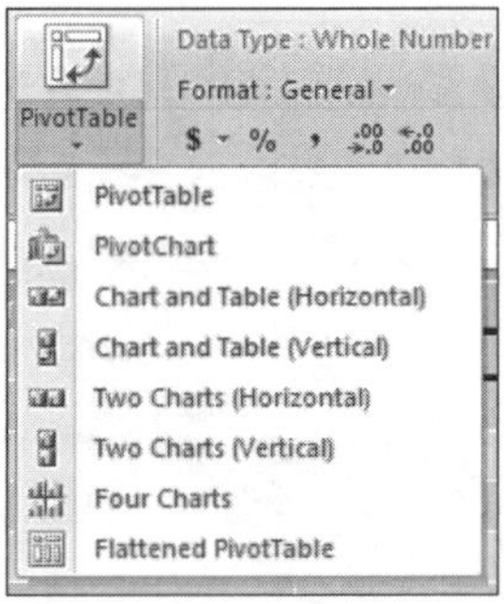

Figure 2.20
You have many options beyond a single table or chart.

Follow these steps.

1. Select PivotTable. You now see the PowerPivot tab back in the Excel window.
2. Choose to put the pivot table on a new worksheet (see Figure 2.21).

Figure 2.21
Choose the location for the pivot table.

There are many things to notice. The icon for a blank pivot table occupies cell B3:D20. This allows room for slicers to go above and left of the pivot table (see Figure 2.22).

Docked on the right side of the screen is the PowerPivot Field List. This is now a third variation of the PivotTable Field List.

> **NOTE**
> Excel already offers two different field lists, one for OLAP data sets and one for PivotCache data sets. Figure 2.23 shows the PowerPivot Field List.

Figure 2.22
The blank pivot table icon appears in B3.

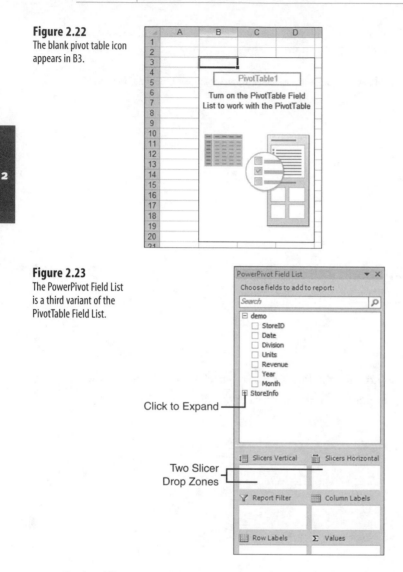

Figure 2.23
The PowerPivot Field List is a third variant of the PivotTable Field List.

Both tables are available in the top of the Field List. The main table is expanded to show the field names, but you can expand the other table and add those fields to this pivot table.

Two new sections in the drop zones offer vertical or horizontal slicers.

> **NOTE**
> For the purposes of the screen shots in this book, I will undock the PowerPivot Field List and float it near the pivot table. To undock the field list, grab the title bar and drag away from the edge of the screen. To later redock the field list, grab the title bar and drag it more than half way off the right side of the Excel window.

Because you are in a pivot table, the PivotTable Tools tabs are available in the Excel Ribbon.

3. Select Revenue from the PowerPivot Field List by adding a check box next to it. Because Revenue is a numeric field, it automatically moves to the Values drop zone at the bottom of the field list. Your pivot table now shows Sum of Revenue, which is the total revenue in the entire 1.8 million row file (see Figure 2.24).

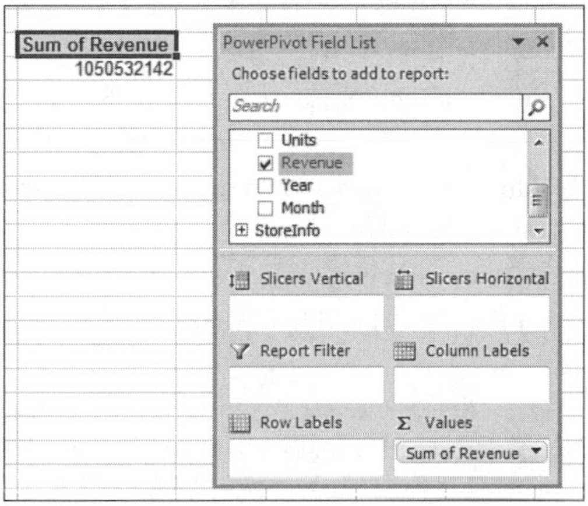

Figure 2.24
Choose a numeric field and Excel sums that field.

4. Expand the StoreInfo table. Select Region from the StoreInfo table. Excel builds a pivot table showing sales by region. At this point, you have a pivot table from 1.8 million rows of data with a virtual link to a lookup table.

5. Drag the Division field from the Demo table to the Column Labels drop zone. Your pivot table is now mashing up data from two different tables (see Figure 2.25).

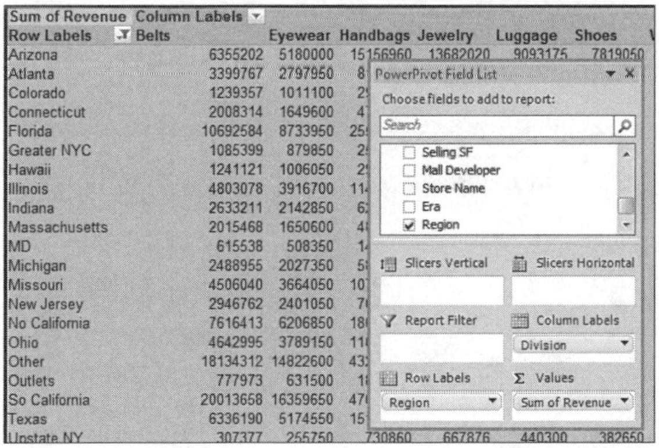

Figure 2.25
This pivot table summarizes 1.8 million rows and data from two tables.

6. Drag the Store Name field to the Row Labels drop zone. Drop Store Name below the Region field.

To show off some more features of the PowerPivot pivot table, let's add some slicer functionality:

1. Drag Year to the Slicers Vertical drop zone.

2. Drag Month to the Slicers Vertical drop zone.

3. Drag Mall Developer to the Slicers Horizontal drop zone.

To clean up the formatting of the pivot table, follow these steps:

1. Go to the PivotTable Tools Design tab in the Ribbon. Select Banded Rows.

2. On the same tab, open the PivotTable Styles gallery and choose a light, medium, or dark color scheme.

3. Go to the Options tab. The Active Field should say Sum of Revenue. If it does not, choose a numeric cell in the pivot table.

4. Click the Field Settings icon in the PivotTable Tools Options tab.

5. In the lower left corner of the Value Field Settings dialog, select the Number Format button.

6. Select the Number category. Select Use 1000 Separator. Select 0 decimal places (see Figure 2.26). Click OK to close the Format Cells dialog. Click OK to close the Value Field Settings dialog.

Figure 2.26
The numeric formatting is hidden two levels deep.

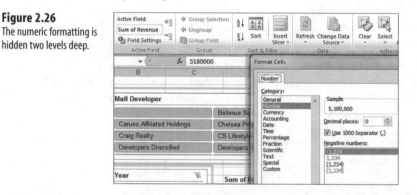

The result is an impressive interactive report, as shown in Figure 2.27.

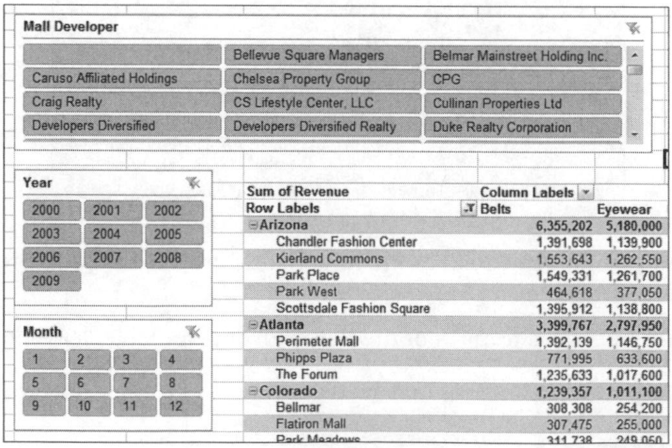

Figure 2.27
The formatted report with some slicers.

7. Select the year 2000 from the Year slicer. The report instantly redraws to show only the stores that were open in the year 2000. The Mall Developer slicer redraws to show only the five developers with whom you had contracts in 2000 (see Figure 2.28).

World-Class Data Compression

When you are creating PowerPivot data sets, all of the data is loaded into computer memory. When you save a PowerPivot workbook, the data from the imported text files is stored in the workbook. Amir Netz from the PowerPivot team came up with an impressive methodology for compressing the data.

Figure 2.28 tells an impressive story. This chapter mashed up a text file that occupies 58MB. It also incorporated the StoreInfo.xlsx file which takes up 19K. All of that data is stored in the StoreMashup.xlsx file in an amazingly small 3.6MB file (see Figure 2.29).

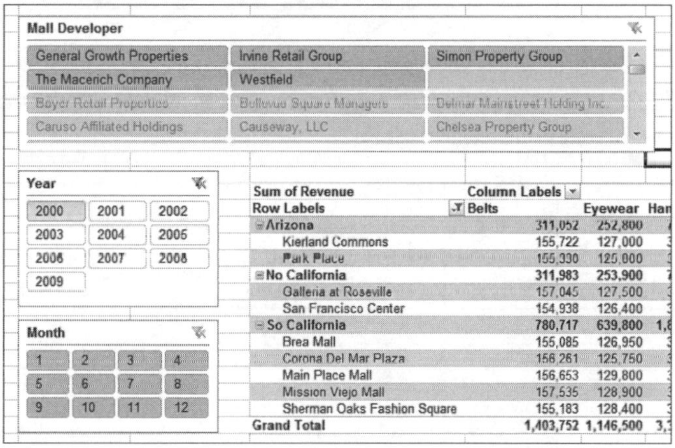

Figure 2.28
Choose a year and the report updates, as well as the other slicers.

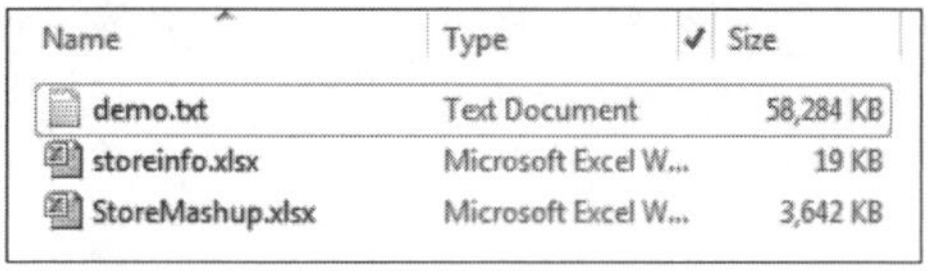

Figure 2.29
58MB of text file fits in a 3.6MB Excel file.

Storing Data Columnwise

When you are storing a database on a medium like a hard drive, it makes sense to keep each record together. Because hard drives are relatively slow, you want that data stored in a contiguous block as shown in Figure 2.30.

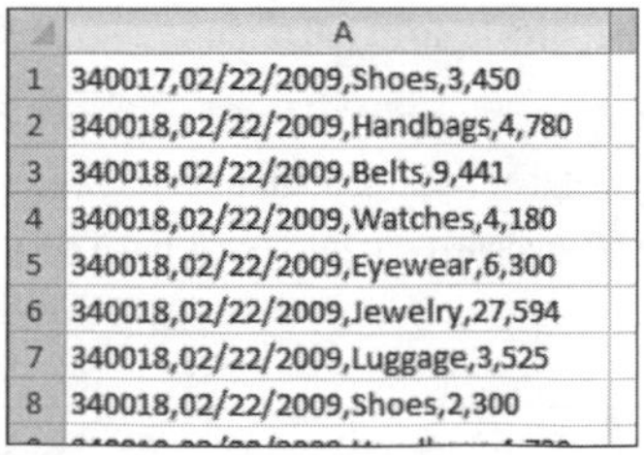

Figure 2.30
In a traditional disk-based database, all of the fields for one record are stored in close proximity to each other.

The problem with storing data in a row-wise fashion is that there is little opportunity for compression. In the entire 1.8 million rows of the text file, there are no records that match 100%.

Early on, the PowerPivot team decided that PowerPivot was only going to be dealing with data in memory. Thus, they don't need to store data in a row-wise fashion.

When you start to look at a single column of data, there are many columns with huge amounts of duplicates. For example, 1.8 million rows of category information really only has nine possible values. There are massive numbers of adjacent values that are exactly the same see Figure 2.31).

Figure 2.31
Look at one column of the data, and there are many possibilities for compression.

	D	E	F	G	H	I	J
211	340056		2/22/2009		Luggage		3
212	340057		2/22/2009		Luggage		3
213	340058		2/22/2009		Luggage		4
214	340059		2/22/2009		Luggage		4
215	340060		2/22/2009		Luggage		3
216	340061		2/22/2009		Luggage		2
217	340017		2/22/2009		Shoes		3
218	340018		2/22/2009		Shoes		2
219	340019		2/22/2009		Shoes		3

If you sort the data by category, you really end up with huge rainbow stripes of records that fit in each category (see Figure 2.32). The space to store the entire column of 1.8 million category values comes down to 9 pointers that say everything from this record to this records is "Jewelry."

Figure 2.32
Conceptually, PowerPivot is reducing the data to rainbow stripes of different values in each column.

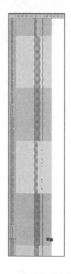

Microsoft calls this VertiPaq compression. (That is kind of a catchy name, isn't it. Vertical packing of the data. Geeky.)

This is why PowerPivot does not do well with long text values in a column. If you have a comment field, remove that field as you are importing the data to allow PowerPivot to do its full compression.

> **NOTE**
> Microsoft is cautiously saying that they might sometimes see 15X compression. The simple example in this chapter was not designed to compress extremely well, but it does demonstrate a 16X compression factor.

I hate to extrapolate, but if the file size limit is 2GB on disk, and if you could somehow keep up the 16X compression, then that is a theoretical maximum of 32GB of data in a single pivot table. That would be 993 million rows of demo.txt type data. You would have to own a serious computer. 64-bit Windows and 64-bit Office to be sure.

Most of us were limited to 65,536 rows just a year or two ago. Now the simple demo file for this book is 27 times larger than that limit, with a theoretical upper limit that is 15,000 times larger than 65,536 rows. I would gladly personally shell out the full purchase price of the PowerPivot client to get access to that much analytical power.

Asymmetric Reporting with PowerPivot

Asymmetric reporting is not possible with pivot tables that are built from pivot caches of Excel data. In Figure 2.33, a small data set in A1:D37 is used to produce the pivot table in columns G:N.

Figure 2.33
Delete those five columns from the report.

Sum of Revenue	Column Labels							
	FY2009			FY2009 Sum	FY2010		FY2010 Sum	Grand Total
Row Labels	Actuals	Budget			Actuals	Budget		
Arizona	550550	600000	1150550		0	633000	633000	1783550
California	3165104	500000	3665104			3666000	3666000	7331104
Colorado	616097	600000	1216097			669000	669000	1885097
Louisiana	814431	825000	1639431		0	902000	902000	2541431
Nevada	1170320	1000000	2170320		0	1194000	1194000	3364320
New Mexico	322168	350000	672168		0	370000	370000	1042168
Oklahoma	186715	200000	386715		0	213000	213000	599715
Texas	2559021	2750000	5309021		0	2920000	2920000	8229021
Utah	632897	650000	1282897		0	706000	706000	1988897
Grand Total	10017303	10475000	20492303		0	11273000	11273000	31765303

Out of seven data columns in the report, you don't want to see five of them. You are interested in last year's actuals and this year's forecast. This is not really possible with a regular pivot table.

You could use PivotTable Tools Options, Options, Totals & Filters, and then clear Show Grand Total For Rows to get rid of the grand total in column N.

Then, you can click a year heading in the pivot table, use PivotTable Tools Options, Field Settings and select None for the Subtotals to get rid of two more columns. But then, you are left with no good way to delete 2009 Budget or 2010 Actuals. If you try to filter out the Budget, it will be removed from both years. If you try to delete column I, you will be met with the warning that you cannot Move a Part of A Pivot Table report message (see Figure 2.34).

Option 1 is to use Home, Format, Column, Hide to hide the columns that you don't want to see. Option 2 is to convert the pivot table to values using Copy and then Paste, Paste Values.

With PowerPivot, a third option becomes available. Because data in the PowerPivot window becomes an online analytical processing (OLAP) cube, you have access to OLAP tools, including named sets.

Figure 2.34
You can get close using regular pivot table tools, but then you are shut down.

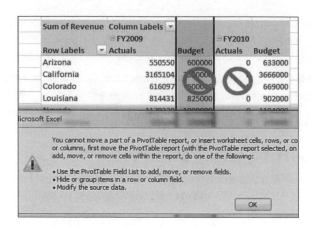

Follow these steps to create an asymmetric report:

1. Open your regular data set in Excel.

2. Select one cell in the data and press Ctrl+T. Confirm that your data has headings. Click OK. The data is formatted and a new Table Tools Design tab appears. On the left side, the Table Name appears as Table 1. Type a new name, such as Financials.

3. On the PowerPivot tab, select Create Linked Table.

4. In the PowerPivot Window, open the Pivot Table drop-down and select Pivot Table.

5. Choose a location for the pivot table.

6. Select State and Revenue from the Pivot Table Field List. Drag Year and Measure to the Column Labels drop zone.

7. You now have a pivot table that looks identical to the one in Figure 2.33. The difference is that Named Sets are not grayed out anymore on the Options tab.

8. Go to PivotTable Tools Options. Open the Fields, Items, and Sets drop-down. Select Create Set Based on Column Items.

9. Type a set name, such as BudAct. The Display Folder can be blank. Excel shows you the 7 columns currently in your pivot table.

10. Select the row for FY2009 Budget, as shown in Figure 2.35. Click Delete Row.

11. Repeat step 10 for the other four rows that you don't want to show in the pivot table. When you are done, you should see only two rows, as shown in Figure 2.36.

12. Click OK to complete the set.

As shown in Figure 2.37, you will now have a pivot table that will report asymmetric sets of columns.

Next Steps

This chapter showed you what is possible with pivot tables. In the next chapter, you will see both the benefits of the drawbacks of using PowerPivot.

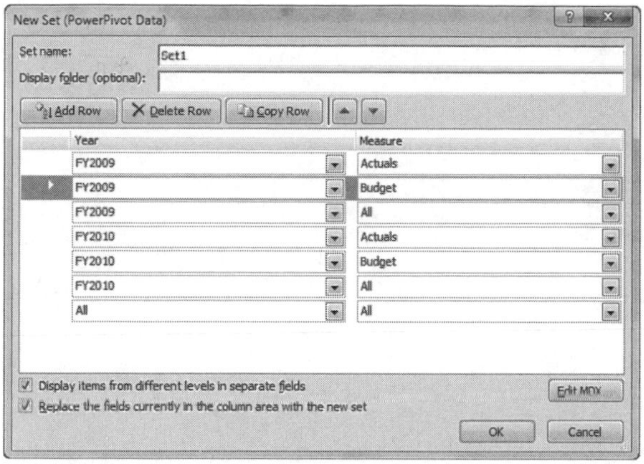

Figure 2.35
Select a pair of values and click Delete.

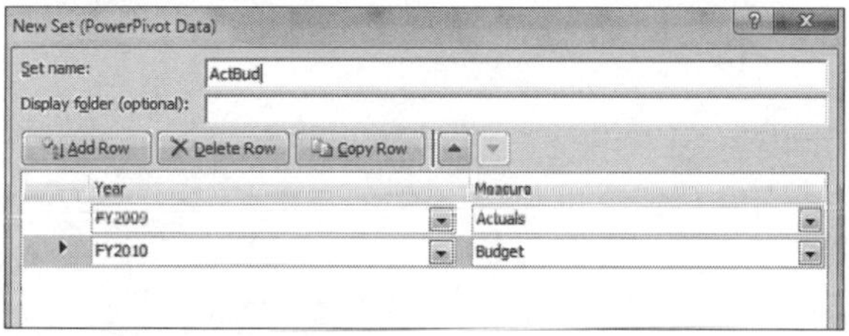

Figure 2.36
Repeat for each item that you want to delete.

Figure 2.37
This pivot table would be very difficult to create without PowerPivot.

Sum of Revenue	Column Labels	
	FY2009	FY2010
Row Labels	Actuals	Budget
Arizona	550550	633000
California	3165104	3666000
Colorado	616097	669000
Louisiana	814431	902000
Nevada	1170320	1194000
New Mexico	322168	370000
Oklahoma	186715	213000
Texas	2559021	2920000
Utah	632897	706000
Grand Total	10017303	11273000

Why Wouldn't I Build Every Future Pivot Table in PowerPivot?

3

I am going to ask you to step into the WayBack machine.

Do you remember at the end of Chapter 2, "The Promise of PowerPivot," somewhere around Figures 2.33 through Figures 2.37, where I showed you how to take a regular Excel data set through PowerPivot to enable the ability to use named sets to create asymmetric reports? When I realized that PowerPivot allowed me to create those types of reports, I asked the question, "Well then, why wouldn't I build every future pivot table in PowerPivot?" By the end of this chapter, you will understand why you might not want to do that.

Now, let me ask you to step into the WayWayBack machine. Do you remember the first five words that I wrote in this book? Here. I will repeat them for you:

"I am a PowerPivot FanBoy."

I had to actually look up the term *FanBoy*. Thanks to UrbanDictionary.com:

1. A passionate fan of various elements of geek culture
2. A person who is completely loyal to a game or company regardless if they suck or not

If you happened to be following my Twitter feed as I discovered how cool the DAX measures are, you have no question that I fit definition number 1.

→ **See** more about DAX measures in Chapter 10, "Using DAX for Aggregate Functions."

However, based on what you learn in this chapter, you'll see that I don't really fit into definition number two. I love pivot tables more than I love PowerPivot.

> **NOTE**   Most data analysis problems can be solved with a pivot table. Pivot tables are the greatest invention in desktop computing. If you've been in one of my Power Excel seminars (or watched the LiveLessons Power Excel DVD from Que), you know that I don't just use pivot tables. I go deep into pivot tables. Everyone wants to know how to make a pivot table. I show you how to go 10 steps beyond that. As I started using PowerPivot pivot tables late in 2009, I started to become a bit annoyed with some of the limitations with pivot tables created by PowerPivot. This isn't PowerPivot's fault. It is a limitation of all pivot tables created from online analytical processing (OLAP) data sources.

This chapter looks at the benefits of PowerPivot and the drawbacks of PowerPivot. I am guessing that the great folks on the PowerPivot team won't like that I spend half a chapter in the world's first PowerPivot book showing you things that you can't do in PowerPivot pivot tables. However, I have a loyalty to the pivot table. For those of you who have read my books and are really using all the features of pivot tables, you are going to hate some of the limitations of PowerPivot pivot tables.

Great Reasons to Use PowerPivot

PowerPivot is groundbreaking. I've probably already gushed about most of these items, but let's cover them again.

Create One Pivot Table from Multiple Tables

Check out that PowerPivot Field List in Figure 3.1. It is showing fields from three different worksheets. You can choose fields from each sheet and put them in the same pivot table! That is incredibly cool.

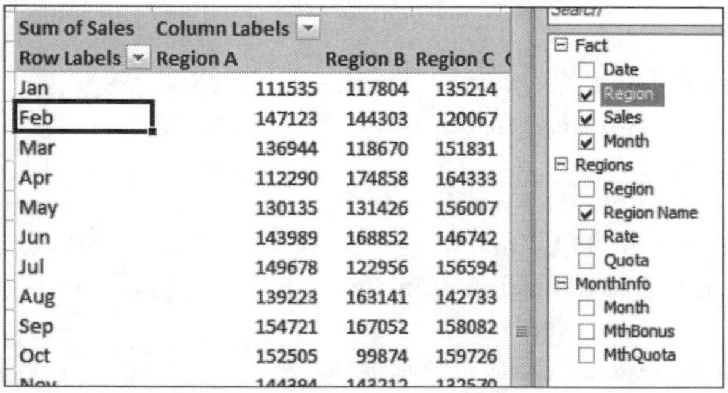

Figure 3.1
Create pivot tables from multiple worksheets.

I will argue with that. First, not everyone can do a VLOOKUP, and PowerPivot now puts business intelligence into the hands of more people. Second, actually doing the VLOOKUPs brings those small lookup tables into your main table and repeats the region names potentially a million times. The PowerPivot model saves memory by not having to repeat the information from the lookup tables on a million rows in the transaction table.

Use Massive Data Volumes

Assuming that you need one row for headings, the most data that you can get into a regular Excel pivot table is 1,048,575 rows of data. PowerPivot can handle an unlimited amount of rows. If you can build a 64-bit machine with 40GB of RAM, you can theoretically fit 900+ million rows in a single pivot data source.

> **NOTE** The Excel guru will point out that without PowerPivot you could connect to an Access database or even use the VBA trick that is documented on page 82 of *Excel Gurus Gone Wild* to combine similar data from Sheet1 and Sheet2 into a single pivot cache.

If you are really considering using one of those tricks to get more than a million rows into a pivot table, you really want to use a tool that was designed with the intention of being able to fit multi-million-row data sets in memory.

Fit More Data into Memory

Amir Netz's VertiPaq data compression scheme allows more data to fit into a smaller footprint in memory. With large data sets, you are fighting two limits.

First, all the data has to fit into a workbook that takes up less than 2GB on the hard drive. Because XLSX and XLSM files are really ZIP files, you can already fit more than 2GB of data into a 2GB workbook.

Second, you are limited by available memory on the computer. Remember that a pivot table is fast because it loads all the data up into memory. Yes, 64-bit computers allow you to break through the 4GB limit on RAM, but at the time of this writing in early 2010, the typical high-end configuration at Best Buy has 8GB to 12GB of RAM. 64-bit machines allow 16 exabytes of RAM (literally, 17 billion gigabytes). When this book hits the bookshelves, you will still be constrained by not-quite-unlimited RAM, and you will appreciate that VertiPaq lets you fit more data into memory.

Use Named Sets to Build Asymmetric Pivot Tables

Named sets are a nice improvement in Excel 2010 pivot tables. They allow you to define a group of regions that should be reported, or they allow you to define a group of columns to show. The problem is that in Excel 2010 they don't work with pivot tables built from regular Excel pivot caches.

In Figure 3.2, the upper pivot table is built from regular Excel data. You cannot hide the 2009 budget without also hiding the 2010 budget. The lower pivot table uses a PowerPivot data set, and named sets make it easy to choose the columns.

Figure 3.2
Named sets become available in PowerPivot pivot tables, enabling asymmetric reporting.

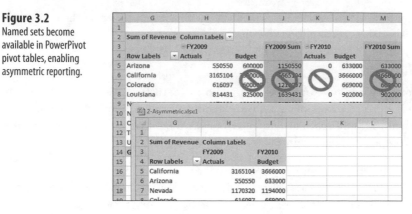

→ For more about named sets, **see** Chapter 12, "Named Sets, GetPivotData, and Cube Formulas."

Join Four Pivot Tables Together Using a Single Set of Slicers

Slicers are the new visual filters available in Excel 2010. Think of them as an improvement on using the page fields in Excel 2003 or report filter fields in Excel 2007.

One of the common themes that Mike Alexander addresses in our book, *Pivot Table Data Crunching* (QUE, ISBN 978-0789743138) is a little bit of VBA code to get two pivot tables to be controlled by one set of report filter fields.

With PowerPivot pivot tables, you can easily have one, two, or four pivot tables that are all controlled by the same set of slicers. These pivot tables can be reporting different measures and using different label fields, yet they all respond to one set of slicers (see Figure 3.3).

If you are trying to create a dashboard, PowerPivot is going to let you do it in just a few clicks.

→ For more about controlling multiple pivot tables with one set of slicers, **see** Chapter 9, "Cool Tricks New with PowerPivot."

Figure 3.3
Control multiple pivot tables with one set of slicers.

PowerPivot Slicer AutoLayout Runs Circles Around Regular Excel Slicers

Build a regular Excel pivot table. Add three slicers to that pivot table. Here is what I can predict about those slicers:

- They will appear tiled on top of each other in the center of the visible Excel window.
- All the slicers will be single-column.
- All the slicers will be tall enough to show eight items, even if there are only three items along the dimension.
- You will be spending many clicks to move those slicers, resize the slicers, change the number of columns, move the slicer, resize the slicer, move the slicer, okay that looks good.

The default slicers for a regular Excel pivot table are shown at the top of Figure 3.4.

Build a PowerPoint pivot table. It is easier to add slicers using the PowerPivot Field List. You don't have to access an icon in the ribbon and then a second dialog box. You just drag fields to either the Vertical Slicer or Horizontal Slicer drop zone.

The slicers added by PowerPivot are intelligently resized. If you only have three items along a dimension, the slicer will only be large enough to show three items. PowerPivot makes some intelligent guesses about the best arrangement for the slicers. In the bottom of Figure 3.4, PowerPivot chose three columns for the Product slicer and two columns for the Region slicer and five columns for the Customer slicer. There is a better chance that you can just accept the default arrangement of the PowerPivot slicers. Because there are 25 customers in the data set, I would probably adjust the Customer slicer to be a bit taller to show 1 more row of items.

Overall, though, you will have a better experience setting up slicers when you are using a PowerPivot pivot table.

> **NOTE**
> You can adjust the slicers for a regular pivot table to appear in the arrangement that defaults from the PowerPivot table, it just requires far more clicks.
>
> Further, if you do find that you have to adjust the PowerPivot slicers, they will drive you mad as they continue to try to automatically adjust.

→ For more about slicers, **see** Chapter 9, "Cool Tricks New with PowerPivot."

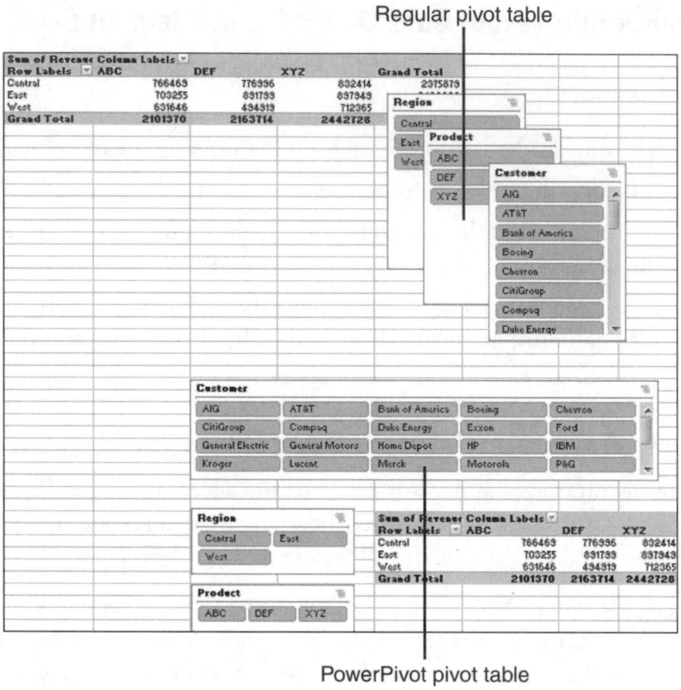

Regular pivot table

Figure 3.4
Default slicers for a regular pivot table (top) and a PowerPivot pivot table (bottom).

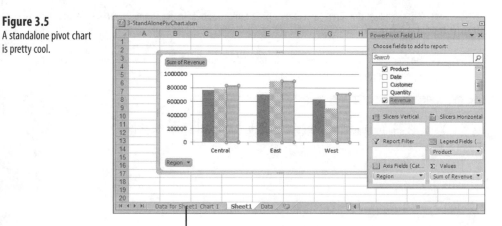

PowerPivot pivot table

PowerPivot Allows for Standalone Pivot Charts

Sort of.

When you insert a single pivot chart with PowerPivot, you do see just the chart and just the PowerPivot Field List. You don't see a pivot table. It is less cluttered (see Figure 3.5).

To create Figure 3.5, start with a table on the Data worksheet. Link the table to PowerPivot. Select to create a pivot chart. Look at the sheet tabs to see what happens.

Figure 3.5
A standalone pivot chart is pretty cool.

Pivot table here

PowerPivot inserts two new worksheets in the workbook. Sheet1 is used to hold the pivot chart. A second sheet called Data for Sheet1 Chart 1 is inserted to hold the pivot table that drives the chart. Now, it is cool that you can drive that pivot table on the back worksheet by using the PowerPivot Field List on the front sheet.

If you use the layout with four charts, you are going to get more back worksheets to hold the pivot tables.

Convert Your PowerPivot Pivot Table to Formulas

Excel 2007 introduced a series of cube functions that cold pull data from an external OLAP database.

If you have a 2D Excel table and link that table to PowerPivot, you've just created a cube.

Build a pivot table, and then use PivotTable Tools Options, OLAP Tools, Convert to Formulas, and your entire pivot table is converted to a series of CUBEVALUE formulas, as shown in Figure 3.6. If you really want to build wild asymmetric reports, these cube formulas would allow it.

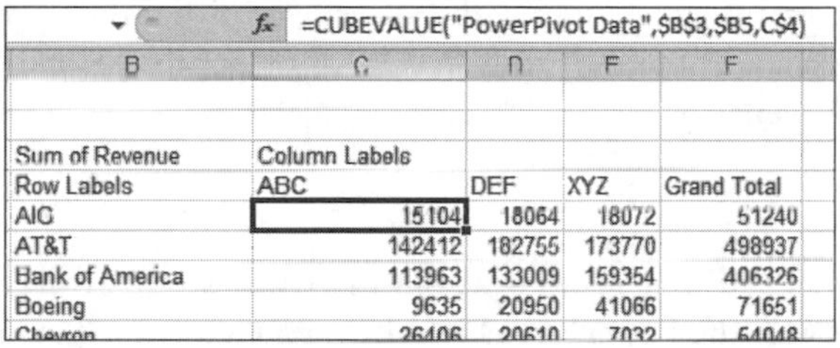

Figure 3.6

Convert your entire pivot table to cube formulas.

		fx	=CUBEVALUE("PowerPivot Data",$B$3,$B5,C$4)		
B	C	D	E	F	
Sum of Revenue	Column Labels				
Row Labels	ABC	DEF	XYZ	Grand Total	
AIG	15104	18064	18072	51240	
AT&T	142412	182755	173770	498937	
Bank of America	113963	133009	159354	406326	
Boeing	9635	20950	41066	71651	
Chevron	26406	20610	7032	54048	

> **NOTE** You can sort of do this in a regular pivot table using =GETPIVOTDATA, but the original pivot table has to persist somewhere in the workbook.

→ Cube Formulas are explained in Chapter 12, "Named Sets, GetPivotData, and Cube Formulas."

Measures Created by DAX Run Circles Around Calculated Fields

You haven't seen a DAX measure yet. The DAX formula language introduces 80 functions. The functions allow for two types of amazing calculations:

- **Time-intelligent calculations:** Compare MTD sales with MTD sales from a year ago. Calculate fiscal year to date sales. Compare this period with the parallel period from 3 years ago. All of these are enabled with DAX measures.

→ For examples of DAX measures, **see** Chapter 10, "Using DAX for Aggregate Functions."

■ **Select any denominator calculations:**In a regular pivot table, you can show this month's sales as a percentage of total sales. Using the new settings in Excel 2010, you can even show an item's sales as a percentage of the parent item's sales. In DAX measures, you can choose to show this month's sales as a percentage of anything. If you want to express all sales reps' sales as a percentage of Amber's sales, you can do that. If you want to show sales divided by the distinct count of customers, you can do that.

→   Chapter 10 provides examples of how to use DAX for calculated fields.

DAX measures really blow calculated fields out of the water. In fact, you could write a whole book about DAX measures. I understand that the headline of "PowerPivot Lets You Pivot 10 Million Rows of Data" will sell more product, but I think the real improvement in PowerPivot is the ability to create DAX measures.

Learn more about DAX measures in Chapter 10, "Using DAX for Aggregate Functions."

The Downside of PowerPivot

There are some frustrating limitations with PowerPivot pivot tables. Many of these are introduced because the pivot table is truly an OLAP pivot table. Some of them are introduced because of PowerPivot.

You Lose Undo

Calling a macro or an add-in tends to wipe out the Undo stack. PowerPivot is an add-in. When you interact with the PowerPivot Field List, you lose your Undo stack.

Workaround: I find that I rarely undo when using a pivot table, because it is relatively easy to go back and re-pivot a field.

However, I can imagine a scenario where you make a huge mistake while editing a data set, notice the change after adding a field to the PowerPivot pivot table, and now you have no way to undo. It will burn me eventually.

> **CAUTION**
>
> Really, you lose Undo! It is easy to be cavalier about not needing Undo in a pivot table, but Undo is there to save you when you do something stupid. There are going to be times when the fact that you lost Undo is going to make you hate PowerPivot.

PowerPivot Is Not Smart Enough to Sort Jan, Feb, Mar, Apr

Every copy of Excel comes with four custom lists:

■ Monday, Tuesday, Wednesday...

■ Mon, Tue, Wed...

■ January, February, March...

■ Jan, Feb, Mar...

You can add new custom lists.

By default, a regular pivot table will sort itself into the sequence specified by a custom list. You might not have realized this is happening, but it is the reason why grouped dates show up as Jan, Feb, Mar.

PowerPivot pivot tables default to showing the months in alphabetic sequence.

> **CAUTION**
>
> If I have to see Apr, Aug, Dec, Feb, Jan, Jul, Jun, Mar, May, Nov, Oct, Sep one more time, I am going to blow a gasket. It is my new favorite rant about insane things that come out of Redmond. How could they not have handled this automatically? Seriously? They talk about time intelligence and they can't even get this one right?

Figure 3.7 shows the default order for months coming out of PowerPivot.

Figure 3.7

PowerPivot won't sort months into the correct sequence.

Sum of Revenue	Column Labels
Row Labels	ABC
Apr	182134
Aug	184452
Dec	195129
Feb	171194
Jan	262726
Jul	154812
Jun	145088
Mar	119131
May	194643
Nov	106523
Oct	196345
Sep	189193
Grand Total	2101370

> **NOTE**
>
> My thanks to Excel guru Colin Baanfield, who figured out that despite the Microsoft Knowledge Base article that states otherwise, you can actually get the months to sort correctly.

Follow these steps:

1. Add Months to your pivot table.
2. Open the drop-down at the top of the Months column.
3. Select More Sort Options.
4. Select Ascending (A to Z) By.
5. Click More Options.

6. Clear the Sort Automatically Every Time the Report Is Updated check box.

7. Open the First Key Sort Order drop-down.

8. Select Jan, Feb, Mar.

9. Click OK to close the More Sort Options (Month) dialog.

10. Click OK to close the Sort (Month) dialog.

That is nine clicks to solve one stupid problem. Considering that it only takes six clicks to create a pivot table, nine clicks is a travesty.

 To see a demo of fixing the month sorting sequence, search for MrExcel PowerPivot 3 at YouTube.

It's Hard to Change the Calculation in the Pivot Table

In a regular pivot table, a field in the Values section has 11 possible calculations: Sum, Count, Average, Max, Min, Product, Count Numbers, StdDev.S, StdDev.P, Var.S, and Var.P.

In a regular pivot table, there are many ways to change the calculation:

■ Select PivotTable Tools Options, Summarize Values As to expose the drop-down in Figure 3.8.

■ Choose a cell that contains a value field and click the Field Settings button in the Ribbon. The Summarize Values By tab offers all 11 functions, as shown in Figure 3.9.

■ If you choose a field in the row labels area and click Field Settings, you can choose Custom Subtotals and choose more than 1 of the 11 functions (see Figure 3.10).

Clicking the field heading in the Values drop zone is not a normal way to change the measure. In Figure 3.11, the only thing in that drop-down is the Field Settings choice that would lead back to Figure 3.9.

Figure 3.8
A new drop-down on the ribbon offers calculations for a regular pivot table.

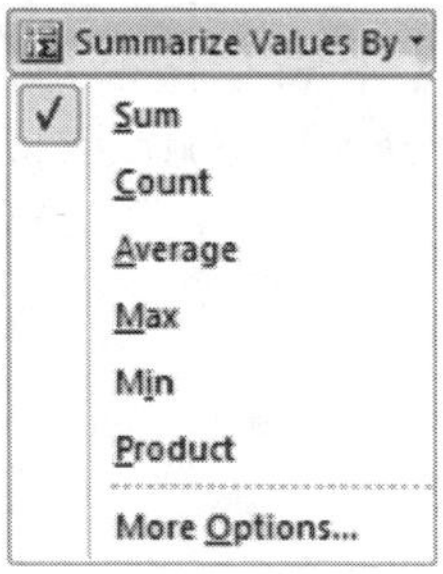

🔲 Summarize Values By ▾
✓ Sum
Count
Average
Max
Min
Product
More Options...

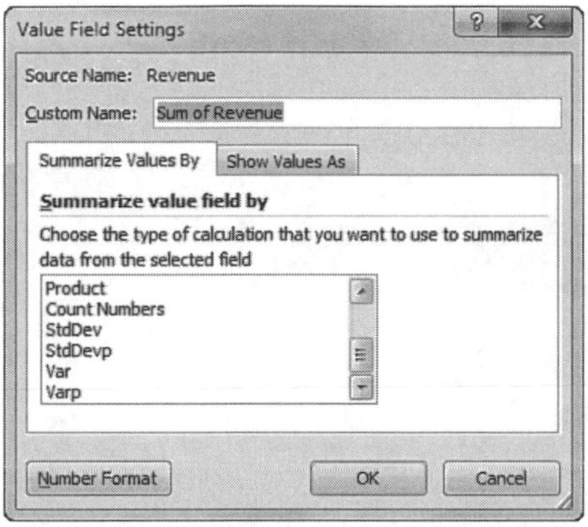

Figure 3.9
The Value Field Settings dialog offers all 11 calculations.

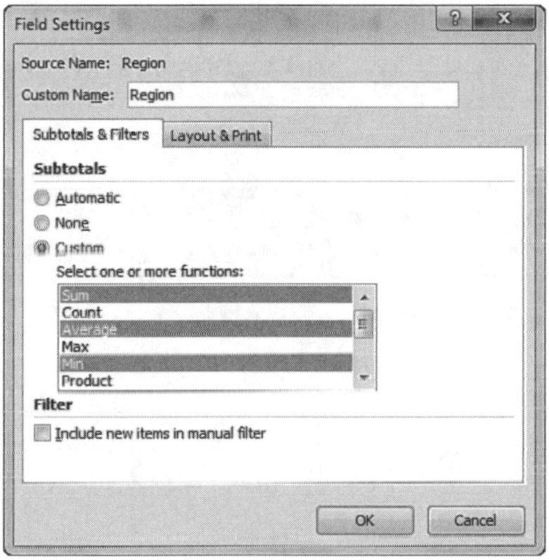

Figure 3.10
You can even add multiple subtotals using the field settings for a row field.

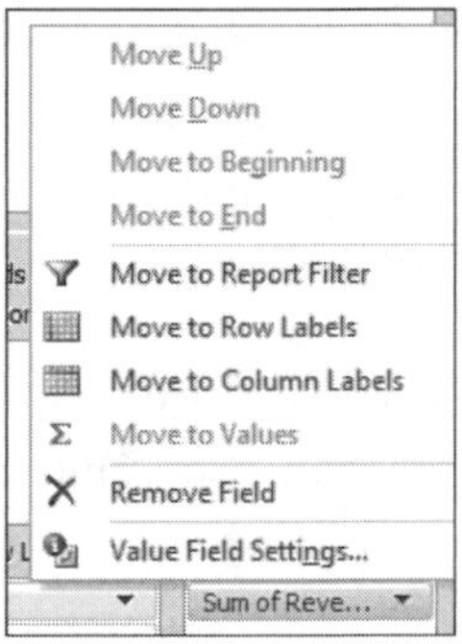

Figure 3.11
Clicking on the Field Heading in the drop zone generally does not lead to a way to change the calculation.

In a PowerPivot pivot table, most of the normal ways to choose the calculation are grayed out. Figures 3.12 through 3.14 show that every method available in a regular pivot table is grayed out with a PowerPivot pivot table.

Figure 3.12
The Summarize Values By
drop-down is grayed out.

Figure 3.13
Calculation choices
grayed out.

3

Figure 3.14
Custom subtotal options
are grayed out.

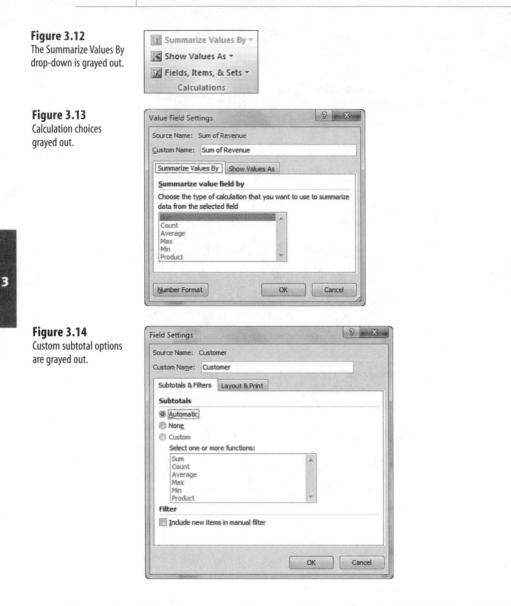

After seeing all those items grayed out, and after reading the "OLAP Pivot Table" Knowledge Base article, you would be pretty convinced that you cannot change the calculation in an OLAP pivot table.

To change the calculation, you have to use this flyout menu attached to the value field heading in the Values drop zone (see Figure 3.15).

You can choose from Sum, Count, Min, Max, and Average.

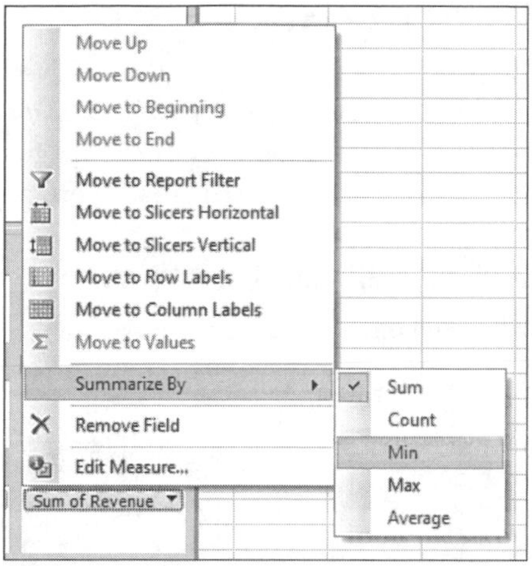

Figure 3.15
Choose from five functions.

NOTE: You can get around this limitation by defining a new DAX measure. As mentioned previously in this chapter, the DAX measures run circles around anything that we had before. They certainly offer Min, Max, Count. They may not offer variance or standard deviation, but you can probably design a DAX measure to do almost everything that you could have done in the missing calculation drop-downs.

→ Chapter 10 includes examples that show how to define a new DAX measure.

You Cannot Create PowerPivot Pivot Tables with VBA

Once the pivot table exists, you can modify the pivot table with a macro.

But you cannot automate PowerPivot with VBA.

There might be a chance that you could do the simplest of single-table pivot tables using PowerPivot, even if you have to use send keys to do Alt+G+C to create a linked table, and then Alt+H+P+T+Enter+Enter to build a default pivot table. But this is a risky proposition.

It would be much tougher to import two tables and set up a relationship using send keys.

Let's say that in general, you won't be using VBA to automate PowerPivot.

You Cannot Edit a Single Cell in the PowerPivot Window

If you spot an error in the PowerPivot window, you cannot edit that value. You have to go back to the original data source, fix the data there, and then reimport.

`GetPivotData` Is Harder to Use with PowerPivot

It is harder to use `GetPivotData` to create report templates when your data is based on PowerPivot.

Are You Insane? Who Actually Uses `GetPivotData`???

Ah, yes. You are right; 99% of the people who get stung with GetPivotData hate the feature and want to turn it off. However, in the last chapter of *Pivot Table Data Crunching for Excel 2010*, I showed how you can take the evil =GetPivotData() formula generated by Microsoft and change it into a cool formula that you can drag throughout your report.

Okay, So If I Somehow Embrace GetPivotData, What's the Problem?

Figure 3.16 shows the initial hard-coded GetPivotData formula:

```
=GETPIVOTDATA("Revenue",Sheet2!$A$3,"Region","East","Product","ABC")
```

Figure 3.16
In the default state, GetPivotData is hard-coded and useless.

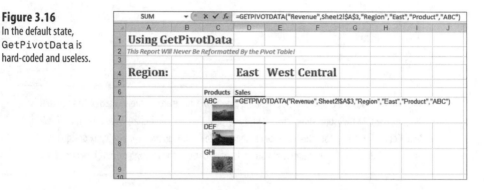

To edit that formula, change the hard-coded "East" and "ABC" to point to cells. In Figure 3.17, the formula is =GETPIVOTDATA("Revenue",Sheet2!$A$3,"Region",D$4,"Product",$C7). You can drag this formula throughout the report template.

Figure 3.17
Edit the formula, and it becomes easy to drag.

So, the problem is that in pivot tables built on PowerPivot data, the GetPivotData formula is tougher to edit. They actually concatenate the field name and the field value into one parameter. This means that you have to edit the formula to concatenate the field name and then a cell address.

Figure 3.18 shows the original formula:

```
=GETPIVOTDATA("[Measures].[Sum of Revenue]",Sheet4!$B$3,"[Sales].[Region]",
"[Sales].[Region].&[East]","[Sales].[Product]","[Sales].[Product].&[ABC]")
```

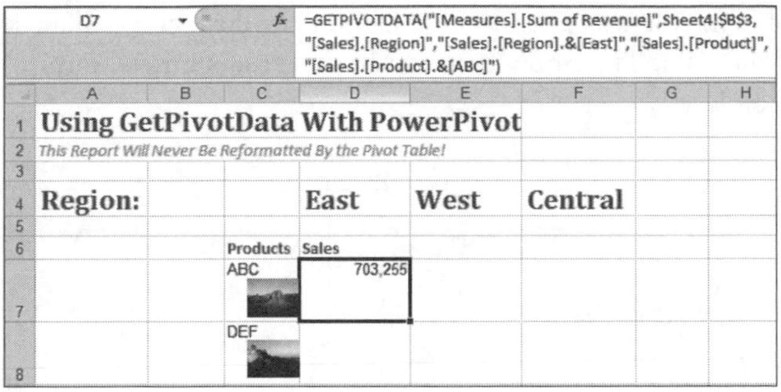

Figure 3.18
The initial default formula is harder to customize.

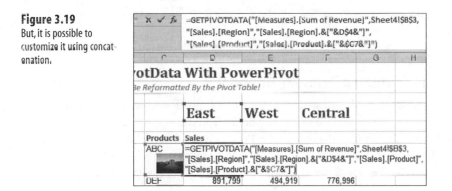

To edit that formula, you want to get rid of the hard coded `"[East]"` and `"[ABC]"`. This is a bit tougher, as you have to concatenate the cells inside of the square brackets. Figure 3.19 shows the final formula:

```
=GETPIVOTDATA("[Measures].[Sum of Revenue]",Sheet4!$B$3,"[Sales].[Region]",
"[Sales].[Region].&["&D$4&"]","[Sales].[Product]","[Sales].[Product].&["&$C7&"]")
```

Figure 3.19
But, it is possible to customize it using concatenation.

So, it is slightly harder to use GetPivotData, but not impossible. Plus, you could simply convert the formulas to cube functions (refer back to Figure 3.6).

Show Items with No Data Is Grayed Out

In Figure 3.20, the left pivot table is based on regular Excel data. Because the Central region had no sales of products B, C, D, and E, those rows do not show up in the pivot table. This creates an unbalanced report.

With a regular pivot table, you can choose a product cell, select Field Settings, Layout and Print, and then select Show Items with No Data.

As you can see in the center pivot table in Figure 3.20, this will fill in the missing product rows.

The pivot table in columns G and H are based on a PowerPivot data set. You cannot add in items without data. The Show Items with No Data is grayed out. This is a limitation of OLAP pivot tables.

Figure 3.20
You cannot use Show Items with No Data in a PowerPivot pivot table.

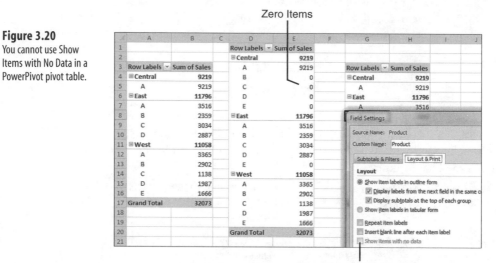

Zero Items

Show Items With No Data

Calculated Fields and Calculated Items Are Grayed Out

You cannot add calculated fields or calculated items to a PowerPivot pivot table. However, the DAX measures run circles around calculated fields. You can also simulate calculated items by adding a new column to the data in the PowerPivot window.

→ **See** Chapter 10 for more information on DAX measures and Chapter 6, "Using Data Sheet View," for details on how to customize the PowerPivot window.

You Cannot Double-Click to Drill Through

In a regular pivot table, you can double-click any cell to drill down on that cell. Excel returns a new worksheet with all the data rows that make up that cell (see Figures 3.21 and 3.22).

Figure 3.21
Double-click the 182,755.

	A	B	C	D
1				
2				
3	Sum of Revenue	Column Labels		
4	Row Labels	ABC	DEF	XYZ	Gran
5	AIG	15104	18064	18072
6	AT&T	142412	182755	173770
7	Bank of America	113963	133 Sum of Revenue
8	Boeing	9635	20 Value: 182755
9	Chevron	26406	20 Row: AT&T
10	CitiGroup	203522	204 Column: DEF
11	Compaq	17250	4380	17620

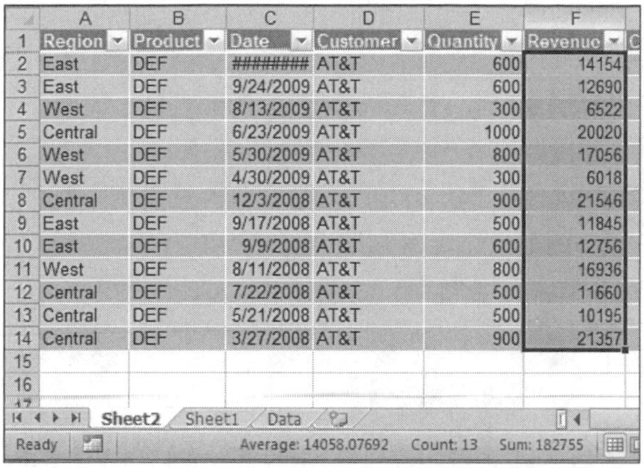

	A	B	C	D	E	F
1	Region	Product	Date	Customer	Quantity	Revenue
2	East	DEF	########	AT&T	600	14154
3	East	DEF	9/24/2009	AT&T	600	12690
4	West	DEF	8/13/2009	AT&T	300	6522
5	Central	DEF	6/23/2009	AT&T	1000	20020
6	West	DEF	5/30/2009	AT&T	800	17056
7	West	DEF	4/30/2009	AT&T	300	6018
8	Central	DEF	12/3/2008	AT&T	900	21546
9	East	DEF	9/17/2008	AT&T	500	11845
10	East	DEF	9/9/2008	AT&T	600	12756
11	West	DEF	8/11/2008	AT&T	800	16936
12	Central	DEF	7/22/2008	AT&T	500	11660
13	Central	DEF	5/21/2008	AT&T	500	10195
14	Central	DEF	3/27/2008	AT&T	900	21357
15						
16						

Figure 3.22
And you get a new worksheet with all the rows that make up the 182,755.

If you try the same trick with a PowerPivot pivot table, Excel says that "Show Details Cannot Be Completed on a Calculated Cell." (See Figure 3.23)

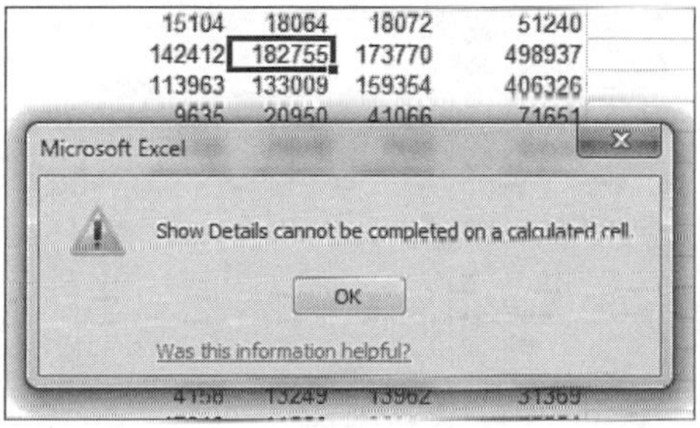

Figure 3.23
You cannot drill down on a PowerPivot pivot table.

Grouping Does Not Work with PowerPivot

You frequently build pivot tables from transactional data. This means that your dates are frequently stored at the daily date level.

In a regular pivot table, you can create date rollups with five clicks:

1. Select a date cell in the pivot table.
2. Click Group Field in the Options tab.
3. Months is already selected. Add Quarter and Year (two clicks) (see Figure 3.24).
4. Click OK.

You now have the summary report shown in Figure 3.25.

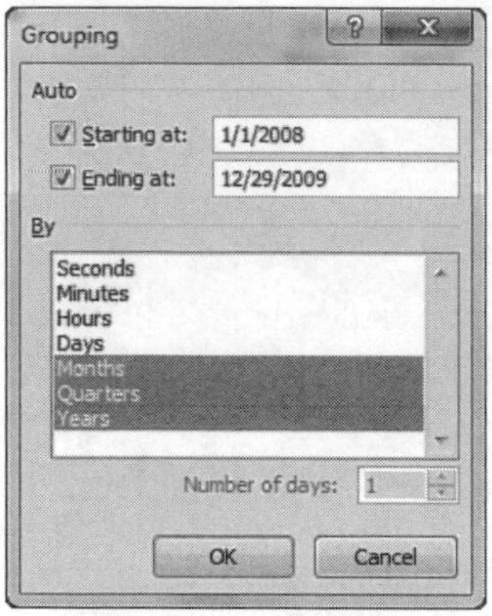

Figure 3.24
Grouping daily dates to months, quarters, and years takes five clicks in a regular pivot table.

Grouping	? ✕

Auto

☑ Starting at: 1/1/2008

☑ Ending at: 12/29/2009

By

Seconds
Minutes
Hours
Days
Months
Quarters
Years

Number of days: 1

OK   Cancel

3

Figure 3.25
Five hundred daily dates are rolled up to 24 months.

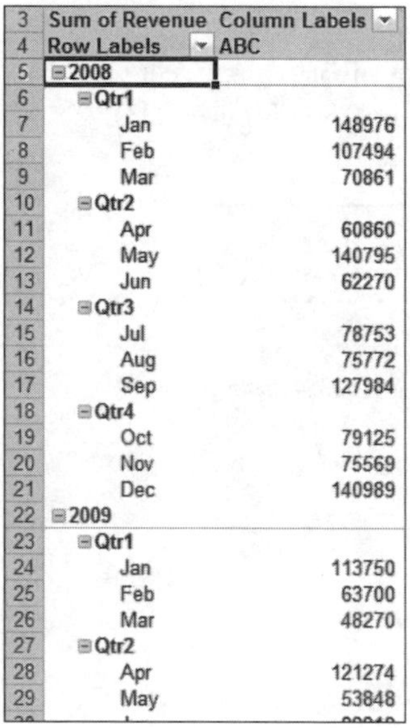

3	Sum of Revenue	Column Labels ▾
4	Row Labels ▾	ABC
5	⊟2008	
6	⊟Qtr1	
7	Jan	148976
8	Feb	107494
9	Mar	70861
10	⊟Qtr2	
11	Apr	60860
12	May	140795
13	Jun	62270
14	⊟Qtr3	
15	Jul	78753
16	Aug	75772
17	Sep	127984
18	⊟Qtr4	
19	Oct	79125
20	Nov	75569
21	Dec	140989
22	⊟2009	
23	⊟Qtr1	
24	Jan	113750
25	Feb	63700
26	Mar	48270
27	⊟Qtr2	
28	Apr	121274
29	May	53848

In a regular pivot table, you can use grouping on a numeric field to create stratifications (see Figure 3.26, with results in Figure 3.27).

Figure 3.26
Group invoice amounts into equal ranges.

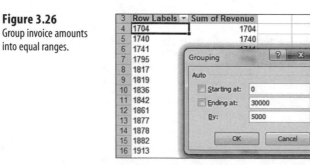

3	Row Labels ▾	Sum of Revenue
4	1704	1704
5	1740	1740
6	1741	
7	1795	
8	1817	
9	1819	
10	1836	
11	1842	
12	1861	
13	1877	
14	1878	
15	1882	
16	1913	

Grouping   ? ✕

Auto

☐ Starting at: 0

☐ Ending at: 30000

By: 5000

OK   Cancel

Figure 3.27
See count and amount of invoices in each size bracket.

	A	B	C
1	**Invoice Stratifications**		
2			
3	**Revenue** ▾	**Sum of Revenue**	**Count of Customer**
4	0-4999	326674	104
5	5000-9999	937212	125
6	10000-14999	1769165	142
7	15000-19999	2149079	123
8	20000-24999	1374732	63
9	25000-30000	150950	6
10	**Grand Total**	6707812	563

You cannot group dates or amounts in a PowerPivot pivot table. To do the same functionality, you would have to add new columns in the PowerPivot window. Adding columns is not incredibly hard, but it is not as easy as selecting a few items in the Grouping dialog.

In Figure 3.28, four calculated columns would allow the reporting that is native to regular pivot tables.

- The year column is =Year([Date])
- The QtrEnding column is =EndOfQuarter([Date])
- The Month column is =Format([Date],"MMM")
- The InvoiceSize column is =INT([Revenue]/5000)*5000&"-"&INT ([Revenue]/5000)*5000+4999

Figure 3.28
To work around the missing grouping feature, add four calculated columns in the PowerPivot window.

`=INT(Table2[Revenue]/5000)*5000&"-"&INT([Revenue]/5000)*5000+4999`

Quantity ▾	Revenue ▾	COGS ▾	Profit ▾	Year ▾	QtrEnding ▾	Month ▾	InvoiceSize ▾
1000	22810	10220	12590	2000	3/31/2008	Jan	20000-24999
100	2257	984	1273	2008	3/31/2008	Jan	0-4999
800	18552	7872	10680	2008	3/31/2008	Jan	15000-19999
400	9152	4088	5064	2008	3/31/2008	Jan	5000-9999
1000	21730	9840	11890	2008	3/31/2008	Jan	20000-24999
400	8456	3388	5068	2008	3/31/2008	Jan	5000-9999
800	16416	6776	9640	2008	3/31/2008	Jan	15000-19999
900	21438	9198	12240	2008	3/31/2008	Jan	20000-24999

Certain On-Worksheet Typing Adjustments Do Not Work in PowerPivot

Frankly, most people don't know that these features work in regular pivot tables, so not many people will miss them.

In Figure 3.29, a regular pivot table shows Sum of Sales for two products and three regions. Notice that the Central region has $75,000 in sales and the East region as $1,500 in sales.

Figure 3.29
A starting pivot table.

	A	B	C	D	E
1					
2					
3	**Sum of Sales**	**Region** ▾			
4	**Product** ▾	**Central**	**East**	**West**	**Grand Total**
5	A	50000	1000	250000	301000
6	B	25000	500	125000	150500
7	**Grand Total**	75000	1500	375000	451500
8					

If you want to rename a measure, you can go to cell A3 and type a new name. Provided that name does match an existing field in the pivot table, the field will be renamed. In Figure 3.30, the Sum of Sales is renamed to Sales. There is a trailing space after Sales to keep that field name different from the original Sales field.

Figure 3.30

Type a new name in A3 to rename the field.

	A	B	C	D	E
1					
2					
3	Sales	Region ▾			
4	Product ▾	Central	East	West	Grand Total
5	A	50000	1000	250000	301000
6	B	25000	500	125000	150500
7	Grand Total	75000	1500	375000	451500

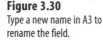

This next trick is completely counterintuitive. Go to cell B4. Type the word **East**, as shown in Figure 3.31.

Figure 3.31

Move a column by typing its name in a new location.

	A	B	C	D	E
1					
2					
3	Sales	Region ▾			
4	Product ▾	East	East	West	Grand Total
5	A	50000	1000	250000	301000
6	B	25000	500	125000	150500
7	Grand Total	75000	1500	375000	451500

When you press Enter, the data for East magically moves from column C to column B as shown in Figure 3.32. The values for Central move to column C. The heading for Central is written to C4.

Figure 3.32

This is a cool trick: The data for East moves where the new heading was typed.

	A	B	C	D	E
1					
2					
3	Sales	Region ▾			
4	Product ▾	East	Central	West	Grand Total
5	A	1000	50000	250000	301000
6	B	500	25000	125000	150500
7	Grand Total	1500	75000	375000	451500

Really, who would be crazy enough to even try such a trick? No one would actually think that it would work.

But, it does work, and once you know it is there, you might try using it a lot. I do.

The trick does not work with PowerPivot pivot tables. Type **East** in B4, and you've screwed up the pivot table (see Figure 3.33).

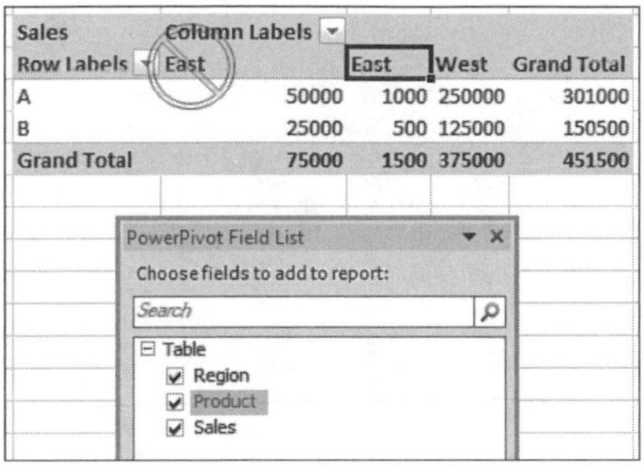

Figure 3.33
The same trick does not work with a PowerPivot pivot table.

Sales	Column Labels ▼			
Row Labels ▼	East	East	West	Grand Total
A		50000	1000	250000	301000
B		25000	500	125000	150500
Grand Total		75000	1500	375000	451500

PowerPivot Field List ▼ ✕

Choose fields to add to report:

Search 🔍

☐ Table
  ☑ Region
  ☑ Product
  ☑ Sales

> **CAUTION**
>
> It is strange that they let you type over those values in a PowerPivot pivot table. It almost seems like a bug.
>
> I always believed that this trick was the keyboard equivalent of dragging field headings to the correct location. That feature (dragging the fields with a mouse) works fine in PowerPivot pivot tables. Again, that might lead you to think that this is supposed to work, but it is a bug.

Greatest Pivot Table Trick of All Time: Show Pages Does Not Work

A tip of the cap to West Coast Excel guru Szilvia Juhasz, who taught me how to use the Show Pages trick. Say that you have a pivot table showing revenue by region and product. Add the Customer field to the Report Filter area, but leave it in the (All) state (see Figure 3.34).

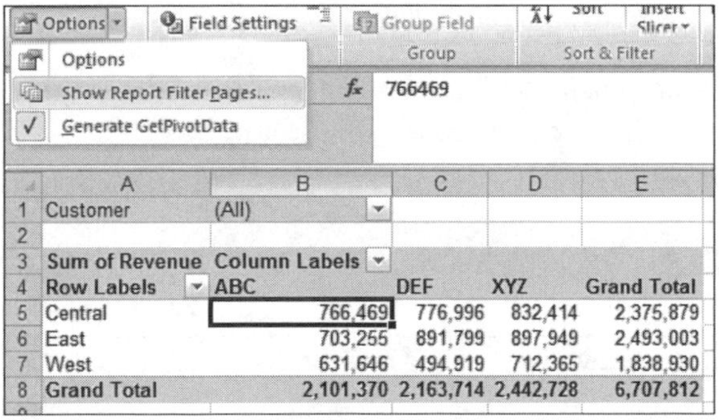

Figure 3.34
Build a report for (All) customers.

	Options ▾	Field Settings	Group Field	Sort Insert Slicer ▾	
	Options		Group	Sort & Filter	
	Show Report Filter Pages...	fx	766469		
✓	Generate GetPivotData				

	A	B	C	D	E
1	Customer	(All)	▾		
2					
3	Sum of Revenue	Column Labels ▾			
4	Row Labels ▾	ABC	DEF	XYZ	Grand Total
5	Central	766,469	776,996	832,414	2,375,879
6	East	703,255	891,799	897,949	2,493,003
7	West	631,646	494,919	712,365	1,838,930
8	Grand Total	2,101,370	2,163,714	2,442,728	6,707,812

Go to the PivotTable Tools Options tab, open the Options drop-down, and select Show Report Filter Pages. When you confirm that you want to show all pages of Customer, Excel leaps into action and produces one new pivot table report for every customer in the database (see Figure 3.35).

Figure 3.35
Excel makes multiple versions of the pivot table, one for each customer.

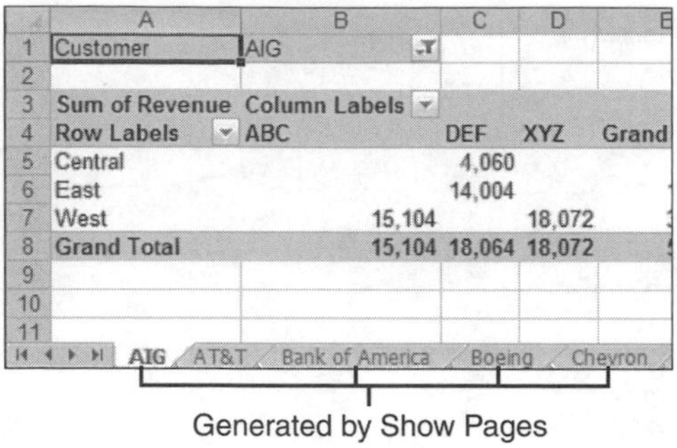

Generated by Show Pages

The Show Pages feature does not work with PowerPivot pivot tables.

The workaround here is to write some VBA to loop through all the items in the report filter field. Doable, but not fun when it was just a couple of clicks away.

Other Minor Annoyances

You lose a few other minor pivot table features when your pivot table is based on PowerPivot:

- Mark Totals with * is not available.
- Background Query is not available.

Normally, if you make some changes in the PivotTable Field List, the focus stays in your worksheet. The PowerPivot Field List seems to take the focus, so after doing anything in your worksheet, you have to go back and click your worksheet.

Bottom Line

Table 3.1 recaps all the benefits and disadvantages of PowerPivot tables. I've added a rating column to indicate just how good a pro is and just how bad each con is.

Table 3.1   Pros and Cons of PowerPivot Tables

Type	Issue	Rating	Pain of Workaround
Pro	Pivot tables from multiple tables	+100	Many VLOOKUPs, added file size.
Pro	Massive data volumes	+100	Use Access.
Pro	Compress more data into memory	+10	None.
Pro	Named sets for asymmetric reporting	+2	Convert pivot tables to values and reformat.

Type	Issue	Rating	Pain of Workaround
Pro	Four pivot charts, one slicer	+10	Use some VBA.
Pro	Slicer AutoLayout	+5	Requires more clicks to format regular slicers.
Pro	Standalone pivot charts (sort of)	+1	Move the table to another sheet manually.
Pro	Convert pivot table to cube formulas	+5	Use `GetPivotData` instead, keep pivot table live.
Pro	DAX measures better than calculated fields	+50	Painful formulas in original data or after.
Con	No Undo	−10	
Con	Won't automatically sort Jan, Feb, Mar	−20	Nine mouse clicks to change.
Con	Don't have easy access 11 calculations	−20	Use DAX to re-create.
Con	Minimal VBA support	−10	
Con	Can't edit underlying data	−1	
Con	Harder to use `GetPivotData`	−1	Still possible to do using concatenation.
Con	Show Items with No Data unavailable	−1	Add fake zero data to original data set.
Con	No calculated fields	−1	DAX is better, but harder.
Con	No calculated items	−1	DAX is better, but harder.
Con	No drill through	−10	
Con	Grouping disabled	−5	Add DAX columns in PowerPivot window.
Con	On-worksheet typing disabled	−1	Drag and drop fields instead.
Con	Show Pages disabled	−20	Write VBA macro.
Con	Mark Totals with * disabled	−1	
	Total of All Ratings:	+181	

In my highly subjective ratings, PowerPivot pivot tables rank at a +181. But, if you don't have to create pivot tables from massive amounts of data, and if you don't have to join tables from multiple worksheets, you can throw out the first two items in the table and they rank at a −19. There are many downsides to PowerPivot pivot tables.

It probably comes down to a "pivot table by pivot table" decision. Do you have to create asymmetric reports or difficult running date calculations? Then you would probably go through PowerPivot. If you don't have to do so, a regular pivot table would work just fine.

Next Steps

In the next chapter, you will learn the various ways to get your data into PowerPivot.

Getting Your Data into PowerPivot

There are a number of ways to get your data into PowerPivot:

- You can link to Excel data that has been converted to a table.
- You can copy and paste Excel data into PowerPoint. Later you can paste append to an existing table.
- You can import from a database such as Access or SQL Server.
- You can import from any SharePoint report that has an Atom symbol in the header.
- You can import from many Atom data feeds. Many Internet databases have Atom feeds, and Atom is a new way to publish data from SQL Server, so there will be increasing examples of corporate data published as Atom feeds.
- From text files, either CSV or tab delimited.
- From Oracle, Teradata, Sybase, Informix, IBM.
- From any ODBC/OLEDB data source.

One question is whether you should copy and paste an Excel table or if you should link to the table.

Getting Excel Data into PowerPivot

You probably have hundreds of Excel data sets that are appropriate for importing into PowerPivot. You need a single row of unique headings followed by rows of data.

When you have this data, you can either link to a table version of the data stored in the workbook, copy and paste, or import from the Excel file.

When you copy and paste, you don't have to alter your original data in Excel. You can copy and paste from any workbook to another workbook. But, because you cannot edit cells in the PowerPivot grid, you cannot make changes to the data in place. You would have to make changes in Excel, recopy, and paste replace. If you get new records, PowerPivot does allow you to paste append.

When you link to a table, you have to alter the data in Excel by making the range into a "table." This refers to the Format as Table command on the Home tab. There are some downsides (and upsides) to defining data as a table, which are discussed later in this chapter. The table has to be stored in the workbook where your PowerPivot model resides. One advantage is that you can refresh the link and any changes to the Excel data will appear in PowerPivot.

You can also import data from an external Excel file. When you import the data, you can either format as a table or create a named range for the import area. Again, if the underlying data changes, you can refresh the link and new data will come into PowerPivot.

Converting Your Data to a Table and Linking

Figure 4.1 shows a typical data set in Excel. You have headings in row 1 followed by rows of data.

Figure 4.1
A typical data set in Excel has one row of headings followed by data.

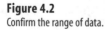

	A	B	C	D	E	F	G	H
1	Region	Product	Date	Customer	Quantity	Revenue	COGS	Profit
2	East	XYZ	1/1/2008	Ford	1000	22810	10220	12590
3	Central	DEF	1/2/2008	Verizon	100	2257	984	1273
4	East	DEF	1/4/2008	Merck	800	18552	7872	10680
5	East	XYZ	1/4/2008	Texaco	400	9152	4088	5064
6	East	DEF	1/7/2008	State Farm	1000	21730	9840	11890
7	East	ABC	1/7/2008	General Motors	400	8456	3388	5068
8	Central	ABC	1/9/2008	General Motors	800	16416	6776	9640

Excel 2003 introduced the concept of an Excel list. In Excel 2007, the Excel list concept was formalized and renamed as an Excel table. If you are willing to format your data as a table, you can get the data into PowerPivot in a couple of clicks.

To format the data as a table, choose one cell in the data set and press Ctrl+T. Excel displays the Create Table dialog where you can confirm the extent of your table and if your table has headers (see Figure 4.2).

Figure 4.2
Confirm the range of data.

Create Table

Where is the data for your table?

=$A$1:$H$564

☑ My table has headers

OK   Cancel

When a range is converted to a table, you automatically get the filter drop-downs in the first 1. Some people hate this because it covers up the right-justified headings. You automatically get a banded row table format (see Figure 4.3).

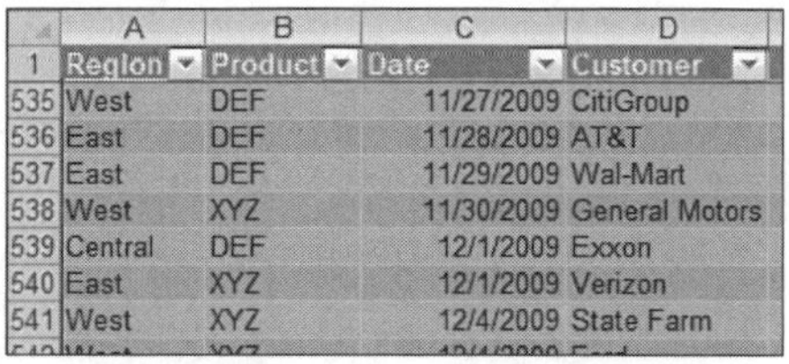

Figure 4.3
Excel applies a banded row format and adds AutoFilter drop-downs.

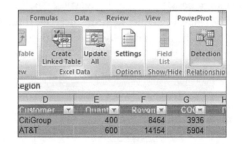

On the left side of the Table Tools Design tab, you will see that Excel has assigned a name to your table, something like Table1. Click in that name box and type a better name, such as Sales.

On the PowerPivot tab, click Create Linked Table, as shown in Figure 4.4.

Figure 4.4
One click to create a PowerPivot table.

The PowerPivot window opens, and your data appears in PowerPivot. The name that you gave the table is used on the worksheet tab. A linked icon appears next to the name to remind you that this is a linked table (see Figure 4.5).

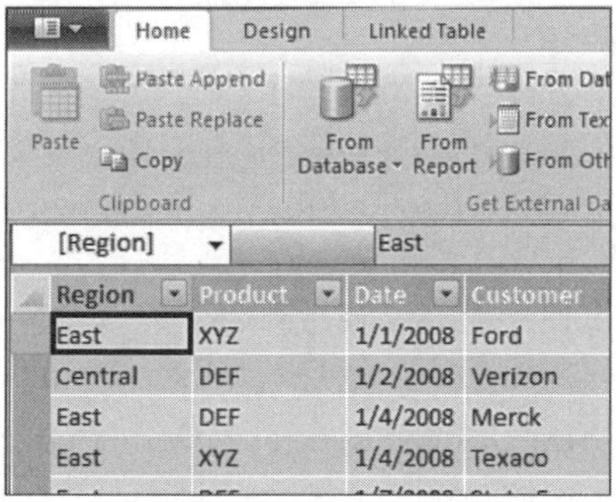

Figure 4.5
The linked data appears in PowerPivot.

To see a demo of linking a table to PowerPivot, search for MrExcel PowerPivot 4 at YouTube.

Ramifications of Converting Your Data to a Table

Many changes happen when you convert your data to a table. If you have not been using lists in Excel 2003 or tables in Excel 2007, you should understand these ramifications.

The ramifications are not all bad:

- If you are not using freeze panes and you scroll down in your data set, the headings from row 1 move up to replace the column letters. This is a nice feature (see Figure 4.6).

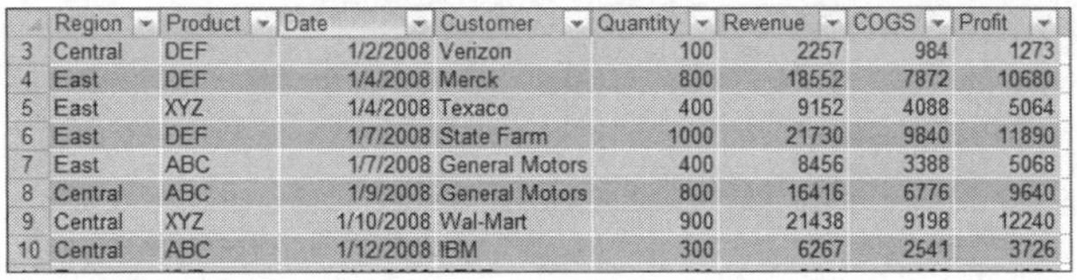

Figure 4.6
If you scroll down in the data, your headings stay visible, replacing column letters A, B, C.

	Region	Product	Date	Customer	Quantity	Revenue	COGS	Profit
3	Central	DEF	1/2/2008	Verizon	100	2257	984	1273
4	East	DEF	1/4/2008	Merck	800	18552	7872	10680
5	East	XYZ	1/4/2008	Texaco	400	9152	4088	5064
6	East	DEF	1/7/2008	State Farm	1000	21730	9840	11890
7	East	ABC	1/7/2008	General Motors	400	8456	3388	5068
8	Central	ABC	1/9/2008	General Motors	800	16416	6776	9640
9	Central	XYZ	1/10/2008	Wal-Mart	900	21438	9198	12240
10	Central	ABC	1/12/2008	IBM	300	6267	2541	3726

- You automatically get a banded row format. You can use the Table Styles gallery on the Table Tools Design tab to change back to a plain formatting (see Figure 4.7). If the formatting really drives you crazy, open the gallery, right-click the thumbnail for the plain style, and select Set as Default. All futures tables on this computer will now have the plain table style.

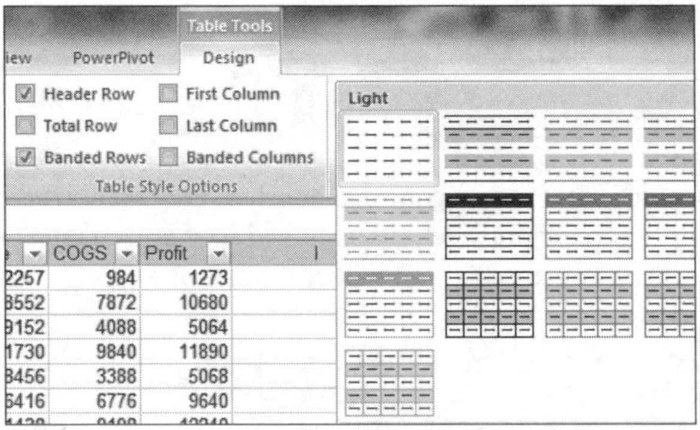

Figure 4.7
You can get rid of the banded rows formatting.

- Custom Views on the View tab will be disabled for the entire workbook. This isn't a popular feature, so it won't affect most people.
- You cannot share a workbook with a table with Review, Share Workbook. Again, workbook sharing disables so much functionality in Excel that it is unlikely you are using it.
- The AutoFilter drop-downs appear by default, often covering up your right-justified headings. You can either center your headings or visit Data, Filter to turn off the drop-downs.
- The first blank row below the table is a special row. Any data that you paste into this row is automatically appended to the table. Any calculations that you add to the first blank column to the right of the table are appended to the table.

> **NOTE**
> This is a good feature. It means that any pivot tables, charts, formulas, or PowerPivot linked tables will get the new rows and columns after a refresh.

- Formulas in tables use a different nomenclature than regular formulas. A formula entered in cell I2 will be copied down to the entire table. Follow these steps:

  1. Type a new heading in cell I1 of **GP%**. When you press Enter, Excel will format column I like the rest of the table.

  2. Format cell I2 as a percentage with one decimal place. You can do this by selecting % on the Home tab and then clicking Increase Decimal once.

  3. In I2, type an equal sign. Click H2. Type a slash for division. Click F2. Take a look at the formula in Figure 4.8. This is the new table nomenclature. =[@ Profit] means the Profit column in the current row. [@Revenue] means the Revenue column in the current row.

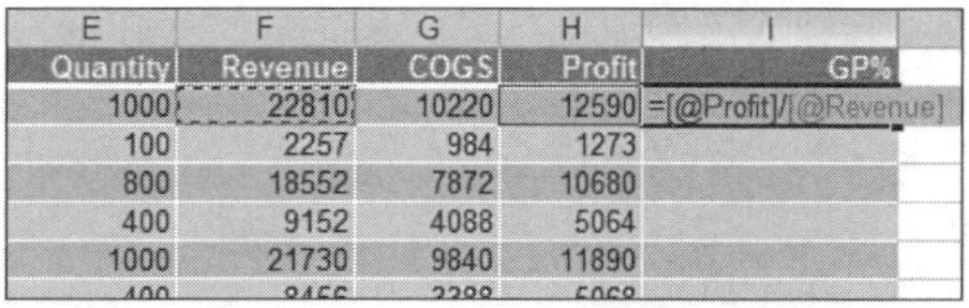

Figure 4.8
Formulas that point inside of tables use a new nomenclature.

E	F	G	H	I
Quantity	Revenue	COGS	Profit	GP%
1000	22810	10220	12590	=[@Profit]/[@Revenue]
100	2257	984	1273	
800	18552	7872	10680	
400	9152	4088	5064	
1000	21730	9840	11890	
400	8456	3388	5068	

4. When you press Enter to accept the formula, that formula is automatically copied throughout the table (see Figure 4.9).

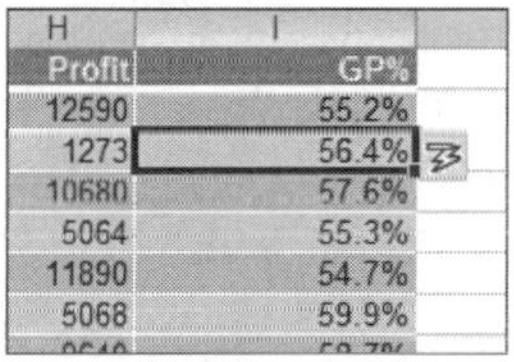

Figure 4.9
The formula is automatically copied throughout the table.

H	I
Profit	GP%
12590	55.2%
1273	56.4%
10680	57.6%
5064	55.3%
11890	54.7%
5068	59.9%
9640	52.7%

NOTE Tables are not bad. They are different. For people who have been used to formulas like =H2/F2, it is a little bizarre to see new formula syntax. If you are not a fan of Custom view or shared workbooks, there really is no reason not to use the tables.

Getting Updated Linked Table Data into PowerPivot

Say that a month has passed and you now have new sales data. Follow these steps to get the data into PowerPivot:

1. Copy the new data.

2. Select the first blank row below your table (see Figure 4.10).

3. Paste that data into the first blank row below your table. The new data will become formatted like the rest of the table. Any formulas on the right side should copy down to the new data (see Figure 4.11).

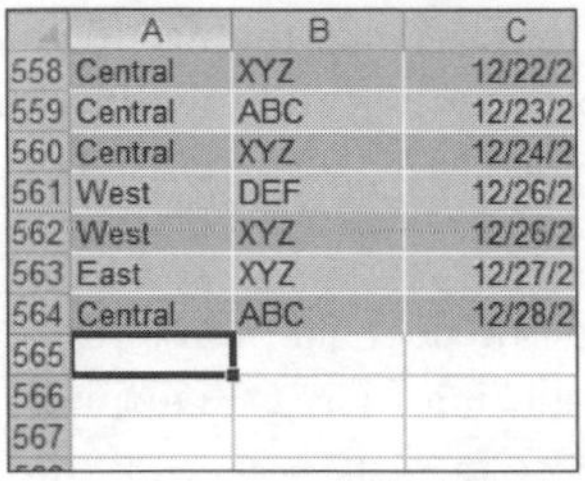

Figure 4.10
Paste adjacent to the
old data.

	A	B	C
558	Central	XYZ	12/22/2
559	Central	ABC	12/23/2
560	Central	XYZ	12/24/2
561	West	DEF	12/26/2
562	West	XYZ	12/26/2
563	East	XYZ	12/27/2
564	Central	ABC	12/28/2
565			
566			
567			

Figure 4.11
The new data will
become part of the table.
Formulas will copy down.

	Region	Product	Date
558	Central	XYZ	12/22/2009
559	Central	ABC	12/23/2009
560	Central	XYZ	12/24/2009
561	West	DEF	12/26/2009
562	West	XYZ	12/26/2009
563	East	XYZ	12/27/2009
564	Central	ABC	12/28/2009
565	East	DEF	1/5/2010
566	West	ABC	1/6/2010
567	East	XYZ	1/6/2010
568	East	DEF	1/6/2010
569	East	ABC	1/7/2010
570	East	XYZ	1/7/2010

4. Go to the PowerPivot tab in the Excel Ribbon. Select the Update All icon next to the
Create Linked Table icon. This will force PowerPivot to refresh the linked tables. The
PowerPivot window will open, and after a brief delay, the record count in the lower left
should update to reflect the correct record count (see Figure 4.12). Updating the data
in the PowerPivot window does not update any pivot tables built from that data.

Figure 4.12
Select to update linked
tables.

Region	Product	Date	Custo
East	XYZ	1/1/2008	Ford
Central	DEF	1/2/2008	Verizo
East	DEF	1/4/2008	Merck
East	XYZ	1/4/2008	Texaco
East	DEF	1/7/2008	State
East	ABC	1/7/2008	Gener
Central	ABC	1/9/2008	Gener
Central	XYZ	1/10/2...	Wal-M
Central	ABC	1/12/2...	IBM
East	XYZ	1/14/2...	AT&T
East	ABC	1/15/2...	Verizo
East	ABC	1/16/2...	CitiGr
West	DEF	1/19/2...	Verizo
East	ABC	1/21/2...	SBC C
West	ABC	1/21/2...	Merck
West	ABC	1/23/2...	Gener
East	ABC	1/24/2...	IBM
Central	ABC	1/25/2...	CitiGr
East	ABC	1/26/2	IBM

Sales

Record: ◄ ◄ 1 of 586 ► ►

5. Return to the Excel window. If you select a pivot table, the PowerPivot Field List should alert you that new data is available and offer a Refresh button. Click the button to refresh (see Figure 4.13).

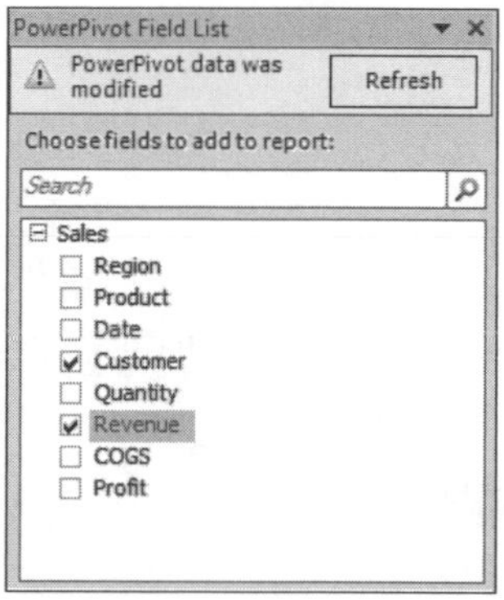

Figure 4.13
This message alerts you that you have to refresh the pivot table, too.

Add Excel Data by Copying and Pasting

When you link to a table in Excel, that data has to be stored in a worksheet in the PowerPivot workbook. Sometimes you might want to keep the source data in its own file and not add a PowerPivot model to that file. One example that comes to mind is if co-workers using Excel 2007 need to access the file. In these cases, you can copy and paste the data into PowerPivot.

Follow these steps:

1. Create a blank Excel workbook that will hold your PowerPivot model.
2. Open the Excel workbook that has the data you want to copy into PowerPivot.
3. Select one cell in the data. Press Ctrl+* to select the entire data set, as shown in Figure 4.14.
4. Press Ctrl+C to copy.
5. Press Ctrl+Tab to switch back to the workbook with the PowerPivot model.
6. Select PowerPivot, PowerPivot Window to open a blank PowerPivot window.

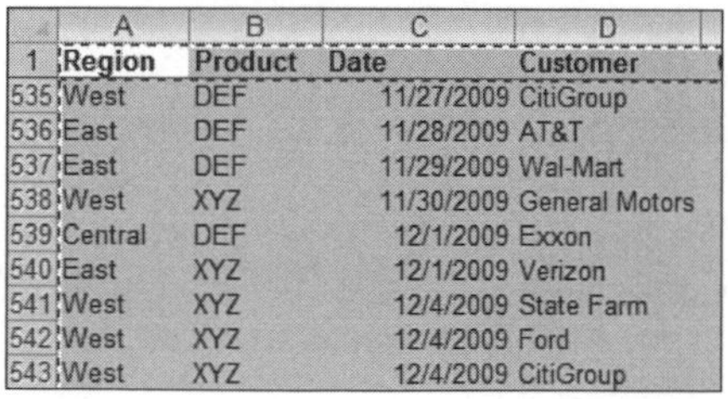

	A	B	C	D
1	Region	Product	Date	Customer
535	West	DEF	11/27/2009	CitiGroup
536	East	DEF	11/28/2009	AT&T
537	East	DEF	11/29/2009	Wal-Mart
538	West	XYZ	11/30/2009	General Motors
539	Central	DEF	12/1/2009	Exxon
540	East	XYZ	12/1/2009	Verizon
541	West	XYZ	12/4/2009	State Farm
542	West	XYZ	12/4/2009	Ford
543	West	XYZ	12/4/2009	CitiGroup

Figure 4.14
Select data in Excel and copy.

7. Select the Paste icon in the PowerPivot window (see Figure 4.15).

PowerPivot
Home
Design
Paste Append
Paste Replace
Paste
Copy
Clipboard

Figure 4.15
Paste in PowerPivot.

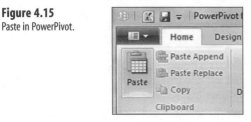

PowerPivot shows a preview of the data and proposes a name, such as Table (see Figure 4.16).

Paste Preview
Preview the data that you are about to paste. You can modify
first row as a header row in the destination table.
Table Name:
Table
Data to be pasted:
Region Product Date
East XYZ 1/1/2008 12:00:...
Central DEF 1/2/2008 12:00:...
East DEF 1/4/2008 12:00:...
East XYZ 1/4/2008 12:00:...
East DEF 1/7/2008 12:00:...
East ABC 1/7/2008 12:00:...
Central ABC 1/9/2008 12:00:...
Central XYZ 1/10/2008 12:00...
Central ABC 1/12/2008 12:00...
East XYZ 1/14/2008 12:00...
East ABC 1/15/2008 12:00...
East ABC 1/16/2008 12:00...
West DEF 1/19/2008 12:00...
Use first row as column headers.

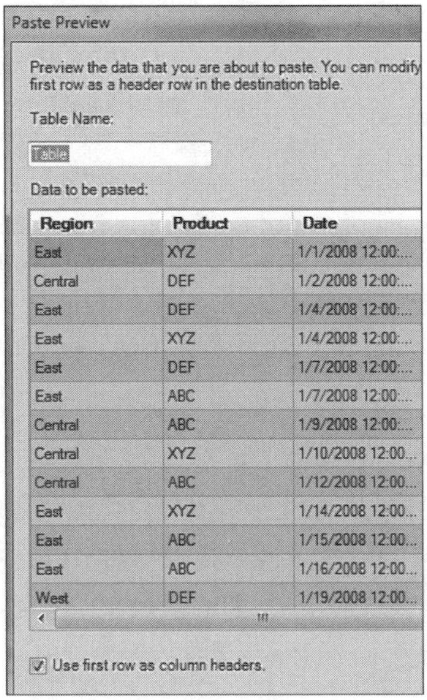

Figure 4.16
The pasted data will start with a default name that you can change.

8. Type a new name for the table, such as Sales, as shown in Figure 4.17.
9. Click OK. The data will appear in the PowerPivot window (see Figure 4.18).

Paste Preview
Table Name:
Sales
Data to be pasted:
Region Product
East XYZ

Figure 4.17
Type a new name for the table.

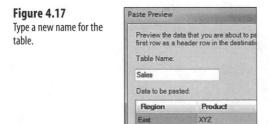

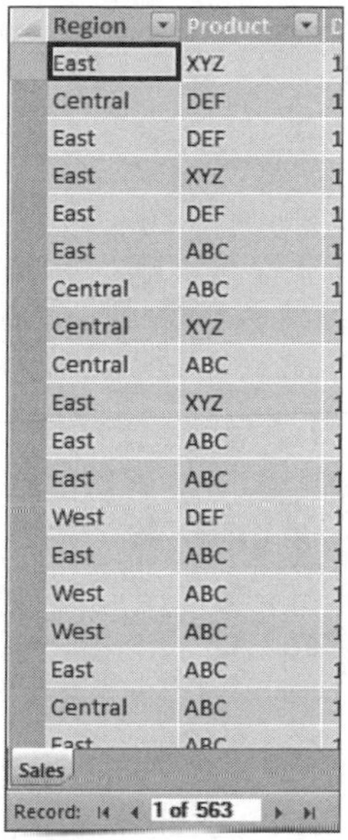

Figure 4.18
The copied data is pasted into PowerPivot.

There is no link from PowerPivot back to your original data. If that data gets updated, it will be up to you to remember to update the data in PowerPivot.

4

Adding New Records to the Table in PowerPivot

After a month, you have new sales data for the new month. Provided the structure of the columns did not change, you can add this data to your PowerPivot table. Follow these steps:

1. Copy the new data from Excel. It is fine to include the headings in the data.
2. Switch to the workbook containing the PowerPivot model.
3. Select PowerPivot Window from the PowerPivot tab in Excel.
4. Select Paste Append (see Figure 4.19).

Figure 4.19
Select to paste append.

The Paste Preview dialog will show you the existing data and the new data. As you can see in Figure 4.20, there is a warning that the "Date" heading is the wrong format for the date column.

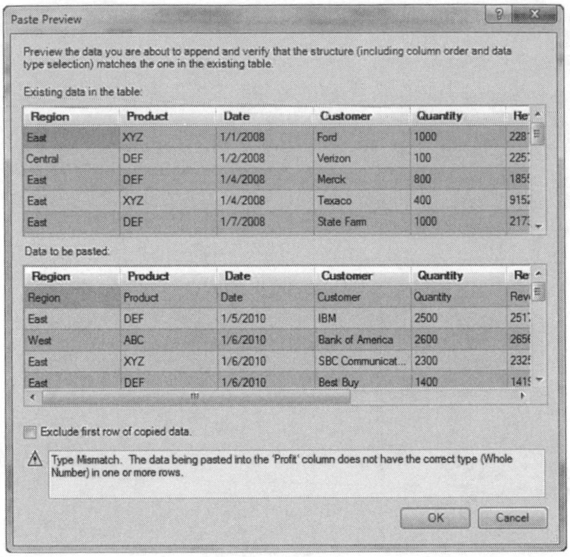

Figure 4.20
The Paste Preview will warn you if any data has the wrong format.

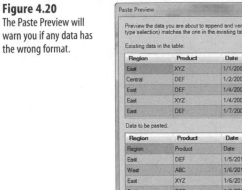

5. Because you want to ignore the headings in the appended data, select the box for Exclude First Row of Copied Data. The Paste Preview warning about a Type Mismatch will disappear (see Figure 4.21).

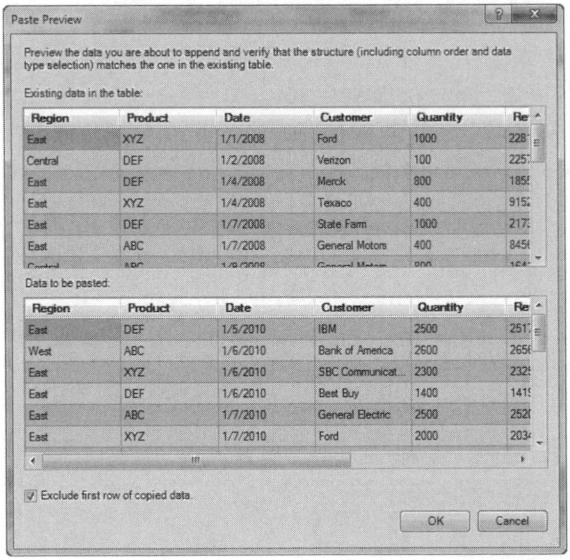

Figure 4.21
Exclude the first row of copied data.

6. Click OK to append the data. The new data is appended after the old data. The record count should reflect the new total record count (see Figure 4.22).

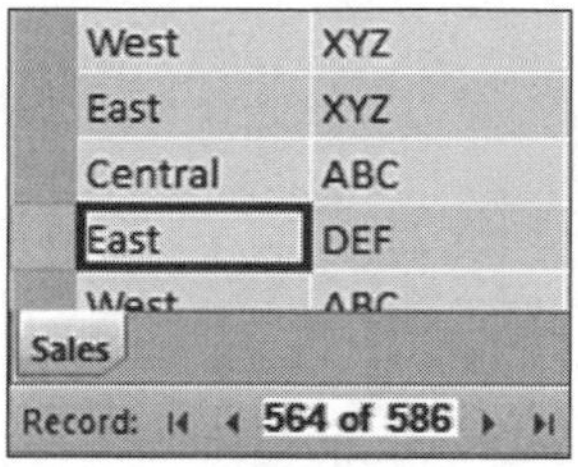

Figure 4.22
The record count shows the correct number of records.

Dealing with Improper Data in the Pasted Data

When you first pasted the data to PowerPivot, each column was identified to have a specific data type. You can choose a column in the PowerPivot window and look in the Formatting group of the Home tab to see the format chosen. In Figure 4.23, the third column has a format of Date. In Figure 4.24, the Revenue column has a format of Whole Number.

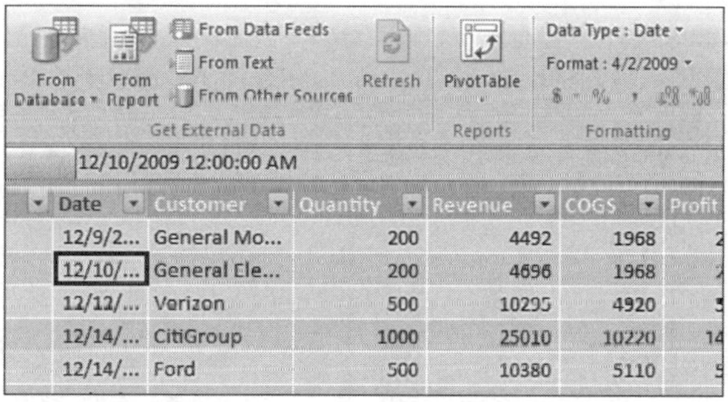

Figure 4.23
The Date column has a data type of Date.

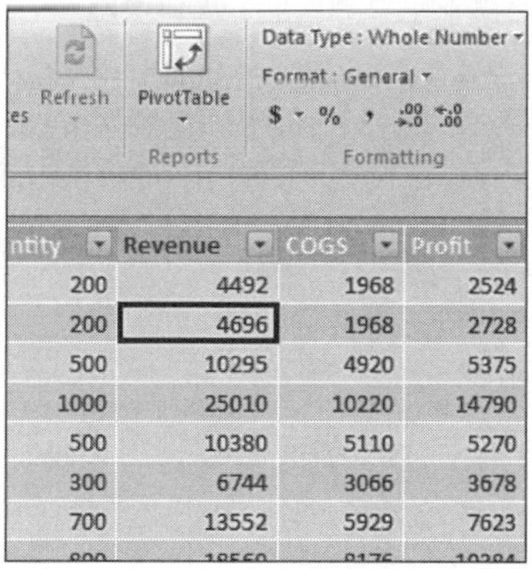

Figure 4.24
The Revenue column has a data type of Whole Number.

PowerPivot chose those formats by inspecting the data. One hundred percent of your data values would have to be dates in order for PowerPivot to choose a Date data type. If you would prefer that revenue be stored as a decimal or as currency, you can change the data type using the drop-down in Figure 4.25.

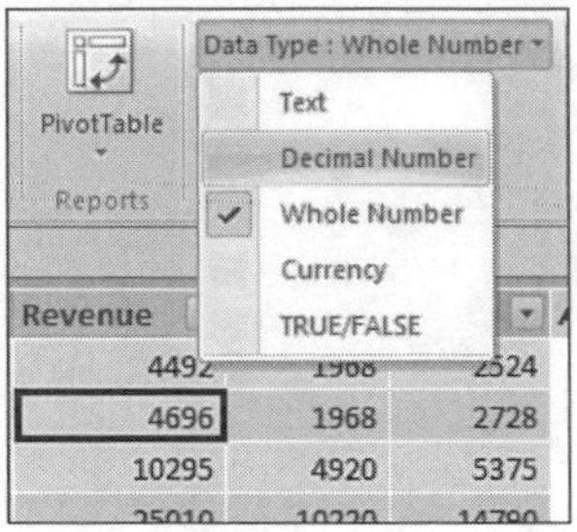

Figure 4.25
You can change the
data type assigned by
PowerPivot.

Let's start over with a slightly different data set. In Figure 4.26 there are two problems highlighted. There is a blank cell in the revenue column in F14. For those of you who have been using regular pivot tables, you know that a blank cell in a numeric column is enough to cause a regular pivot table to count instead of sum. In cell C12, the legacy computer system allowed someone to key in a nonexistent date of January 32, 2010.

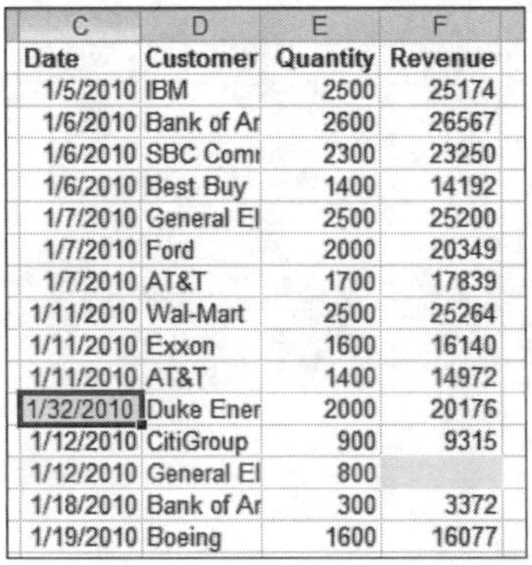

Figure 4.26
This data has some data
type integrity issues.

C	D	E	F
Date	Customer	Quantity	Revenue
1/5/2010	IBM	2500	25174
1/6/2010	Bank of Ar	2600	26567
1/6/2010	SBC Comr	2300	23250
1/6/2010	Best Buy	1400	14192
1/7/2010	General El	2500	25200
1/7/2010	Ford	2000	20349
1/7/2010	AT&T	1700	17839
1/11/2010	Wal-Mart	2500	25264
1/11/2010	Exxon	1600	16140
1/11/2010	AT&T	1400	14972
1/32/2010	Duke Ener	2000	20176
1/12/2010	CitiGroup	900	9315
1/12/2010	General El	800	
1/18/2010	Bank of Ar	300	3372
1/19/2010	Boeing	1600	16077

When you copy and paste that data to PowerPivot, the blank cell in the Revenue column does not cause a problem. The data type remains a whole number (see Figure 4.27).

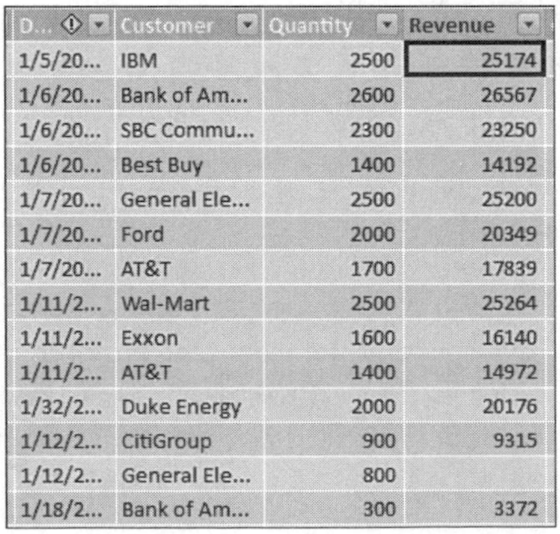

Figure 4.27
A blank cell in a numeric
column is okay.

D...	Customer	Quantity	Revenue
1/5/20...	IBM	2500	25174
1/6/20...	Bank of Am...	2600	26567
1/6/20...	SBC Commu...	2300	23250
1/6/20...	Best Buy	1400	14192
1/7/20...	General Ele...	2500	25200
1/7/20...	Ford	2000	20349
1/7/20...	AT&T	1700	17839
1/11/2...	Wal-Mart	2500	25264
1/11/2...	Exxon	1600	16140
1/11/2...	AT&T	1400	14972
1/32/2...	Duke Energy	2000	20176
1/12/2...	CitiGroup	900	9315
1/12/2...	General Ele...	800	
1/18/2...	Bank of Am...	300	3372

The invalid date causes problems. The data type is converted to Text. However, PowerPivot offers to add a calculated column and convert the text dates to real dates (see Figure 4.28).

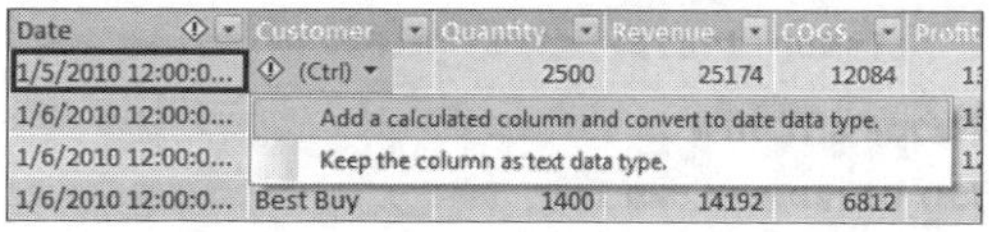

Figure 4.28
The dates are converted to text, and PowerPivot offers to add a formula to convert them back.

If you allow PowerPivot to create the formula, it uses the `DATEVALUE` function to produce real dates. The invalid date of 1/32/2010 is converted to a blank cell (see Figure 4.29).

Figure 4.29
At least you have an audit trail of why the new column has a blank date.

```
=IF(NOT(ISERROR(DATEVALUE([Date]))),DATEVALUE([Date]))
```

Date	Customer	Quantity	Revenue	COGS	Profit	CalculatedColumn1
1/5/2010 12:00:0...	IBM	2500	25174	12084	13090	1/5/2010
1/6/2010 12:00:0...	Bank of Am...	2600	26567	12752	13815	1/6/2010
1/6/2010 12:00:0...	SBC Commu...	2300	23250	11160	12090	1/6/2010
1/6/2010 12:00:0...	Best Buy	1400	14192	6812	7380	1/6/2010
1/7/2010 12:00:0...	General Ele...	2500	25200	12096	13104	1/7/2010
1/7/2010 12:00:0...	Ford	2000	20349	9768	10581	1/7/2010
1/7/2010 12:00:0...	AT&T	1700	17839	8563	9276	1/7/2010
1/11/2010 12:00:...	Wal-Mart	2500	25264	12127	13137	1/11/2010
1/11/2010 12:00:...	Exxon	1600	16140	7747	8393	1/11/2010
1/11/2010 12:00:...	AT&T	1400	14972	7187	7785	1/11/2010
1/32/2010	Duke Energy	2000	20176	9684	10492	
1/12/2010 12:00:...	CitiGroup	900	9315	4471	4844	1/12/2010

If you create a pivot table from this data, the pivot table correctly sums the Revenue column. One extra row appears at the top of the pivot table because of the blank Date field. (See Figure 4.30)

Figure 4.30
The pivot table is smart enough to sum rather than count.

Row Labels	Sum of Revenue
	20176
1/5/2010	25174
1/6/2010	64009
1/7/2010	63388
1/11/2010	56376
1/12/2010	9315
1/18/2010	3372
1/19/2010	16077
1/21/2010	19444
1/26/2010	30950
1/27/2010	44642
1/29/2010	29300
Grand Total	**382223**

Overall, this was not a horrible outcome. PowerPivot dealt with the bad data in a reasonable way and even helped you build a formula to deal with the dates.

Dealing with Bad Data in Appended Data

Suppose that the first copy and paste goes well and the Date column is assigned a Date type. Now, you try to append data that contains errors such as those back in Figure 4.26.

As you paste append, the Paste Preview window warns you that one or more dates are invalid, as shown in Figure 4.31.

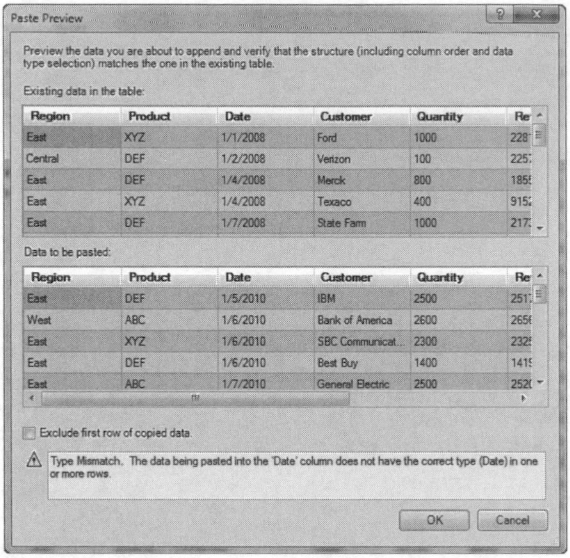

Figure 4.31
The Paste Preview window warns you that you have invalid dates.

If you try to continue, PowerPivot will refuse to paste the data. After the table has been created and that column has been set as a date, PowerPivot will not let you paste non-date data into that column (see Figure 4.32).

In this case, you have to go back to Excel, correct the invalid dates, and copy and paste append again.

Figure 4.32
The paste will fail.

Changing Pasted Data

After pasting the data to Excel and creating a pivot table, you realize that there is a mistake in the data. One account was miscoded to the wrong region, or a data transposition error caused the 19,000 sale to be recorded as 91,000.

Although I love to say that PowerPivot lets you deal with millions of rows in a grid that feels like Excel, the fact is that the PowerPivot grid is not Excel. You can sort, filter, and scroll like Excel. You can add formulas to an entire column like Excel. But you cannot edit a single cell like Excel.

You cannot even delete an entire row. You can delete entire columns, but not entire rows.

To change the data, you can go back to the original data set, make the change, copy the data. Then in PowerPivot, you can choose to paste replace, as shown in Figure 4.33

Figure 4.33
You have a Paste Replace option.

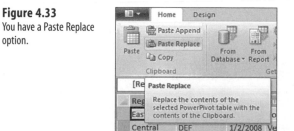

If your copied data includes headings, you will see a warning that there is a type mismatch. Click the box for Exclude First Row of Copied Data in the Paste Preview dialog (see Figure 4.34).

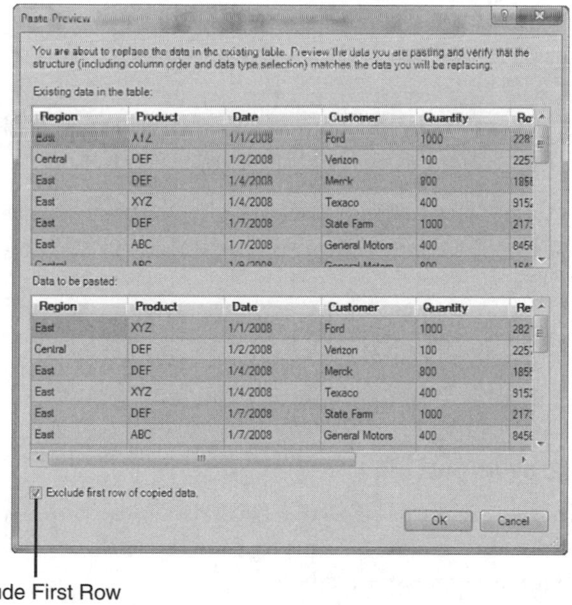

Figure 4.34
If your copied data includes headings, choose to exclude the first row.

Exclude First Row

Handling If the Original Data Source Is Lost

If you have data in the PowerPivot window but you no longer have access to the original Excel data, you can get the data out of PowerPivot to edit. Just follow these steps:

1. Go to the PowerPivot window.
2. Select the icon in the top left of the window to select the entire table (see Figure 4.35).
3. Use the Copy icon.
4. Return to Excel.
5. Select a blank section of a worksheet and paste. You can now edit the data.
6. Select all the data using Ctrl+*.
7. Return to PowerPivot.
8. Paste replace.

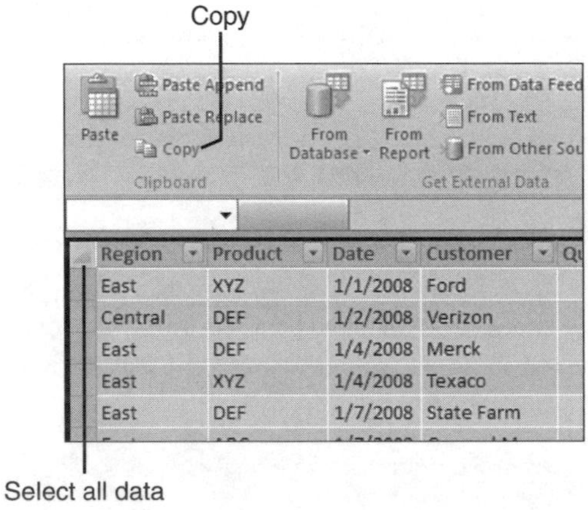

Figure 4.35
Select the whole table.

Copy

Select all data

> **CAUTION**
>
> As you are bouncing back and forth between Excel and PowerPivot, it is easy to get mixed up and to return to PowerPivot from the wrong workbook.
>
> Say that you have a PowerPivot model in Book1. You copy the data from the PowerPivot window and return to Excel. You create a new workbook called Book2. Paste the data to Book2. Edit the data. Copy the data.
>
> You need to return to Book1 before you launch the PowerPivot window. If you launch the PowerPivot window from Book2, your data will seem to be missing, since there is no PowerPivot data in Book2.

Adding Excel Data by Importing

There is a third method for getting your Excel data into PowerPivot. This method is a bit more hidden from view. It almost seems that the PowerPivot team didn't want to promote this method, but it has some specific benefits.

In this method, you import data from an external workbook. Here are some advantages:

■ You don't have to convert the data to a table. It does help to apply a range name to the data. Applying a named range is not as sweeping as using the table command.

- The original data workbook can live out on a departmental network drive, and people can still continue to use that workbook in all the ways that they used to use the workbook. You aren't going to freak anyone out because you changed the format of the workbook that they use all the time.

- A copy of the data is stored in the PowerPivot workbook similar to the copy and paste method, but PowerPivot also remembers the link back to the original workbook. If you go to PowerPivot and choose Refresh All, the current version of the data is brought into Excel.

Naming the Range

Normally, you would not think that it would be important to name your range. In my first experiment with importing, I had a 563-row data set that was imported as a 650-row data set, with the first 90 rows being blank. I have no idea what had happened to this data set over the 4 years that I've been using it to convince PowerPivot that the data extended 90 rows past the true end of the data.

Because this happened to me once, I am now always taking the extra step of applying a range name to the data. This certainly has downsides, though, because any time you add new data to the bottom of the data set, you will either have to add it above the last row in the data set, or make sure to change the named range.

One workaround is to convert the data to a table. The table name will always grow with the data.

The second workaround is to always be extremely careful when you insert new rows do that you add them above the last row.

The third workaround could have been to use a dynamic range name using the OFFSET formula as a named range. Unfortunately, the PowerPivot team confirms that they will not be supporting the use off OFFSET in version 1 of PowerPivot.

Importing the Excel Data to PowerPivot

Open the PowerPivot window. On the Home tab, in the Get External Data group, there is an icon for From Other Sources.

Click that icon and you are presented with a long list of data sources from which PowerPivot can import. Scroll down to the bottom of the list and you will see Microsoft Excel, as shown in Figure 4.36.

Browse to your Excel file and indicate that the first row contains column headers, as shown in Figure 4.37.

Choose the proper range name and click OK. PowerPivot will import a copy of your data into the PowerPivot window, as shown in Figure 4.38.

4

Figure 4.36
Select From Other
Sources, Microsoft Excel.

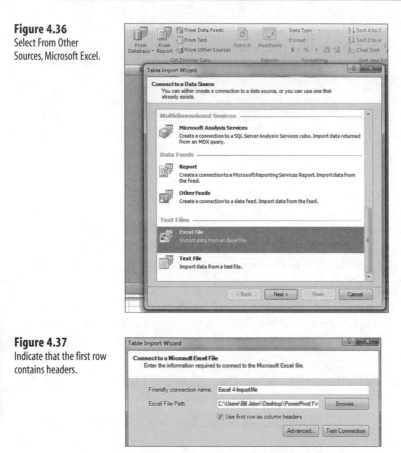

Figure 4.37
Indicate that the first row
contains headers.

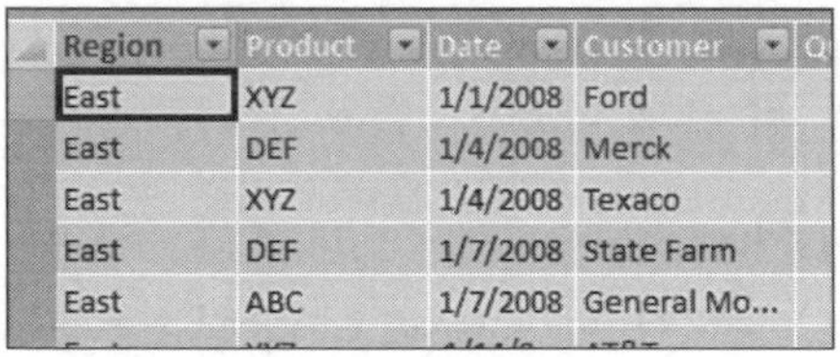

Figure 4.38
This is a copy of your Excel
worksheet.

Refreshing the Imported Data in PowerPivot

If the data in the Excel workbook later changes, you can come back to PowerPivot and select Refresh from the Get External Data group of the PowerPivot Home tab (see Figure 4.39).

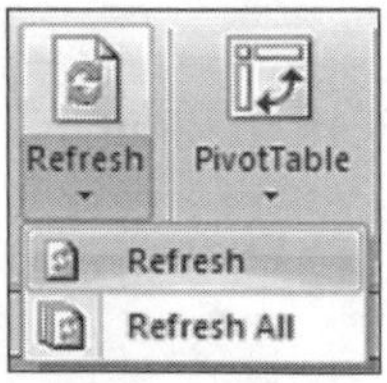

Figure 4.39
Select Refresh to reread
the file from disk.

PowerPivot will display the Data Refresh dialog. You can watch the progress as rows are imported. Eventually, PowerPivot should report success, as shown in Figure 4.40.

Figure 4.40
PowerPivot replaces the data with current data from the workbook.

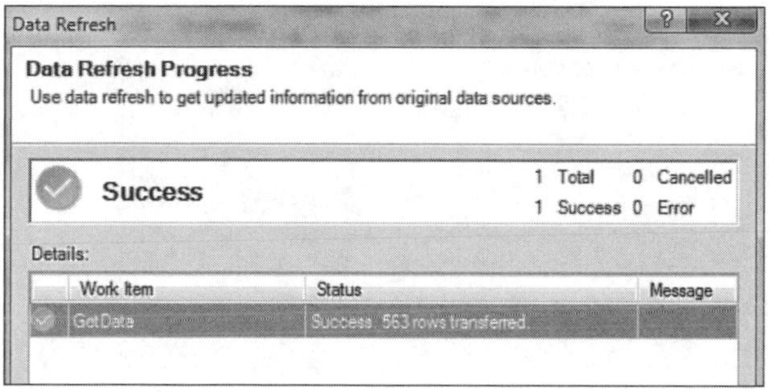

Importing Data from SQL Server

To import tables from SQL Server, follow these steps:

1. Open the PowerPivot window.
2. Select From Database, From SQL Server. The Table Import Wizard will appear.
3. Open the Server Name drop-down. PowerPivot will pause while it attempts to retrieve a list of installed servers. Choose a server from the list.
4. Your SQL Server administrator will tell you if you should use Windows authentication of SQL Server authentication.
5. Open the Database Name drop-down. Again, PowerPivot will pause while it loads up a list of available databases. Choose one database from the list. The Table Import Wizard should look something like Figure 4.41. Click Next.

Figure 4.41
Choose a server and database.

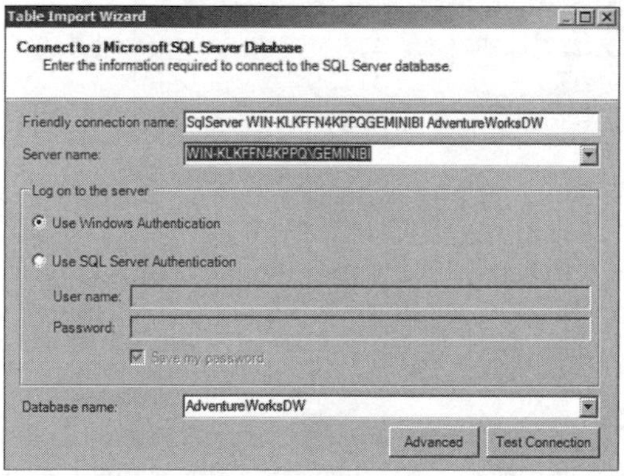

6. In the next step, indicate that you want to select from a list of tables and views, as shown in Figure 4.42. Click Next.

7. Scroll through the list to find your main transaction table. In Figure 4.43, FactInternetSales is selected.

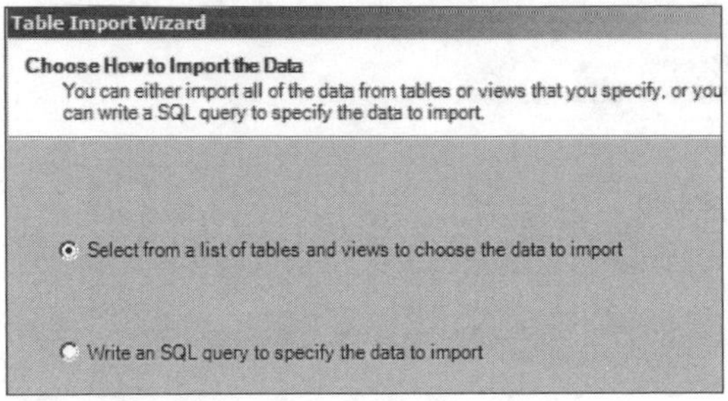

Figure 4.42
Choose existing tables or write your own SQL.

8. Click the Select Related Tables button. PowerPivot will examine the SQL Server dictionary and find all tables with relationships to your selected table. In Figure 4.44, there are six related tables.

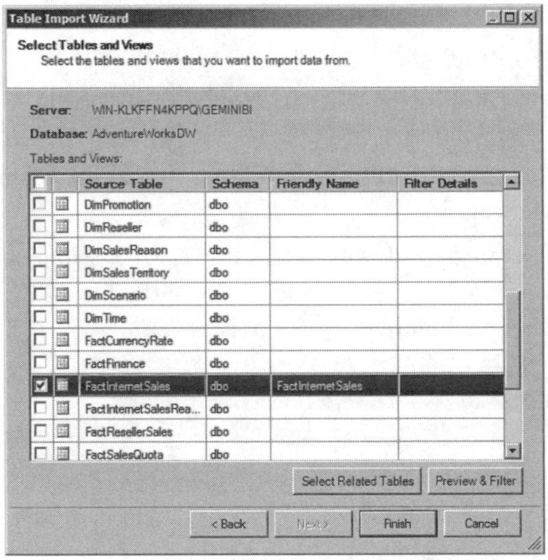

Figure 4.43
Choose the main transaction table.

9. Click Finish. You will watch as each individual table is imported. Eventually, PowerPivot will report Success, as shown in Figure 4.45

Importing a Text File

You can import data from text files or CSV files using PowerPivot. Back in Chapter 2, "The Promise of PowerPivot," the example walked through importing a 1.8 million row demo.txt file.

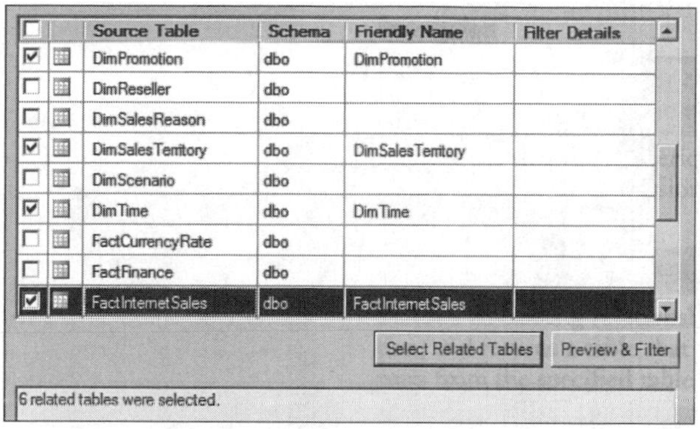

Figure 4.44
Click the Related Tables button to gather all linked tables.

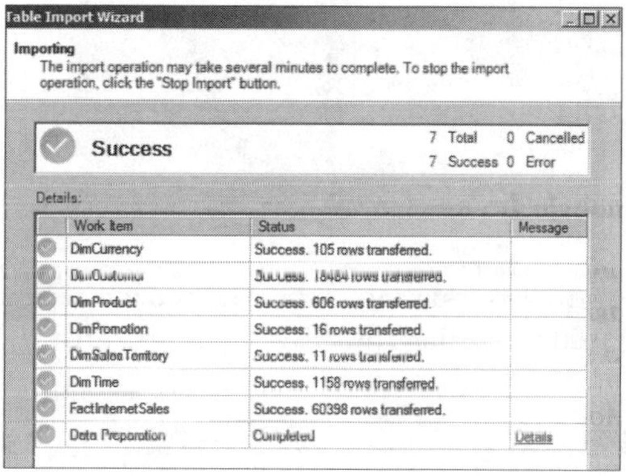

		Source Table	Schema	Friendly Name	Filter Details	
☑	▦	DimPromotion	dbo	DimPromotion		
☐	▦	DimReseller	dbo			
☐	▦	DimSalesReason	dbo			
☑	▦	DimSalesTerritory	dbo	DimSalesTerritory		
☐	▦	DimScenario	dbo			
☑	▦	DimTime	dbo	DimTime		
☐	▦	FactCurrencyRate	dbo			
☐	▦	FactFinance	dbo			
☑	▦	FactInternetSales	dbo	FactInternetSales		

Select Related Tables   Preview & Filter

6 related tables were selected.

Figure 4.45
All seven tables are imported to PowerPivot.

Table Import Wizard

Importing
The import operation may take several minutes to complete. To stop the import operation, click the "Stop Import" button.

✓ **Success**   7 Total   0 Cancelled
             7 Success 0 Error

Details:

	Work Item	Status	Message
◉	DimCurrency	Success. 105 rows transferred.	
◉	DimCustomer	Success. 18484 rows transferred.	
◉	DimProduct	Success. 606 rows transferred.	
◉	DimPromotion	Success. 16 rows transferred.	
◉	DimSalesTerritory	Success. 11 rows transferred.	
◉	DimTime	Success. 1158 rows transferred.	
◉	FactInternetSales	Success. 60398 rows transferred.	
◉	Data Preparation	Completed	Details

4

In this example, you will import the same file, but will use filters to import only a subset of the data:

1. In the PowerPivot window, select From Text. The Table Import Wizard displays.

2. Select Use First Row as Column Headers.

3. Use the Browse button and locate your text file. PowerPivot will show you a preview of the first 50 records.

4. Clear the Units field to prevent PowerPivot from bringing this data into the grid.

5. Open the Division drop-down. There will be a long pause while PowerPivot loads a list of all possible divisions in the 1.8 million row file.

6. In the Filter drop-down, clear Select All. Then, select only the Handbags check box, as shown in Figure 4.46.

Figure 4.46
You can filter which
records are imported.

7. Click Finish. PowerPivot starts counting as the data is imported into PowerPivot. As
   Figure 4.47 shows, 100,000 matching rows have been imported.

Figure 4.47
PowerPivot reports prog-
ress during the import.

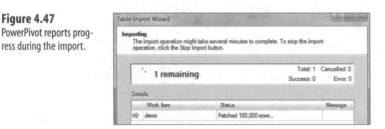

Eventually, PowerPivot will report success. In this case, you have imported 258,984 rows
out of the 1.8 million row data set (see Figure 4.48).

Figure 4.48
Only 200K records out
of 1.8 million were
imported.

Importing from Atom Data Feeds

Two competing feed structures are available on most web pages. One is called RSS, and the other is called Atom. Microsoft has decided to support Atom feeds in PowerPivot.

You might be able to find some external Atom feeds that you can pull into PowerPivot. But, if your company has SharePoint, it is likely that you are going to be able to find more valid Atom feeds in your SharePoint reports. The new version of SharePoint will often embed an Atom icon in the header of SharePoint reports. This means that you can use that feed to get the underlying summary data that went into the report.

In Figure 4.49, a data feed from usgs.gov provides all magnitude 2.5 earthquakes in the past 7 days.

As you specify the data feed, always use the Test Connection button to make sure that the data feed is formatted correctly.

Figure 4.49
This earthquake data from the USGS is updated daily.

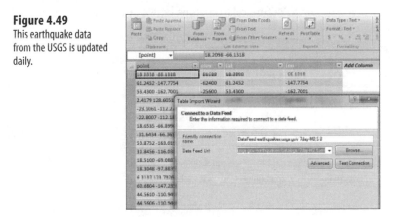

Importing from Other Sources

The From Other Sources choice in the PowerPivot window allows you to import from these databases:

- Microsoft SQL Server
- Microsoft SQL Azure
- Microsoft SQL Server Parallel Data Warehouse
- Microsoft Access
- Oracle
- Teradata
- Sybase

- Informix
- IBM DB2
- Any other OLEDB/ODBC data source
- Microsoft Analysis Services
- Microsoft Reporting Services Reports
- Other data feeds
- Excel files
- Text files

For each database, be prepared to provide a path to the data source and any relevant authentication or passwords.

Next Steps

In the next chapter, you will learn how to define relationships between various tables in PowerPivot.

Creating and Managing Relationships

One of the massive benefits of PowerPivot is the possibility of creating pivot tables from multiple tables. When you have two or more tables, you are going to rely on the concept of relationships to join the tables together.

Good news: Relationships are easier to define than VLOOKUPs are to set up.

Mildly good news: In some simple cases, PowerPivot can autodetect the relationship correctly.

Good news: If you don't want to rely on automatic detection of relationships, you can define the relationships yourself.

This chapter also introduces a DAX function called RELATED and walks through a fairly complex example of joining two tables that generally do not play well together.

Trying to Autodetect Relationships

You will see an example here of how autodetect is supposed to work.

In this example, there are three tables, as shown in Figure 5.1.

- Sales table has invoice number, rep ID, and amount.
- The rep table maps rep ID to rep name and state.
- The state table provides a bonus rate applicable to each state.

Ideally, you would like to join the Rep field in column B with the Rep field in column E. Then, join the State in column G with the State in column I.

Figure 5.1
Three tables that need to be joined together.

Invoice	Rep	Amount		Rep	Name	State		State	BonusRate
1001	R3	3000		R1	Rob	OH		OH	0.05
1002	R4	8000		R2	Bill	OH		WA	0.04
1003	R1	3000		R3	Charley	WA		OR	0.03
1004	R1	9000		R4	Dale	OR		MI	0.02
1005	R3	3000		R5	Allan	WA		CA	0.01
1006	R1	3000		R6	Josh	CA			
1007	R1	4000							

Link the three tables to PowerPivot, as discussed in Chapter 4:

1. Choose to create a pivot table.
2. Select Amount from the Sales table.
3. Select Name from the Reps table.
   The resulting pivot table in Figure 5.2 is dead wrong.

Figure 5.2
Without a link between the tables, you get total sales for all reps ($554K) reported as the sales for each rep.

Row Labels ▼	Sum of Amount
Allan	554000
Bill	554000
Charley	554000
Dale	554000
Josh	554000
Rob	554000
Grand Total	554000

To be fair, though, the PowerPivot Field List tells you that a relationship may be needed, as shown in Figure 5.3.

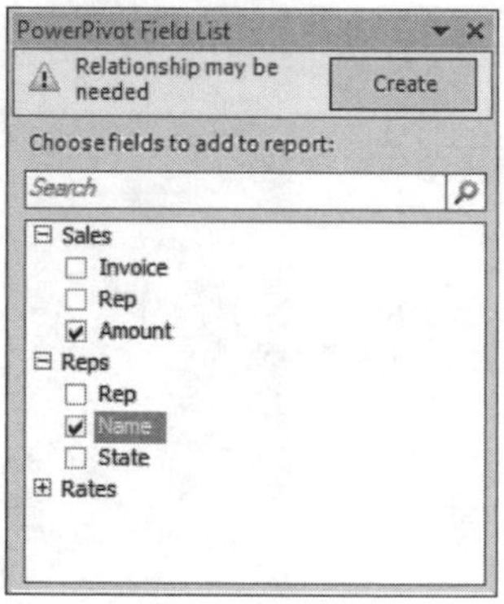

Figure 5.3
PowerPivot suggests that you create a relationship.

5

4. Click the Create button shown in Figure 5.3. PowerPivot thinks for a moment, and then reports that a relationship was detected and created (see Figure 5.4).

It doesn't actually tell you what the relationship that was detected. If you have a need to see the relationship (and you probably should), launch the PowerPivot window. Go to the Design tab. Click Manage Relationship. The dialog will show you that PowerPivot linked the Rep field in the Sales table with the Rep field in the Rep table (see Figure 5.5). Fields in this dialog appear as TableName[FieldName].

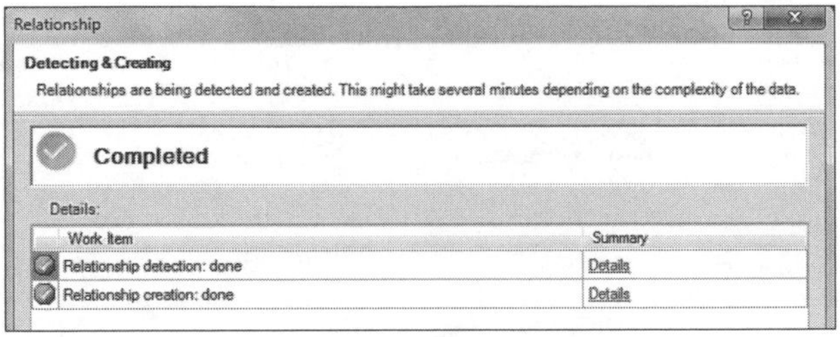

Figure 5.4
PowerPivot auto-detected a relationship.

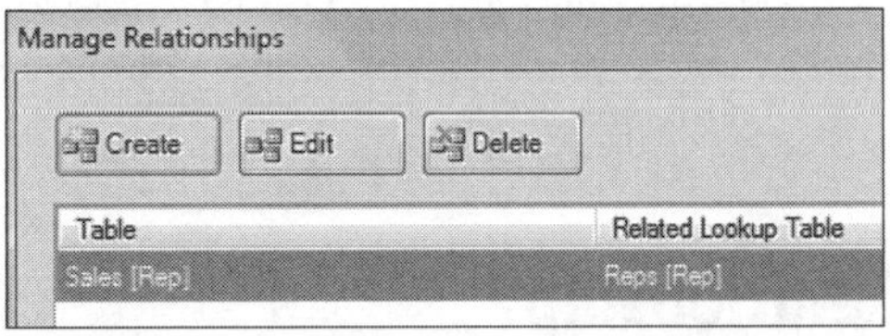

Figure 5.5
PowerPivot got this relationship correct.

After using PowerPivot for a while, I have some theories about why this relationship was detected:

■ The relationship is from the home table to a lookup table.

■ Both the home table and the lookup table had one column name in common.

Back in the Excel window, the Sum of Amount column is now reporting the correct information for each sales rep (see column C of Figure 5.6).

PowerPivot did so well with the first relationship, you might try to bring in data from the third table. Try to report the Bonus Rate in the pivot table. As you can see in column D of the table, you are getting the total of all bonus rates in the Rates table reported for each rep.

Figure 5.6
Trying to add in data from the third table does not work.

Row Labels	Sum of Amount	Sum of BonusRate
Allan	105000	0.15
Bill	144000	0.15
Charley	94000	0.15
Dale	101000	0.15
Josh	35000	0.15
Rob	75000	0.15
Grand Total	554000	0.15

Again, PowerPivot offers that a relationship may need to be created. Click the Create button. This time, you strike out as PowerPivot cannot figure out that State should map to State (see Figure 5.7).

You hate to be negative, but right now, you are batting .500 on the relationship autodetection situation. I really don't like that when they suspect that there needs to be a relationship, they put bad data in the pivot table. If you are a conscientious data analyst, you will

Figure 5.7
PowerPivot cannot make the hop from Reps to Rates.

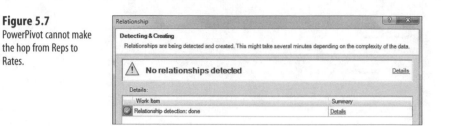

recognize that the data cannot be right. But, I am sure you have co-workers who are happy to get a result and mail the report out to three dozen people without considering if the result it correct.

Manually Defining a Relationship

Creating a manual relationship in the PowerPivot window requires only a few mouse clicks.

By preselecting the field that you want to link from, the whole process can be as simple as 4 mouse clicks.

You want to link from the State field in the rep table to the State field in the Rates table:

1. Open the PowerPivot window and navigate to the Reps sheets.

2. Select one cell in the State field.

3. On the Design tab, select Create Relationship, as shown in Figure 5.8.

Figure 5.8
Select the From field and select Create Relationship.

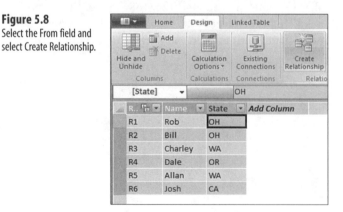

4. Because you preselected the State field, the Create Relationship dialog opens with the first two drop-downs already populated. The Table shows Reps, and the Column shows State. Open the Related Lookup Table drop-down and select Rates.

Because the Rates table has a matching field, Excel will automatically populate the Related Lookup Column (see Figure 5.9). The total click count inside this dialog box is three; one to open the drop-down, one to select Rates, and one to click Create.

After you set up the relationship, the PowerPivot Field List shows that the PowerPivot Data Was Modified and offers to let you refresh (see Figure 5.10).

 To see a demo of creating a relationship in PowerPivot, search for MrExcel PowerPivot 5 at YouTube.

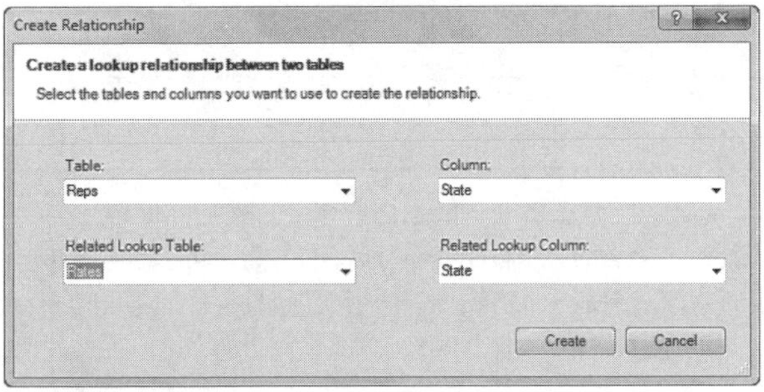

Figure 5.9
Choose which fields should be matched.

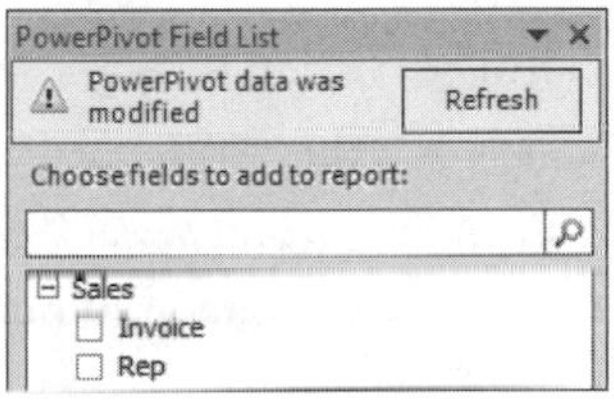

Figure 5.10
After defining a relationship, you need to refresh.

Calculating Between Tables

The correct place to calculate a bonus amount is back in the Sales table. Click in the Add Column column. You might think that you could try a formula like =Sales[Amount]*Rates [BonusRate] (see Figure 5.11).

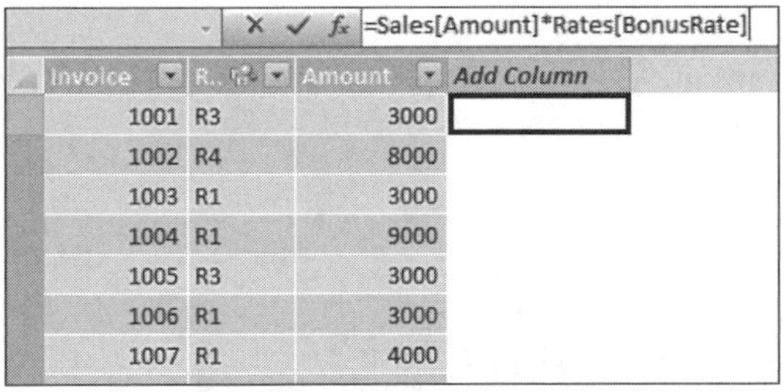

Figure 5.11
After defining the relationship, you would think this formula would work.

Invoice	R..	Amount	Add Column
1001	R3	3000	
1002	R4	8000	
1003	R1	3000	
1004	R1	9000	
1005	R3	3000	
1006	R1	3000	
1007	R1	4000	

=Sales[Amount]*Rates[BonusRate]

However, that formula does not work. When you press Enter, all the rows calculate as an error. If you open the Ctrl drop-down and ask to see the error, PowerPivot informs you that it cannot determine the value for Bonus Rate (see Figure 5.12).

Figure 5.12
This formula fails.

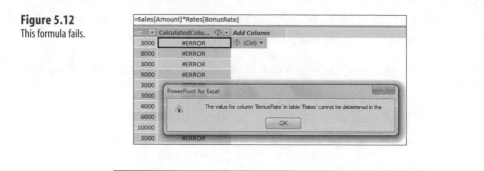

This formula was one of the first things that I tried in PowerPivot and I was a little hacked off that it was not working. After all, had I chosen one of the fields in the Rates table as a label field in my pivot table, then PowerPivot could have figured it out. But here, in the process of calculating a new column, PowerPivot can't get it.

PowerPivot provides a new formula language called DAX. There are 71 functions in DAX and many of the functions are very similar to functions in Excel.

But to solve this problem, you have to use a new function called RELATED. In his PowerPivotPro blog, Rob Collie referred to RELATED as a "one-argument VLOOKUP," and that essentially is what it does.

By saying that you want the RELATED(Rates[BonusRate]), you are telling PowerPivot to "go figure it out." PowerPivot should use all the relationships defined to figure out how to get the related rates. In this case, it means to essentially do a VLOOKUP from rep ID to the Rep table and then from the State field to the Rates field.

There are two sides of this argument going on in my head:

■ Why do I have to use RELATED at all?

■ But, since I have to use it, I have to admit that simply specifying RELATED(field) and letting PowerPivot figure it out is pretty cool!

In Figure 5.13, adding the RELATED function allows PowerPivot to return the correct value.

Figure 5.13
Use the RELATED function to jump to another table.

Invoice	R..	Amount	CalculatedColumn1	Add Column
1001	R3	3000	120	
1002	R4	8000	240	

Chapter 6, "Using Data Sheet View," does into more detail on all the DAX functions that can be used in the data sheet.

Back in the pivot table, add the new Bonus calculation to the pivot table and everything adds up correctly (see Figure 5.14).

Figure 5.14
The Bonus calculation works correctly.

Row Labels ▼	Sum of Amount	Sum of Bonus
Allan	105000	4200
Bill	144000	7200
Charley	94000	3760
Dale	101000	3030
Josh	35000	350
Rob	75000	3750
Grand Total	554000	22290

Defining a Difficult Relationship

In this data model, you have three tables.

- Sales table contains Date, Product, RepID, and Sales amount.
- The Rep table maps RepID to Rep Name.
- The Bonus table lists the products down the side and the months going across the top (see Figure 5.15).

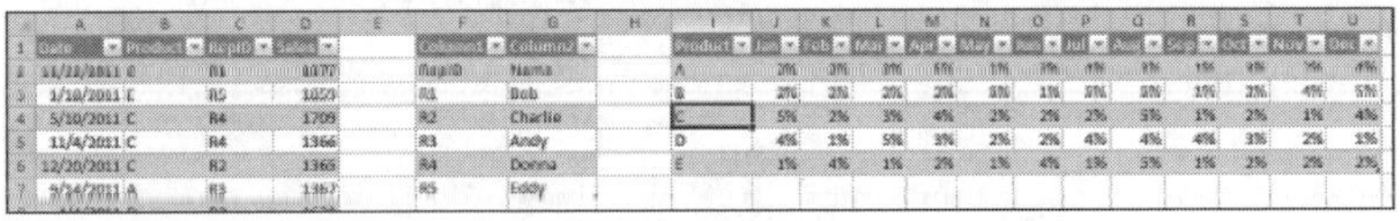

Figure 5.15
Define a relationship between these three tables.

You want to be able to find the right bonus rate based on the product in column B and the month of the date in column A.

This is possible, but not necessarily easy.

For the first thing, the rates table is in the wrong format. Instead of having months go across the table, you need months going down the table. There should be 60 rows in the final table, 5 products × 12 months.

Unwinding a Lookup Table

You need to change the 5-row lookup table in Figure 5.15 into a 60-row table with values like those shown below:

Product	Month	Rate
A	Jan	2%
A	Feb	2%
A	Mar	3%
A	Apr	5%
...		
B	Jan	2%

5

The technique to do this involves a special kind of pivot table called a *multiple consolidation range pivot table*. This pivot table is no longer offered in the Office Ribbon, but you can still invoke it using a shortcut key.

> **NOTE** I have to give a tip o' the cap to Mike Alexander, my co-presenter on the Power Analyst Boot Camps, for showing me this technique.

To unwind the product/month/rate table, follow these steps:

1. Press Alt+D+P to invoke the Excel 2003 command of Data, PivotTable. Excel will show the old PivotTable and PivotChart Wizard dialog, as shown in Figure 5.16.

Figure 5.16
Someone at Microsoft had to redraw the art for this dialog that was then removed from the ribbon.

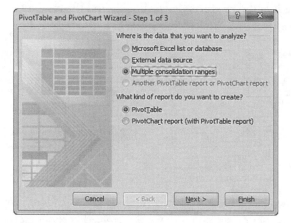

2. Select Multiple Consolidation Ranges from the dialog and click Next.
3. In step 2a of the wizard, click I Will Create the Page Fields, as shown in Figure 5.17. Click Next.

Figure 5.17
You are actually telling a fib. You aren't going to create any page fields.

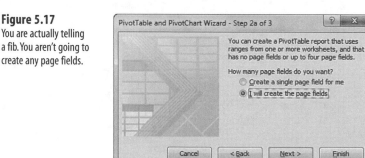

4. In step 2b of the wizard, use the Refers to icon and specify the range that contains your table, I1:U6. Click the Add button (see Figure 5.18).

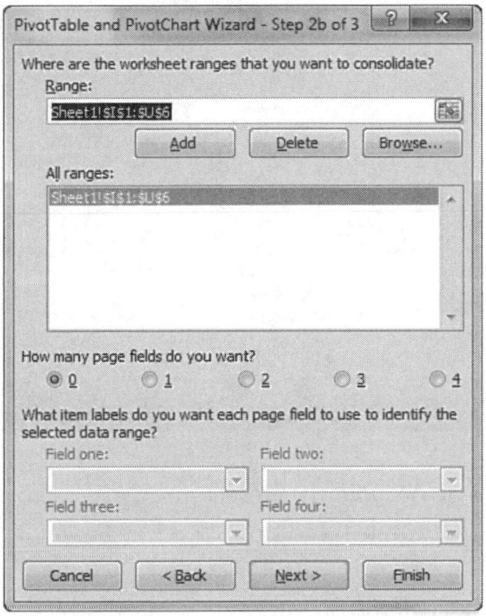

Figure 5.18
You normally would specify the multiple ranges here, but you only need to specify one.

5. Click Next to go to step 3 of the wizard.
6. Specify that you want to put the pivot table on an existing worksheet and specify cell I9 (see Figure 5.19).

Figure 5.19
Choose any existing blank range for the output.

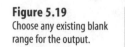

7. Click Finish. Excel creates a pivot table that looks exactly like the table that you started with, with the addition of some totals (see Figure 5.20).

Original Data

Figure 5.20
This is the point where you give Mike Alexander a stupid look.

Product	Jan		Feb	Mar	Apr	May	Jun	Jul	Aug	Sep	Oct	Nov	Dec	
A	2%		2%	3%	5%	1%	3%	4%	3%	1%	3%	2%	4%	
B	2%		2%	2%	2%	5%	1%	5%	5%	1%	2%	4%	5%	
C	5%		2%	3%	4%	2%	2%	2%	5%	1%	2%	1%	4%	
D	4%		1%	5%	3%	2%	2%	4%	4%	4%	3%	2%	1%	
E	1%		4%	1%	2%	1%	4%	1%	5%	1%	2%	2%	2%	

Sum of Value	Column Labels													
Row Labels	Jan		Feb	Mar	Apr	May	Jun	Jul	Aug	Sep	Oct	Nov	Dec	Grand Total
A			0.02	0.02	0.03	0.05	0.01	0.03	0.04	0.03	0.01	0.03	0.02	0.04	0.33
B			0.02	0.02	0.02	0.02	0.05	0.01	0.05	0.05	0.01	0.02	0.04	0.05	0.36
C			0.05	0.02	0.03	0.04	0.02	0.02	0.02	0.05	0.01	0.02	0.01	0.04	0.33
D			0.04	0.01	0.05	0.03	0.02	0.02	0.04	0.04	0.04	0.03	0.02	0.01	0.35
E			0.01	0.04	0.01	0.02	0.01	0.04	0.01	0.05	0.01	0.02	0.02	0.02	0.26
Grand Total			0.14	0.11	0.14	0.16	0.11	0.12	0.16	0.22	0.08	0.12	0.11	0.16	1.63

Pivot table after 52 steps

NOTE

Seriously, I could not figure out where Mike Alexander was heading when he got to this point in his demo. This trick seemed far more useless than most of Mike's tricks!

Here is a quiz question: What happens if you double-click a cell in a regular pivot table?

Answer: You get a new worksheet with all the detail rows that make up that cell.

Quiz question 2: What would happen if you would double-click the Grand Total column in the Grand Total row?

Answer: You would get every single record in the data set. It would be a pointless activity with a regular pivot table. But...watch what happens when you do it in a multiple consolidation range pivot table.

8. Double-click the Grand Total Grand Total (cell V16). When you drill through the total cell, Excel gives you every record in the data set, but as you can see in Figure 5.21, the new worksheet contains the data as it exists in memory. This is a 60-row by 3-column table and is the exact format that you need!

Figure 5.21
Amazingly, the result of the drill through is the unwound lookup table.

	A	B	C
1	Row	Column	Value
2	A	Jan	0.02
3	A	Feb	0.02
4	A	Mar	0.03
5	A	Apr	0.05
6	A	May	0.01
7	A	Jun	0.03
8	A	Jul	0.04

9. Change the headings in the new table to Product, Month, and Bonus Rate.

10. Click Ctrl+T to make the range into a table (see Figure 5.22).

Figure 5.22
Change the headings and you are done.

	A	B	C
1	Product	Month	Bonus
2	A	Jan	0.02
3	A	Feb	0.02
4	A	Mar	0.03
5	A	Apr	0.05

Building a Concatenated Key Relationship

Link the three tables from the previous example to PowerPivot. You will have tables called Sales, Reps, and Rates. The Sales table is shown in Figure 5.23. Instead of letting PowerPivot figure out the links, you want to set them up manually:

Figure 5.23
Link from the sales table to the Reps and Rates tables.

Date	Product	RepID	Sales
11/22/...	C	R1	1377
1/18/2...	E	R5	1059
5/10/2...	C	R4	1709
11/4/2...	C	R4	1366
12/20/...	C	R2	1365
9/14/2...	A	R3	1367
4/4/2011	D	R2	1631
12/16/...	A	R4	1852
3/1/2011	A	R3	1875
8/15/2...	B	R2	1026
5/4/2011	A	R3	1568
10/13/...	B	R3	1219
9/22/2...	C	R3	1416
4/21/2...	C	R4	1528
7/26/2...	A	R3	1943
1/3/2011	D	R4	1236
9/30/2...	C	R2	1936
8/31/2...	E	R2	1347
11/16/...	D	R2	1763

Sales | Reps | Rates

5

1. Select the RepID column in the Sales table.

2. From the Design tab in PowerPivot, select Create Relationship. The dialog box appears with Sales and RepID prepopulated.

3. Select Reps from the Related Lookup Table drop-down. PowerPivot fills in RepID in the Related Lookup Column, as shown in Figure 5.24.

   PowerPivot cannot use two fields in each table for establishing a relationship. You will have to concatenate the two fields together into a single calculated column.

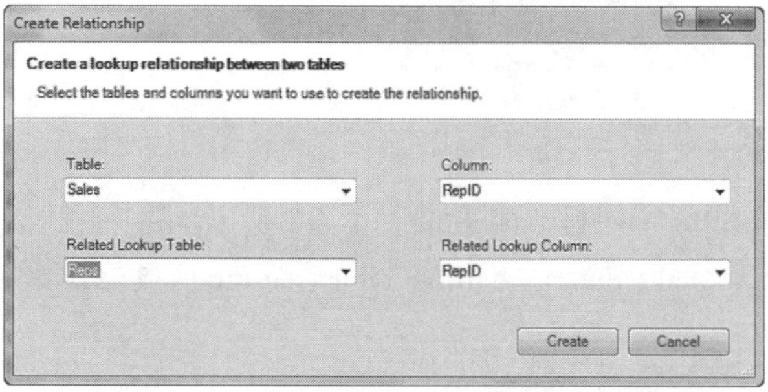

Figure 5.24
Build the first relationship.

DAX contains 71 functions that are nearly identical to existing functions in Excel. Out of those 71 functions, 69 of them have the same name as the corresponding Excel function. Of the two that don't match, they renamed the DATEDIF function to YEARFRAC, which is good, because DATEDIF has a nasty reputation for returning incorrect values. However, I can figure out no logical reason for them to rename the TEXT function to FORMAT. So, for those Excel gurus who are reading along and realize that you need =TEXT(Sales[Date],"MMM"), you are absolutely correct. Just be aware that the T-E-X-T function is misspelled in PowerPivot as F-O-R-M-A-T.

4. In the Sales table, select what is essentially cell E2 and type a new formula. Type **=Format(** and click the Date field. Type a comma, then **"MMM")&**. Click the Product field. Your formula should look like =Format(Sales[Date],"mmm")&Sales[Product]. Press Enter.

5. Right-click the column and select Rename.

6. Type a new column name, such as MonthProd, as shown in Figure 5.25.

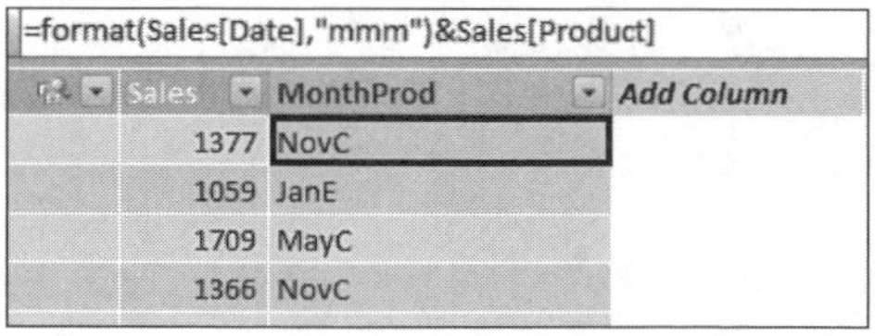

Figure 5.25
Add a new calculated column to the Sales table.

7. Select the worksheet for Rates.

8. Add a new calculated column of =Rates[Month]&Rates[Prod].

9. Right-click the column and select Rename.

10. Change the name of the column to **MonthProd**.

11. Select the worksheet for Sales.

12. Click the MonthProd column.

13. On the PowerPivot Design tab, select Create Relationship. The Create Relationship dialog launches with Sales and MonthProd preselected.

14. Open the Related Lookup Table drop-down and select Rates. PowerPivot will automatically select MonthProd from the Related Lookup column. The dialog should look like Figure 5.26.

Figure 5.26
Link between the two concatenated key columns.

15. In the Sales worksheet, add a new calculated column with a formula of =Sales[Sales]* RELATED(Rates[BonusRate]). Rename this column to be called **Bonus** (see Figure 5.27).

Figure 5.27
Calculate a bonus as the sales amount times the rate from the lookup table.

	Sales	MonthProd		Bonus	Add Column
=Sales[Sales]*RELATED(Rates[BonusRate])					
	1377	NovC		13.77	
	1059	JanE		10.59	
	1709	MayC		34.18	
	1366	NovC		13.66	
	1365	DecC		54.6	

16. Select the PivotTable drop-down and select Single PivotTable.

17. Build a pivot table with Rep Name in the row labels and Bonus in the Values area (see Figure 5.28).

Figure 5.28
This pivot table joins three tables and a fairly complex concatenated key relationship.

Row Labels	Sum of Bonus
Andy	9621.94
Bob	10989.95
Charlie	8979.18
Donna	9807.77
Eddy	9857.62
Grand Total	**49256.46**

5

Is This Harder Than a VLOOKUP?

I was excited about PowerPivot because it would allow people who had not mastered a VLOOKUP to join data sets together.

Certainly, doing simple relationships such as linking the RepID in Sales to the RepID in the Reps table is easier than doing a VLOOKUP.

Using the RELATED function means doing a little bit of training, but RELATED is definitely easier than using VLOOKUP because you only have to specify the field that you want to find.

Then, we come down to the steps between Figure 5.16 and Figure 5.28. Are those steps harder than doing a VLOOKUP? Possibly.

I am going to argue that it would not have been a simple VLOOKUP to get the proper rate from the original table. It might have taken a combination of an INDEX, two MATCH functions, and a TEXT function, or at the very least a VLOOKUP in combination with the MONTH function:

Method 1:

```
=INDEX($J$2:$U$6,MATCH(B2,I$2:I$6,0),MATCH(TEXT(A2,"MMM"),J$1:U$1,0))
```

Method 2:

```
=VLOOKUP(B2,$I$2:$U$6,MONTH(A2)+1,FALSO)
```

Both of those approaches are tougher than a VLOOKUP. Which would I rather do? Get someone to be able to write one of those two formulas or build the relationship in PowerPivot? There are close. Maybe the Method 2 formula is simpler.

Questions About Relationships

Can you have multiple relationships between two tables? No. Only one relationship is allowed between two tables. If you need to set up two relationships, import the lookup table twice, each with a different table name, and set up one relationship to each copy of the table.

Are many-to-many relationships supported? Not directly. You cannot use the Create Relationships icon to define a many-to-many relationship. You can define a DAX measure that equates to a logical many-to-many relationship.

DAX measures are covered in more detail in Chapter 10, "Using DAX for Aggregate Functions."

Does renaming a table in the PowerPivot window break existing relationships? No. The relationships will automatically change to reflect the new table names. However, any calculated columns that reference the old name will not be updated. So, you should rename your tables before you start building calculated columns.

Does case matter when creating relationships? Will ABC map to Abc? Just as with VLOOKUP, case does not matter. In Figure 5.29, a variety of customer ID's in column A are joined in PowerPivot with the all-caps customer ID's in D2:D4. As you can see from the resulting pivot table in D7, all the customer records match up.

Figure 5.29
ABC maps to Abc without a problem.

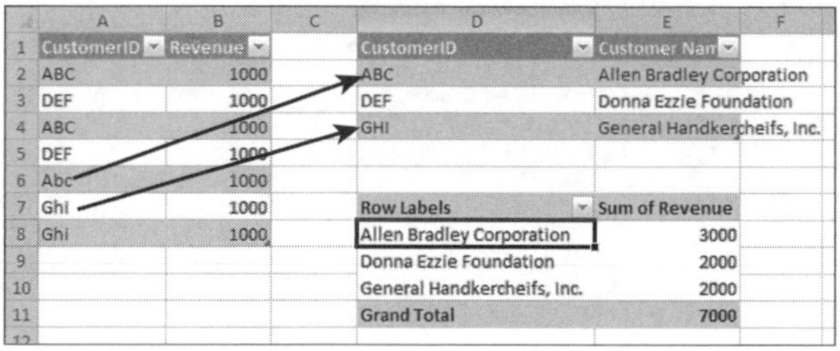

Do trailing spaces matter when creating relationships? Amazingly, they do not. In Figure 5.30, the customer IDs in column A have three trailing spaces each. The customer ID's in D2:D3 have no trailing spaces. After joining the data in PowerPivot and creating the pivot table in D6, you can see that all the customer ID's were matched up. This is impressive, since those trailing spaces would trip up VLOOKUP formulas.

Figure 5.30
Trailing spaces are ignored when matching data.

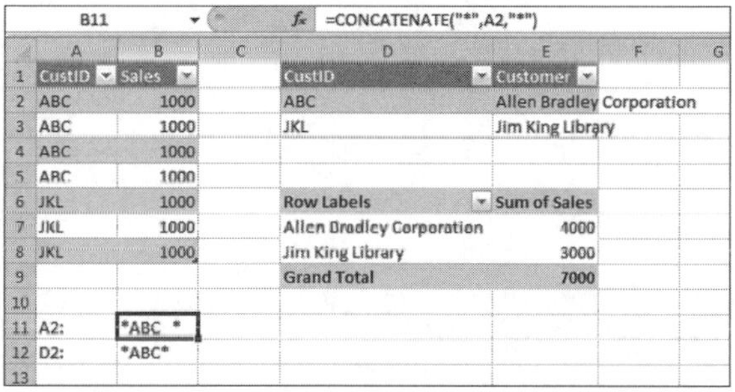

Will numbers link to numbers stored as text? No. But, you will be warned about this when defining the relationship. If a column contains a mix of numbers and text as in column A of Figure 5.31, the column will be imported as text. If the column of the lookup table contained all numeric values, it could be possible that the column would be imported with a data type of whole numbers. When you create the relationship, PowerPivot will refuse to allow the relationship. You will have to convert the data type for the lookup table to text, and then the relationship will be allowed (see Figure 5.31).

Figure 5.31
Joining numbers to text numbers will not work.

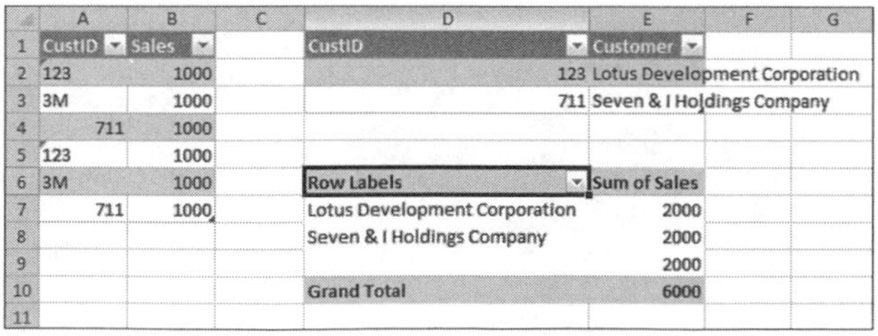

5

Next Steps

Chapter 6 deals with the few commands available in the PowerPivot window, plus 71 DAX functions that you can use to create calculated columns.

5

Using Data Sheet View

This chapter is mostly about adding calculated columns in the PowerPivot data sheet. There are 71 DAX functions defined in this chapter, with examples.

Another 64 DAX functions are described in Chapter 10, "Using DAX for Aggregate Functions," and Chapter 11, "Using DAX for Date Magic."

Before launching into the DAX function reference, this chapter covers the commands available in the PowerPivot window. These include scrolling, sorting, formatting, and filtering.

Working with Data in the PowerPivot Window

The data sheet view in PowerPivot feels a bit like an Excel grid. You can scroll through rows, sort, filter, and apply numeric formatting. You can also hide columns, delete columns, and add new columns. You can freeze columns.

But there is a lot that you cannot do. You cannot edit a single cell. You cannot change the color of cells. You cannot add cell comments. You cannot print the worksheet.

This section talks about how to use the right side of the Home tab in PowerPivot (see Figure 6.1) and the left side of the Design tab (see Figure 6.2).

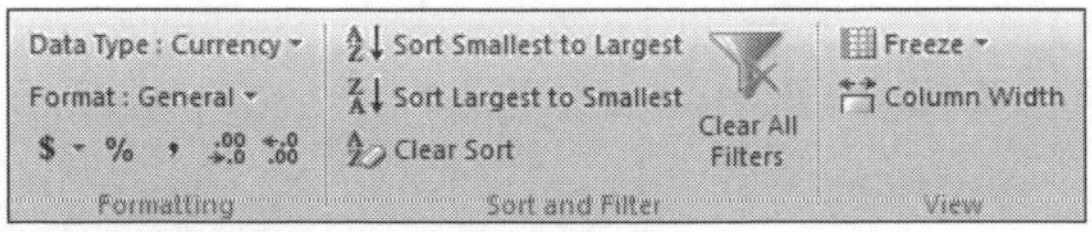

Figure 6.1
The Formatting, Sort and Filter, and View groups in the Home tab.

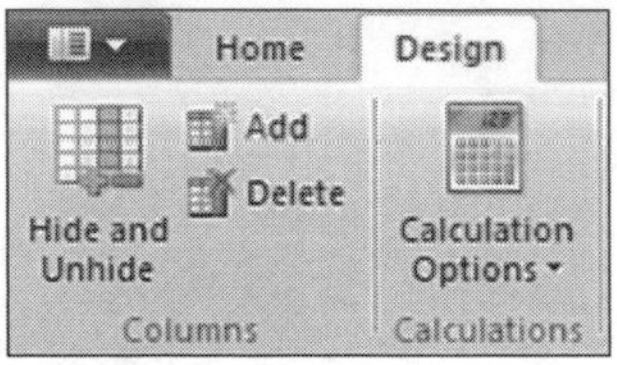

Figure 6.2
The Columns group in the Design tab.

Applying Numeric Formatting

The Formatting group of the Home tab offers a Data Type and a Format drop-down, as well as quick icons for currency, percentage, comma, and increase/decrease decimal.

The Data Type drop-down shown in Figure 6.3 is more important than just formatting. DAX understands seven types of data. When you choose something from the Data Type drop-down, you are actually changing the data type of the column.

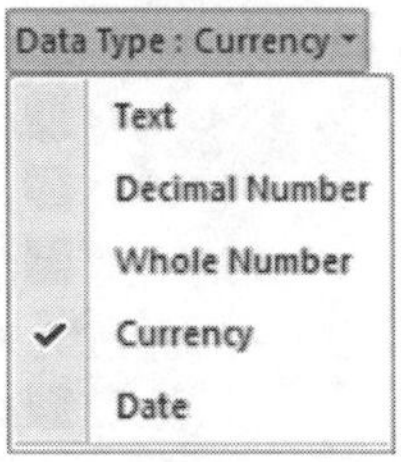

Figure 6.3
Choosing something from the Data Type drop-down changes the way data in the column is stored.

DAX supports these data types:

- **I8 (8-byte integer):** Numbers that have no decimal places. Integers can be positive or negative, but must be whole numbers. This is represented in the drop-down as Whole Number. This data type allows from –9.2 quintillion to +9.2 quintillion.

- **R8 (8-byte real number):** Real numbers with decimal places. The number of decimals is not defined. Represented in the drop-down as Decimal Number.

- **Boolean:** False and true or 1 and 0. Represented in the drop-down as TRUE/FALSE.

- **String:** Character data. Represented by Text in the drop-down.

- **Date:** Dates and times in a SQL Server datetime representation. Represented in the drop-down as Date.

- **CY:** Currency. Represented in the drop-down as Currency.

- **Blank:** A blank is a data type that replaces blank cells in Excel, nulls in SQL, and empty strings. You can create a Blank by using the BLANK function or test for Blank using ISBLANK function. Although Blank may appear in other columns, you cannot format an entire column as Blank, so it is not available in the drop-down.

When you select from the Data Type drop-down, you might change the format of how the number is displayed. You are definitely changing how the number is stored in memory.

Figure 6.4 shows the Format drop-down. Some of these selections will also change the data type. Choosing Currency from the drop-down will automatically change the data type to Currency.

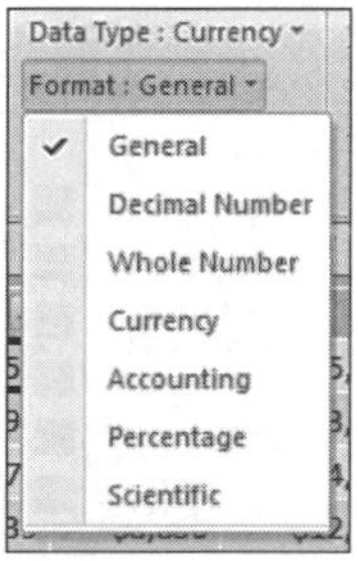

Figure 6.4
Select the Format of the column.

The remaining icons control which currency symbol is used, applies a percentage format, adds a thousands separator, and controls the number of decimals in the display (see Figure 6.5).

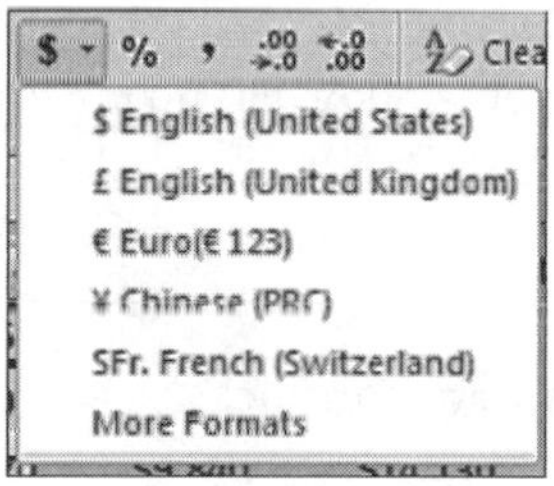

Figure 6.5
Control how the numbers are displayed in the PowerPivot window.

Format in the PowerPivot Window Does Not Carry Through to the PivotTable!

In my humble opinion, you are focusing on the wrong thing if you are spending a lot of time formatting things in the PowerPivot data sheet. The formatting changes that you make in the data sheet will not affect the initial number format used in the pivot table.

You cannot print from the data sheet, so there is almost zero reason for you to need to format the data in the PowerPivot grid.

Data Type in the PowerPivot Window Will Affect Calculations

When you perform a calculation between two different data types, PowerPivot will use a table to determine the resulting data type. For example, a whole number plus currency will yield currency. A real number plus currency will yield a real number. But, currency times a real number will return a currency data type.

6

Rules for Blanks

- If you add two blank cells in Excel, the result is zero. Add two blank cells in DAX, and the result is a blank.
- Blank * 5 in Excel is zero. Blank * 5 in DAX is Blank.
- 5/Blank in Excel is a DIV/0 error. In DAX, it is infinity.
- Blank or True in DAX is True.
- Blank and True in DAX is Blank.

Sorting Data in the PowerPivot Window

You can sort one column at a time in the PowerPivot window. The AZ and ZA buttons work just as they would in Excel.

If you want to sort by Date within Product within Region, you would sort backward as follows:

1. First sort by Date.
2. Then, sort by Product. All the ties are for product ABC are sorted by the previous date sequence.
3. Then, sort by Region.

Again, any sorting that you do in the PowerPivot window has no effect on the pivot table that you create from the PowerPivot data.

Filtering in the PowerPivot Window

The filtering options in the PowerPivot window are horrible.

If any of this stuff that you are doing in the PowerPivot grid actually mattered, I would be complaining loudly about the lack of filtering ability in the PowerPivot window.

However, the filtering that you do in the PowerPivot window does not affect your pivot table. So, this filtering is just for your preliminary browsing of the data.

In Excel 2010, the filter drop-downs offer a Search box, a hierarchical date filter, and a boatload of virtual date filters, as shown in Figure 6.6.

In the PowerPivot grid, the Filter drop-down offers the ridiculous day-by-day check boxes (see Figure 6.7). You can choose Equals, Not Equals, or an Excel 97-era Custom Filter dialog (see Figure 6.8).

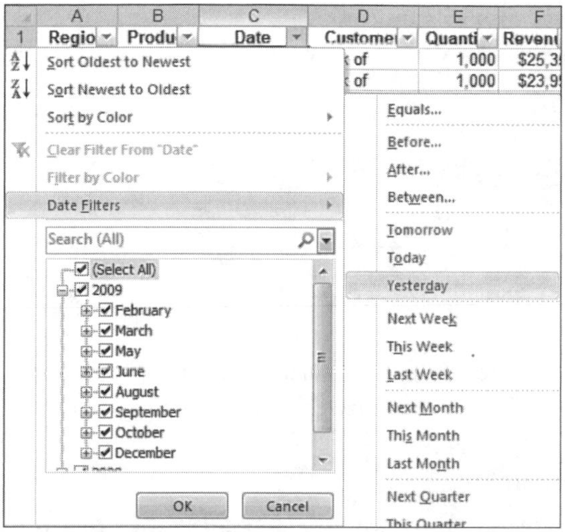

Figure 6.6
In Excel 2010, there are many ways to filter a column.

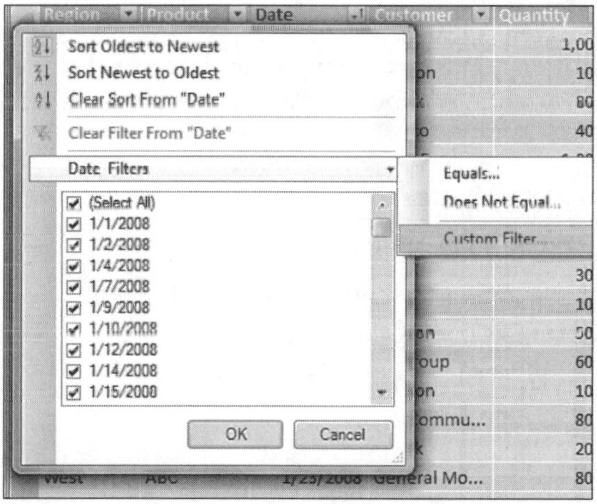

Figure 6.7
To filter out everything except the second quarter of 2009, you will be selecting 70 different dates.

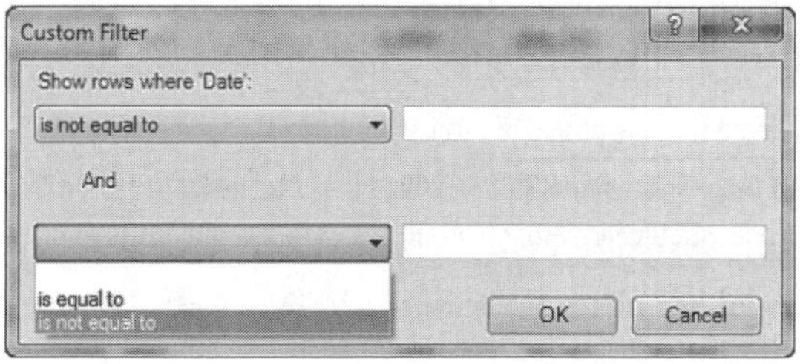

Figure 6.8
The custom filter dialog is really lacking.

The one good filter trick available in PowerPivot is the Excel 2007 Filter by Selection. To use this technique, right-click a certain value and select Filter, Filter by Selected Cell Value (see Figure 6.9).

Figure 6.9
Filter by selection is a good trick.

This would be a great icon to add to the Quick Access toolbar, if future versions of PowerPivot would allow you to customize the Quick Access toolbar.

You Can't Print from PowerPivot

You can't print from the PowerPivot window. The formatting that you do in the grid does not flow through to the pivot table. Why would they even offer the sort, filter, format options in PowerPivot?

It is with a little trepidation that I even mention this. Suppose that you a data set with five million rows. You really want to analyze that data in Excel. Of course, the data set is too big to get into Excel.

You could follow these steps:

1. Import the five million rows to PowerPivot.
2. Apply a filter that will get the data down to about a million records.
3. Use the triangle icon in the upper-left corner of the grid to select all rows.
4. Use the Copy icon on the PowerPivot Home tab.
5. Return to Excel.
6. Paste.
7. Return to PowerPivot. Apply a different filter in step 2 and repeat.

> **CAUTION**
>
> Only the filtered rows are pasted to Excel. The formats that you applied in the PowerPivot window are brought over. I am sure that they did not intend for PowerPivot to be the "get huge data sets into Excel" tool, but with the formatting, sorting, andv filtering options, it would be a good tool for getting oversized data sets into Excel.

Rearranging Columns

You can rearrange columns in the grid. Follow these steps:

1. Click the heading for a column. The mouse pointer changes to a four-headed arrow.

2. Click the heading and drag left or right. When the column is in the correct location, release the mouse button.

Freezing Columns

In the Excel interface, you can freeze rows and columns at the top and left of the screen. In PowerPivot, you cannot freeze rows. You can only freeze columns at the left side of the screen.

In an interesting twist, if you select a column in the middle of the screen and select to freeze that column, the column will automatically move to the left side of the screen. If there is already one frozen column, the new frozen column will appear to the right of the previously frozen columns.

When a column is frozen, you cannot move it to the right of an unfrozen column. You would have to unfreeze the column first.

Changing Column Widths

There are four different ways of adjusting the columns widths.

- Select a column, and then select the Column Width icon in the Home tab. You will then be presented with a bizarre Column Width dialog where you are supposed to set the column width in pixels. Since the beginning of time, Excel people have been setting column widths in the mythical unit of "the average width of the digits 0 to 9 in the default font of the worksheet." Looking at the Revenue column in Figure 6.9, you would guess it has an Excel width of about 9.5. The Column Width dialog says that it has a width of 90 pixels. This throws you for a loop the first time you see it, but you get used to it.

- Hover the mouse between two column headings. The mouse pointer changes to a two-headed horizontal arrow. Click and drag to adjust the column to the left of the arrow.

- Hover the mouse in the same location as above. Double-click and the column will adjust to handle the longest value in the column.

- Right-click a column heading and select Column Width to display the Column Width dialog shown in Figure 6.10.

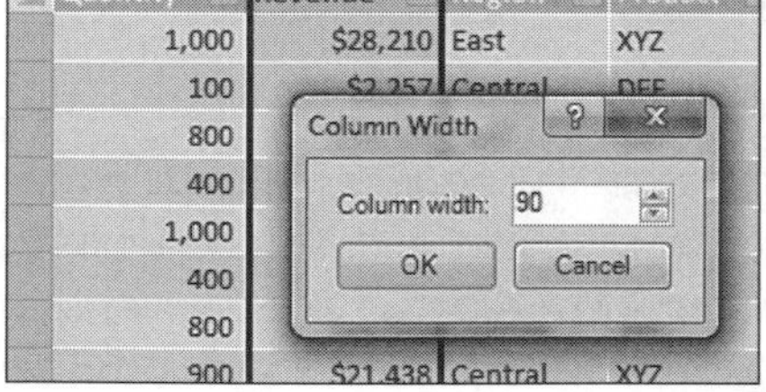

Figure 6.10
Column widths are measured in pixels in PowerPivot.

You also might be refreshed to learn that PowerPivot does not show the maddening #####
signs when a column is too narrow for a value. In Figure 6.11, the Cost and Profit columns
are too narrow to show all the digits. PowerPivot adds an ellipsis to the end of the visible
digits to let you know that there are more digits (see Figure 6.11).

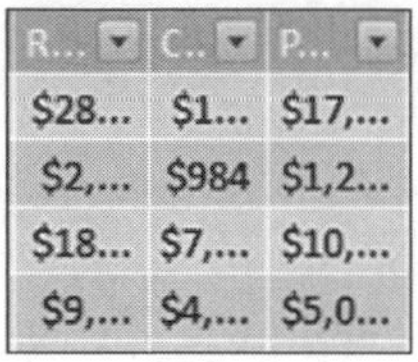

Figure 6.11
If a column is too narrow,
Excel adds an ellipsis.

Hiding Columns at Two Levels

The Hide and Unhide columns icon on the Design tab is a clever improvement over hidden
columns in Excel. When you click the icon, you are given a dialog box of all the columns
in the table. You have a series of check boxes where you can hide the column in either the
PowerPivot window or the pivot table (see Figure 6.12).

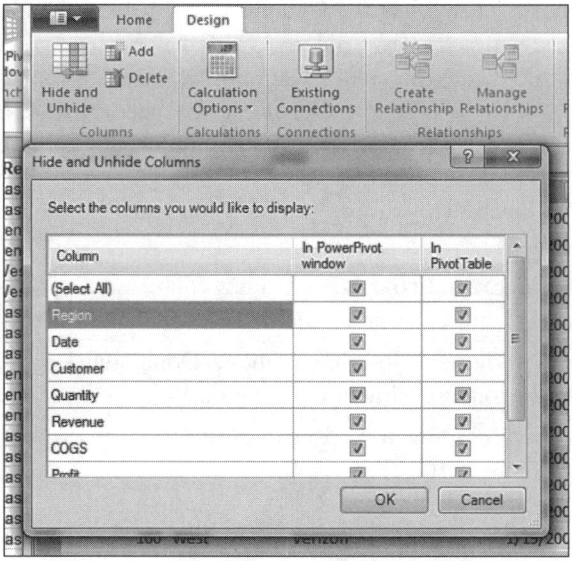

Figure 6.12
You can hide columns in
PowerPivot or in the pivot
table.

> **TIP**
>
> You can imagine all sorts of scenarios where you might have temporary columns in the PowerPivot
> window that are not appropriate for use in the pivot table. By clearing them from the final column of
> the Hide and Unhide Columns dialog, you can prevent the people using the pivot table from dealing
> with those fields in the PowerPivot Field List.

Using PowerPivot Undo and Redo

The Undo and Redo drop-downs at the right side of the Design tab allow you to undo and redo a surprising number of changes. The Undo list in Figure 6.1v3 shows the addition of a calculated column and the deletion of the calculation column. You can actually undo the deletion of a calculated column.

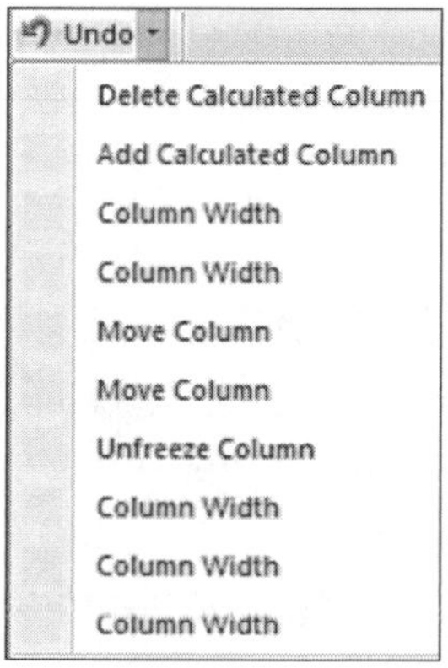

Figure 6.13
You can undo or redo many actions in the PowerPivot window.v

However, you cannot undo the deletion of a data column. Further, if you delete a real data column, the PowerPivot Undo stack will be cleared.

Deleting Columns

You can delete two kinds of columns in the PowerPivot window.

- If you delete a calculated column, you can undo your choice by using the Undo drop-down on the Design tab.
- If you delete a true data column, you are asked to confirm that you want to permanently delete the column. If you select OK, the undo stack is cleared and the data is permanently removed.

Using the Context Menu

If you right-click a cell in the grid, you are given a weak context menu with Copy and Filter.

The good context menu appears when you right-click a heading. You have options to create a relationship, navigate to the related table, and many other commands that are located elsewhere on the tabs in the Ribbon (see Figure 6.14).

6

Figure 6.14
A context menu appears when you click a column heading.

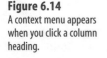

Region	▼	Customer	▼
East		Create Relationship...	
Central		Navigate to Related Table	
East		Copy	
East		Delete Columns	
East		Rename Column	
East		Freeze Columns	
East		Unfreeze All Columns	
Central		Hide Columns ▶	
Central		Unhide Columns...	
Central		Column Width...	
East		Filter ▶	
East			

Adding New Columns Using DAX Formulas

If you choose the Add icon to add a new column, it is just like clicking in the Add Column column. So, when you want to add a column, just click in any cell in the blank column to the right of the table.

You will build your formula in the DAX language. When you press Enter, the formula will be copied throughout the column.

A column can only have one formula.

DAX stands for Data Analysis Expressions. DAX handles various operators and 135 functions. A number of the functions are very similar to Excel functions. Many of the functions are new.

If there is something confusing about DAX, it is this: There are two kinds of formulas that can be created using DAX, as follows:

■ Calculated columns are created in the PowerPivot grid. These functions will most likely use 71 of the 135 functions. When you enter a calculation in the PowerPivot grid, the calculation is actually copied and calculated for every row in the grid. If you have a 10 million row data set and add 3 calculated columns, PowerPivot will be calculating 30 million formula results.

■ DAX measures are created in the pivot table. A DAX measure is only calculated once for each cell in the resulting pivot table. Sixty-four of the 135 functions are most likely to be used when creating DAX measures.

> **NOTE**
> The remainder of this chapter will document the 71 DAX functions that are most likely to be used when adding calculated columns. There might be instances where there is some crossover.

Operators in the DAX Language

The DAX language contains several operators. Many are similar to Excel:

■ +-*/ for addition, subtraction, multiplication, and division

- & for text concatenation
- ^ for exponents
- =, >, <, >=, <=, <> as comparison operators

DAX also supports three additional operators for evaluating Boolean expressions:

- && creates an AND condition between two expressions that each have a True/False result. `([Region]="West")&&([Product]="ABC")`
- || creates an OR condition between two expressions that each have a True/False result. `([Region]="West")¦¦([Product]="ABC")`
- ! is the NOT operator. This will turn True into False and False into True. `!([Region]="West")`

Building Formulas in the PowerPivot Grid

To start entering a formula, click in the Add Column column and type an equal sign.

At this point, you have several choices.

- You can click a column and PowerPivot will insert that column name in the formula (see Figure 6.15).

Figure 6.15
Click a column to insert the column name in the formula.

=Sales[Revenue]			
Customer	Date	Revenue	
Ford	1/1/2008	$28,210	
Verizon	1/2/2008	$2,257	

- You can type an operator.
- You can click the fx icon to the left of the formula bar to bring up the Insert Function Wizard (see Figure 6.16).

Figure 6.16
Click the fx icon to bring up the Insert Function dialog.

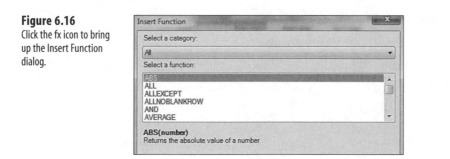

- You can start typing a function name or a table name. The AutoComplete brings up a list of possible fields and functions that match the letters that you've typed (see Figure 6.17).

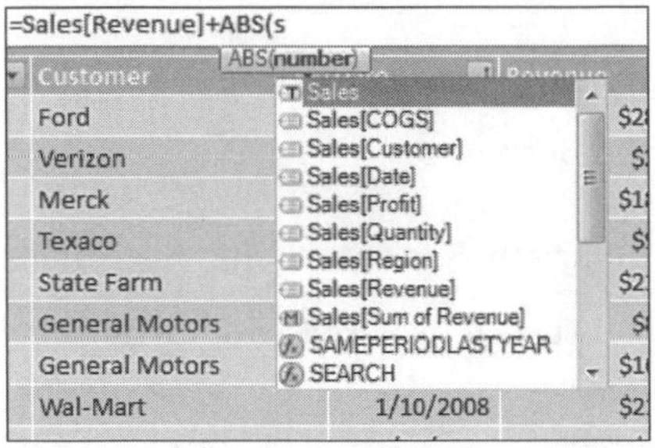

Figure 6.17
Start to type a table name to get a list of fields in that table.

> **CAUTION**
>
> There are a few things that don't work like they do in regular Excel, including the following:
>
> Going back to the days of Lotus 1-2-3, you could use the arrow keys to point to a cell while building a formula. This does not work in the PowerPivot window.
>
> The concept of absolute references does not work in DAX. You cannot press F4 to add dollar signs to your formula.
>
> There are no defined named in DAX, so you cannot use F3 to paste names in your formula.

DAX Function Reference

This chapter documents the 71 functions that are likely to be used in building calculated columns in DAX.

Date and Time Functions

There are 17 date and time functions. Sixteen of these functions are similar to Excel. However, the `YearFrac` function is new in PowerPivot.

Table 6.1 Alphabetic List of Date and Time Functions

Function	Description
`DATE(<year>, <month>, <day>)`	Returns the specified date in datetime format.
`DATEVALUE(date_text)`	Converts a date in the form of text to a date in datetime format.
`DAY(<date>)`	Returns the day of the month, a number from 1 to 31.
`EDATE(<start_date>, <months>)`	Returns the date that is the indicated number of months before or after the start date. Use `EDATE` to calculate maturity dates or due dates that fall on the same day of the month as the date of issue.

Function	Description
EOMONTH(<start_date>, <months>)	Returns the date in datetime format of the last day of the month, before or after a specified number of months. Use EOMONTH to calculate maturity dates or due dates that fall on the last day of the month.
HOUR(<datetime>)	Returns the hour as a number from 0 (12:00 a.m.) to 23 (11:00 p.m.).
MINUTE(<datetime>)	Returns the minute as a number from 0 to 59, given a date and time value.
MONTH(<datetime>)	Returns the month as a number from 1 (January) to 12 (December).
NOW()	Returns the current date and time in datetime format.
SECOND(<time>)	Returns the seconds of a time value, as a number from 0 to 59.
TIME(hour, minute, second)	Converts hours, minutes, and seconds given as numbers to a time in datetime format.
TIMEVALUE(time_text)	Converts a time in text format to a time in datetime format.
TODAY()	Returns the current date.
WEEKDAY(<date>, <return_type>)	Returns a number from 1 to 7 identifying the day of the week of a date. By default the day ranges from 1 (Sunday) to 7 (Saturday).
WEEKNUM(<date>, <return_type>)	Returns the week number for the given date and year according to the specified convention. The week number indicates where the week falls numerically within a year.
YEAR(<date>)	Returns the year of a date as a four digit integer in the range 1900-9999.
YEARFRAC(<start_date>, <end_date>, <basis>)	Calculates the fraction of the year represented by the number of whole days between two dates. Use the YEARFRAC worksheet function to identify the proportion of a whole year's benefits or obligations to assign to a specific term.

DATE(<year>, <month>, <day>)

Returns the specified date in datetime format.

> **NOTE** Use four-digit years whenever possible. Unlike Excel, a year of 07 will be treated as 1907 rather than 2007.

If month is greater than 12, the date function will return a date from a future year. =DATE(2010,14,17) will return February 17, 2011.

If the month is less than 1, the date function will return a month from an earlier year. Note these examples:

=DATE(2010,0,31) will return December 31, 2009.

=DATE(2010,-1,1) will return November 1, 2009.

If the day is greater than the number of days in the month, DATE will return a date in a future month. =DATE(2011,1,33) will return February 2, 2011.

A day of 0 is treated as the last day of the previous month: =DATE(2011,3,0) will return February 28, 2011.

Negative days will subtract the appropriate number of days from the last day of the previous month.

You will frequently use DATE to calculate new dates. Say that employee benefits begin to accrue on the January 1 following the hire date. You can calculate this with =DATE(YEAR([HireDate])+1,1,1).

To calculate the 15th of the month after the hire date, use =DATE(YEAR([HireDate]),MONTH([HireDate])+1,15).

To calculate the last day of the month prior to a date, use =DATE(YEAR([HireDate]),MONTH([HireDate]),0).

Other functions such as EOMONTH and EDATE can be used to calculate specific dates. These functions are discussed in the "Using EOMONTH or EDATE to Calculate Maturity Dates" section, later in this chapter.

DATEVALUE(date_text)

Converts a date in the form of text to a date in datetime format.

Date_text is a text string that looks like a date (for example, "1/1/2008" or "30-Dec-2011"). Figure 6.18 shows a variety of date formats that work with DATEVALUE.

Using NOW and TODAY to Calculate the Number of Days Until a Certain Date

DAX offers two functions for calculating the current date: NOW and TODAY. These functions are excellent for figuring out the number of days until a deadline or how late an open receivable might be.

Syntax: =NOW() and TODAY()

NOW returns the datetime of the current date and time. TODAY returns the datetime number of the current date. The TODAY function returns today's date, without any time attached. The NOW function returns the current date and time.

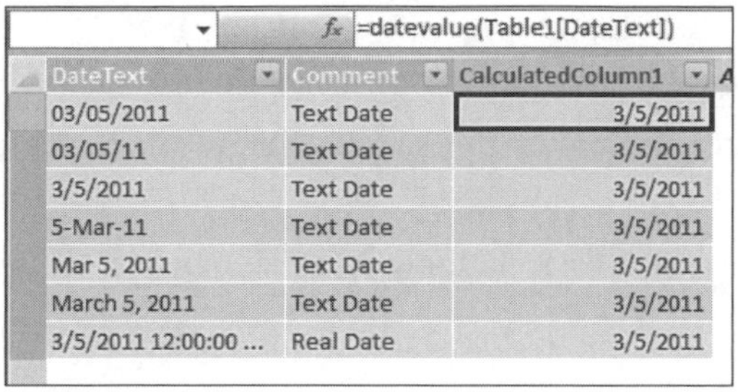

	DateText	Comment	CalculatedColumn1
	03/05/2011	Text Date	3/5/2011
	03/05/11	Text Date	3/5/2011
	3/5/2011	Text Date	3/5/2011
	5-Mar-11	Text Date	3/5/2011
	Mar 5, 2011	Text Date	3/5/2011
	March 5, 2011	Text Date	3/5/2011
	3/5/2011 12:00:00 ...	Real Date	3/5/2011

Figure 6.18
Any of these text date formats work with DATEVALUE.

There is an important distinction when you are performing calculations with the functions.

In Figure 6.19, you are calculating the days from today to a deadline. If you subtract `NOW()` from the deadline, you will get a fractional number of days. If you subtract `TODAY()` from the deadline, you will get a whole number of days.

Although most people would say that a deadline of tomorrow is 1 day away, formulas based on `NOW()` would tend to say that the deadline is 0.6969 days away. This can be deceiving. If you are going to use the result of `NOW` or `TODAY` in a date calculation, you should use `TODAY` to prevent Excel from reporting fractional days.

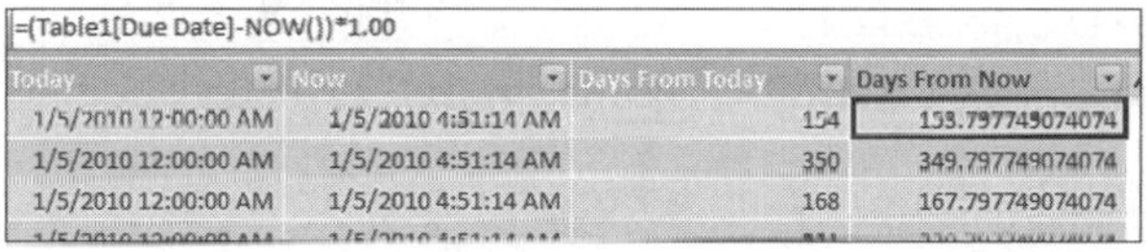

=(Table1[Due Date]-NOW())*1.00

Today	Now	Days From Today	Days From Now
1/5/2010 12:00:00 AM	1/5/2010 4:51:14 AM	154	153.797749074074
1/5/2010 12:00:00 AM	1/5/2010 4:51:14 AM	350	349.797749074074
1/5/2010 12:00:00 AM	1/5/2010 4:51:14 AM	168	167.797749074074

Figure 6.19
Comparison of NOW versus TODAY.

Note that when you subtract two fields that are of datetime type, the result will be formatted as a datetime. Unfortunately, none of the date formats shown in Figure 6.20 allow you to show the date as a numeric like you would do in Excel. To force the calculation to show the number of days, multiply the difference by a real number, such as 1.00.

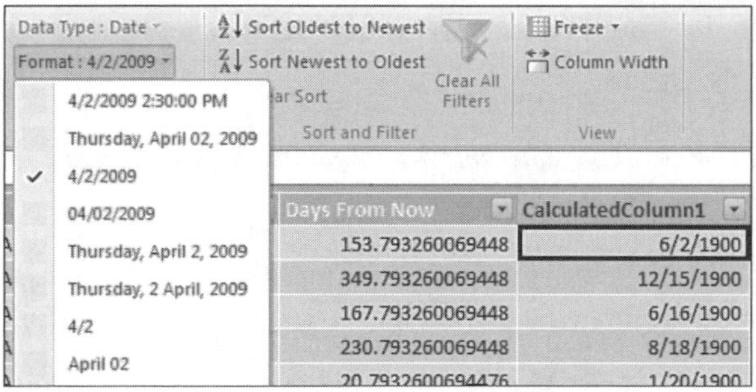

Figure 6.20
`=[HireDate]-Today()` gets classified as a date, and you are stuck with these date formats, none of which are what you need.

The somewhat annoying solution is to change this formula

```
=[HireDate]-Today()
```

To

```
=([HireDate]-Today())*1
```

When you multiply a datetime number times an integer, the datetime format is converted to an integer.

If you need a decimal portion of days, multiply by a real number. Change this formula

```
=[HireDate]-Now()
```

To

```
=([HireDate]-Now())*1.00
```

Using YEAR, MONTH, DAY, HOUR, MINUTE, and SECOND to Break a Date/Time Apart

Because PowerPivot pivot tables do not offer date grouping, you will be using these functions extensively in your data grid to break dates into years, months, and days:

- ■ =YEAR(<date>) returns the year portion as a four-digit year.
- ■ =MONTH(<date>) returns the month number, from 1 through 12.
- ■ =DAY(<date>) returns the day of the month, from 1 through 31.
- ■ =HOUR(<datetime>) returns the hour, from 0 to 23.
- ■ =MINUTE(<datetime>) returns the minute, from 0 to 59.
- ■ =SECOND(<datetime>) returns the second, from 0 to 59.

In Figure 6.21, the Due Date column is broken into year, month, and day by using YEAR, MONTH, and DAY functions.

Figure 6.21
Breaking daily dates into years, months, or days.

	fx =format(Table1[Due Date],"DDD")					
Due Date	Year	Month	Day	Format MMM	Format DDD	Sorts Well
6/7/2010	2010	6	7	Jun	Mon	06 Jun
12/20/2010	2010	12	20	Dec	Mon	12 Dec
6/21/2010	2010	6	21	Jun	Mon	06 Jun
8/24/2010	2010	8	24	Aug	Tue	08 Aug
1/29/2010	2010	1	29	Jan	Fri	01 Jan
4/15/2010	2010	4	15	Apr	Thu	04 Apr

 To see a demo of breaking dates into years, months, and days in the PowerPivot grid, search for MrExcel PowerPivot 6 at YouTube.

You would likely break the dates into years and months so that you can include the year or month field in a slicer to filter the pivot table.

I frankly think that forcing the Months slicer to have values of 1 through 12 looks really bad. In Figure 6.21, this formula produces a three digit month abbreviation:

```
=Format([DueDate],"MMM")
```

You are going to have to use a custom list to get these month names to sort into the proper sequence, but it's worth it.

If you don't want to fool around with a custom list, you could use the following:

```
=FORMAT(MONTH([Due Date]),"00 ")&FORMAT([Due Date],"MMM")
```

This will produce month names such as 12 Dec or 06 Jun. These will sort into proper sequence in the slicer.

In Figure 6.22, the table includes a start time and an end time. The following formulas are used:

- **Duration:**=[Stop]-[Start]
- **Hour:**=HOUR([Duration])
- **Minute:**=MINUTE([Duration])
- **Second:**=SECOND([Duration])
- **Decimal Hours:**=([Start]-[Stop])*24

Figure 6.22
Calculate duration, whole hours, minutes, or decimal hours.

Start	Stop	Duration	Hour	Minute	Second	Decimal Hours
4:57:27 PM	5:38:31 PM	00:41:04	0	41	4	0.684
10:28:23 AM	4:12:44 PM	05:44:21	5	44	21	5.739
10:30:20 AM	1:56:31 PM	03:26:11	3	26	11	3.436
2:37:11 PM	3:58:12 PM	01:21:01	1	21	1	1.350
11:35:02 AM	12:29:26 PM	00:54:24	0	54	24	0.907
2:30:26 PM	4:17:53 PM	01:47:27	1	47	27	1.791

Calculating the Day of the Week Using WEEKDAY

The WEEKDAY function returns a number from 1 to 7 to indicate the day of the week. Three different arrays of results can be returned:

- =WEEKDAY(<date>) will return 1 for Sunday through 7 for Saturday.
- =WEEKDAY(<date>,2) will return 1 for Monday through 7 for Sunday.
- =WEEKDAY(<date>,3) will return 0 for Monday through 6 for Sunday.

In Figure 6.23, the columns compare the three forms of WEEKDAY.

Figure 6.23
Weekday calculations.

[Sortable]	fx	=weekday(Table1[SaleDate],2)&"-"&format(Table1[SaleDate],"DDD")				
SaleDate	Weekday	Weekday 2	Weekday 3	Format DDD	Sortable
Sunday, February 13, 2011	1	7	6	Sun	7-Sun
Monday, February 14, 2011	2	1	0	Mon	1-Mon
Tuesday, February 15, 2011	3	2	1	Tue	2-Tue
Wednesday, February 16, 2011	4	3	2	Wed	3-Wed

The formulas used in the figure are as follows:

- **Weekday:**=WEEKDAY([SaleDate])
- **Weekday 2:**=WEEKDAY([SaleDate],2)
- **Weekday 3:**=WEEKDAY([SaleDate],3)

- **Weekday:**`=FORMAT([SaleDate],"DDD")`
- **Weekday:**`=WEEKDAY([SaleDate],2)& FORMAT([SaleDate],"DDD")`

The `3` argument is great for calculating the "week of" date. See the next section for an example.

Calculating the Week Number Using WEEKNUM

At least the DAX help is honest. They come right out and say that this function is going hack off the people in Europe. The Excel `WEEKNUM` function has been calculating the week number incorrectly compared to the ISO standard. DAX copied this logic, but notes it in the DAX help.

DAX and Excel assign a week number of 1 to January 1 of each year. It doesn't matter whether January 1 is on a Sunday, a Monday, or a Friday, the result of `WEEKNUM` for January 1 will always be 1.

WEEKNUM(<date>, <return_type>)

If the return_type is 1 or omitted, then the new week begins on Sunday. If the `return_type` is 2, the new week begins on Monday.

In Europe, they generally use the ISO convention where week 1 is the first week where 4 or more days fall in January.

Figure 6.24 compares some week number calculations.

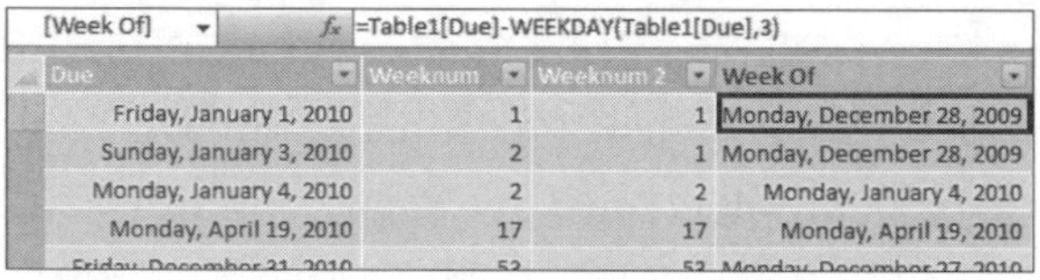

[Week Of] =Table1[Due]-WEEKDAY(Table1[Due],3)

Due	Weeknum	Weeknum 2	Week Of
Friday, January 1, 2010	1	1	Monday, December 28, 2009
Sunday, January 3, 2010	2	1	Monday, December 28, 2009
Monday, January 4, 2010	2	2	Monday, January 4, 2010
Monday, April 19, 2010	17	17	Monday, April 19, 2010
Friday, December 31, 2010	53	53	Monday, December 27, 2010

Figure 6.24
Three ways to calculate the week.

For many people, it is difficult to conceptualize something like Week 31. Is that in July? August? The final column in the figure skips `WEEKNUM` and uses the `3` argument in `WEEKDAY` to calculate a Week Of date.

Formulas used in Figure 6.24 are as follows:

- **Weeknum:**`=WEEKNUM([Due])`
- **Weeknum 2:**`=WEEKNUM([Due],2)`
- **Week Of:**`=[Due]-WEEKDAY([Due],3)`

In Figure 6.24, the first rows illustrate the difference between the `return_type` of 1 and 2. Friday January 1, 2010 is week number 1 in both conventions. With a `return_type` of 1, week 2 begins on Sunday, January 3. With a `return_type` of 2, week 2 begins on Monday, January 4.

Using EOMONTH or EDATE to Calculate Maturity Dates

The EOMONTH function will return the date at the end of the month that is some number of months from a given date. Using =EOMONTH(<date>,0) will return the end of the given month. Using -1 will give you the end of the previous month.

The EDATE function returns a date that is a specified number of months after a given date. This is used to calculate the maturity of 3-month or 6-month bonds. For example, the ending date 3 months after February 17, 2010 is May 17, 2010. On the face of it, this would be an incredibly simple calculation, if it weren't for bond sales that occur on the 31st of a month. If you need the EDATE 3 months after January 31, 2011, you cannot use April 31, 2011. The banking rules say that this bond would mature on the last day of April, so the result would be April 30, 2011.

```
EDATE(<start_date>, <months>)
EOMONTH(<start_date>, <months>)
```

Figure 6.25 illustrates calculations using EDATE or EOMONTH.

Figure 6.25
Calculate ending month dates or bond maturity dates.

[3 Months]	▼	*fx*	=EDATE(Table1[SaleDate],3)	
SaleDate	**LastMonth**	**ThisMonth**	**3 Months End**	**3 Months**
1/5/2011	12/31/2010	1/31/2011	4/30/2011	4/5/2011
3/31/2011	2/28/2011	3/31/2011	6/30/2011	6/30/2011
5/22/2010	4/30/2010	5/31/2010	8/31/2010	8/22/2010
5/11/2011	4/30/2011	5/31/2011	8/31/2011	8/11/2011
2/26/2010	1/31/2010	2/28/2010	5/31/2010	5/26/2010
4/20/2011	3/31/2011	4/30/2011	7/31/2011	7/20/2011
5/15/2010	4/30/2010	5/31/2010	8/31/2010	8/15/2010
7/19/2011	6/30/2011	7/31/2011	10/31/2011	10/19/2011
1/16/2011	12/31/2010	1/31/2011	4/30/2011	4/16/2011
8/27/2010	7/31/2010	8/31/2010	11/30/2010	11/27/2010
1/19/2010	12/31/2009	1/31/2010	4/30/2010	4/19/2010

The formulas used in Figure 6.25 are as follows:

- **LastMonth:**=EOMONTH([SaleDate],-1)
- **ThisMonth:**=EOMONTH([SaleDate],0)
- **3 Months End:**=EOMONTH([SaleDate],1)
- **3 Months:**=EDATE([SaleDate],3)

Notice that the EDATE for January 5 is April 5. The EDATE for January 31 is April 30, because there is no April 31.

Using YEARFRAC to Calculate Elapsed Time

If you work in a human resources department, you might be concerned with years of service to calculate a certain benefit. Excel provides one function, YEARFRAC, that can calculate decimal years of service in five different ways.

```
=YEARFRAC(<start_date>, <end_date>, <basis>)
```

6

The YEARFRAC function calculates the fraction of the year represented by the number of whole days between two dates (start_date and end_date). You use the YEARFRAC worksheet function to identify the proportion of a whole year's benefits or obligations to assign to a specific term.

This function takes the following arguments:

- start_date:This is a date that represents the start date.
- end_date:This is a date that represents the end date.
- basis:This is the type of day count basis to use.

  - If basis is 0 or omitted, Excel uses a 30/360 plan, modified for American use. In this plan, the employee earns 1/360 of a year's credit on most days. The employee earns no service on the day after any 31st of the month. In a leap year, the employee earns 2/360 of a year for showing up on March 1. In a non–leap year, the employee earns 3/360 of a year for showing up on March 1.

  - If basis is 1, the actual number of elapsed days is divided by the actual number of days in the year. This method works well and ensures that the year fraction ends up being 1 on the anniversary date, whether it is a leap year or not.

  - If basis is 2, the actual number of elapsed days is divided by 360. If someone would show up and work for 30 years straight for one employer, this method would give that person an extra 0.4528 years of credit. Sisogenes would be spinning in his grave.

  - If basis is 3, the actual number of elapsed days is divided by 365. This works great for three out of every four years. It is slightly wrong in leap years.

  - If basis is 4, Excel uses a 30/360 plan, modified for European use. This is similar to the default basis of 0. In this plan, the employee gets no credit for working any 31st of the month. The employee still gets triple credit for working March 1 (to make up for the 29th and 30th of February). In a leap year, March 1 is worth only double credit.

Troubleshooting PowerPivot: December 30, 1899

If you enter a calculation and all the results are December 30, 1899, don't panic. Many of the date and time functions return only the time portion of a date and time. Unfortunately, PowerPivot tends to format these times using a Date format, as shown in Figure 6.26.

In Excel, day 1 is considered to be January 1, 1900.

Thus, a value of 1.25 would be 6AM on January 1, 1900.

If your time calculation comes up with an answer of 6AM, this will get stored as 0.25. You can see where this would get displayed as 6AM on December 31, 1899.

Why, then, are the dates being shown as December 30, 1899?

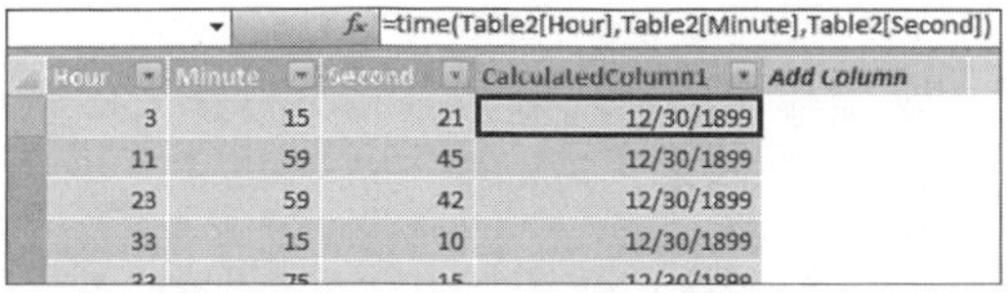

Figure 6.26
If you see dates in 1899, the answer really contains time.

There was no leap year in 1900, but the designers of Lotus 1-2-3 did not know this. Enter the numbers 1 through 61 in Excel and format those numbers as a date. The serial number of 61 reports a date of March 1, 1900. The serial number of 60 reports a nonexistent date of February 29, 1900. All the dates reported by Excel from January 1, 1900 through February 28, 1900 are off by a day. When Excel was introduced in 1985, they had to mimic the incorrect behavior of the market-leading Lotus 1-2-3.

PowerPivot makes an adjustment for this error.

In PowerPivot

=DATE(1900,3,1) is reported as March 1, 1900.

=DATE(1900,2,29) is reported as February 28, 1900!

=DATE(1900,2,28) is reported as February 27, 1900!

Everything continues off by 1 day:

=DATE(1900,1,2) is reported as January 1, 1900!

=DATE(1900,1,1) is reported as December 31, 1989.

Thus, the conceptual value of 0.25 is reported as 6AM on December 30, 1989 and displayed in the PowerPivot window as 12/30/1899.

The 1-day adjustment is made in PowerPivot to allow both PowerPivot and Excel to sync and report Day 61 as March 1, 1900.

Bottom line, when you see December 30, 1899, it means that you have only a time in the calculated column. Use the Format drop-down to choose one of the time formats, and the answers will appear (see Figure 6.27).

Using TIME to Calculate a Time

The TIME function is similar to the DATE function. It calculates a time given a specific hour, minute, and second.

```
=TIME(<hour>,<minute>,<second>)
```

The TIME function returns the datetime value for a particular time. This function takes the following arguments:

- hour:This is a number from 0 to 23, representing the hour. Numbers greater than 23 will use the remainder after dividing hour by 24.

Figure 6.27
Change the format to a time to get the real result.

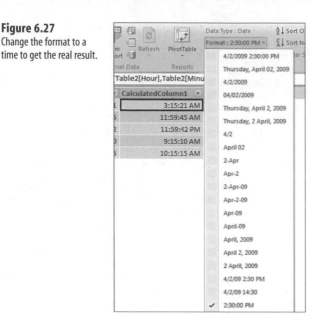

■ minute:This is a number from 0 to 59, representing the minute. Values greater than 59 are allowed and are converted to hours and minutes.

■ second:This is a number from 0 to 59, representing the second. Values greater than 59 are allowed and are converted to hours, minutes, and seconds.

As with the DATE function, DAX can handle situations in which the minute or second argument calculates to more than 60. For example, =TIME(12,72,120) evaluates to 1:14 PM. Figure 6.28 shows various results of the TIME function.

Figure 6.28
Convert hours, minutes, and seconds to a real time.

[Time]		fx =time([Hour],[Minute],[Second])		
Hour	Minute	Second	Time	Add Column
3	15	21	3:15:21 AM	
3	79	45	4:19:45 AM	
3	79	130	4:21:10 AM	
33	15	10	9:15:10 AM	
33	75	65	10:16:05 AM	

Notice that in the last two records, the hours of 33 are converted to a value of 9 in the function. 33 hours is the same as 9AM tomorrow. Because the TIME function does not return any date information, =TIME(33,1,1) is the same as =TIME(9,1,1).

Although TIME throws out hour values in excess of 24 hours, the TIME function will deal appropriately with minutes or seconds in excess of 60. In the second row, 79 minutes is converted to 1 hour and 19 minutes. In the third row, 130 seconds are converted to 2 minutes and 10 seconds.

Using TIMEVALUE to Convert Text Times to Real Times

It is easy to end up with a column of text values that look like times. Similar to DATEVALUE, you can use the TIMEVALUE function to convert these to real times.

Syntax:=TIMEVALUE(time_text)

The TIMEVALUE function returns the time represented by a text string. The argument time_ text is a text string that represents a time in any one of the Microsoft Excel time formats. For example, "6:45 PM" and "18:45" are text strings within quotation marks that represent time. (See Figure 6.29) Date information in time_text is ignored.

The TIMEVALUE function does not deal well with a time such as "45:30". While most people would interpret this as meaning 45 minutes and 30 seconds. In Excel, this is treated vas 45 hours and 30 minutes. In DAX, this is treated as an error.

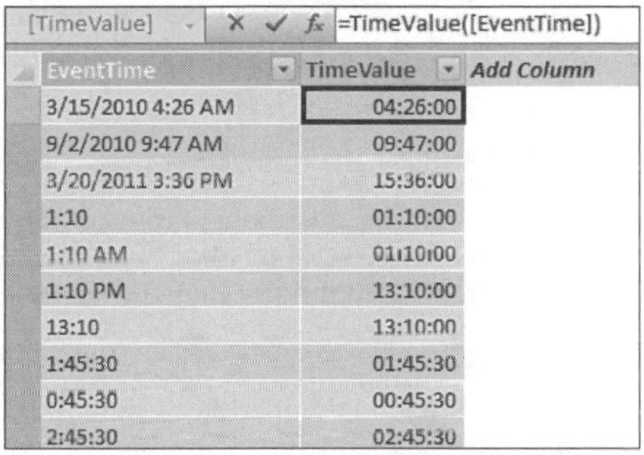

Figure 6.29
Convert text that looks like time to real times.

Examples of Math and Trigonometry Functions

DAX offers 22 math and trigonometry functions, all of which are identical to functions in Excel.

Table 6.2 includes an alphabetic list of the math and trig functions

Table 6.2   Math and Trigonometry Functions

Function	Description
ABS(<number>)	Returns the absolute value of a number.
CEILING(<number>, <significance>)	Rounds a number up, to the nearest integer or to the nearest multiple of significance.
EXP(<number>)	Returns e raised to the power of a given number. The constant e equals 2.71828182845904, the base of the natural logarithm.
FACT(<number>)	Returns the factorial of a number, equal to the series 1*2*3*...*, ending in the given number.
FLOOR(<number>, <significance>)	Rounds a number down, toward 0, to the nearest multiple of significance.

continues

Table 6.2 Continued

Function	Description
INT(<number>)	Rounds a number down to the nearest integer.
LN(<number>)	Returns the natural logarithm of a number. Natural logarithms are based on the constant e (2.71828182845904).
LOG(<number>,<base>)	Returns the logarithm of a number to the base you specify.
LOG10(<number>)	Returns the base-10 logarithm of a number.
MOD(<number>, <divisor>)	Returns the remainder after a number is divided by a divisor. The result always has the same sign as the divisor.
MROUND(<number>, <multiple>)	Returns a number rounded to the desired multiple.
PI()	Returns the value of Pi, 3.14159265358979, accurate to 15 digits.
POWER(<number>, <power>)	Returns the result of a number raised to a power.
QUOTIENT(<numerator>, <denominator>)	Performs division and returns only the integer portion of the division result. Use this function when you want to discard the remainder of division.
ROUND(<number>, <num_digits>)	Rounds a number to the specified number of digits.
ROUNDDOWN(<number>, <num_digits>)	Rounds a number down, toward 0.
ROUNDUP(<number>, <num_digits>)	Rounds a number up, away from 0.
SIGN(<number>)	Determines the sign of a number, the result of a calculation, or a value in a column. The function returns 1 if the number is positive, zero if the number is 0, or -1 if the number is negative.
SQRT(<number>)	Returns the square root of a number.
TRUNC(<number>,<num_digits>)	Truncates a number to an integer by removing the decimal, or fractional, part of the number.
RAND()	Returns a random number greater than or equal to 0 and less than 1, evenly distributed. The number that is returned changes each time the cell containing this function is recalculated.
RANDBETWEEN(<bottom>,<top>)	Returns a random number between the numbers you specify.

Using ROUND, ROUNDDOWN, ROUNDUP, INT, TRUNC, FLOOR, CEILING, MROUND, and SIGN to Remove Decimals or Round Numbers

A wide variety of functions—including ROUND, ROUNDDOWN, ROUNDUP, INT, TRUNC, FLOOR, CEILING, and MROUND—can be used to round a result or to remove decimals from a result. Three of those functions have to be used in conjunction with the SIGN function.

=SIGN(<number>) returns a 1 for positive numbers and a -1 for negative numbers. You wouldn't think this would be useful, but you will have to use it with other functions in this section.

```
=INT(<number>)
```

The INT function returns the integer that is smaller or equal to number. For positive values, this is the same as removing the numbers after the decimal place. However, for negative values, INT will choose the negative integer smaller than number. =INT(-2.2) is -3.

```
=TRUNC(<number>,<num_digits>)
```

The TRUNC function will truncate a number after so many decimal digits. If num_digits is not specified, the number is truncated to have no decimal places. =TRUNC(2.2) is 2, and =TRUNC(-2.2) is -2.

```
=ROUND(<number>,<num_digits>)
=ROUNDUP(<number>,<num_digits>)
=ROUNDDOWN(<number>,<num_digits>)
```

Three functions—ROUND, ROUNDUP, and ROUNDDOWN—round a number to a specified number of decimal places. They all take the following arguments:

- number:This is the number you want to round.

- num_digits:This specifies the number of digits to which you want to round number.

With ROUND, if the number of digits is zero, the number is rounded to the nearest integer, following these rules:

- Values up to 0.49 are rounded toward zero. For example, ROUND(1.49,0) results in 1, and ROUND(-1.49,0) results in -1.

- Values of 0.5 and above are rounded away from zero. For example, ROUND(1.5,0) results in 2, and ROUND(-1.5,0) results in -2.

If the num_digits is positive, the number is rounded to have the specified number of decimal places. If the number of digits is negative, the number is rounded to the left of the decimal point. For example, ROUND(117,-1) is rounded to the nearest 10, or a value of 120.

To override the rounding rules, you can use ROUNDDOWN or ROUNDUP:

- The ROUNDDOWN function always rounds toward zero. For example, =ROUNDDOWN(1.999,0) rounds to 1, and =ROUNDDOWN(-19.999,0) rounds to -19. You might use this function when judging a contest in which if the entrant does not completely finish a task, he or she does not get credit for the unfinished portion of the task.

- The result of the ROUNDUP function always rounds away from zero. For example, =ROUNDUP(1.01,0) rounds up to 2, and =ROUNDUP(-1.01,0) rounds to -2. You might use this function when calculating prices because if the customer uses any fractional portion of a product, he or she is charged for the complete product.

6

Using a negative number for the number of digits provides an interesting result. If you need to round a number to the nearest thousand, you can indicate that it should be rounded to -3 decimal places. For example, ROUND(1234567,-3) would be 1,235,000.

```
=CEILING(number,significance)
=FLOOR(number,significance)
=MROUND(number,multiple)
```

The last three rounding functions round a number to a certain multiple. They require you to enter the number and the multiple to which to round. They all take the following arguments:

- number:This is the number you want to round.

- multiple **or** significance:This is the nearest multiple that you want to round toward. Note that if number is negative, multiple or significance must also be negative!

There are problems with the CEILING and FLOOR function, which were fixed in Excel 2010. Unfortunately, DAX implemented the Excel 2007 version of CEILING and FLOOR, which are still wrong.

=CEILING(2.1,1) will round the 2.1 up to 3.

=CEILING(6.1,2) will round the 6.1 to the next multiple of 2, or 8.

The problem comes for negative numbers. If you use =CEILING(-2.1,-1), the result is -3. The ISO standard says that ceiling should be higher than the number. The number higher than -2.1 is actually -2, not -3.

FLOOR should round down to the next lower multiple of significance. Although this works fine for positive numbers, it rounds to a higher number for negative numbers.

MROUND is great for rounding to the nearest 5 or some other multiple. =MROUND(12.1,5) will round to 10.

> **TIP**
>
> It is a huge annoyance that multiple or significance must have the same sign as the number that you are rounding. If you don't know if you will have negative numbers mixed in, you run the risk of getting errors for the negative numbers. The workaround is to multiply the multiple or significance by the SIGN of the number. Figure 6.30 shows examples of the rounding functions.

Formulas used in Figure 6.30 are as follows:

Figure 6.30
Various rounding functions.

[MRound 5]	▼	*f*ₓ	=MROUND(Table1[Qty],5*SIGN(Table1[Qty]))						
Qty ▼	INT ▼	Trunc ▼	Round ▼	RoundDown ▼	RoundUp ▼	Ceiling ▼	Floor ▼	MRound 5 ▼
-2.9	-3	-2	-3	-2	-3	-3	-2	-5
-2.5	-3	-2	-3	-2	-3	-3	-2	-5
-2.1	-3	-2	-2	-2	-3	-3	-2	0
2.1	2	2	2	2	3	3	2	0
2.5	2	2	3	2	3	3	2	5
2.9	2	2	3	2	3	3	2	5

6

- **Int:**=INT([Qty])
- **Trunc:**=TRUNC([Qty])
- **Round:**=ROUND([Qty],0)
- **RoundDown:**=ROUNDDOWN([Qty],0)
- **RoundUp:**=ROUNDUP([Qty],0)
- **Ceiling:**=CEILING([Qty],SIGN([QTY])
- **Floor:**=FLOOR([Qty],SIGN(Qty])
- **MRound5:**=MROUND([Qty],5*SIGN([Qty]))

Generating Random Numbers

DAX offers two functions for generating random numbers: RAND and RANDBETWEEN. These can be useful for performing Monte Carlo simulations.

=RAND() will return a random number between 0 and 1, evenly distributed. The number might include 0 but will never include 1. Traditionally, if you wanted to generate random numbers between 1 and 10, you would have to use =INT(RAND()*10)+1.

=RANDBETWEEN(<bottom>,<top>) will return a random integer between the two integers specified. If you want to introduce a random variation to a column that varies + or – 5%, you could use =[Qty]*RANDBETWEEN(95,105)/100.

Calculating Roots and Powers

DAX includes a built-in function, SQRT, for calculating square roots. You can use the POWER function to figure out all other roots and powers.

=SQRT(<number>) calculates the square root of number.

=POWER(<number>, <power>) raises number to a power.

To calculate the compounded interest rate of an investment after four years, use the following:

    =POWER(1+[IntRate],4)

Note that the power argument can be negative. When you raise a number to the negative third power, it is the same as taking the cube root. =POWER(125, -3) is 5.

Calculating Quotients and Remainders

Do you remember when you were first starting to learn how to do division way back in elementary school? If you had to calculate 23 divided by 5, you might express the answer as 4 with a remainder of 3.

DAX offers two functions to return the whole number and the remainder.

6

In Figure 6.31, a quantity and a case size are shown. To calculate the number of full cases, use the following:

```
=QUOTIENT([Qty],[Case Size])
```

To return the number of items left over after packing full cases, use this:

```
=MOD([Qty],[Case Size])
```

MOD stands for Modulo. Mathematicians would express the equation as 11 Modulo 5. In DAX, use =MOD(11,5). Because 5 goes into 11 twice with a remainder of 1, the result of the MOD function is 1.

Figure 6.31

Use QUOTIENT and MOD for calculating full cases and remainders.

		f_x =Quotient([Qty],[Case Size])		
Qty	Case Size	Full Cases	Remainder	Ac
11	5	2	1	
38	7	5	3	
25	8	3	1	
15	3	5	0	
41	4	10	1	
35	3	11	2	
39	6	6	3	
49	5	9	4	
23	5	4	3	

Using PI to Calculate Cake or Pizza Pricing

How many more ingredients are in a 16-inch pizza than an 8-inch pizza? Be careful; it is not double!

The formula for the area of a circle is $\varpi \times r2$. The radius of a circle is half the diameter. The function =PI() returns the constant for PI. You use =PI()*(B7/2)^2 to calculate the number of square inches in a 16-inch pizza. As shown in Figure 6.32, the 16-inch size contains nearly four times the area of an 8-inch pie.

Figure 6.32

Most pizza shops don't have a dedicated cost accountant.

	[Area]		f_x =PI()*([Pizza Size]/2)^2
Pizza Size	Area	Add Column	
8	50.27		
10	78.54		
12	113.10		
16	201.06		

If your company makes anything round (drink coasters, drum heads, wedding cakes, pizzas, or Frisbees), you want to use =PI() when calculating your product cost.

The PI function returns the number 3.14159265358979, the mathematical constant ϖ, accurate to 15 digits.

Measure the Magnitude of Error Using ABS

If you have to measure a forecast versus actual results, you need to measure the magnitude of the error. You might have been low on 7 products by 1,000 units each and high on 7 other products by 1,000 units each. If you simply added the deltas, you would have no error. You need to add the magnitude of error for each item.

=ABS(<number>) returns the absolute value of number.

The ABS function measures the size of the error. Positive errors are reported as positive, and negative errors are reported as positive, too. You can use =ABS([Forecast]-[Actual]) to calculate the magnitude of the error.

Calculating Permutations with FACT

=FACT(<number>) calculates the factorial of the number.

=FACT(6) is 6 × 5 × 4 × 3 × 2 × 1 or 720.

Factorials are useful in figuring out the number of permutations of a set of items.

Calculating Logarithms

A logarithm raises a number, the base, to a certain power.

10^1 is 10. The base 10 logarithm of 10 is 1.

10^2 is 100. The base 10 logarithm of 100 is 2.

What base 10 logarithm would give you 98? Use =LOG10(98) to learn that 98 is 10 raised to the 1.991226 power.

DAX offers four functions for dealing with logarithms. LOG10 calculates the logarithms based on raising 10 to a certain power. LOG can calculate the logarithm for any base. LN and EXP deal with a special logarithm.

    LOG10(number)

The LOG10 function returns the base 10 logarithm of a number. The argument number is the positive real number for which you want the baseb10 logarithm.

    LOG(number,base)

DAX makes it simple to calculate the logarithm for any base, using the LOG function. The formula =LOG(15,2) could be used to express 15 as a base 2 logarithm.

In science, only two logarithms are used frequently. The first is the base 10 logarithm discussed previously. The second is a natural logarithm where numbers are expressed as a power of the number e. e is a special number. You can calculate e by adding up all the numbers in the series of $1 + [1 / (1!)] + [1 / (2!)] + [1 / (3!)] + [1 / (4!)] + [1 / (5!)] + [1 / (6!)] + [1 / (7!)] + [1 / (8!)] + [1 / (9!)] + [1 / (10!)] + ...$

6

Luckily, 10! is 3.7 million, so 1 / (10!) is a very small number: 0.000000275573. After about 1 / (17!), the numbers are small enough that they are beyond Excel's 15-digit precision.

This infinite series converges toward a number around 2.718281. This number is known as the transcendental number and is abbreviated as e. Logarithms for base e are known as natural logarithms. =EXP(1) returns the approximation of e.

> **NOTE** Natural logarithms are very popular in science because anything with a constant rate of growth follows a curve described by natural logarithms. Radioactive isotopes, for example, decay along a curve described by natural logarithms.
>
> While common logarithms with base 10 are called *logs*, natural logarithms with base e are written as *ln* (often pronounced *lon*). You calculate natural logarithms by using the LN function.

```
LN(number)
```

The LN function returns the natural logarithm of a number. Natural logarithms are based on the constant e (that is, 2.71828182845904). The argument number is the positive real number for which you want a natural logarithm.

With common logarithms, you can easily convert the logarithm back to the original number by using =10^x. However, it is fairly difficult to write 2.71828182845904^x. Therefore, Excel provides the function EXP to raise e to any power.

```
EXP(number)
```

The EXP function returns e raised to the power of number. The constant e equals 2.71828182845904, the base of the natural logarithm. The argument number is the exponent applied to the base e.

EXP is the inverse of LN, the natural logarithm of number.

Examples of Text Functions

DAX provides 18 text functions. 17 of them are identical to their Excel counterparts. The Excel TEXT() function has been renamed to FORMAT() in DAX.

Table 6.3 provides an alphabetic list of DAX text functions.

Table 6.3   DAX Text Functions

Function	Description
CODE(<text>)	Returns a numeric code for the first character in a text string, in the character set used by your computer.

Function	Description
CONCATENATE(<text1>, <text2>,...)	The CONCATENATE function joins multiple text strings into one text string. The joined items can be text, numbers or Boolean values represented as text, or a combination of those items. You can also use a column reference if the column contains appropriate values.
EXACT(<text1>,<text2>)	Compares two text strings and returns True if they are exactly the same, False otherwise. EXACT is case sensitive but ignores formatting differences. You can use EXACT to test text being entered into a document.
FIND(<find_text>, <within_text>, <start_num>)	Returns the starting position of one text string within another text string. FIND is case sensitive.
FIXED(<number>, <decimals>, <no_commas>)	Rounds a number to the specified number of decimals and returns the result as text. You can specify that the result be returned with or without commas.
FORMAT(<value>, <format_string>)	Converts a value to text according to the specified format.
LEFT(<text>, <num_chars>)	Returns the specified number of characters from the start of a text string.
LEN(<text>)	Returns the number of characters in a text string.
LOWER(<text>)	Converts all letters in a text string to lowercase.
MID(<text>, <start_num>, <num_chars>)	Returns a string of characters from the middle of a text string, given a starting position and length.
REPLACE(<old_text>, <start_num>, <num_chars>, <new_text>)	REPLACE replaces part of a text string, based on the number of characters you specify, with a different text string.
REPT(<text>, <num_times>)	Repeats text a given number of times. Use REPT to fill a cell with a number of instances of a text string.
RIGHT(<text>, <num_chars>)	RIGHT returns the last character or characters in a text string, based on the number of characters you specify.
SEARCH(<search_text>, <within_text>, [start_num])	Returns the number of the character at which a specific character or text string is first found, reading left to right. SEARCH is case sensitive.
SUBSTITUTE(<text>, <old_text>, <new_text>, <instance_num>)	Replaces existing text with new text in a text string.
TRIM(<text>)	Removes all spaces from text except for single spaces between words.
UPPER (<text>)	Converts a text string to all uppercase letters.
VALUE(<text>)	Converts a text string that represents a number to a number.

6

Examples of Text Functions

When they think of Excel, most people think of numbers. Excel is great at dealing with numbers, and it lets you write formulas to produce new numbers. Excel offers a whole cadre of formulas for dealing with text.

You might sometimes be frustrated because you receive data from other users and the text is not in the format you need. Or, the mainframe might send customer names in uppercase, or the employee in the next department might put a whole address in a single cell. Excel provides text functions to deal with all these situations and more.

Formatting Numbers or Dates Using FORMAT (a.k.a. TEXT)

DAX copied 81 functions from Excel. For 80 of those functions, they used the same name. This is the one function that gets a new name. The Excel TEXT function is now called FORMAT.

FORMAT will take a number or a date and present it in a specific format. This function is extremely useful for calculated columns in the PowerPivot window. Because online analytical processing (OLAP) pivot tables do not allow you to group daily dates up to months and years, you will need to do this in the PowerPivot grid, and FORMAT is an excellent way to achieve the result.

```
=FORMAT(<value>, <format_string>)
```

If you check PowerPivot help, there are a number of built-in format_strings that you can use for numbers and for dates. You can also use most strings that you would type in the custom number box of the Excel Format Cells dialog.

Here are the most useful format strings:

- =Format([Date],"MMM") will convert a date to Jan, Feb....
- =Format([Date],"YYYY") will convert a date to 2010, 2011....
- =Format([Date],"DDD") will convert a date to Mon, Tue, Wed....
- =Format([Date],"YYMM") will show a date as a two-digit year and month.

There are many built-in formats. Here are some of interest:

- s converts a date to a sortable index: 2011-02-17T11:15:31.
- Yes/No converts True/False to Yes/No.
- On/Off converts True/False to Yes/No.

Joining Text with the Ampersand (&) Operator

The ampersand (&) operator is worth mentioning again here because it is the most important tool for dealing with text. The & is an operator that you use to join text.

Suppose that you have a table with [FirstName] and [LastName]. To join those together, use =[FirstName]&" "&[LastName].

Some people prefer to use the CONCATENATE function rather than the &. This function does not perform the way that I want it to perform, and I generally avoid it, but it is described in the following section.

```
=CONCATENATE (<text1>,<text2>,...)
```

The CONCATENATE function joins several text strings into one text string. The arguments text1, text2, and so on are 1 to 30 text items to be joined into a single text item.

Using **LOWER** or **UPPER** to Convert Text Case

Two functions, LOWER and UPPER, convert text to or from capital letters. =UPPER([Name]) will convert all characters to uppercase.

```
=LOWER(<text>)
```

The LOWER function converts all uppercase letters in a text string to lowercase. The argument text is the text you want to convert to lowercase. LOWER does not change characters in text that are not letters.

```
=UPPER(<text>)
```

The UPPER function converts text to uppercase. The argument text is the text you want converted to uppercase.

Using **TRIM** to Remove Trailing Spaces

If you frequently import data, you might be plagued with a couple of annoying situations. You may have trailing spaces at the end of text cells. Although "ABC" and "ABC" might look alike when viewed in the grid, they cause equality functions to fail. TRIM removes leading and trailing spaces.

```
=TRIM(text)
```

The TRIM function removes all spaces from text except for single spaces between words. You use TRIM on text that you have received from another application that may have irregular spacing.

Using the **CODE** Function to Learn the Character Number for Any Character

Each font set offers 255 different characters, numbered from 1 through 255. Old-time computer folks might know some of the popular codes off the top of their heads. For example, a capital A is 65. The capital letters run from 65 to 90, a space is 32, a lowercase letter a is 97, and the other lowercase letters run from 98 through 122.

In the early days of personal computers, every computer was packed with a list of the ASCII codes for each character. Today, with the character map, no one has to memorize character codes. However, in some instances, you might want to learn exactly what character you are seeing in a cell. The CODE function returns the character code for one character at a time.

```
=CODE(<text>)
```

The CODE function returns a numeric code for the first character in a text string. The returned code corresponds to the character set used by your computer. The argument text is the text for which you want the code of the first character. This is an important distinction. CODE returns the code for only the first character in a cell. =CODE("A") and =CODE("ABC") return only 65 to indicate the capital letter A.

Using LEFT, MID, or RIGHT to Split Text

One of the newer rules in information processing is that each field in a database should contain exactly one piece of information. Throughout the history of computers, there have been millions of examples of people trying to cram many pieces of information into a single field. Although this works great for humans, it is pretty difficult to have Excel to sort a column by everything in the second half of a cell.

Say that you have a part number field that contains a three-character vendor code, a dash, and a five-digit part number.

=LEFT([PartNumber],3) will isolate the vendor code.

=RIGHT([PartNumber],5) will isolate the numeric part number.

=MID([PartNumber],5,5) is an alternate formula for the part number.

Excel offers three functions—LEFT, MID, and RIGHT—that allow you to isolate just the first or just the last characters, or even just the middle characters, from a column.

```
=LEFT(<text>,<num_chars>)
```

The LEFT function returns the first character or characters in a text string, based on the number of characters specified. This function takes the following arguments:

- text:This is the text string that contains the characters you want to extract.
- num_chars—This specifies the number of characters you want LEFT to extract. num_chars must be greater than or equal to zero. If num_chars is greater than the length of text, LEFT returns all of text. If num_chars is omitted, it is assumed to be 1.
```
=RIGHT(<text>,<num_chars>)
```

The RIGHT function returns the last character or characters in a text string, based on the number of characters specified. This function takes the following arguments:

- text:This is the text string that contains the characters you want to extract.
- num_chars—This specifies the number of characters you want RIGHT to extract. num_chars must be greater than or equal to zero. If num_chars is greater than the length of text, RIGHT returns all of text. If num_chars is omitted, it is assumed to be 1.
```
=MID(<text>,<start_num>,<num_chars>)
```

MID returns a specific number of characters from a text string, starting at the position specified, based on the number of characters specified. This function takes the following arguments:

- text:This is the text string that contains the characters you want to extract.
- start_num:This is the position of the first character you want to extract in text. The first character in text has start_num 1, and so on. If start_num is less than the length of

text, but start_num plus num_chars exceeds the length of text, MID returns the characters up to the end of text.

- num_chars—This specifies the number of characters you want MID to return from text. If num_chars is negative, MID returns an error.

Using LEN to Find the Number of Characters in Text

It seems pretty obscure, but you will find the LEN function amazingly useful. The LEN function determines the length of characters in a cell, including any leading or trailing spaces.

```
=LEN(<text>)
```

The LEN function returns the number of characters in a text string. The argument text is the text whose length you want to find. Spaces count as characters.

There are instances in which LEN can be used in conjunction with LEFT, MID, or RIGHT to isolate a portion of text.

Using SEARCH or FIND to Locate Characters in a Particular Cell

Two nearly identical functions can scan through a text cell, looking for a particular character or word. Many times, you just want to know if the word appears in the text. These functions go further than telling you whether the character exists in the text; they tell you at exactly which character position the character or word is found. The character position can be useful in subsequent formulas with LEFT, RIGHT, or REPLACE.

First, let's look at an example of using FIND to determine whether a word exists in another cell. Say that you have a database of customers. The database was created by someone who doesn't know Excel and jammed every field into a single cell.

You want to find customers in California. =FIND("CA",[Customer]) will either return the character position where CA is found or an error. To convert this to something useful, use the following:

```
=NOT(ISERROR(FIND("CA",[Customer])))
```

> **CAUTION**
>
> The trick with this application of FIND is to look for something that is only likely to be found in California records. If you had customers in Cairo, Illinois, they would have also been found by the FIND command you just used. The theory with this sort of search is that you can quickly check through the few matching records to find false positives.

FIND and SEARCH are similar to one another. The FIND function does not distinguish between uppercase and lowercase letters. FIND identifies CA, ca, Ca, and cA as matches for CA. If you need to find a cell with exactly AbCdEf, you need to use the SEARCH command rather than FIND. Also, SEARCH allows for wildcard characters in find_text. A question mark (?) finds a single character, and an asterisk (*) finds any number of characters.

6

The FIND function makes it easy to find the first instance of a particular character in a cell. However, if your text values contain two instances of a character and you need to find the second instance, your task is a bit more difficult. Suppose that your part number has three segments: ABC-123-0987 as shown in Figure 6.33.

1. To find the first dash, use =FIND("-",[PartNum]). Give this field a name of **FirstDash**.

2. To find the second dash, use the optional start_num parameter to the FIND function. The start_num parameter is a character position. You want the function to start looking after the first instance of a dash. This can be calculated as [FirstDash]+1. Thus, the formula to find the second dash is =FIND("-",[PartNum],[FirstDash]+1).

3. After you find the character positions of the dashes, isolate the various portions of the part number. To get the first part of the part number, use =LEFT([PartNum],[FirstDash]-1). This basically asks for the left characters from the part number, stopping at one fewer than the first dash.

4. To get the middle part of the part number, use =MID([PartNum],[FirstDash]+1,[NextDash]-[FirstDash]-1). This asks Excel to start at the character position one after the first dash and then continue for a length that is one fewer than the first dash subtracted from the second dash.

5. To get the third segment of the part number, use =RIGHT([PartNum],LEN([PartNum])-[NextDash]). This calculates the total length of the part number, subtracts the position of the second dash, and returns those right characters.

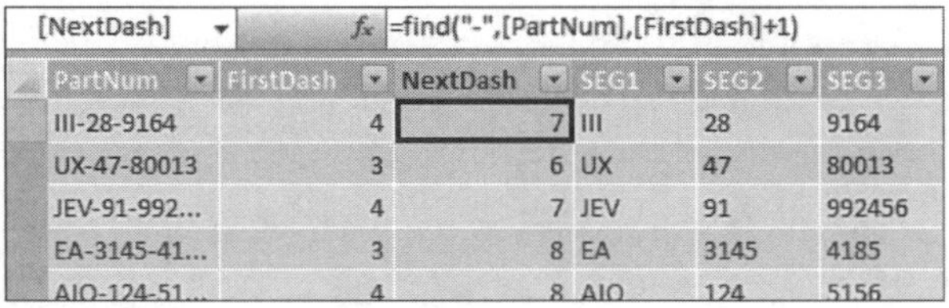

Figure 6.33
Formulaically isolating data between the first and second dashes can be done, but it helps to break each number down into small parts.

[NextDash] ▾		fx =find("-",[PartNum],[FirstDash]+1)			
PartNum ▾	FirstDash ▾	NextDash ▾	SEG1 ▾	SEG2 ▾	SEG3 ▾
III-28-9164	4	7	III	28	9164
UX-47-80013	3	6	UX	47	80013
JEV-91-992...	4	7	JEV	91	992456
EA-3145-41...	3	8	EA	3145	4185
AIO-124-51...	4	8	AIO	124	5156

```
=FIND(<find_text>,<within_text>,<start_num>)
```

FIND finds one text string (find_text) within another text string (within_text) and returns the number of the starting position of find_text from the first character of within_text. You can also use SEARCH to find one text string within another, but unlike SEARCH, FIND is case sensitive and doesn't allow wildcard characters.

The FIND function takes the following arguments:

■ find_text: This is the text you want to find. If find_text is "" (that is, empty text), FIND matches the first character in the search string (that is, the character numbered start_num or 1). find_text cannot contain any wildcard characters.

■ within_text: This is the text that contains the text you want to find.

■ start_num—This specifies the character at which to start the search. The first character in within_text is character number 1. If you omit start_num, it is assumed to be 1.

If find_text does not appear in within_text, FIND return an error. If start_num is not greater than zero, FIND returns an error. If start_num is greater than the length of within_text, FIND returns an error.

```
=SEARCH(<find_text>,<within_text>,<start_num>)
```

SEARCH returns the number of the character at which a specific character or text string is first found, beginning with start_num. You use SEARCH to determine the location of a character or text string within another text string so that you can use the MID or REPLACE functions to change the text.

The SEARCH function takes the following arguments:

■ find_text:This is the text you want to find. You can use the wildcard characters question mark (?) and asterisk (*) in find_text. A question mark matches any single character; an asterisk matches any sequence of characters. If you want to find an actual question mark or asterisk, you type a tilde (~) before the character. If find_text is not found, an error is returned.

■ within_text:This is the text in which you want to search for find_text.

■ start_num:This is the character number in within_text at which you want to start searching. If start_num is omitted, it is assumed to be 1. If start_num is not greater than zero or is greater than the length of within_text, an error is returned.

Using SUBSTITUTE and REPLACE to Replace Characters

When you have the ability to find text, you might want to replace text. DAX offers two functions for this: SUBSTITUTE and REPLACE. The SUBSTITUTE function is easier to use and should be your first approach.

```
=SUBSTITUTE(<text>, <old_text>, <new_text>, <instance_num>)
```

The SUBSTITUTE function substitutes new_text for old_text in a text string. You use SUBSTITUTE when you want to replace specific text in a text string; you use REPLACE when you want to replace any text that occurs in a specific location in a text string.

The SUBSTITUTE function takes the following arguments:

■ text:This is the text or the reference to a cell that contains text for which you want to substitute characters.

■ old_text:This is the text you want to replace.

■ new_text:This is the text you want to replace old_text with.

■ instance_num—This specifies which occurrence of old_text you want to replace with new_text. If you specify instance_num, only that instance of old_text is replaced. Otherwise, every occurrence of old_text in text is changed to new_text.

For example, =SUBSTITUTE("Sales Data","Sales","Cost") would generate "Cost Data".

The SUBSTITUTE function works similarly to a traditional find and replace command. Compared to the SUBSTITUTE function, the REPLACE function is difficult enough to make even an old programmer's head spin.

```
=REPLACE(<old_text>,<start_num>,<num_chars>,<new_text>)
```

REPLACE replaces part of a text string, based on the number of characters specified, with a different text string. This function takes the following arguments:

- old_text:This is text in which you want to replace some characters.
- start_num:This is the position of the character in old_text that you want to replace with new_text.
- num_chars:This is the number of characters in old_text that you want REPLACE to replace with new_text.
- new_text:This is the text that will replace characters in old_text.

To successfully use REPLACE, you have to use functions to determine the location and number of characters to replace. In most circumstances, SUBSTITUTE is easier to use.

Using REPT to Repeat Text Multiple Times

The REPT function will repeat a character or some text a certain number of times.

```
=REPT(<text>,<number_times>)
```

The REPT function repeats text a given number of times. You use REPT to fill a cell with a number of instances of a text string. This function takes the following arguments:

- text:This is the text you want to repeat.
- number_times:This is a positive number that specifies the number of times to repeat text. If number_times is 0, REPT returns "" (that is, empty text). If number_times is not an integer, it is truncated. The result of the REPT function cannot be longer than 32,767 characters.

Using EXACT to Test Case

For the most part, Excel isn't concerned about case. To Excel, ABC and abc are the same thing. To some people, these two text cells may not really be equivalent. If you work in a store that sells the big plastic letters that go on theater marquees, your order for 20 letter a characters should not be filled with an order for 20 letter A characters.

Excel forces you to use the EXACT function to compare these two cells to learn that they are not exactly the same.

```
=EXACT(<text1>,<text2>)
```

The EXACT function compares two text strings and returns TRUE if they are exactly the same and FALSE otherwise. EXACT is case sensitive but ignores formatting differences. This function takes the following arguments:

- text1:This is the first text string.
- text2:This is the second text string

Using **FIXED** to Format a Number as Text

This is a strange function. I am not entirely sure why it made the cut to be in DAX. This function will take a number, format it with or without commas, use a certain number of decimals, and then convert that formatted number to text. It seems like you could do this in the final pivot table without too much trouble.

```
=FIXED(<number>,<decimals>,<no_commas>)
```

The FIXED function rounds a number to the specified number of decimals, formats the number in decimal format using a period and commas, and returns the result as text. The major difference between formatting a cell that contains a number with the Format Cells dialog and formatting a number directly with the FIXED function is that FIXED converts its result to text. A number formatted with the Format Cells dialog is still a number. This function takes the following arguments:

- number:This is the number you want to round and convert to text.
- decimals:This is the number of digits to the right of the decimal point. Numbers in Microsoft Excel can never have more than 15 significant digits, but decimals can be as large as 127. If decimals is negative, number is rounded to the left of the decimal point. If you omit decimals, it is assumed to be 2.
- no_commas:This is a logical value that, if TRUE, prevents FIXED from including commas in the returned text. If no_commas is FALSE or omitted, the returned text includes commas as usual.

Using the **VALUE** Function

The VALUE function converts text that looks like a number to a number. If you have an imported column which contains mostly numbers but a few text cells, PowerPivot will convert the entire column to text. Use VALUE() to convert the numeric cells back to numbers.

=VALUE() converts text that looks like a number or a date to the number or the date.

Examples of Logical Functions

The logical function includes the IF function and five other functions which can be used with IF. This group also includes the relatively new IFERROR function to handle error values.

Table 6.4 provides a complete list of logical functions.

6

Table 6.4   Logical Functions in DAX

Function	Description
AND(<logical1>,<logical2>,...)	Checks whether all arguments are TRUE, and returns TRUE if all arguments are TRUE.
BLANK()	Returns a blank.
FALSE()	Returns the logical value FALSE.
IF(logical_test>,<value_if_true>, <value_if_false>)	Checks if a condition provided as the first argument is met. Returns one value if the condition is TRUE, and returns another value if the condition is FALSE.
IFERROR(<value>, <value_if_error>)	Returns value_if_error if the first expression is an error and the value of the expression itself if otherwise.
NOT(<logical>)	Changes FALSE to TRUE, or TRUE to FALSE.
OR(<logical1>,<logical2>,...)	Checks whether one of the arguments is TRUE to return TRUE. The function returns FALSE if all arguments are FALSE
TRUE()	Returns the logical value TRUE.

Performing Conditional Calculations with IF

The IF function checks a logical test that is specified as the first argument of the function. If the logical test is true, the second argument is used as the result. If the logical test is false, then the third argument is used.

```
=IF(<logical_test>,<value_if_true>, <value_if_false>)
```

■ logical_test:Any value or expression that can be evaluated to TRUE or FALSE.

■ value_if_true:The value that is returned if the logical test is TRUE. If omitted, TRUE is returned.

■ value_if_false:The value that is returned if the logical test is FALSE. If omitted, FALSE is returned.

Say that you want to pay a 2% bonus any time that the sale amount meets or exceeds $20,000. The logical test would be [Sales]>=20000. The DAX formula would be as follows:

```
=IF([Sales]>=20000,0.02*[Sales],0)
```

The IF function attempts to return a single data type in a column. Therefore, if the values returned by value_if_true and value_if_false are of different data types, the IF function will implicitly convert data types to accommodate both values in the column. For example, the formula IF(<condition>,TRUE(),0) returns a column of ones and zeros and the results can be summed, but the formula IF(<condition>,TRUE(),FALSE()) returns only logical values.

You can nest additional IF functions in the second or third argument. If you wanted to pay a 2% bonus for sales > $20000 and a 1% bonus for sales > $10000, then you would use the following:

```
=IF([Sales]>=20000,0.02*[Sales], IF([Sales]>=10000,0.01*[Sales],0))
```

Testing for Multiple Conditions with AND

You will frequently have to check that multiple conditions are true in the logical test portion of the IF statement. You can combine those logical tests in the AND function. Separate each logical condition with a comma.

To test that sales are greater than $20,000 and that gross profit percent is over 50%, use the following:

```
=AND([Sales]>20000,[GPPct]>0.5)
```

= AND(<logical1>,<logical2>,...) tests to see whether all the arguments are true and returns TRUE if they are all true.

Testing for Any Conditions with OR

In other cases, you might want to test to see whether any of several conditions are true. The OR function will evaluate several conditions and return TRUE if any of the logical conditions are true.

Have you ever seen a bonus plan like this:

```
=IF(OR([Sales]>20000,[RepName]="Joey"),0.02*[Sales],0)
```

Of course, this usually happens when the boss's son is Joey.

What About NAND and Other Boolean Logic Functions?

DAX provides the NOT() function, as well as the TRUE() and FALSE() functions. Using combinations of NOT, AND, and/or OR, you can construct NAND, NOR, XOR and other Boolean logic functions.

= NOT(<logical>) changes TRUE to FALSE, and FALSE to TRUE.

=TRUE() returns TRUE.

=FALSE() returns FALSE.

=BLANK() returns a Blank.

Efficiently Testing for Errors with IFERROR

The IFERROR function was a new function in Excel 2007. It is a much faster way to test for an error than any of the information functions presented below.

6

Before the introduction of IFERROR, you would often have to write a calculation that performed the calculation once to see if it was an error and then perform the calculation again if it was not an error.

```
=IF(ISERROR(<calculation>),0,<calculation>)
```

If you have a million rows and only 50 of them result in an error, you are doing almost 2 million calculations.

The IFERROR function first evaluates the <calculation> for all rows. Then, for the few rows that evaluate to errors, the value_if_error is calculated.

```
=IFERROR(value, value_if_error)
```

Examples of Information Functions

DAX provides six information functions, all duplicates of functions in Excel. These will frequently be used as the first argument in the IF function.

Table 6.5 provides an alphabetic list of the information functions.

Table 6.5   Information Functions in DAX

Function	Description
ISBLANK(<value>)	Checks whether a value is blank, and returns TRUE or FALSE
ISERROR(<value>)	Checks whether a value is an error, and returns TRUE or FALSE
ISLOGICAL(<value>)	Checks whether a value is a logical value, (TRUE or FALSE), and returns TRUE or FALSE
ISNONTEXT(<value>)	Checks whether a value is not text (blank cells are not text), and returns TRUE or FALSE
ISNUMBER(<value>)	Checks whether a value is a number, and returns TRUE or FALSE
ISTEXT(<value>)	Checks whether a value is text, and returns TRUE or FALSE

For example, if you want to use a default rate of 3% any time that the commission rate field is invalid, you could use the following:

```
=IF(ISNUMBER([Rate]),[Rate],0.03)
```

Grabbing Values from a Related Table

All the functions used so far in this chapter have been functions to calculate a column using data inside of one table.

It is possible with DAX to use functions that navigate to related tables.

The workbook used in this section has three tables:

■ The Sales table has 563 rows of data.

- The Industry table maps the 27 customers to an industry.
- The Rates table maps the six industries to a bonus rate. The company is offering higher bonuses for sales in emerging industries.

Using One Value from a Related Table

Say that you want to add a calculated column to the Sales table to calculate the bonus. The bonus is the Revenue amount from the Sales table multiplied by the Bonus Rate amount in the Rates table.

To find the bonus rate, you have to find the industry sector for this customer in the Industry table and then use that sector to navigate to the Rates table. The great news is that you don't have to know this navigation route to set up the formula.

When you use RELATED(Rates[Bonus Rate]), this tells PowerPivot to follow the defined relationships to go out and return a value from another table.

In Figure 6.34, a formula of =[Revenue]*RELATED(Rates[Bonus Rate]) performs a calculation using a number from the current table times a number in a related table.

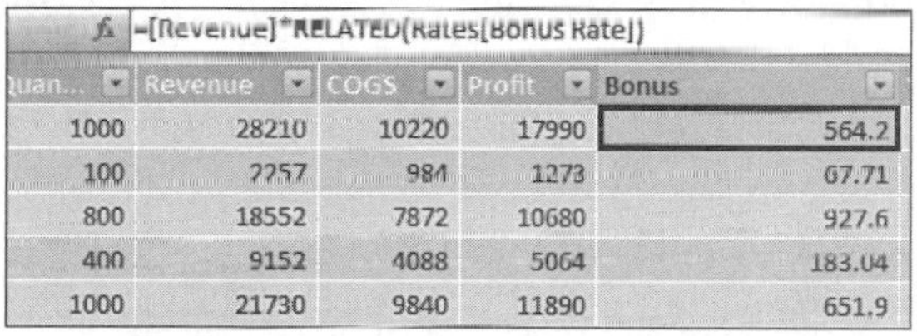

Figure 6.34
The RELATED function tells PowerPivot to follow defined relationships to get a value from a foreign table.

Getting Multiple Values from a Related Table

Sometimes you will want to retrieve multiple records from a related table.

Figure 6.35 shows the Industry table. There are 27 records in this table, one for each customer in the Sales table. If you want to see the total sales for each customer, each row in the Industry table must retrieve several rows from the Sales table.

In this case, the RELATEDTABLE function will retrieve all the matching records from the other table. After you have those several records, you will have to use one of the external statistical functions such as COUNTAX to summarize the many results down to a single number. These functions are like wrapper functions in Excel.

In Figure 6.35, the Customer Revenue column uses =SumX(RelatedTable(Sales),Sales [Revenue]). The # of Orders column uses =COUNTAX(RelatedTable(Sales),Sales[Reve nue]).

→ SUMX, COUNTAX, and COUNTROWS are explained in Chapter 10 "Using DAX for Aggregate Functions."

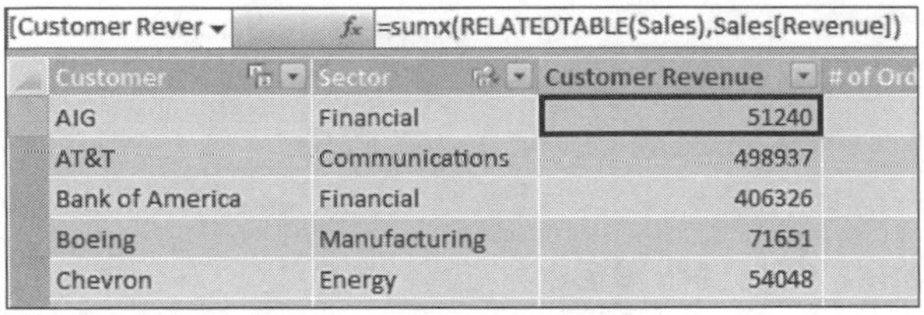

Figure 6.35
The RELATED function tells PowerPivot to follow defined relationships to get a value from a foreign table.

[Customer Rever ▾		*fx* =sumx(RELATEDTABLE(Sales),Sales[Revenue])	
Customer ⌂ ▾	Sector ⌂ ▾	Customer Revenue ▾	# of Ord
AIG	Financial	51240	
AT&T	Communications	498937	
Bank of America	Financial	406326	
Boeing	Manufacturing	71651	
Chevron	Energy	54048	

Filtering Multiple Values from a Related Table

The CALCULATETABLE function allows you to get multiple values from a related table, but to apply filters to that table.

CALCULATETABLE(<expression>, <filter1>, <filter2>,...) evaluates a table expression in a context modified by filters.

The <expression> generally will be a RELATEDTABLE function.

Filters will apply to columns in the related table.

Because this function returns a table, you have to include it in a wrapper function.

In Figure 6.36, this formula calculates the number of records in the Sales table that have a product of ABC:

    =CountRows(CalculateTable(RelatedTable(Sales),Sales[Product]="ABC"))

Figure 6.36
CalculateTable applies a filter to a foreign table.

=countrows(CALCULATETABLE(RELATEDTABLE(Sales),Sales[Product]="ABC"))			
or ⌂ ▾	Customer Revenue ▾	# of Orders ▾	ABC Records ▾
ncial	51240	4	1
munications	498937	40	14
ncial	406326	28	9

Table 6.6 shows the functions used to get data from an external table.

Table 6.6   DAX Functions to Get Data from External Table

Function	Description
AVERAGEX(<table>, <expression>)	Calculates the average (arithmetic mean) of a set of expressions evaluated over a table
CALCULATETABLE(<expression>, <filter1>, <filter2>,...)	Evaluates a table expression in a context modified by filters.
COUNTAX(<table>, <expression>)	The COUNTAX function counts nonblank results when evaluating the result of an expression over a table.
COUNTX(<table>, <expression>)	Counts the number of rows that contain a number or an expression that evaluates to a number, when evaluating an expression over a table.

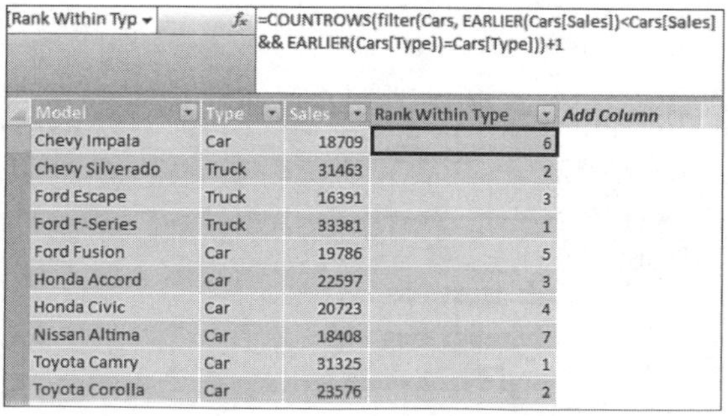

Function	Description
MAXX(<table>, <expression>)	Evaluates an expression for each row of a table and returns the largest numeric value.
MINX(<table>, < expression>)	Returns the smallest numeric value that results from evaluating an expression for each row of a table.
RELATED(<column>)	Returns a related value from another table
RELATEDTABLE(<table>)	Follows an existing relationship, in either direction, and returns a table that contains all matching rows from the specified table.
SUMX(<table>, <expression>)	Returns the sum of an expression evaluated for each row in a table.

Using the Recursive Functions

There are two last functions designed for column calculations: EARLIER and EARLIEST.

EARLIER(<column>, <number>) is useful for nested calculations where you want to use a certain value as an input and produce calculations based on that input. In PowerPivot, you can compare the value of the current row to all the rows in the table.

<column> is a column or an expression that evaluates to a column.

<number> is the evaluation level. Defaults to 1.

EARLIER is a recursive function. If you have a 10-row table, the column might have to evaluate 10x10 values or 100 values. If you have a 1,000-row table, the column might have to evaluate 1,000,000 values. If you have a 100,000,000-row data set, the calculation will never finish.

The formula in Figure 6.37 calculates a rank within type. The formula is as follows:

```
=CountRows(Filter(Cars, Earlier(Cars[Sales])<Cars[Sales] && Earlier(Cars[Type]
)=Cars[Type]))+1
```

Figure 6.37
There is no RANK function in DAX. The EARLIER function allows you to calculate a RANK.

6

The EARLIER function forces PowerPivot to loop through each value in the Sales column one at a time.

The first time through the loop, EARLIER(Sales) would be 18709 and EARLIER(Type) would be Car. The Filter then looks through the Cars table for records matching Type=Car and 18709<Sales. Five cars fall into this category. To prevent the top ranked car from returning a blank, add 1 to the result.

The second time through the loop, EARLIER(Sales) would be 31463 and EARLIER(Type) would be Truck.

This example uses only one level of recursion. If you use a number argument of 2, you could add a second loop.

The EARLIEST function would let you specify one additional level of recursion, something like EARLIER(,-1).

Table 6.7 shows the recursion functions.

Table 6.7   Recursion Functions in DAX

Function	Description
EARLIER(<column>, <number>)	Returns the current value of the specified column in an outer evaluation pass of the mentioned column
EARLIEST(<table_or_column>)	Returns the current value of the specified column in an outer evaluation pass of the mentioned column

Using Other Functions

Of the 64 other functions in the DAX language, 11 are existing functions such as SUM, COUNT, AVERAGE, and so on.

> **NOTE** These 11 existing functions are not covered here because they are not appropriate in the PowerPivot grid.

Think about using SUM in the PowerPivot grid. If you have 12 columns of monthly numbers, as shown in Figure 6.38, there is no way to use =SUM(B2:M2). You would have to do something crazy like =SUM([Jan],[Feb],[Mar]).... If you were actually going to do that, you would just use =[Jan]+[Feb]+[Mar], right?

Figure 6.38
The SUM function really
would not work here.
It will work as a DAX
measure, as discussed in
Chapter 10.

	Mar	A...	M...	Jun	Jul	Aug	Sep	Oct	Nov	Dec	Q1
59	1918	1572	1596	1692	1908	1864	1394	1505	1198	1259	4618
57	1508	1202	1150	1468	1904	1379	1225	1988	1751	1215	5310
74	1273	1276	1216	1035	1716	1160	1112	1888	1031	1430	3410
93	1249	1358	1926	1701	1837	1182	1103	1383	1509	1271	4685
60	1584	1030	1755	1516	1584	1664	1643	1981	1172	1878	4696

The other 64 functions will come up again in Chapters 10 and 11. This is really where the DAX language shines.

Next Steps

In the next chapter, you leave the PowerPivot window and start building pivot tables in the Excel window.Natural logarithms are very popular in science because anything with a constant rate of growth follows a curve described by natural logarithms. Radioactive isotopes, for example, decay along a curve described by natural logarithms.

While common logarithms with base 10 are called *logs*, natural logarithms with base e are written as *ln* (often pronounced *lon*). You calculate natural logarithms by using the LN function.

Building Pivot Tables

After completing the preceding chapter, your data has been loaded into PowerPivot and you have added some calculated columns. Now it is time to produce some pivot tables with all of that data.

Depending on your background, you've probably built either PivotCache pivot tables or online analytical processing (OLAP) pivot tables. The pivot tables that you create with PowerPivot are a hybrid of both types. Although they are technically OLAP pivot tables, the PowerPivot Field List is going to make you think that they are regular pivot cache pivot tables.

Elements of a Pivot Table

A pivot table is comprised of four zones:

- The Row Labels fields are fields that appear down the left side of the report. These are typical text fields from the data set. In Figure 7.1, both Customer and Product appear down the left side of the report. If you have just upgraded from Excel 2003, you would have known these as row fields.

- The Column Labels fields are fields that stretch across the top of the report. In other spreadsheets, this is known as the crosstab field. Again, these are fields that are typically text fields from the data set. Usually, fields with a short list of unique items will be used for column labels, while fields with longer lists of unique items will be used in the Row Label area. In Excel 2003, these were column fields.

- The Values area of the pivot table is everything that lies at the intersection of the row labels and column labels. This is almost always a numeric field, although you can put a text field here if you want to count the number of values in a field. In Excel 2003, these were data fields.

■ The Report Filter area of the pivot table appears above the columns area. It may have a number of fields that can be used to filter the report. In Excel 2003, these were page fields.

Arranging Field Headings to Build a Report

You build a report by arranging field headings in four drop zones in the bottom of the PivotTable Field List. The order of fields in the Row Labels drop zone defines the order that fields appear along the left side of the report.

Figure 7.1 shows the four areas of the pivot table and the drop zones in the field list.

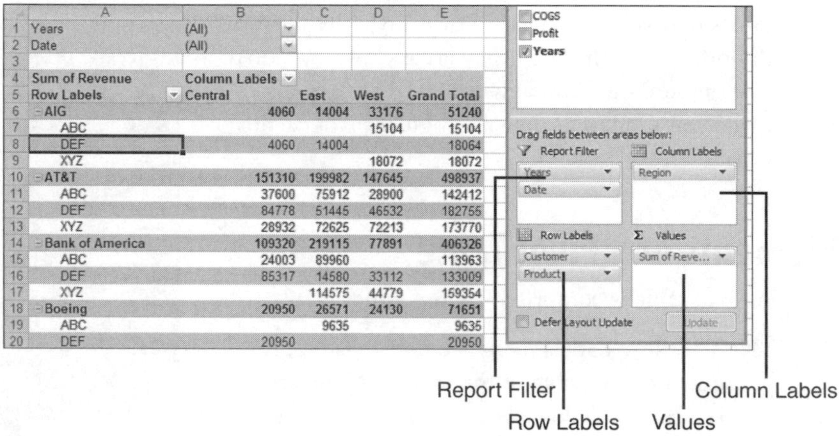

Figure 7.1
A traditional pivot table is comprised of four areas and is controlled through a PivotTable Field List.

OLAP pivot tables are used to summarize cube files. In the language of cube files, the text labels are called dimensions. The numeric fields that you can sum are called measures. The OLAP PivotTable Field List contains four drop zones just like the regular PivotTable Field List, but there are certain limitations, You can only drop measures in the Values drop zone. You can only drop dimensions in the Row Labels, Column Labels or Report Filter section of the pivot table.

Figure 7.2 shows the OLAP PivotTable Field List.

Using the PowerPivot Field List to Create Reports

When you create a report from PowerPivot data, the add-in presents you with a third type of Field List called the PowerPivot Field List (see Figure 7.3).

Figure 7.2
The OLAP field list has
some bizarre limitations.

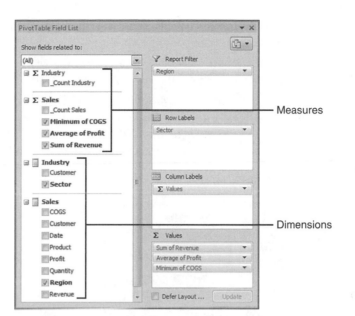

Measures

Dimensions

Figure 7.3
The PowerPivot Field List
is designed to look like
a regular field list and to
protect you from some
of the challenges of the
OLAP field list.

This field list has some interesting improvements.

- You are shielded from measures vs. dimensions. If you drag a field to the Values area, the add-in makes it into a measure behind the scenes.
- Two new drop zones offer Slicers Vertical and Slicers Horizontal. This is a good improvement over the Excel 2010 slicers.

7

- You are not able to rearrange the field list and the drop zones as you can in the other two field lists.

- The regular pivot tables offer a "secret" drop-down if you hover over a field in the field list. This drop-down is missing from the PowerPivot Field List.

- The regular pivot tables offer a visible drop-down on the field when it is in a drop zone. The PowerPivot Field List offers this drop-down with four extra menu items. Two of those menu items are Move to Slicers Vertical and Move to Slicers Horizontal. The other two items are of critical importance: Summarize By and Edit Measure (see Figure 7.4).

Figure 7.4
This is the only place where you can change the calculation of a field.

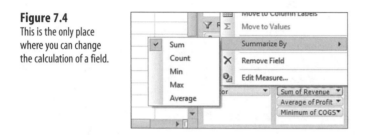

In addition to the PowerPivot Field List, you have access to the tools available on the two PivotTable tabs. These offer many settings for formatting the pivot table.

Building a Pivot Table

In this section, you will learn how to use the PowerPivot Field List to build a pivot table that links data from two different tables. If you want to work along, use the 7-DataBefore.xlsx file from the sample files.

A Look at the Underlying Data

The data set for this chapter consists of a sales table with fields of Region, Product, Date, Customer. Numeric fields include Quantity, Revenue, COGS, and Profit. Three calculated columns convert the date to Year, Month, and Weekday (see Figure 7.5).

Figure 7.5
The Sales table includes some calculated fields based on the date field.

Region	Product	Date	Custo...	Quan...	Revenue	COGS	Profit	Year	Mo...	Weekday
East	XYZ	1/1/2008	Ford	1000	28210	10220	17990	2008	Jan	Tue
Central	DEF	1/2/2008	Verizon	100	2257	984	1273	2008	Jan	Wed
East	DEF	1/4/2008	Merck	800	18552	7872	10680	2008	Jan	Fri
East	XYZ	1/4/2008	Texaco	400	9152	4088	5064	2008	Jan	Fri
East	DEF	1/7/2008	State Farm	1000	21730	9840	11890	2008	Jan	Mon
East	ABC	1/7/2008	General Mo...	400	8456	3388	5068	2008	Jan	Mon

The Customer field is linked to a second Industry table. This maps each customer in the database to a Sector field.

Between the two tables, the Customer field appears twice. If you select the Industry table, then use the Hide and Unhide icon on the Design tab in the PowerPivot window, you can choose to remove the second Customer field from the PowerPivot Field List.

> **TIP** This is optional, but it will lessen the clutter in the field list. If you are linking to SQL Server data with all sorts of key fields that are not appropriate in the pivot table, this dialog is a great place to hide them from the pivot table interface (see Figure 7.6).

Figure 7.6
Prevent columns from appearing in the pivot table field list.

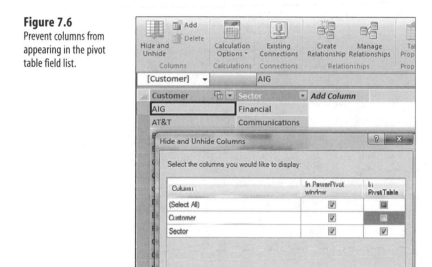

Defining the Pivot Table

There are two identical drop-down menus that you can use to insert a pivot table into the workbook. Figure 7.7 shows the drop-down in the Home tab of the PowerPivot Window. Above the PowerPivot window, you can see the identical drop-down in the PowerPivot tab of the Excel Ribbon. You can use either drop-down.

Depending on your selection in the drop-down, the PowerPivot add-in will create anywhere from 1 to 4 pivot tables in your workbook that share a common slicer cache.

For this first example, select the Single Pivot Table option at the top of the list.

You will be asked if the pivot table should be created on a new worksheet or placed on an existing worksheet, as shown in Figure 7.8. If you want to go to a specific location in an existing worksheet, the RefEdit control in the Create PivotTable dialog seems a bit nonstandard. You are forced to actually click the RefEdit before you can click a cell in the worksheet.

For now, select to put the PivotTable on a new worksheet.

Figure 7.7
Instead of using the PivotTable icon on the Insert tab, use one of these two drop-downs to set up a link to your PowerPivot data.

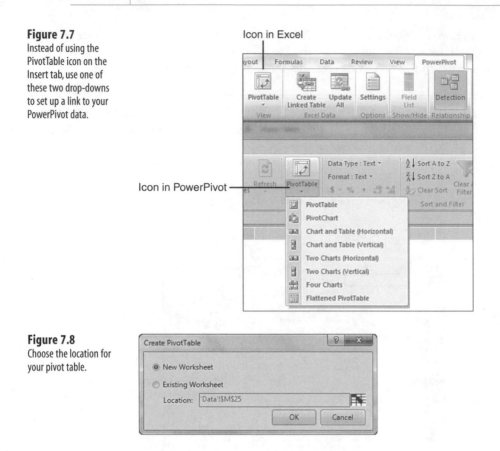

Icon in Excel

Icon in PowerPivot

Figure 7.8
Choose the location for your pivot table.

You will see the blank pivot table icon in cell B3 of a new worksheet. The icon shows you the system generated name for the pivot table (PivotTable6 in my case). The icon also instructs you to turn on the PivotTable Field List in order to work with the pivot table (see Figure 7.9). You can ignore that instruction.

The PowerPivot add-in has hidden the OLAP PivotTable Field List, but it is showing the PowerPivot Field List instead. Normally, this icon would tell you to start dragging fields in the PivotTable Field List. That is what you should do next.

Docked on the right side of the screen is the PowerPivot Field List. The fields in the home table are shown. The lookup tables appear in the list with a plus sign next to them (see Figure 7.10). If you click the + sign, you will see the fields available in the lookup table.

> **NOTE**
> Normally, you can leave the PowerPivot Field List docked on the right side of the screen. Because of the physical width of this book, my field list will be undocked and floating next to the pivot table. This will allow the figures to show the field list and the result in the pivot table. To undock the field list, drag the title bar into the worksheet. Redocking the Field List is difficult. You have to grab the left side of the title bar and drag the field list more than 60% off the right of the screen.

Figure 7.9
Ignore the instructions to
turn on the Field List.

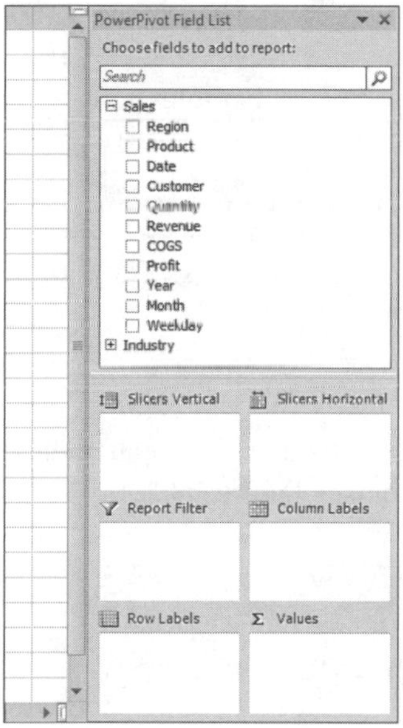

Figure 7.10
The PowerPivot Field List
shows up docked on the
right side of the screen.

By Default, Text Fields Go to Row Labels and Numeric Fields Go to Values

In the old days, you built a pivot table by dragging fields into the appropriate place on the report. In Excel 2007, that paradigm changed and you build a report by dragging fields into the appropriate drop zone in the Field List.

However, if you understand the default behavior of various fields, you can build the first pivot table without doing any dragging.

Each check box in the top of the field list can be selected. If you select a field that is text or a date, that field will automatically move to become the next field in the Row Labels area.

7

If you select a field which is numeric, that field will automatically move to the Values area with a calculation of Sum.

Let's say that you want to see a report showing revenue by Customer and Product. This requires three clicks:

1. Select the check box next to the Customer field. An alphabetic list of the unique customers appears in the left column of the pivot table (see Figure 7.11).

Figure 7.11
With one click, you have a unique list of customers.

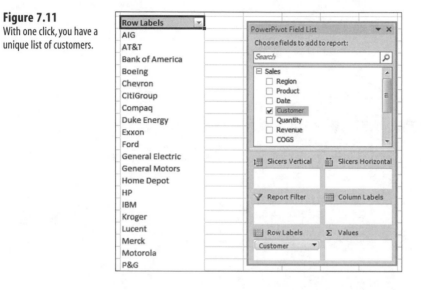

2. Select the check box next to the Revenue field. The revenue field will move to the Values area and will be shown as a Sum (see Figure 7.12).

Figure 7.12
If you select the Revenue check box, you will already have a nice summary report.

Row Labels	Sum of Revenue
AIG	51240
AT&T	498937
Bank of America	406326
Boeing	71651
Chevron	54048
CitiGroup	613514
Compaq	39250
Duke Energy	57516
Exxon	704359
Ford	628194
General Electric	568851
General Motors	750163
Home Depot	31369
HP	55251
IBM	427349
Kroger	46717
Lucent	62744
Merck	42316
Motorola	31021

3. Select the Product field check box. Product moves to be the last field in the Row Labels area. You will see a listing of the revenue associated with each product for each customer (see Figure 7.13).

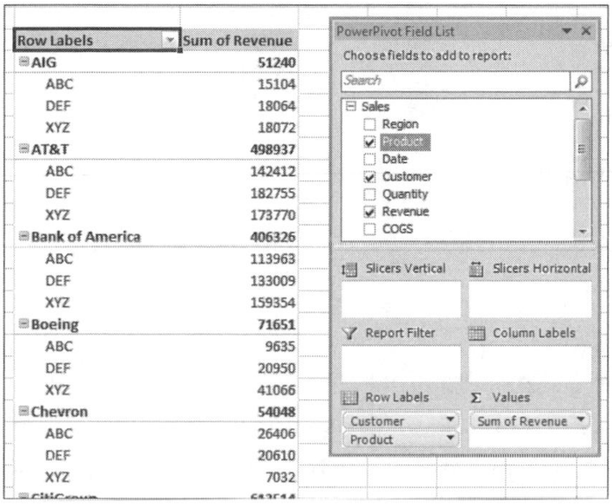

Figure 7.13
Choose another text field and you will see products within each customer.

Putting the Pivot in Pivot Table

Before MrExcel.com became my full-time gig, I spent 12 years in various financial analyst positions for a fast-growing company. In this case, "fast-growing" meant that I had more managers than most would expect. Thus, I speak with authority when I say that managers are some of the most annoying people in the world.

A manager might ask you for one analysis, but when you deliver that analysis, they decide that they really wanted something different. As my data analyst career included a few years before pivot tables were added to Excel, I became an expert in doing unnatural things with a spreadsheet, often performing several iterations before coming up with something that answered my manager-du-jour's questions. I was one of the first Lotus Improv customers and later embraced pivot tables when they were introduced in Excel. When a manager asks you to adjust the report, it is often just a couple of clicks in the pivot table.

The report in Figure 7.13 is customer focused. For each customer, you see a list of products. If you report was destined for the product managers in the marketing department, you would want a report that is more product focused. It will take just one drag of the mouse to produce a vastly different report.

Take the Product field in the Row Labels drop zone and drag it so that it is above the Customer field in the same drop zone. You have now produced a report that focuses on products. For each product, you see a list of customers who purchased that product (see Figure 7.14).

7

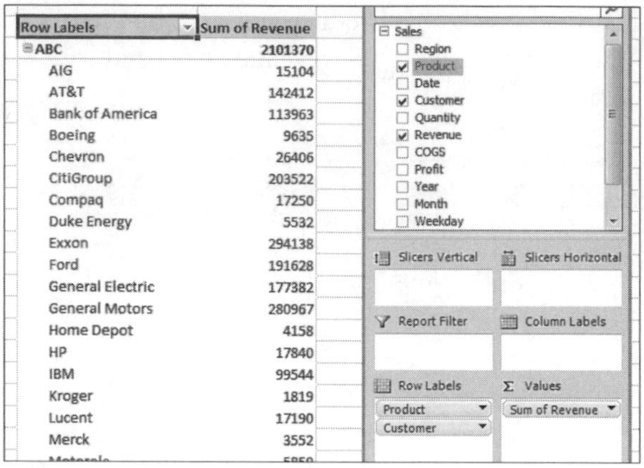

Figure 7.14
Rearrange the order of fields in the Row Labels drop zone and you have a product-focused different report.

Dragging from the Field List to a Drop Zone

This next example shows why these reports have "pivot" in their name. Take the Product field and drag it to the Column Labels drop zone. You now have a crosstab report, with customers down the left side and products across the top (see Figure 7.15).

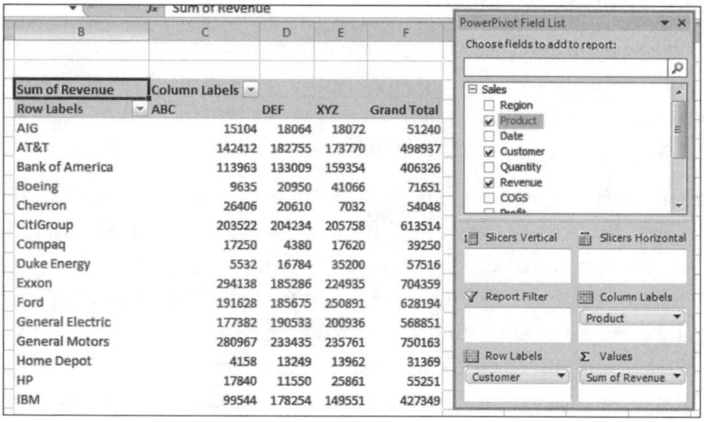

Figure 7.15
Drag the Product field to the Column Labels drop zone to produce a cross-tab report.

Scroll through the top half of the Field List and click the plus sign next to the Industry table so you can see the fields there.

If you just select the check box for the Sector field, what will happen? Because it is a text field, it will become the last item in the Row Labels drop zone. Because each customer belongs to only one sector, this would be an incredibly ugly and un-useful report.

Because you can predict that the default action would not be appropriate, you can drag the field from the Field List and drop it in the Row Label drop zone but above the Customer field. This produces a useful report that breaks the customer lists into various industry sectors (see Figure 7.16).

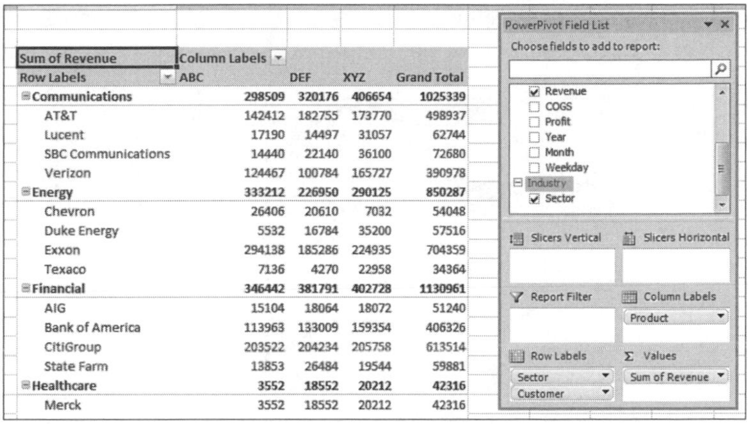

Figure 7.16
Drag the Sector field above the Customer field in the Row Labels area.

Sum of Revenue	Column Labels			
Row Labels	ABC	DEF	XYZ	Grand Total
⊟ Communications	298509	320176	406654	1025339
AT&T	142412	182755	173770	498937
Lucent	17190	14497	31057	62744
SBC Communications	14440	22140	36100	72680
Verizon	124467	100784	165727	390978
⊟ Energy	333212	226950	290125	850287
Chevron	26406	20610	7032	54048
Duke Energy	5532	16784	35200	57516
Exxon	294138	185286	224935	704359
Texaco	7136	4270	22958	34364
⊟ Financial	346442	381791	402728	1130961
AIG	15104	18064	18072	51240
Bank of America	113963	133009	159354	406326
CitiGroup	203522	204234	205758	613514
State Farm	13853	26484	19544	59881
⊟ Healthcare	3552	18552	20212	42316
Merck	3552	18552	20212	42316

Using the Report Filter

The report in Figure 7.16 contains a lot of good information. The VP of Sales is going to love that report and show it to one of his regional managers. You already know what is going to happen; the regional manager is going to ask whether he can get that report, but just for his region.

This is easy to do using the Report Filter field.

Drag the Region field to the Report Filter drop zone. Not much happens in your pivot table. None of the numbers change. Everything moves down two rows and a new pair of cells appear in B3:C3. B3 will say region and C3 contains a drop-down that says All (see Figure 7.17).

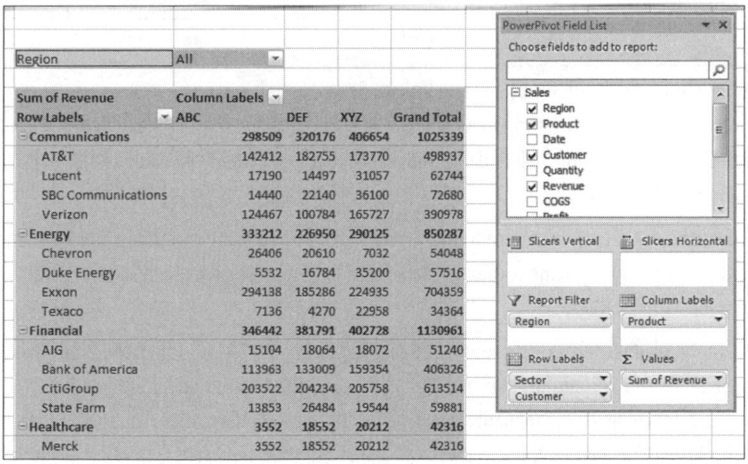

Figure 7.17
Initially, not much happens with a field in the report filter.

Region	All			
Sum of Revenue	Column Labels			
Row Labels	ABC	DEF	XYZ	Grand Total
⊟ Communications	298509	320176	406654	1025339
AT&T	142412	182755	173770	498937
Lucent	17190	14497	31057	62744
SBC Communications	14440	22140	36100	72680
Verizon	124467	100784	165727	390978
⊟ Energy	333212	226950	290125	850287
Chevron	26406	20610	7032	54048
Duke Energy	5532	16784	35200	57516
Exxon	294138	185286	224935	704359
Texaco	7136	4270	22958	34364
⊟ Financial	346442	381791	402728	1130961
AIG	15104	18064	18072	51240
Bank of America	113963	133009	159354	406326
CitiGroup	203522	204234	205758	613514
State Farm	13853	26484	19544	59881
⊟ Healthcare	3552	18552	20212	42316
Merck	3552	18552	20212	42316

7

Open the drop-down in cell C3. Click the + next to All and you will see a list of Regions, as shown in Figure 7.18.

Figure 7.18
Expand the All item in the Report Filter to access a list of regions.

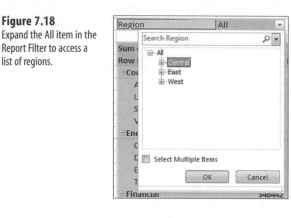

Select Central from the report filter and the numbers are recalculated to show you only sales to the Central region (see Figure 7.19). You can repeat this process to produce reports for the East and West regions.

Figure 7.19
Repurpose the report for the Central region manager.

Region	Central ⟙			
Sum of Revenue	**Column Labels** ▾			
Row Labels ▾	**ABC**	**DEF**	**XYZ**	**Grand Total**
⊟ **Communications**		78559	151679	51127	281365
AT&T		37600	84778	28932	151310
Lucent				7167	7167
SBC Communications			22140		22140
Verizon		40959	44761	15028	100748
⊟ **Energy**		136774	99521	121000	357295
Chevron			20610		20610

Troubleshooting Excel: Blanks in the Values Area

As your pivot table starts getting more granular, you will usually run into the problem shown in Figure 7.19. Take a look at cell C9 in that figure. This cell is blank. That means that there were no records in the Central region where Lucent bought any of Product ABC.

Because this cell is in a range of cells that should contain revenue information, a blank cell is not at all appropriate. Excel help teaches you that a numeric column should contain zeros instead of blanks. Yet, in pivot tables, Microsoft litters the pivot table with blank cells.

The empty cell does tell you one very subtle thing and one very blatant thing. The subtle thing; a blank cell indicates that there were no records for that combination. A zero cell indicates that Lucent bought some ABC but then later returned it for credit. If your manager is looking for this type of information, you should run a report of returns and not use this format. The blatant thing that you can learn from the empty cells is that the fine people who develop Excel don't actually have to produce accounting reports for a living.

In just about every pivot table that you create, you will find yourself repeating these steps:

1. Select one cell inside the pivot table so that the PivotTable Tools tabs are available.

2. On the Options tab, look in the lower-left corner for an icon and a drop-down labeled Options. Click the Options icon, not the drop-down. Excel displays the PivotTable Options dialog that is now broken into six tabs.

3. On the first tab, Layout and Format, there is a setting For Empty Cell Show. Type a *0* in this box, as shown in Figure 7.20.

4. Click OK. The empty cells are now replaced with zeros.

Figure 7.20
Change blank cells to zeros.

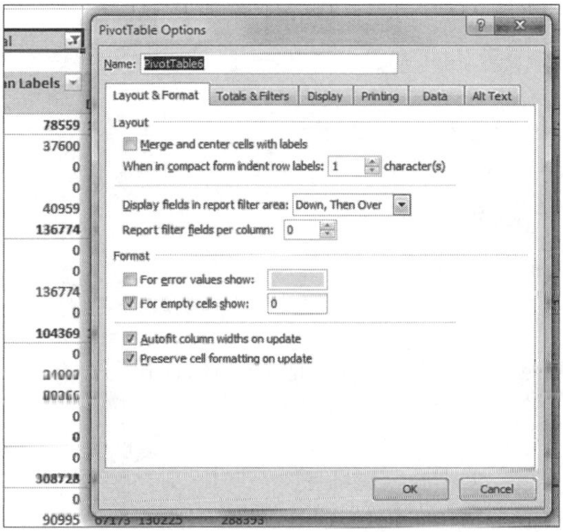

Report Filters Versus Slicers

In Excel 2007, the Report Filter drop-down offered a cool new trick. You could select the Select Multiple Items check box and choose more than one item from the filter. In Figure 7.21, the report will show all sales for the Central and East regions.

Although this addition to Excel 2007 was conceptually cool, the words (multiple items) in cell C3 was nearly useless. Once the drop-down was closed and the report was printed, no one could actually tell which multiple items were selected!

In Figure 7.22, the Region field is moved from the Report Filter field to the Slicers Horizontal drop zone. It is now very clear which regions are included and which regions are not included.

7

Figure 7.21
Starting in Excel 2007, you could choose to enable multiple items in the report filter.

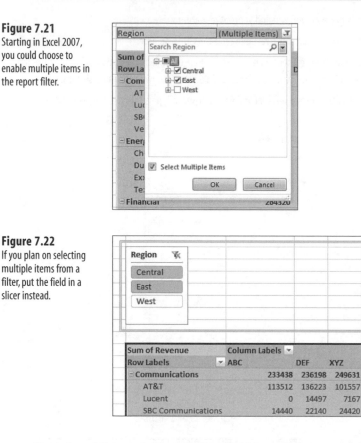

Figure 7.22
If you plan on selecting multiple items from a filter, put the field in a slicer instead.

Does the addition of slicers in Excel 2010 mean that report filters are obsolete? Probably not. If you are in the habit of selecting only one item from the filter, then having the item in the report filter gives you the same functionality as the slicer without taking up eight rows at the top of your report.

The super-cool Show Report Filter Pages located in the Options drop-down also allows you to make hundreds of pivot tables in a single click, so until Microsoft extends that feature to slicers, the report filter still has a great reason to exist. Sadly, OLAP pivot tables, and hence PowerPivot pivot tables, do not support this functionality.

Explanation of Column B

I realize that much of the world will be upgrading directly from Excel 2003 to Excel 2010. Since you missed Excel 2007, you are probably wondering what the heck is going on in column B of the pivot table.

Column B of the pivot table is showing both Sector and Customer information in the same column.

All good data analysts everywhere are screaming inside their head when they see reports like this. Seriously, the only thing worse than having blanks instead of zeros in the revenue portion of the report are the people who try to save space by jamming two completely different fields in one column.

> **NOTE**
> If you don't understand why this is bad, you should realize that many people create pivot tables as an intermediate step on the way to some other analysis. These pivot tables live for about 15 seconds, and then are converted to values using Copy, Paste Values. We can then use those tight summary tables as lookup tables. Putting Sector and Customer in the same column makes it impossible to sort the data after it has been converted to values.

Here is the theory behind this seemingly insane decision. There are two tiny icons in the Active Field group of the PivotTable Tools Options tab. One is a green plus sign, and the other is a red minus sign. If you would select a sector in the pivot table and click the red minus sign, Excel will collapse the report and show you only the sectors, as shown in Figure 7.23. Each sector has a tiny plus sign, so you can expand one sector, or click the green plus icon in the ribbon to expand all the sectors.

Figure 7.23
Collapse the Sector column and the customers are hidden.

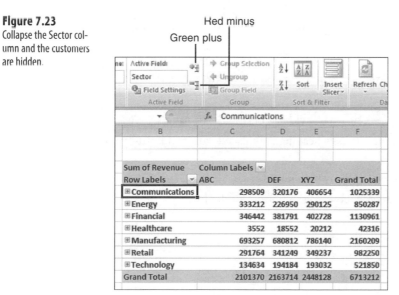

> **NOTE**
> While I am sitting here trying to defend a feature that I clearly hate, I can hear the skeptics out there screaming that you already could have achieved this affect by clearing and then selecting the Customer field in the pivot table field list. And, you are also probably screaming that using the check box in the Field List works no matter what cell is active in the pivot table, so that method is actually far superior. I hear you. I agree with you. I am just trying to rationalize why Microsoft would do this to us and why they would go so far as to make it be the default view of all new pivot tables.

7

Returning the Column Labels to Sanity

What you are seeing in column B is a new layout called Compact Layout. In legacy versions of Excel, you could choose between Tabular Layout and Outline layout. Excel 2007 introduced the Compact Layout and made it be the default.

You can, of course, change back to Tabular layout. Follow these steps:

1. Select one cell inside the pivot table so that the PivotTable Tools tabs are available.

2. Select the Design tab.

3. The third icon from the left is the Report Layout drop-down. Open this drop-down and select Show in Tabular Form (see Figure 7.24).

Figure 7.24
Return to Tabular layout.

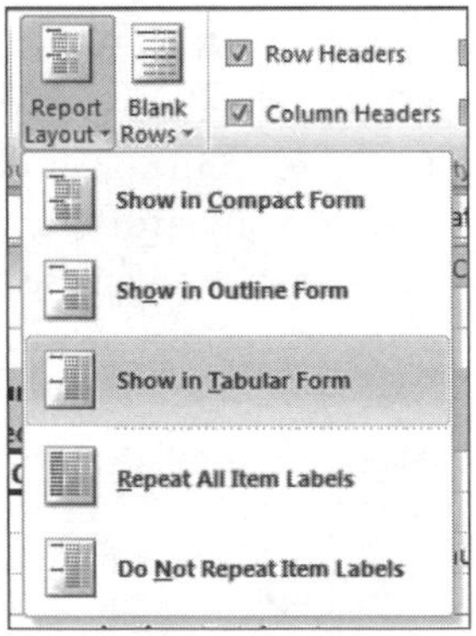

As shown in Figure 7.25, several things happen:

- The bizarre Column Labels heading is replaced with real headings of Sector and Customer.

- Customers move to their own column C.

- Totals for each Sector move to the bottom of the list.

Figure 7.25
In tabular view, everything goes back to the familiar Excel 2003 layout.

Sum of Revenue		Product			
Sector	Customer	ABC	DEF	XYZ	Grand Total
⊟ Communications	AT&T	142412	182755	173770	498937
	Lucent	17190	14497	31057	62744
	SBC Communications	14440	22140	36100	72680
	Verizon	124467	100784	165727	390978
Communications Total		298509	320176	406654	1025339
⊟ Energy	Chevron	26406	20610	7032	54048
	Duke Energy	5532	16784	35200	57516
	Exxon	294138	185286	224935	704359

New Trick with Column Labels

If you are feeling like Figure 7.25 is like going back to the good old days, then you are already feeling good about complaining about the blank cells in B6 through B8.

NOTE My first book, in 2002, was *Guerilla Data Analysis Using Microsoft Excel*. I spent a good bit of time in that book complaining about those blank cells in column B and provided several really obscure tricks for filling those blank cells in. I constantly hounded the Excel project managers at Microsoft for a way to fill those cells.

Did you see the bottom two options in Figure 7.24? Yes, new in Excel 2010, you can now select Repeat All Item Labels and the blank cells in the row labels area are filled in with the values from above. This is a great addition to Excel 2010 (see Figure 7.26).

Figure 7.26
Filling in the blank cells in column B is now easy in Excel 2010.

Sum of Revenue	
Sector	Customer
⊟Communications	AT&T
Communications	Lucent
Communications	SBC Communications
Communications	Verizon
Communications Total	
⊟Energy	Chevron
Energy	Duke Energy
Energy	Exxon
Energy	Texaco
Energy Total	

Is There a Way to Permanently Sack the Compact Layout?

One of the common questions that I get in my Power Excel seminars is how people can change the default behavior of pivot tables. People want to know if they can permanently kill the compact layout, or at least not make it the default layout.

Previously, the answers were not really practical:

- You could store your workbooks as Excel 2003 files. This forces Excel into compatibility mode. In this mode, you automatically get the tabular layout. You even get the ability to drag and drop fields right into the report (see Figure 7.27). This won't work with PowerPivot, however, because all that functionality is grayed out when you are in compatibility mode.
- You could create your pivot tables using VBA. Pivot tables created using VBA will, for compatibility reasons, be created in tabular layout.

So, in the regular Excel interface, you are pretty much stuck with the compact layout as the default.

However, PowerPivot offers a choice in the PivotTable drop-down (refer back to Figure 7.7) called a flattened pivot table. When you select this, you are given a single pivot table with tabular view chosen.

Figure 7.28 shows a flattened pivot table. After selecting the check boxes for the six fields, you end up with a pivot table with three columns fields and three numeric fields.

Figure 7.27
The old pivot table interface is lurking in Excel 2010.

Figure 7.28
Flattened pivot tables select tabular layout by default.

Sector	Region	Product	Sum of Revenue	Sum of Profit	Sum of COGS
Communic	Central	ABC	78559	42985	35574
Communic	Central	DEF	151679	83783	67896
Communic	Central	XYZ	51127	28643	22484
Communic	Central Total		281365	155411	125954
Communic	East	ABC	154879	87966	66913
Communic	East	DEF	84519	46143	38376
Communic	East	XYZ	198504	107546	90958
Communic	East Total		437902	241655	196247
Communic	West	ABC	65071	36273	28798
Communic	West	DEF	83978	45602	38376
Communic	West	XYZ	157023	88549	68474
Communic	West Total		306072	170424	135648
Communications Total			1025339	567490	457849
Energy	Central	ABC	136774	76637	60137

   To see a demo of a flattened pivot table, search for MrExcel PowerPivot 7 at YouTube.

Two Important Rules with Pivot Tables

If you are new to pivot tables, there are two critical things you need to understand that are discussed in the following sections.

Pivot Tables Do Not Recalculate When Underlying Data Changes

Although most of the Excel workbook will recalculate in response to changing a cell, pivot tables are not in the recalculation chain.

Normally, if you change any data, you have to select the pivot table, go to the PivotTable Tools Options tab, and choose either the large Refresh icon or open the drop-down attached to the Refresh icon, and then select Refresh All. (See Figure 7.29).

With PowerPivot, pivot tables there are extra steps involved in the refresh:

- If your pivot table is created from linked tables, you can use the Update All icon on the PowerPivot tab.
- If your pivot table is created from data that was copied and pasted to PowerPivot, you need to redo the copy and then paste replace in the PowerPivot window.
- If your data is from any other external source, you need to go to the PowerPivot window and use the Refresh drop-down there to refresh.

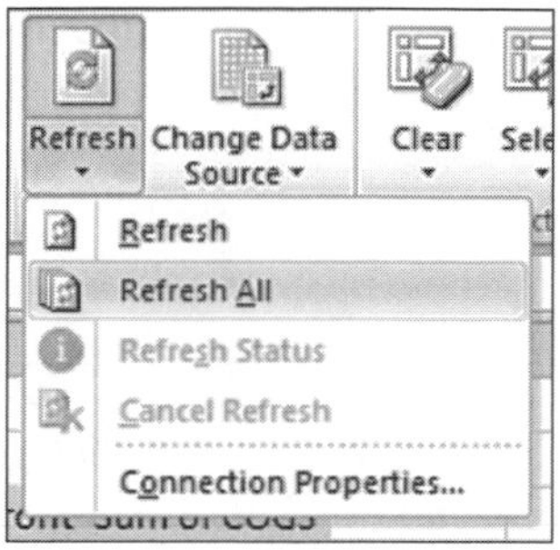

Figure 7.29
Normally, you have to refresh pivot tables.

CAUTION ────────────────────────────

Refreshing the data in PowerPivot does not refresh the pivot table! You have to go back to the pivot table and use the Refresh icon in the ribbon or the Refresh button that appears on the PowerPivot Field List.

You Cannot Move or Change Part of a Pivot Table

Suppose you decide to insert some blank rows or columns in the middle of your pivot table. Perhaps you would like to add some space or a new Excel calculation there.

The Insert commands are grayed out when you are inside the pivot table. Of course, it is easy to get around this by moving outside of the pivot table. However, if you try to insert columns that would interfere with the pivot table, you receive the ubiquitous dialog box shown in Figure 7.30.

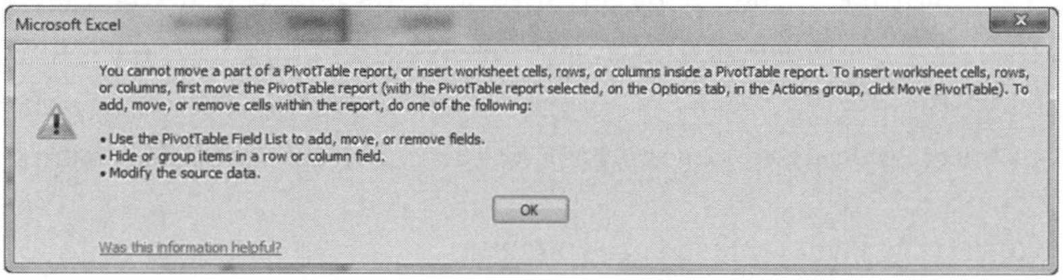

Figure 7.30
Try to insert a column that interferes with the pivot table and you get this dialog.

I know this dialog is too wide to actually be readable in the book. Let's take a quick look at the suggestions in the dialog:

You cannot move a part of a PivotTable report, or insert worksheet cells, rows, or columns inside a PivotTable report. To insert worksheet cells, rows, or columns, first move the PivotTable Report (with the PivotTable report selected, on the Options Tab, in the Actions group, click Move Pivot Table). To add, move, or remove cells within the report, do one of the following:

- ■ Use the PivotTable Field List to add, move, or remove fields.
- ■ Hide or group items in a row or column field.
- ■ Modify the source data.

Was this Information Helpful?

That is sort of funny. Did you actually read it? I haven't read the dialog in years. So, Microsoft is offering four different suggestions, and none of the suggestions are what people actually do at this point.

Convert the Pivot Table to Values

The most popular course of action at this point is to convert the pivot table to values. You've gotten what you needed out of the pivot table. It has the answers that you need and now you need to calculate something else that might not be possible using the regular pivot table tools.

To convert a pivot table to values, you must select the entire pivot table. This includes the Report Filter fields if you have any, but not the slicers. Select that entire range. Use the Copy icon on the Home tab to copy the pivot table. Open the Paste drop-down and select Paste Values.

> **TIP**   The Paste drop-down has been replaced with a series of incomprehensible symbols in Excel 2010. You want the first icon in the third row, the one with 123 on the icon.

The downside to converting the pivot table to values is that you can no longer refresh the pivot table. If your underlying data changes, you need to re-create the pivot table, but that is easy enough to do.

In Excel 2010, using PowerPivot Pivot Tables, there is one new option, discussed next.

Convert the Pivot Table to Cube Formulas

If you have an Excel 2010 pivot table based on either PowerPivot or OLAP, you can follow these steps:

1. Choose one cell inside the pivot table.
2. Go to the Options tab.
3. On the right side, open the OLAP Tools drop-down.
4. Select Convert to Formulas.

Don't panic when your pivot table temporarily changes to a series of cells that say "Getting Data." In a few seconds, all the values will come back.

Check out the formula bar in Figure 7.31. The range of your pivot table has been converted to a series of CUBEMEMBER and CUBEVALUE formulas that continue to retrieve data from the data in PowerPivot. You are, however, free to insert new rows and columns as desired.

Figure 7.31
Instead of converting your pivot table to values, convert it to live cube formulas.

				f_x =CUBEVALUE("PowerPivot Data",$D4,E$3)			
B	C	D	E	F	G	H
Sector	Region	Product	Sum of Revenue		Sum of Profit	Sum of COGS
Communi(	Central	ABC	78559		42985	35574
Communi(	Central	DEF	151679		83783	67896
Communi(	Central	XYZ	51127		28643	22484
Communi(	Central Total		281365		155411	125954
Communi(	East	ABC	154879		87966	66913
Communi(	East	DEF	84519		46143	38376
Communi(	East	XYZ	198504		107546	90958
Communi(	East Total		437902		241655	196247

Working with Pivot Charts

Pivot charts have a similar field list to pivot tables. You will notice these changes:

- The Row Labels drop zone is now called Axis Fields (Categories).
- The Column Labels drop zone is now called Legend Fields (Series).

Figure 7.32 shows the default pivot chart when you choose one text field and one numeric field. The text field moves to the Axis Fields drop zone, and the items in that field stretch out along the horizontal axis of the chart.

Figure 7.32
The fields in the former Row Labels area become categories along the horizontal axis.

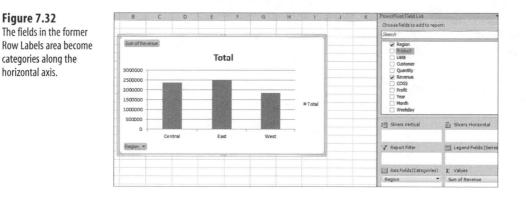

If you add a text field to the Legend Fields drop zone, each item along that dimension becomes a new series in the chart. The series appear in the legend along the right side of the chart.

Figure 7.33 shows the default chart with one field in the Axis Field and one field in the Legend field.

7

NOTE I changed the chart to a pattern fill so the differences would show up in this book.

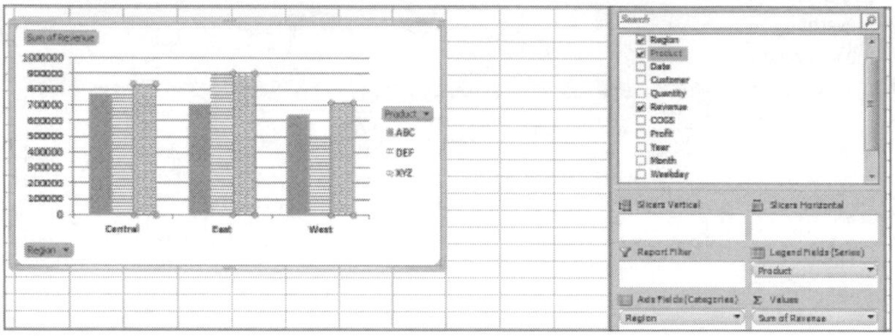

Figure 7.33
Add a field to the Legends drop zone, and those items become series in the chart.

Ninety-nine percent of people using Excel have a clustered column chart set at their default chart, so the columns for ABC appear next to the columns for DEF. If you would prefer to have a stacked column chart, select the Design tab, then the Change Chart Type icon, and choose a new chart type. Figure 7.34 shows the pivot chart with a stacked column chart.

Figure 7.34
Use the Change Chart Type icon on the Design tab to change to a new chart type.

TIP If you want all of your future pivot charts to default to stacked column charts, pause for a moment in the Change Chart Type dialog. After choosing the Stacked Column Chart, click the Set as Default Chart button in the lower left corner of the dialog.

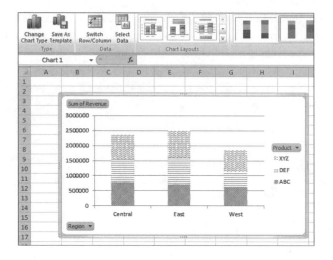

Is it possible to have multiple fields in the Axis Fields drop zone? It gets convoluted, but if your series have few enough items, there might be situations where the chart is readable. In Figure 7.35, both Region and Product are in the Axis field and Sector is in the Legend field.

Figure 7.35
It is possible to add two fields to the Axis zone.

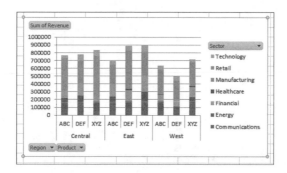

> **CAUTION**
>
> You should not try to add two fields to either the Legend Fields or the Values drop zones. The pivot chart will end up concatenating every combination of the fields in the legend and values zones into a confusingly high stack of column segments.

You can add fields to the Report Filter area. In Figure 7.36, the Year button in the top left corner of the chart shows that Year is a Report Filter field and even that a year has been selected. However, you will have no idea which year is selected, so you really should consider using Slicers instead of the Report Filter field.

Figure 7.36
Report filters on the pivot chart don't show what has been selected, so go with slicers instead.

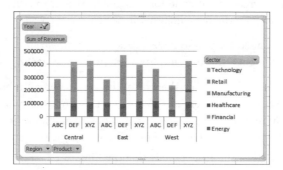

> **NOTE**
>
> Most of the buttons on the pivot chart are useless. The buttons were actually removed in Excel 2007, but found their way back in Excel 2010.

7

If you go to the PivotChart Tools Analyze tab, open the Field Buttons drop-down, you can choose Hide All (see Figure 7.37).

Figure 7.37
Remove the buttons
from the pivot chart for a
cleaner appearance.

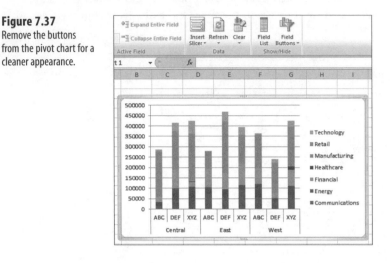

> **NOTE**
> The one cool thing with pivot charts in PowerPivot is that most pivot charts have a pivot table attached to them. These pivot charts also have a pivot table attached, but the pivot table is hidden on a back worksheet.

Behind the Scenes with PowerPivot Field List and Add-In

Normally, OLAP pivot tables are reading a special type of database called a *cube*. You need a database administrator to create a cube file for you and to define the dimensions and measures that are available to you, the data analyst when creating the pivot table.

PowerPivot removes the need for you to have a database administrator. The PowerPivot add-in actually creates the cube file and simplifies the process of dealing with the cube file:

- When you choose one of the pivot tables from the PowerPivot Ribbon, the PowerPivot add-in creates and cube file and defines a connection string to the OLAP cube. The add-in asks you where to insert the pivot table. They then choose to hide the OLAP PivotTable Field List and show you the PowerPivot Field List.

- When you drag a field to the Row Labels, Report Filter, or Column Labels drop zones in the PowerPivot Field List, the PowerPivot add-in hops into action, making the exact same changes to the now hidden OLAP PivotTable Field List.

- When you drag a field to the Values drop zone, the add-in has to define a new measure in the OLAP cube. If you change the Summarize By from Sum to Average, it is the add-in that redefines the measure. This all happens instantly, so to you, it feels like you are dragging fields to a field list.

■ When you drag a field to one of the Slicers drop zones, the add-in defines a new slicer, analyzes the number of items in the slicer, the length of the slicer, and how many other slicers exist. The add-in decides on a number of columns to use in the slicer, as well as the height and width of the slicer.

■ When you interact with most items on the PivotTable Tools tabs, you are actually interacting with the pivot table and the add-in stays out of the way. If you try to use the tab to add your own slicer, you will see the ugly default slicer appear momentarily, and then the add-in steps in and resizes and repositions the slicer.

■ Watch your screen closely when you close Excel. As the PowerPivot add-in unloads itself, it has to bring the OLAP PivotTable Field List back. You might see it flash onto the screen just before your workbook closes.

Next Steps

The following chapter shows you some of the cool tricks that are native to all pivot tables.

7

Cool Tricks Native to Pivot Tables

Excel gurus use a lot of cool tricks with Excel pivot tables. Some of my absolute favorite pivot table tricks don't work with online analytical processing (OLAP) pivot tables, so they don't apply to PowerPivot reports. However, there are still plenty of cool tips and tricks in this chapter and the next. If you add just a few of these to your tool chest, you will be running circles around 98% of the people using Excel.

Applying Sorting Rules to Pivot Tables

By default, most fields that you add to the Row Labels or Column Labels fields will appear in your pivot table in alphabetic sequence. This makes perfect sense, but it often is not the optimal way to show the data.

Presenting Customers with the Largest Sales at the Top

Figure 8.1 shows a pivot table with Customer and Revenue. The customers appear in alphabetic sequence. You would like to see the largest customers at the top.

Figure 8.1
By default, customers appear in alphabetic sequence.

Row Labels	Sum of Revenue
AIG	51240
AT&T	498937
Bank of America	406326
Boeing	71651
Chevron	54048
CitiGroup	613514
Compaq	39250

To sort the customers, follow these steps:

1. Open the Row Labels drop-down in cell B3.
2. Select More Sort Options (see Figure 8.2). Excel displays the Sort (Customer) dialog where it says that the current sort is Data Source Order.

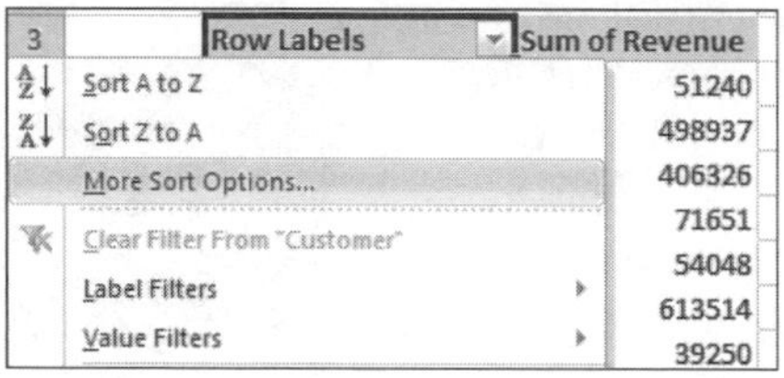

Figure 8.2
Select More Sort Options.

3	Row Labels ▼	Sum of Revenue
A↓	Sort A to Z	51240
Z↓	Sort Z to A	498937
	More Sort Options...	406326
		71651
▼K	Clear Filter From "Customer"	54048
	Label Filters ▶	613514
	Value Filters ▶	39250

3. Change the sort order to Descending (Z to A).
4. Open the drop-down and select Sum of Revenue, as shown in Figure 8.3.

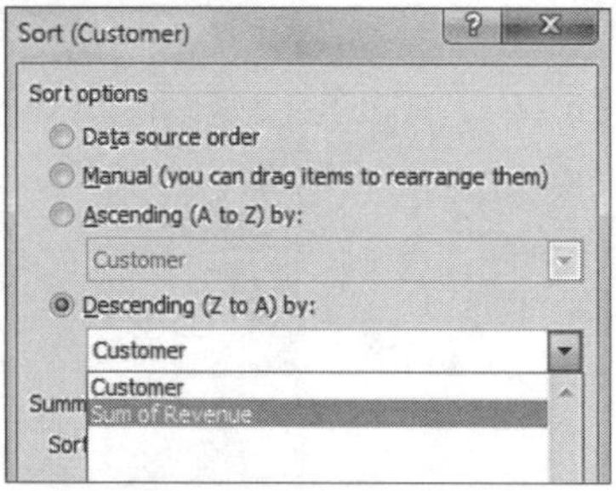

Figure 8.3
Select to sort by descending revenue.

Sort (Customer)   ? X

Sort options
 ○ Data source order
 ○ Manual (you can drag items to rearrange them)
 ○ Ascending (A to Z) by:
   [Customer   ▼]
 ● Descending (Z to A) by:
   [Customer   ▼]
   Customer
 Summ Sum of Revenue
 Sor

5. Click OK.

As shown in Figure 8.4, the customers will be sorted into high-to-low sequence.

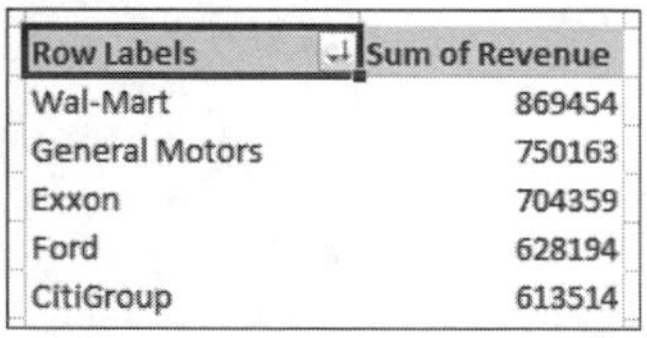

Figure 8.4
You've established a rule to govern how the pivot table should be sorted.

Row Labels ▾	Sum of Revenue
Wal-Mart	869454
General Motors	750163
Exxon	704359
Ford	628194
CitiGroup	613514

Why go to all of this trouble when you could simply click the ZA button in the Data tab?

The advantage of setting up a sorting rule is that the pivot table will continue to sort into the correct sequence as you add more pivot fields to the report. In Figure 8.5, after adding Product as the outer row field, you still see the customers sorted high-to-low within Customer. Exxon is the largest customer for Product ABC.

Figure 8.5
A sorting rule continues to sort correctly even after you add fields to the pivot table.

Row Labels	Sum of Revenue
⊟ ABC	2101370
Exxon	294138
General Motors	280967
Wal-Mart	276847
CitiGroup	203522

Sorting Month Names into the Proper Sequence

> **NOTE**
>
> Just a quick moment of silence while we recall how easy it is to group daily dates up to months that sort correctly in regular pivot tables.
>
> <moment of silence>
>
> Thanks for respecting that moment of silence.

Back in Chapter 3, "Why Wouldn't I Build Every Future Pivot Table in PowerPivot?" I complained about how easy it *used* to be to sort month names, so I am not going to complain about it further. Let's talk about how to work around it.

If you have a date field in your original data set, you will want to add two calculated columns, as described in Chapter 6, "Using Data Sheet View":

- **Year:** =Year([Date])
- **Month:** =Format([Date],"MMM")

> **NOTE**
>
> I realize that some other people are counseling you on their blogs to calculate the months with =MONTH([Date]), but I think that having months appear as 1, 2, 3, ..., 12 in a management report looks like it was designed by some IT guy who knows more about SQL Server than Excel.

> **CAUTION**
>
> If you remove any field from the pivot table, even temporarily, the sort settings are discarded. This is unlike the behavior with regular pivot tables that will remember the sort order as you remove a field and later re-add it. Thus, don't remove the month field after applying a sort.

If you regularly create Excel pivot tables, you know the next fact, but you probably never stopped to consider it: regular Excel pivot tables will automatically sort the pivot tables in custom list sequence.

Because every copy of Excel ships with four custom lists, month names like Jan, Feb, Mar will always appear in the correct sequence in regular Excel pivot tables.

OLAP pivot tables do not automatically sort into custom list sequence. Thus, you end up with a pivot table like the one in Figure 8.6; the months are arranged alphabetically, with Apr, Aug, Dec, Feb, and so on.

Figure 8.6
OLAP pivot tables don't sort by custom lists be default.

Sum of Revenue	Column Labels		
Row Labels	2008	2009	Grand Total
Apr	276640	292003	568643
Aug	311745	286891	598636
Dec	288115	340184	628299
Feb	312065	236565	548630
Jan	278622	274936	553558
Jul	385767	295851	681618
Jun	165569	241883	407452
Mar	269796	216561	486357
May	332076	287443	619519
Nov	231872	301880	533752
Oct	304246	308986	613232
Sep	256440	217076	473516
Grand Total	3412953	3300259	6713212

> **NOTE**
> These next eight clicks really hack me off. I've taken the fact that pivot table sort into custom list sequence for granted for the past 15 years. Imagine if someone came along with a great new invention but all of a sudden you had to start clicking the mouse eight times every time that you wanted to take a breath. Frustrating.

To sort the months into correct sequence, follow these steps:

1. Open the Row Labels drop-down in cell B4.
2. Click More Sort Options.
3. In the Sort dialog, select Ascending by Month.
4. In the bottom-left corner of the dialog, select More Options (see Figure 8.7).

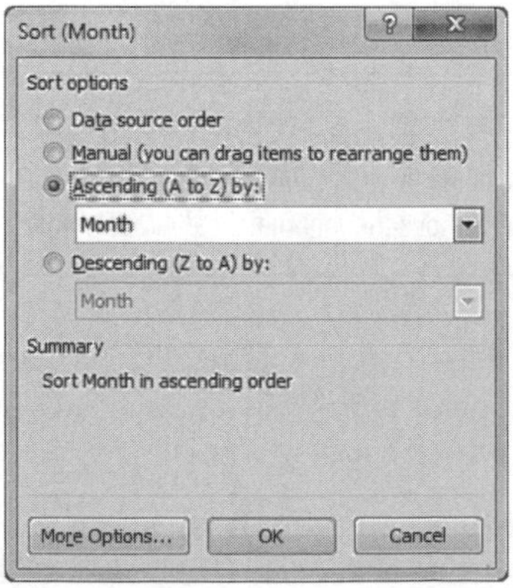

Figure 8.7
Select More Options in the sort dialog.

5. The More Sort Options dialog starts with the Sort Automatically check box selected, as shown in Figure 8.8. You must clear that check box to enable the drop-down in step 6.

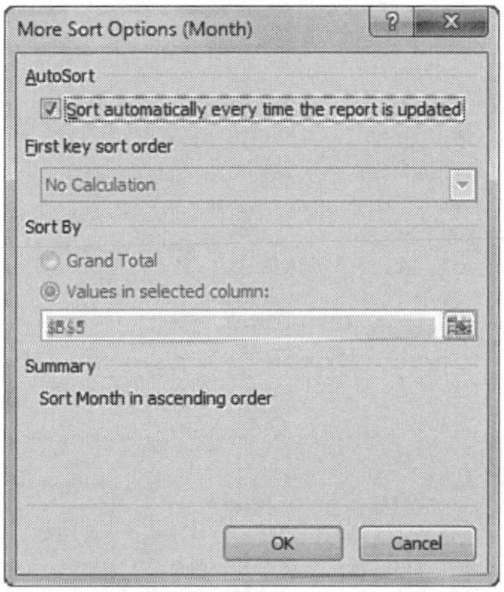

Figure 8.8
Clear the Sort
Automatically check box.

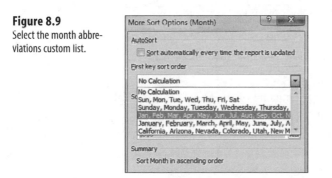

6. Open the First Key Sort order dialog and select Jan, Feb, Mar (see Figure 8.9).

Figure 8.9
Select the month abbre-
viations custom list.

7. Click OK to close More Sort Options.

8. Click OK to close Sort Options.

Your pivot table is now sorted into the proper sequence, as shown in Figure 8.10

Adding a Custom List to Control Sort Order

In Figure 8.11, the regions appear in alphabetic order of Central, East, West. What if the company standard is to show the East region first, then Central, then West?

Figure 8.10
After eight clicks, the pivot table is sorted in the proper sequence.

Sum of Revenue	Column Labels		
Row Labels	2008	2009	Grand Total
Jan	278622	274936	553558
Feb	312065	236565	548630
Mar	269796	216561	486357
Apr	276640	292003	568643
May	332076	287443	619519
Jun	165569	241883	407452
Jul	385767	295851	681618
Aug	311745	286891	598636
Sep	256440	217076	473516
Oct	304246	308986	613232
Nov	231872	301880	533752
Dec	288115	340184	628299
Grand Total	3412953	3300259	6713212

Figure 8.11
There is no good way to sort Central into the middle. (Unless they would rename Central as Middle!)

Sum of Revenue	Column Labels				
Row Labels	2008	2009	Grand Total		East
Central	1248944	1126935	2375879		Central
East	1353025	1145378	2498403		West
West	810984	1027946	1838930		
Grand Total	3412953	3300259	6713212		

It is easy to set up a custom list. Follow these steps:

1. Type the correct sequence for the regions in a blank section of the worksheet.
2. Select the list in your worksheet as shown in cells G4:G6 of Figure 8.11.
3. Select File, Options.
4. Click Advanced in the left navigation panel of the Excel Options dialog.
5. Scroll to the bottom of the dialog where you will see the Edit Custom Lists button (see Figure 8.12). Click this button.

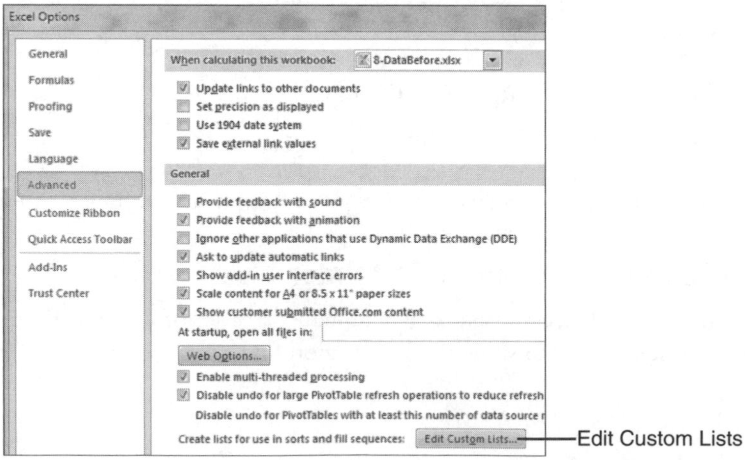

Figure 8.12
This button was moved from the first screen of Excel options to this obscure location.

Edit Custom Lists

If you actually selected the list range back in step 2, the address of that range will be in the Import text box.

6. Click the Import button. You should see your custom list at the bottom of the Custom Lists list box (see Figure 8.13).

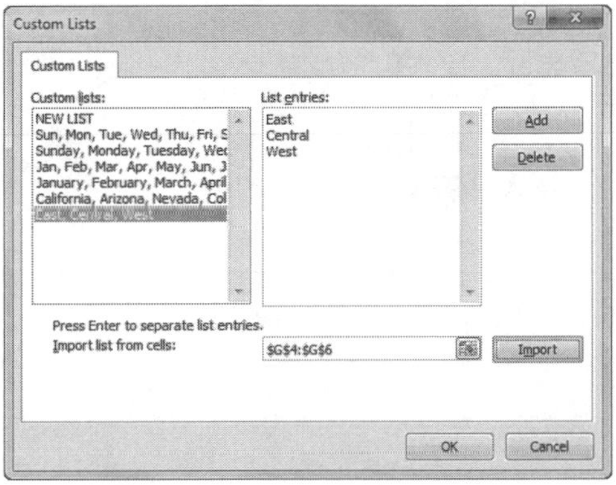

Figure 8.13
Import your regions as a custom list.

7. Click OK to close the Custom Lists dialog and OK to close Excel Options.

Your computer will now understand that regions should be sorted into East, Central, West sequence.

Your regular pivot tables will automatically sort into the custom list sequence.

For your PowerPivot pivot tables, you need to go through the eight-click process described in the "Sorting Month Names into the Proper Sequence" section, earlier in this chapter. When you get to the step previously shown in Figure 8.9, your new custom list will be offered in the drop-down, as shown in Figure 8.14.

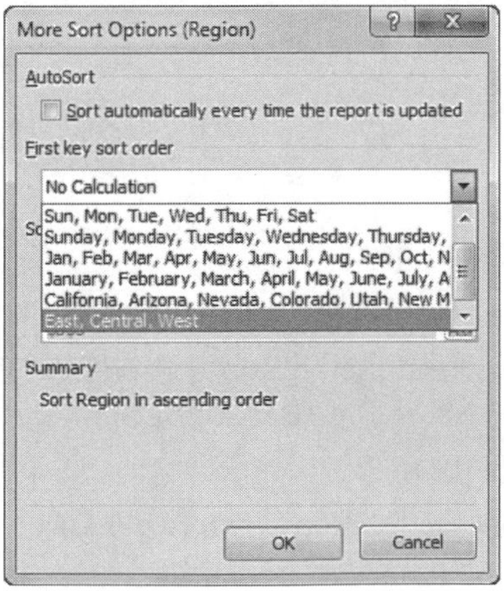

Figure 8.14
Your custom list is now in the More Sort Options.

The good news is that you only have to set up the custom list once per computer. The bad news is that you have to go through the eight-step sort process every time you add the region field to a pivot table. Figure 8.15 shows a pivot table with regions in the correct sequence.

Figure 8.15
This pivot table is sorted into the correct sequence because of the custom list.

Sum of Revenue	Column Labels			
Row Labels	2008	2009	Grand Total	
East	1353025	1145378	2498403	
Central	1248944	1126935	2375879	
West	810984	1027946	1838930	
Grand Total	3412953	3300259	6713212	

NOTE Custom lists can be as short as 2 items or as long as 96 items.

Showing the Top Five Customers

Excel offers a Top10 Filter that enables you to show the top or bottom customers, region, products in a pivot table.

In Figure 8.16, you have a report with Customers in the Row Labels, the Revenue and Profit in the Values area.

Figure 8.16
A report shows all customers, arranged by revenue.

Row Labels	Sum of Revenue	Sum of Profit
Wal-Mart	869454	487284
General Motors	750163	415549
Exxon	704359	392978
Ford	628194	353216
CitiGroup	613514	338409
General Electric	568851	316329
AT&T	498937	278959
IBM	427349	238018
Bank of America	406326	227741

To use the Top 10 filter, follow these steps:

1. Open the Row Labels drop-down in cell B3.
2. Open the Value Filters flyout menu.
3. At the bottom of the Value Filters menu, select Top 10 (see Figure 8.17). The Top 10 Filter dialog starts out offering to Show Top 10 Items by Sum of Revenue.
4. Use the spin button to change the 10 to 5.
5. Choose the appropriate field from the By drop-down (see Figure 8.18).
6. Click OK.

Figure 8.17
Select to Filter by Top 10 Values.

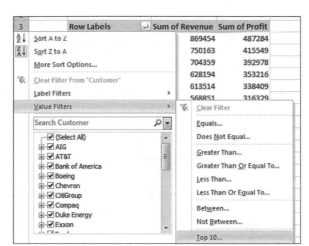

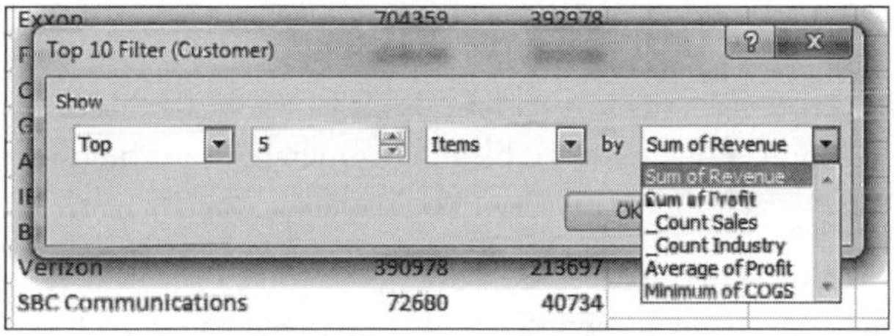

Figure 8.18
Customize the filters.

The result shown in Figure 8.19 is a report of only the top five customers based on revenue.

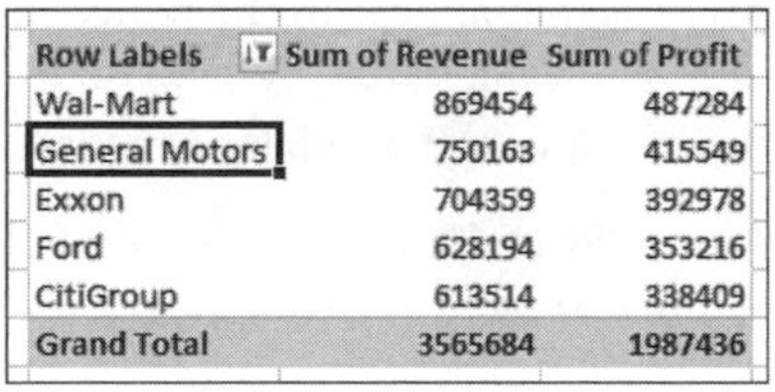

Figure 8.19
A Top 5 Customers report.

Row Labels	Sum of Revenue	Sum of Profit
Wal-Mart	869454	487284
General Motors	750163	415549
Exxon	704359	392978
Ford	628194	353216
CitiGroup	613514	338409
Grand Total	3565684	1987436

 To see a demo of creating a top 10 report, search for MrExcel PowerPivot 8 at YouTube.

Notes About the Top 10 Filter

Here are some interesting notes about the Top 10 Filter.

■ The third drop-down in the dialog offers Items, Percent, or Sum. Percent can be used to show the customers who make up the top 80% of revenue. The Sum option, which was added to Excel 2007, opens the possibility of allowing you to specify that you want to see how many customers it takes until you see $5 million of revenue. Obviously, when you use Sum, you should no longer use the spin button up arrow to increase from 10 to 5,000,000. You can click in the second box and type a value.

■ The fourth drop-down always offers the values fields that are currently in the pivot table. It always offers a count of each table that is in the data set. (This was added internally by the PowerPivot add-in and should be ignored.) It also offers any value field that has existed in this pivot table since it was created. Average of Profit and Minimum of COGS is something that I had temporarily put in the pivot table way back near the beginning of Chapter 7, "Building Pivot Tables." If you want to create a report showing the five customers who have the five smallest orders, but you want to show the total revenue from those customers, you could temporarily add Minimum of Revenue to the pivot table, take it out, then come back to the Top 10 Filter and filter by Minimum of Revenue.

Changing the Calculation in the Pivot Table

Regular pivot tables offer 11 main calculations and 15 subcalculations. OLAP pivot tables offer 1 main calculation. PowerPivot tables fall somewhere in the middle. They offer 5 built-in ways to show each field plus the 15 subcalculations.

Chapter 10, "Using DAX for Aggregate Functions," discusses how pivot tables offer a complete DAX language that will allow infinite different ways to calculate a measure.

For now, you'll see the main 5 calculations plus the 15 subcalculations.

Easiest Way to Force a Count

If you want to count the number of records that appear in the table, you can force the pivot table to count by dragging a text field to the Values area. When you drop a text field in the Values area, PowerPivot shows you the count of the number of records.

In Figure 8.20, the Customer field is in the Row Labels area. By dragging the Region field to the Values area, you will see the number of records that appear for each customer.

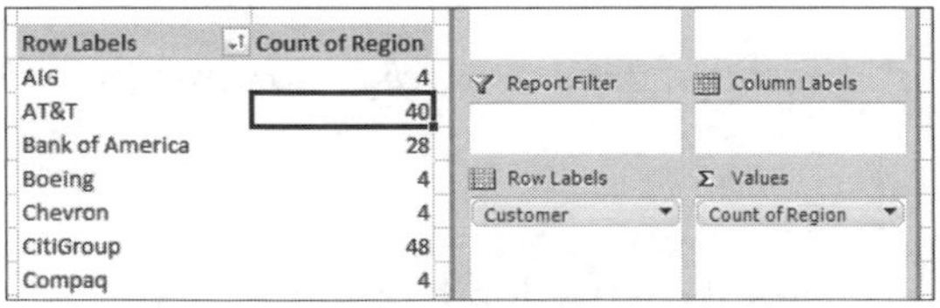

Figure 8.20
Drag a text field to the Values area to force a count.

> **NOTE** This is a count of the total number of records for each customer. It is not a count of the distinct number of regions for each customer. You can now do a Count Distinct using DAX.

→ **See** Chapter 10 for details about working with DAX.

Using Sum, Count, Min, Max, or Average

Figure 8.21 looks like a crazy report. Put Customers in the Row Labels area. Select the Revenue check box to move Revenue to the Values area. Then, drag the Revenue field to the Values area four more times. You now have five identical columns in your report, all showing Sum of Revenue.

Figure 8.21
Drag the Revenue field to the report five times.

This trick is completely new in PowerPivot.

In the Values drop zone, open the drop-down attached to Sum of Revenue 1. Select Edit Measure (see Figure 8.22).

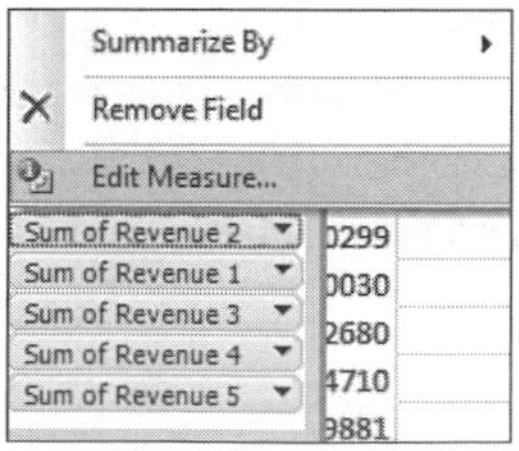

Figure 8.22
Changing the calculation now happens from this drop-down in the Values drop zone.

In the Measure Settings dialog, change the calculation from Sum to Count.

Also, change the custom name of Count of Revenue 1 to just **Count of Revenue** (see Figure 8.23).

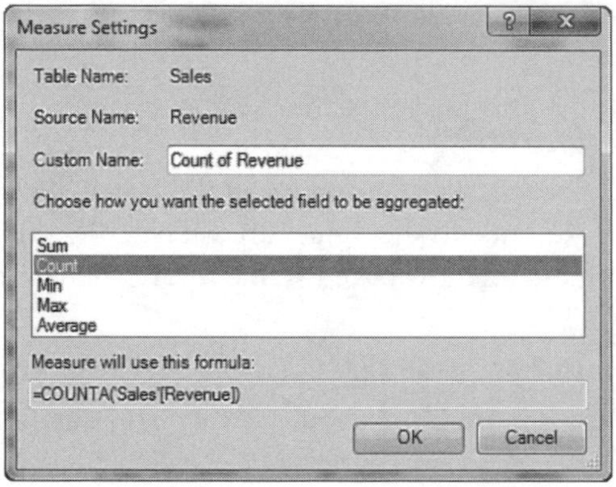

Figure 8.23
Select to count.

Measure Settings	? X

Table Name: Sales

Source Name: Revenue

Custom Name: Count of Revenue

Choose how you want the selected field to be aggregated:

Sum
Count
Min
Max
Average

Measure will use this formula:

=COUNTA('Sales'[Revenue])

OK   Cancel

Repeat these steps for the other four Revenue fields, each time changing the calculation and the custom name.

> **TIP**
> Nothing says that custom names have to use awkward names like Count of Revenue. Feel free to use descriptive names such as Smallest Order, Largest Order, Average Order, and so on.

Figure 8.24 shows a report with five different calculations of revenue.

Figure 8.24
You can create five different calculations of revenue.

Row Labels	Smallest Order	Largest Order	Average Order	Total Revenue	# Orders
AIG	4060	18072	12810	51240	4
AT&T	1740	25310	12473.425	498937	40
Bank of America	6156	25350	14511.64286	406326	28
Boeing	9635	24130	17912.75	71651	4
Chevron	7032	20610	13512	54048	4
CitiGroup	1817	25010	12781.54167	613514	48
Compaq	4380	17250	9812.5	39250	4

> **NOTE**
> Behind the scenes, the PowerPivot add-in has to do a lot of work when you change the measure using this dialog. The add-in goes back to the cube file and defines a new DAX measure. After the measure has been added, it renames the measure. So, you might briefly see your measure appear with the wrong name, then with the right name. It is another one of those processes that is supposed to look easy, but the add-in is handling a lot of the behind-the-scenes work for you.

Changing the Show Values as Drop-Down

Microsoft put a lot of work into the Show Values drop-down for Excel 2010. First, they actually created the drop-down, as most of these settings were buried three levels deep where no one would ever find them. If you had used them before, you will be pleased to know that they added several new items to the drop-down, including the much-requested Percent of Parent Item.

Follow these steps to try out the various calculation options:

1. Build a report with Sector in the Row Labels Area and Revenue in the Values area.

2. Drag Revenue to the Values Area a second time.

3. Put the cell pointer on the second column of revenue values.

4. Go to the PivotTable Tools Option tab.

5. Open the Show Values As drop-down.

6. Select % of Grand Total (see Figure 8.25).

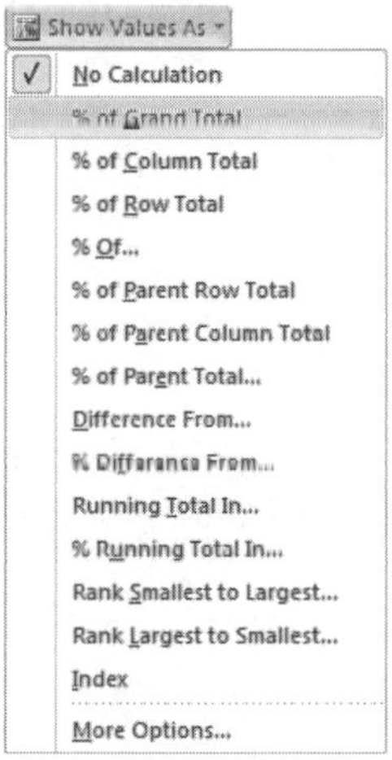

Figure 8.25
Excel 2010 offers 15 different ways to show values in the pivot table.

The result in Figure 8.26 is the correct calculation with a horrible title. The Communications sector is 15.27% of the total.

Figure 8.26
The second revenue column is showing percentage of total.

Row Labels	Sum of Revenue	Sum of Revenue 1
Communications	1025339	15.27%
Energy	850287	12.67%
Financial	1130961	16.85%
Healthcare	42316	0.63%
Manufacturing	2160209	32.18%
Retail	982250	14.63%
Technology	521850	7.77%
Grand Total	6713212	100.00%

To rename the field, go to cell M3 and type a new heading, something like % of Total. There might be a bug in the PowerPivot Field List where the field continues to show Sum of Revenue 1. However, if you display the OLAP Field List, you will see that the field name actually did change in the OLAP Field List.

> **TIP** To see the OLAP Field List, click the Field List icon on the right side of the Options tab.

Base Fields and Base Items

As you try out the 15 different calculations in the Show Values As drop-down, you will find that some (like % of Grand Total) simply calculate without any further information.

Other calculations require you to specify a Base Field.

For example, you ask Excel to Rank Largest to Smallest, you will have to confirm that you want to calculate that rank based on the rank within the sectors (see Figure 8.27).

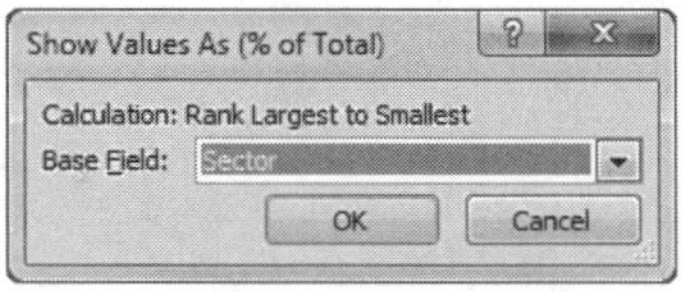

Figure 8.27
When you ask for a Rank, you have to specify a base field.

Change the heading, and you will have a column that shows the rank of each sector. Manufacturing is the largest sector, and Healthcare is smallest (see Figure 8.28).

Figure 8.28
Rank is a new pivot table calculation in Excel 2010.

Row Labels	Sum of Revenue	Rank
Communications	1025339	3
Energy	850287	5
Financial	1130961	2
Healthcare	42316	7
Manufacturing	2160209	1
Retail	982250	4
Technology	521850	6
Grand Total	6713212	

Other calculations in the drop-down require both a base field and a base item. For example, you can express sales as a percentage of the Manufacturing number. In Figure 8.29, you have to specify both a base field and the base item.

One of the new calculations in Excel 2010 pivot tables is the % of Parent item. Figure 8.30 shows a report with two row fields and a % of Parent.

Figure 8.29
Sometimes you have to specify both a base field and base item.

3	Row Labels	Sum of Revenue	% of Manufacturing
4	Communications	1025339	47.46%
5	Energy	850287	39.36%
6	Financial	1130961	52.35%
7	Healthcare	42316	1.96%
8	Manufacturing	2160209	100.00%
9	Retail	982250	45.47%
10	Technology	521850	24.16%
11	**Grand Total**	6713212	

Show Values As (% of Manufacturing)

Calculation: % Of

Base Field: Sector

Base Item: Manufacturing

OK Cancel

Figure 8.30
% of Parent item is a new calculation in Excel 2010.

3	Row Labels	Sum of Revenue	% of Parent
4	Central	2375879	35.39%
5	ABC	766469	32.26%
6	DEF	776996	32.70%
7	XYZ	832414	35.04%
8	East	2498403	37.22%
9	ABC	703255	28.15%
10	DEF	891799	35.69%
11	XYZ	903349	36.16%
12	West	1838930	27.39%
13	ABC	631646	34.35%
14	DEF	494919	26.91%
15	XYZ	712365	38.74%
16	**Grand Total**	6713212	100.00%

In this report, the 32.26% in M5 means that the ABC sales of 766,469 are 32.26% of the 2,375,879 in cell L4.

The percentage shown for the Central region total in row 4 is the percentage of the grand total in row 16.

One last calculation frequently proves useful. In the % Of drop-down, you can choose to have the base item be the next or previous item in the list.

In Figure 8.31, the MTD column is calculated using Running Total in the Date field. The % of Yesterday column uses the % Of calculation with a base field of date and a base item of (previous). The $11,240 sold on January 2 is 109.71% of the $10,245 sold on January 1.

The 100% shown for January 1 is not actually correct. A little white font applied to that cell is probably the best way to solve that problem.

8

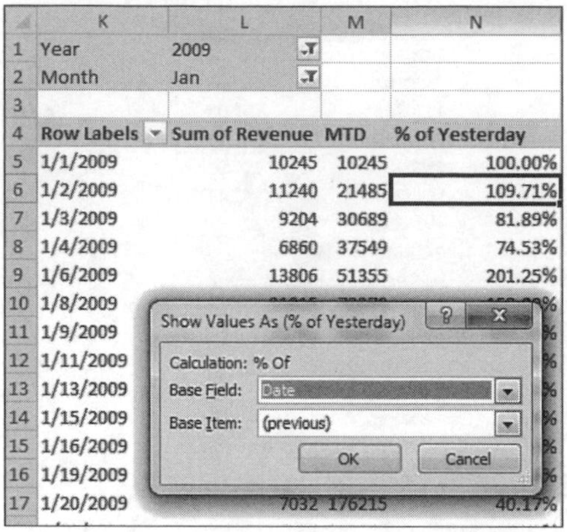

Figure 8.31
Running Total and %
of Previous calculations
make this report.

Pivot Table Formatting

The formats in Excel 2010 pivot tables are a massive improvement over the 14 autoformats offered in Excel 2003 pivot tables.

This section covers the various formatting options in pivot tables.

Change the Numeric Formatting for a Field

The numbers in the pivot tables are generally showing up with the revenue in general format. These numbers are really big enough that they should be showing up with commas at the very least.

Here is how to change the number format in a pivot table:

1. Add the field to the Value area of the pivot table.

2. Select a cell in the pivot table that contains either the heading for the field or one of the values for the field.

3. With that cell selected, select the Field Settings icon in the PivotTable Tools Option tab. The Show Values Tab of the Value Field Settings dialog is where you used to have to change the calculations for a field. This dialog is almost obsolete in Excel 2010, except that it is the entry point for numeric formatting.

4. In the lower-left corner of the Value Field Settings dialog, click Number Format (see Figure 8.32).

You then have the Number tab of the Format Cells dialog, as shown in Figure 8.33

Figure 8.34 shows the results. Only the Revenue field is formatted. You have to repeat steps 2 through 4 for the other Values fields.

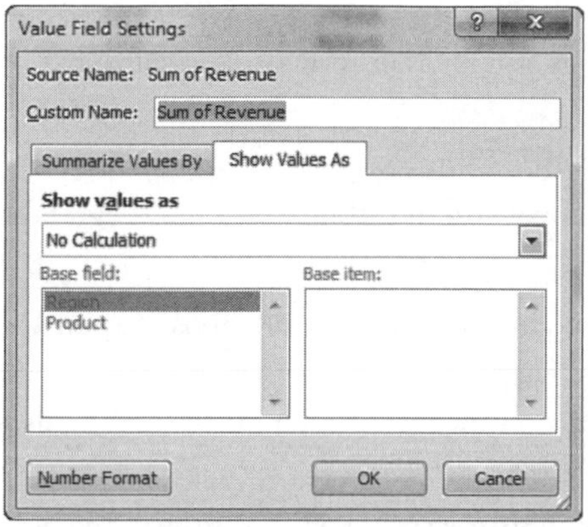

Figure 8.32
I think this whole dialog still exists so that there is a place for the Number Format button to live.

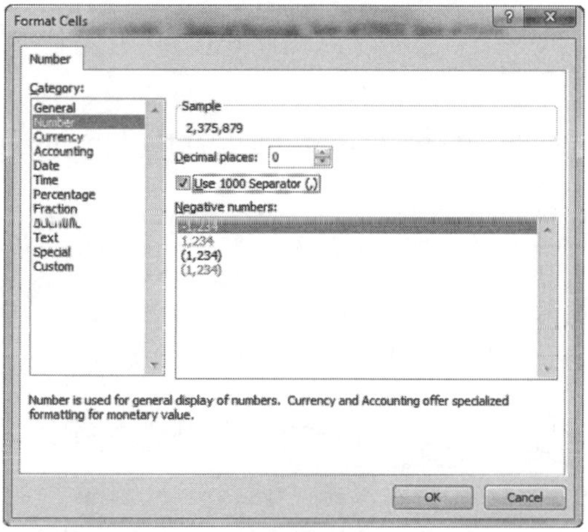

Figure 8.33
Choose a format.

Figure 8.34
You have to format each field one at a time.

Row Labels ▼	Sum of Revenue	Sum of COGS	Sum of Profit
⊟ Central	2,375,879	1053874	1322005
ABC	766,469	340494	425975
DEF	776,996	343416	433580
XYZ	832,414	369964	462450
⊟ East	2,498,403	1110419	1387984
ABC	703,255	309155	394100
DEF	891,799	396552	495247
XYZ	903,349	404712	498637
⊟ West	1,838,930	814101	1024829
ABC	631,646	282051	349595
DEF	494,919	222384	272535
XYZ	712,365	309666	402699
Grand Total	6,713,212	2978394	3734818

You are certainly wondering why you don't just select C4:E16 and format the whole pivot table at once time? The traditional answer is that going through the other steps will permanently change the format of the field. Even if you add new fields to the pivot table, the new revenue values will continue to be formatted correctly.

Permanent is a relative term with PowerPivot pivot tables. If you remove a field from the pivot table, both the sort settings and number formatting are lost.

Formatting Changes on the Design Tab

There are many formatting changes spread throughout the Design tab, including the following:

- If you open the Blank Rows drop-down, you can choose to add a blank row after each outer row field subtotal.

- If you open the Subtotals drop-down, you can move the subtotals in the compact layout to the bottom of each group.

- If you open the Grand Totals drop-down, you can turn off the grand total row and/or grand total column.

- Using the four check boxes in the PivotTable Style Options, you can turn on or off banded rows / banded columns.

Figure 8.35 shows a pivot table with blank rows, totals at the bottom, and banded rows.

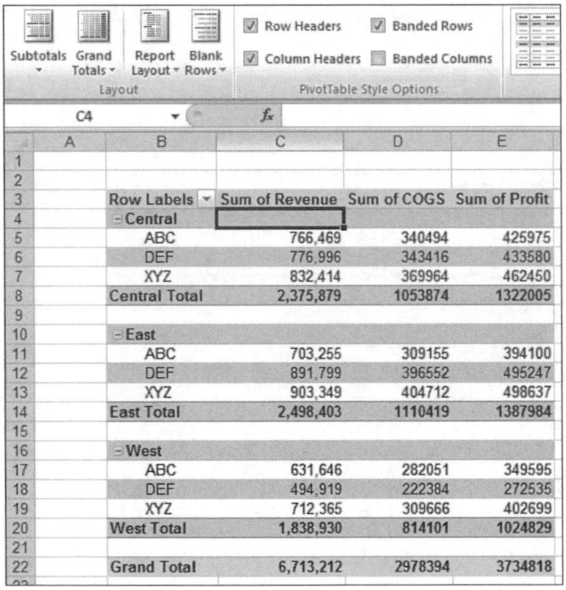

Figure 8.35
This pivot table shows off some of the various formatting options.

The big formatting changes are in the huge PivotTable Styles gallery (see Figure 8.36). These style thumbnails change in response to which of the four check boxes are selected in the PivotTable Style Options.

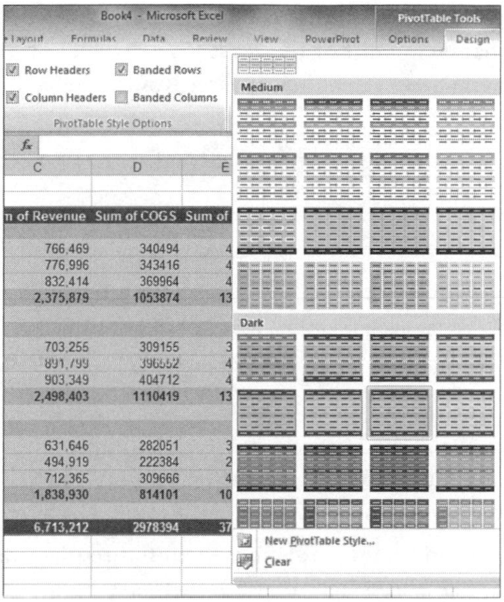

Figure 8.36
Live Preview works in
this gallery. Hover over
a thumbnail to see the
change in the pivot table.

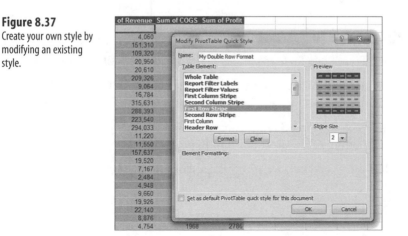

If you can't find a suitable thumbnail in the gallery, you can make your own. Follow these steps:

1. Right-click any thumbnail and select Duplicate. Excel makes a copy of the thumbnail and assumes that you want to make some changes. They launch the Modify Pivot Table Quick Style dialog.

2. Type a new name for your style. In Figure 8.37, the new name is My Double Row Format.

Figure 8.37
Create your own style by
modifying an existing
style.

3. Select a Table Element from the list. For many items, you can click the Format button to apply a format for that element. For the First Row Stripe, you can use the Stripe Size drop-down to assign a new value. Select First Row Stripe and select a stripe size of 2.

4. Select Second Row Stripe and select a stripe size of 2.

5. Click OK.

> **TIP**
>
> You might be surprised to learn that clicking OK in step 5 does *not* apply your new style to the pivot table. That would make too much sense! I am sure a lot of people go through all the hassle of defining a new style just to kill time when the Internet is down and *don't* choose the style.

6. Open the gallery again. Your new style is at the very top of the gallery, in a section called Custom. Click the style to select it.

7. If you love your new style and want it to apply to all future pivot tables that you create, you can right-click the style and select Set as Default (see Figure 8.38).

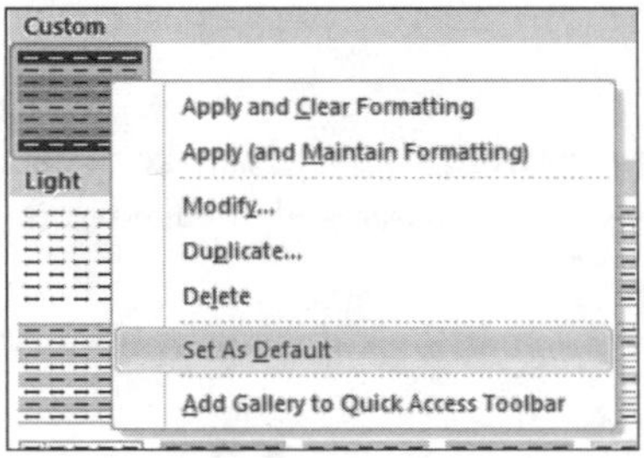

Figure 8.38
You can choose a style as a default.

Not Enough Styles? Multiply by 20

All of those styles in the PivotTable Styles gallery consists of variations of six basic colors.

If none of those colors are to your liking, go to the Page Layout tab and open the Colors drop-down. There, you will find 41 different built-in sets of colors (see Figure 8.39).

If you would rather use colors that match your company logo, you can select Create New Theme Colors from the bottom of the drop-down in Figure 8.39.

You then can define text colors and six accent colors, as shown in Figure 8.40.

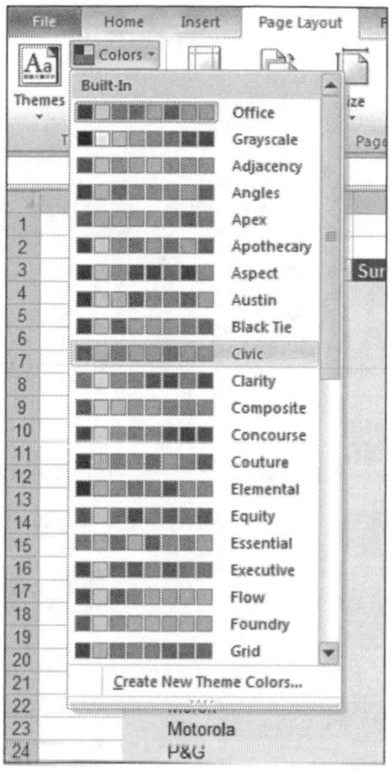

Figure 8.39
Change to a new theme, and you get new colors in the PivotTable Styles dialog.

Figure 8.40
You can define your own set of colors for a custom theme.

Applying Data Visualizations and Sparklines

Excel 2007 added data visualizations and Excel 2010 added sparklines. Both of these are available in pivot tables.

Figure 8.41 shows a data bar visualization and a set of sparkcolumns.

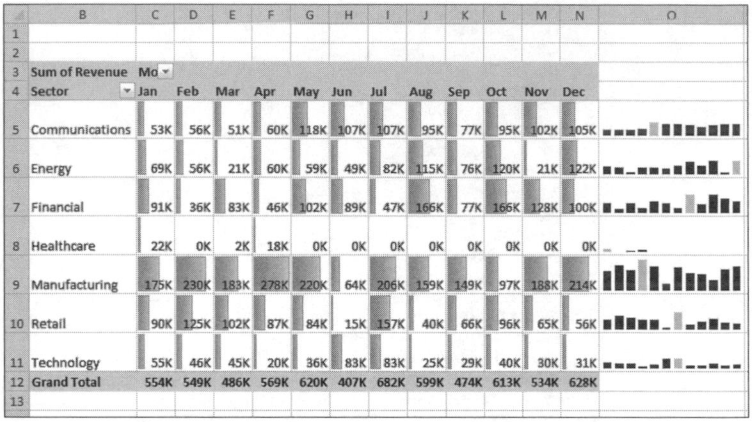

Figure 8.41
Data bars in the pivot table and sparkcolumns to the right of the table.

	B	C	D	E	F	G	H	I	J	K	L	M	N	O
3	Sum of Revenue	Mo												
4	Sector	Jan	Feb	Mar	Apr	May	Jun	Jul	Aug	Sep	Oct	Nov	Dec	
5	Communications	53K	56K	51K	60K	118K	107K	107K	95K	77K	95K	102K	105K	
6	Energy	69K	56K	21K	60K	59K	49K	82K	115K	76K	120K	21K	122K	
7	Financial	91K	36K	83K	46K	102K	89K	47K	166K	77K	166K	128K	100K	
8	Healthcare	22K	0K	2K	18K	0K	0K	0K	0K	0K	0K	0K	0K	
9	Manufacturing	175K	230K	183K	278K	220K	64K	206K	159K	149K	97K	188K	214K	
10	Retail	90K	125K	102K	87K	84K	15K	157K	40K	66K	96K	65K	56K	
11	Technology	55K	46K	45K	20K	36K	83K	83K	25K	29K	40K	30K	31K	
12	Grand Total	554K	549K	486K	569K	620K	407K	682K	599K	474K	613K	534K	628K	

To create the data bars, follow these steps:

1. Select the range of C5:N11.
2. Select Home, Conditional Formatting, Data Bars.
3. Choose one of the data bar colors.
4. Select Conditional Formatting, Manage Rules.
5. Click the Data Bar rule and select Edit Rule.
6. The top of the Edit Formatting Rule offers three choices when the visualization is in a pivot table. Select the third option, All Cells Showing "Sum of Revenue" Values for <field 1> and <field 2> (see Figure 8.42).
7. Click OK twice.

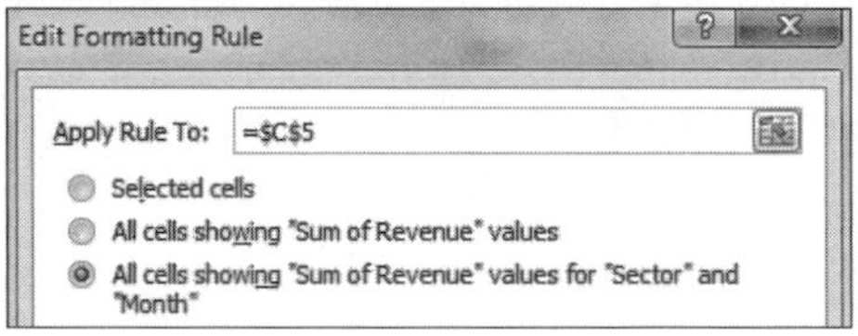

Figure 8.42
Apply the formatting to only the detail cells in the pivot table.

To create the sparkcolumns, follow these steps:

1. Select cells C5:N11.
2. Go to the Insert tab, to the Sparklines group. Select Column. Excel displays the Create Sparklines dialog.
3. The Data Range will be prepopulated. Specify a location range of O5:O11. Click OK. You will have sparkcolumns, but be careful because groups of sparkcolumns have some evil default settings.

4. On the Sparkline Tools Design tab, open the Axis drop-down and select Same for All Sparklines as the Vertical Axis Maximum Value option. Select Custom Value for the Minimum and specify a minimum of 0.

5. Select the High Point check box in the Show group.

6. Open the Marker Color drop-down. Select High Point, Green. This will show the largest month in each cell as a green marker.

7. Make rows 5:11 taller. Make column O wider. Sparkbars do much better when they are larger than the default size of a cell.

Next Steps

The following chapter shows you how to work with the multiple pivot table layouts that are possible with PowerPivot.

Cool Tricks New with PowerPivot

9

The PowerPivot add-in enables you to build multiple pivot table elements on one worksheet that are all controlled by the same set of slicers.

This is just your run-of-the-mill pivot table and pivot chart that have been moved to be adjacent to each other. You can build pivot charts that show different summaries and have them all respond to a single set of slicers.

The PowerPivot add-in has a drop-down that offers eight layouts. You've already seen the single pivot table, single pivot chart, and flattened pivot table in this book. That leaves five multi-element layouts:

- Chart on the left, table on the right
- Chart on the top, table on the bottom
- Two charts side by side
- Two charts arranged vertically
- Four charts arranged in a quadrant pattern

Are you limited to these arrangements? What if you want two pivot tables? What if you want six charts? You can pull this off, but you have to be careful to do it in the correct sequence. I can't answer this completely until I talk about slicers for a little bit.

The slicers in PowerPivot have some behavior that is freakish. I can see where they were trying to be helpful, but the slicers have a tendency to act like a stubborn 4-year-old who is convinced he knows best.

This chapter will give you some limited ideas for coercing the automatic slicers. You might decide that the automatic slicers are too much of a pain and to create your own slicers where you have absolute control.

Back to the question of whether you can build a layout that is not in the Figure 9.1 gallery:

- If you want to use automatic slicers, you must add the slicers before you try to add extra pivot tables or pivot charts. The automatic slicers will not appear if there are unexpected extra pivot charts below the original pivot chart.

- If you start from an existing layout, build out the automatic slicers, and then you can add a new pivot table or pivot chart and in a few clicks have that pivot table respecting the existing slicers.

- If you reject the automatic slicers, you can build as many pivot tables or charts in any sequence.

Building a Report with Two Pivot Charts

After loading your data into PowerPivot, use the PivotTable drop-down in either the Home tab of the PowerPivot window or the PowerPivot tab of the Excel Ribbon.

As shown in Figure 9.1, the drop-down offers eight layout choices.

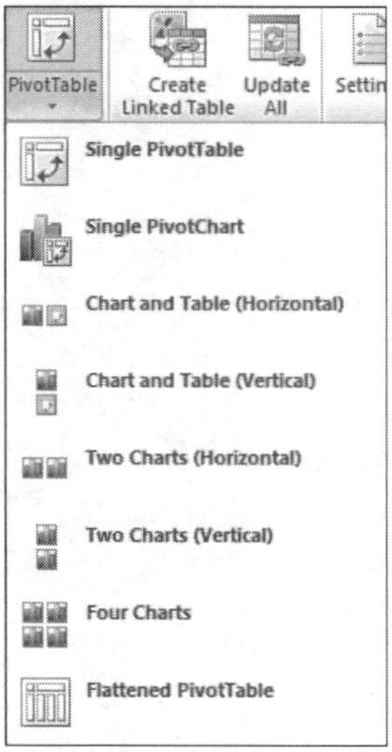

Figure 9.1
PowerPivot offers eight built-in layouts.

For this example, select Two Charts (Horizontal).

Figure 9.2 shows the resulting screen. There are many things to notice:

- Two blank pivot charts appear on the screen.
- One of the charts is selected (in this case, Chart 1).
- One PowerPivot Field List appears. This field list is tied to the selected chart.

■ Three worksheet tabs have been added. You are looking at Sheet1. Two additional worksheets to the left are called Data for Sheet1 Chart 1 and Data for Sheet1 Chart 2. Those other worksheets hold the pivot tables for the pivot charts on Sheet1.

Figure 9.2
Each pivot chart has a new worksheet to hold the pivot table associated with the chart.

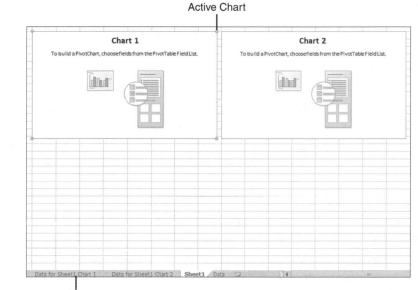

Active Chart

Data worksheet for Chart 1

Follow these steps:

1. While Chart 1 is selected, choose fields in the PowerPivot Field List to build that chart. In Figure 9.3, Region and revenue create a chart by region.

Figure 9.3
Choose fields for the first chart.

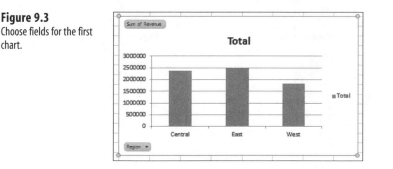

2. Click Chart 2. You should see handles around Chart 2, and the bottom four drop zones of the PowerPivot Field List should be cleared of any fields that you added to Chart 1. The Slicer drop zones do not get cleared, but the Legend, Axis, Values, and Report Filter should get cleared out. If they do not, perform the extra step in step 3.

9

3. If the PowerPivot Field List still has data from another pivot table, click the worksheet tab that contains data for Chart 2. On that tab, put the cell pointer inside the pivot table. This should clear out the PowerPivot Field List. Go back to the worksheet with the charts and the field list will remain cleared out.

4. Add fields for the second chart. In Figure 9.4, Product and Revenue were selected.

Figure 9.4
Add fields to the next chart.

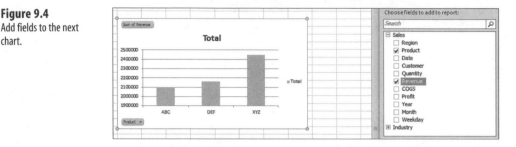

You can now bounce back and forth between the two charts, doing any formatting changes.

Chart Formatting Changes

Once you have fields on each chart, you can do any chart formatting changes. In Figure 9.5, you will notice these changes to both charts:

■ The default column charts are changed to pie charts. Select a chart. Use the Design tab, select Change Chart Type, and select a pie chart.

■ The titles are improved. Click a title, type the new title in the formula bar, and press Enter.

■ The PivotChart buttons have been removed. Select each chart. On the Analyze tab, open the Field Buttons drop-down and select Hide All.

Figure 9.5
Two pivot charts co-exist, but without any slicers.

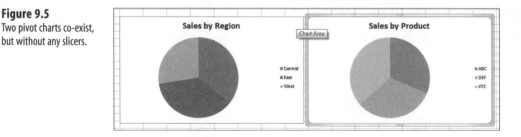

To use the other multiple element layouts, you should follow a similar sequence; add fields to the first element, then click the next element and add fields, and so on. After you've added fields to all of the pivot tables and pivot charts, you can then undertake other tasks such as formatting.

> **CAUTION**
>
> If you go in some other sequence, it is possible to confuse the PowerPivot add-in and end up without a PowerPivot Field List. If you suddenly see an online analytical processing (OLAP) version of the PowerPivot Field List, you've accidentally done a sequence of events that caused the PowerPivot Field List to disappear. In my tests, the Field List icon in the PowerPivot tab is often grayed out. If you go back to the worksheet that holds the data for a pivot chart, you might be able to get the PowerPivot Field List to come back. Otherwise, save the workbook, close the workbook, close Excel, and reopen.

Adding Slicers and Understanding Slicer AutoLayout

The advantage of PowerPivot is having multiple pivot charts controlled by a single set of slicers.

The PowerPivot slicers definitely have some cool tricks. But these tricks can become annoying if you don't understand what is happening.

Drag the Region field to the horizontal slicer drop zone.

Three things happen:

- The PowerPivot add-in moves all of the pivot table and pivot chart elements down by 109 pixels. This is about 1.8 inches of screen space. If there is something in the way, such as another rogue pivot table that you've added, PowerPivot will refuse to add the slicer.

- PowerPivot uses the Insert Shapes feature to add a new rectangle to your worksheet. This rectangle will be 109 pixels tall and 500 pixels wide. The rectangle will start at the upper-left corner where the pivot chart used to be. This leaves a measly 10-pixel gap between the slicer and the top of the pivot chart.

- PowerPivot will add a slicer inside the rectangle. Depending on the length of the items in the slicer, and the number of items in the slicer, PowerPivot will decide the proper number of columns for the slicer, and the optimal width for the slicer. For the horizontal slicer, a field that contains 26 one-letter codes might get as many as 9 columns in the slicer. For a vertical slicer, you might see three-column slicers for items that are a single character or two-column slicers for items that have two characters such as state codes or three-characters such as telephone area codes.

Figure 9.6 shows the horizontal slicer.

Similar things happen if you add a field the vertical slicer drop zone:

- The left side of your pivot charts move 140 pixels to the right.
- A new 130 pixel wide by 340 pixel tall rectangle is added where the pivot chart used to be.

■ A slicer is inserted inside the rectangle, with the size and number of columns calculated by PowerPivot. In the vertical slicer, fields that contain one-character codes will get a slicer with three columns. Two- and three-character fields will get two columns. All others will get a vertical slicer with one column.

Figure 9.6
A horizontal slicer added by PowerPivot.

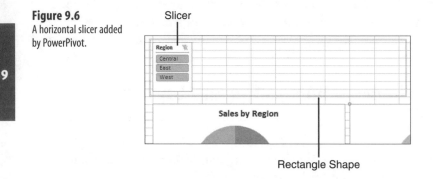

Figure 9.7 shows the vertical slicer.

Figure 9.7
A vertical slicer.

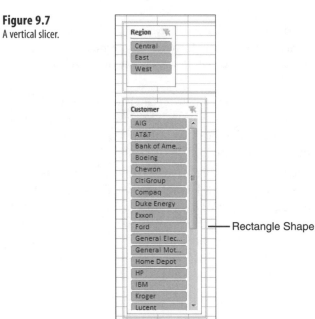

Cannot Directly Change the Size of Slicers

You are allowed to change the color the slicers.

Attempting to change the size or the number of columns in the slicer is futile.

If you click a slicer, the Slicer Tools Options tab appears. Using the icons on the right side of the ribbon, you can change the number of columns and the height and width of the slicer (see Figure 9.8).

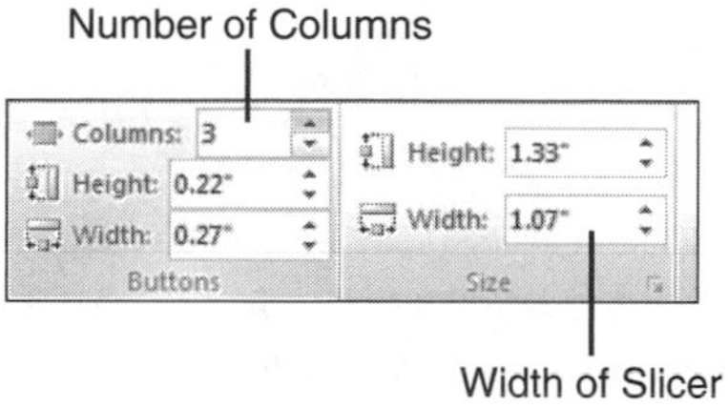

Figure 9.8
Slicer Tools Options tab.

Number of Columns

Width of Slicer

Suppose you want to get the regions to appear in a slicer that has three columns. Your first step might be to use the spin button in the ribbon to dial the number of columns up to three. This creates three slicer buttons that are too small to hold any text at all (see Figure 9.9).

Figure 9.9
Adjusting the number of columns results in buttons that are too small.

Your next move is to drag the slicer resize handles to make the slicer wider. Figure 9.10 shows the result less than a second after dragging the handle to the right.

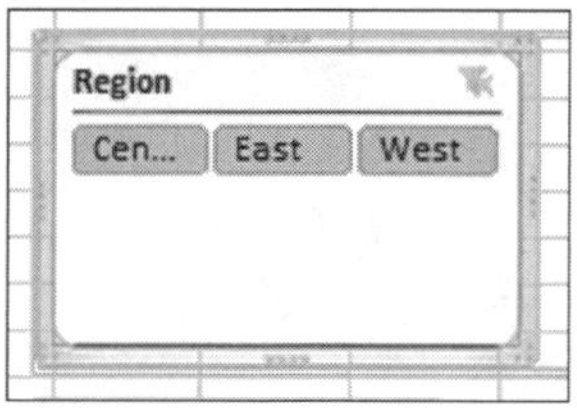

Figure 9.10
You think that you can resize the slice.

When you let go of the slicer resize handle, the PowerPivot add-in leaps into action, trying to figure out the best size for the slicers that have been added to the pivot table.

> **NOTE**
> The figures in this book don't do it justice to this feature. However, PowerPivot nicely animates the action of the slicer resizing back to a one-column slicer, as shown in Figure 9.11.

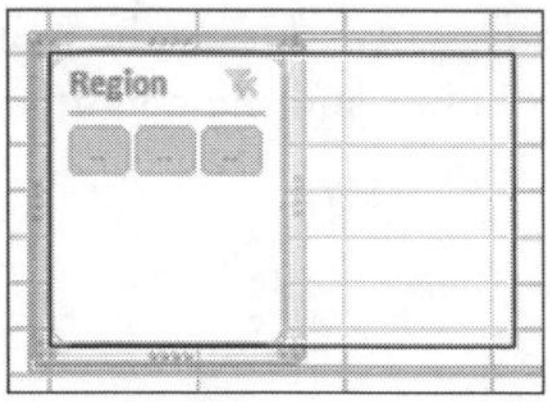

Figure 9.11
When you release the
resize handle, PowerPivot
animates the action of
changing the slicer back.

> **NOTE**
> I've already suggested to Microsoft that although I love what the slicer autolayout feature does 92% of the time, it would be nice to have an option to turn it off so that you can tweak the final slicers, either by changing the number of columns or the height and width.

Controlling the Size of the Bounding Rectangle

While you cannot change the size of the slicers that are in an AutoLayout, you can change the size and shape and location of the bounding rectangle.

Although every horizontal slicer starts out with a size of 500 pixels wide by 109 pixels tall, the PowerPivot add-in can handle the possibility that the rectangle might be a different size.

Before calculating the optimal columns and width for the slicer, PowerPivot considers the current size of the slicer bounding rectangle.

Therefore, if you want the region slicer to be three columns wide by one row tall, you can resize the bounding rectangle.

When you click the bounding rectangle, you will have eight resize slicers, as shown in Figure 9.12.

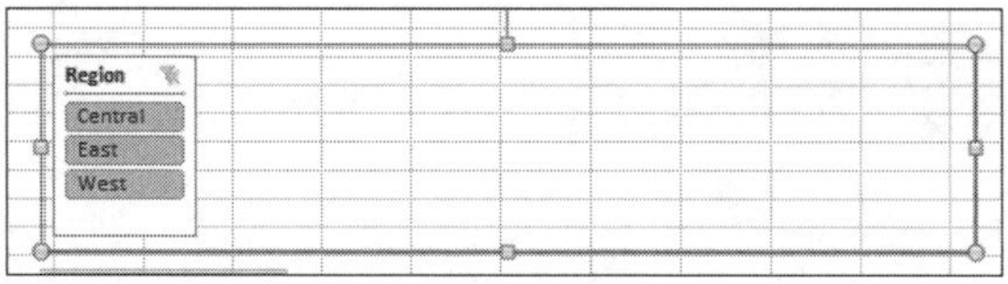

Figure 9.12
Click the bounding
rectangle.

Grab the top-right corner of the rectangle and resize the rectangle so that it has less height. When you release the rectangle, PowerPivot calculates that this slicer looks best as a three-column slicer (see Figure 9.13).

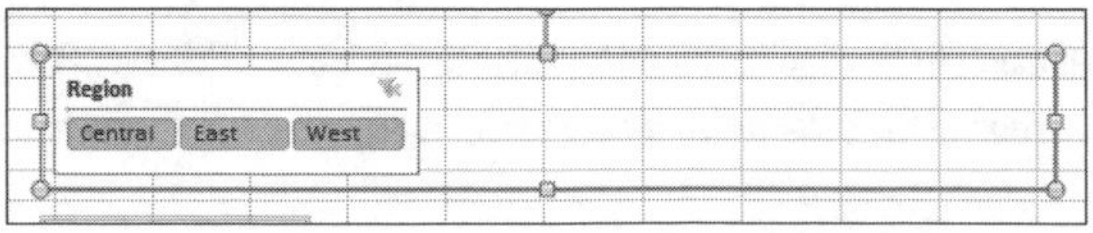

Figure 9.13
By changing the rect-
angle, you can finesse the
PowerPivot add-in toward
calculating the desired
number of columns.

You are able to change the width of the Excel columns. You can drag pivot charts to new locations or sizes. You can drag the bounding rectangle to a new location. If you make column A wider, you can actually resize the vertical slicer enough that it will show up with three columns, as shown in Figure 9.14.

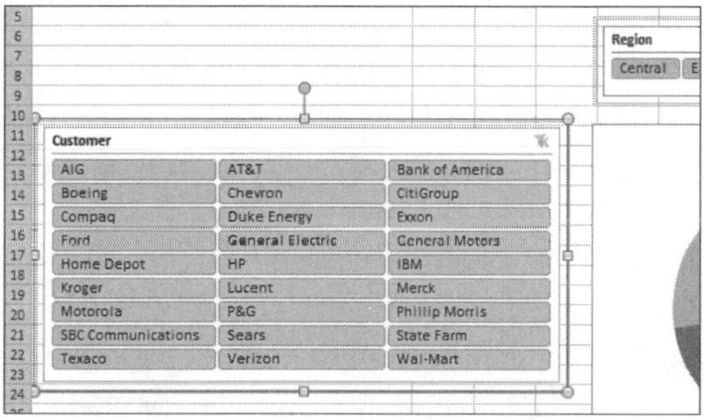

Figure 9.14
You can change the size of the vertical slicer to increase the number of columns in that slicer.

> **TIP**
> If you ever become completely frustrated with the slicer AutoLayout and just wish you could finesse a slicer, there is a solution. Click the slicer title. Drag the slicer completely outside the bounds of the bounding rectangle. You now have absolute control over the slicer using the Slicer Tools tab!

The bounding rectangle is designed to become transparent when you click outside of the pivot table or pivot chart. (See Figure 9.15) If you are trying to selecting the slicer bounding rectangle and you've clicked outside of the pivot table, the rectangle is not there to select.

Figure 9.15
The bounding rectangle is not there when you've clicked outside of the pivot chart.

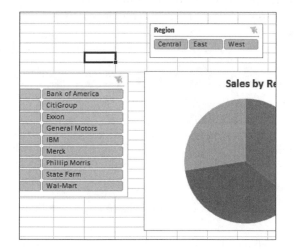

Strategy for Dealing with AutoLayout of Slicers

Here is a quick recap of the rules for the slicers in AutoLayout mode:

- It is easier if you let PowerPivot add the slicers in for you.
- There has to be 100 pixels below your pivot table or pivot chart to add the horizontal slicers and 100 pixels to the right of your pivot charts to add vertical slicers. Do not add any new pivot tables to those areas until you've added the slicers.
- If you want to change the field in a slicer, add a new field first, and then remove the unwanted field. Doing so prevents PowerPivot from shifting and then reshifting the pivot tables and pivot charts.
- You are allowed to adjust the color of the slicers.
- You cannot use the slicer tools to adjust the size or columns in the slicer. Instead, adjust the size of the bounding rectangle to try to coerce the slicer into behaving as you want.
- When you populate either of the slicer drop zones, PowerPivot adds the slicer bounding rectangle. Provided you never let the slicer drop zone become empty, PowerPivot will not change the size or location of the slicer bounding rectangle.
- Provided you never let the slicer drop zone become completely empty, you can move and completely resize the slicer rectangles. You can actually have two vertical slicer rectangles or two horizontal slicer boxes by making the vertical slicer rectangle short and wide or making the horizontal rectangle tall and narrow.
- You can drag a slicer completely outside of the bounding rectangle to stop the AutoLayout behavior.

Your strategy should be to use the drop zones to add slicers before you add new pivot tables outside the layout. Once PowerPivot draws in the default rectangles, you can resize the rectangles as needed, provided you never completely empty the slicer drop zone in the PowerPivot Field List.

Adding a Pivot Chart to an Existing Layout

Say that you've maxed out your PowerPivot layout. You've created a report with four pivot charts. You would like to add more charts to the layout.

If your charts are going to have slicers, make sure that those slicers are in place and stay in place during the following steps:

1. Put the cell pointer below your existing charts.
2. On the Insert tab, open the PivotTable drop-down and select PivotChart, as shown in Figure 9.16.
3. In the Create PivotTable with PivotChart dialog, select that you want to Use an External Data Source. This enables the Choose Connection button, as shown in Figure 9.17.

Figure 9.16
To add a fifth pivot chart, skip the PowerPivot tab and go to the Insert tab.

Figure 9.17
Select external data source.

4. The Existing Connections dialog will indicate that there is an existing connection to PowerPivot Data. This connection gets created as soon as you add your first table to the PowerPivot window. Select that connection, as shown in Figure 9.18.

Figure 9.18
Use the PowerPivot Data connection.

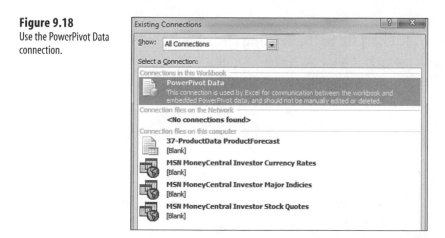

5. Back in the Create dialog box, select to create the pivot chart on an existing worksheet and click OK. While the pivot table gets created in the correct location, the pivot chart is assigned a different location, as shown in Figure 9.19. This is okay because you can fix it later.

Figure 9.19
Excel puts the table and
chart on the existing
sheet.

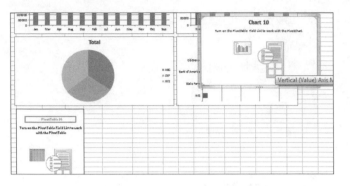

6. Use the PowerPivot Field List to build your chart (see Figure 9.20).

> N O T E
> Even though you did not build the pivot table in step 6 through the PowerPivot tab, you get the
> improved field list interface because you used the PowerPivot Data source.

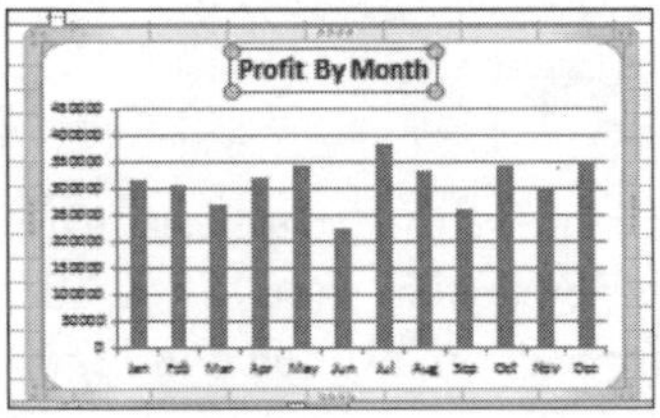

Figure 9.20
Build your chart using the
PowerPivot Field List.

Hooking the New Pivot Chart Up to the Existing Slicers

You've added a fifth pivot chart to the worksheet, but it is not using the same slicers yet. It
turns out that it is pretty easy to hook a pivot table up to existing slicers.

Make sure that your cell pointer is inside the new pivot table.

On the PivotTable Tools Options tab, open the Insert Slicer drop-down and select Slicer
Connections, as shown in Figure 9.21.

Figure 9.21
You don't want a
new slicer. Edit the
connections.

The Slicer Connections dialog appears. It shows all three slicers in the workbook. None are currently attached to this pivot table (see Figure 9.22).

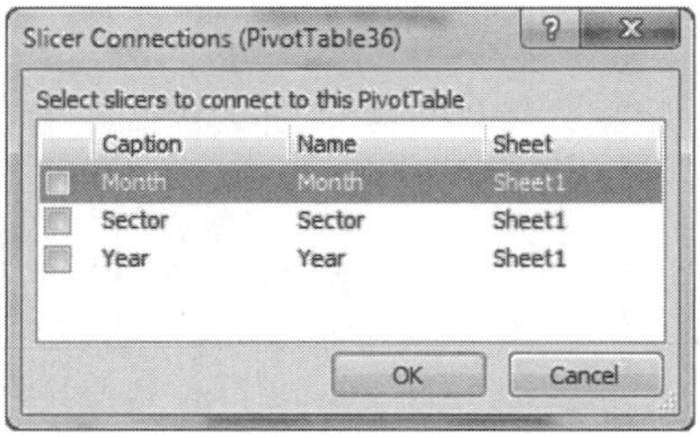

Figure 9.22
None of the three existing slicers are driving this pivot table.

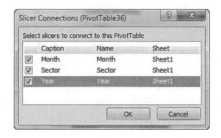

Select all three check boxes in Figure 9.23 and click OK. Your new pivot table and pivot chart are now tied into the same slicers as the other four pivot charts.

Figure 9.23
Select all three slicers.

> **NOTE**
> Microsoft sure made a big deal about PowerPivot allowing multiple pivot tables to be driven from the same slicers. When you get right down to it, that is pretty easy to do, isn't it?

To see a demo of adding a fifth pivot chart to a layout, search for MrExcel PowerPivot 9 at YouTube.

Moving the Pivot Table to a Back Worksheet

The other feature that the PowerPivot folks touted about PowerPivot is the ability to have a standalone pivot chart. As you've already seen, it isn't really a standalone pivot chart. It is a pivot chart on one sheet with the pivot table on another sheet. Let's see how tough that really is:

1. Insert a new worksheet in your workbook. Give the sheet any name. I used Extra Sheet for Pivot Table, but frankly Sheet5 would have worked as well.

2. Go back to your pivot table. Select any cell inside the pivot table.

3. On the PivotTable Tools Options tab, select Move PivotTable (see Figure 9.24).

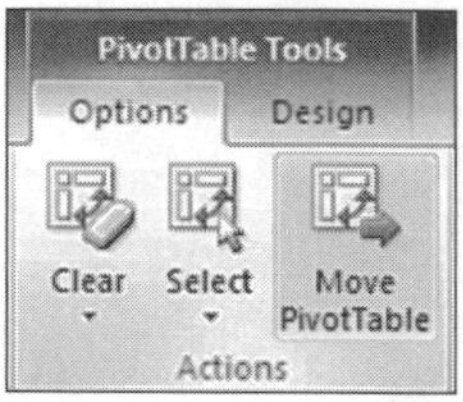

Figure 9.24
Select to move your pivot table.

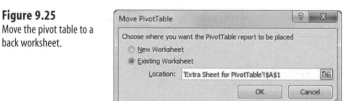

4. Microsoft shows you the Move Pivot Table dialog. Select to move the pivot table to an existing worksheet. Use the RefEdit control to point to cell A1 on the new worksheet (see Figure 9.25).

Figure 9.25
Move the pivot table to a back worksheet.

Move PivotTable

Choose where you want the PivotTable report to be placed
- ○ New Worksheet
- ● Existing Worksheet
    Location: 'Extra Sheet for PivotTable'!$A$1

OK   Cancel

You can now move the Pivot Chart to the correct location.

Figure 9.26 shows a PowerPivot workbook with five charts driven from the same slicers.

Figure 9.26
Five charts in a PowerPivot layout.

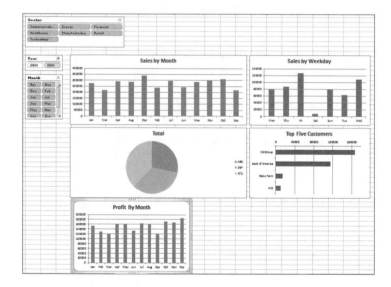

Adding a Pivot Table to an Existing Layout

The steps for adding a new pivot table are very similar to adding a new pivot chart.

When you place your cursor in the correct location and use Insert PivotTable, the pivot table will appear at the correct location.

Figure 9.27 shows a layout with five charts and a pivot table.

Figure 9.27
Five charts and a pivot table.

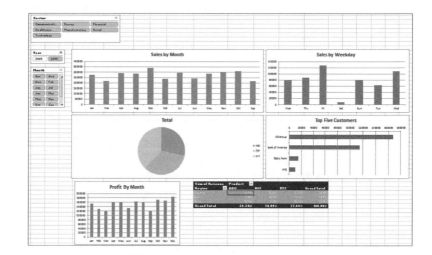

Can the PowerPivot Layout Be Skipped Entirely?

This is a great question.

As soon as you put a table in the PowerPivot window, the PowerPivot Data connection is available when you use Insert PivotTable.

In Figure 9.28, I avoided the PowerPivot layout.

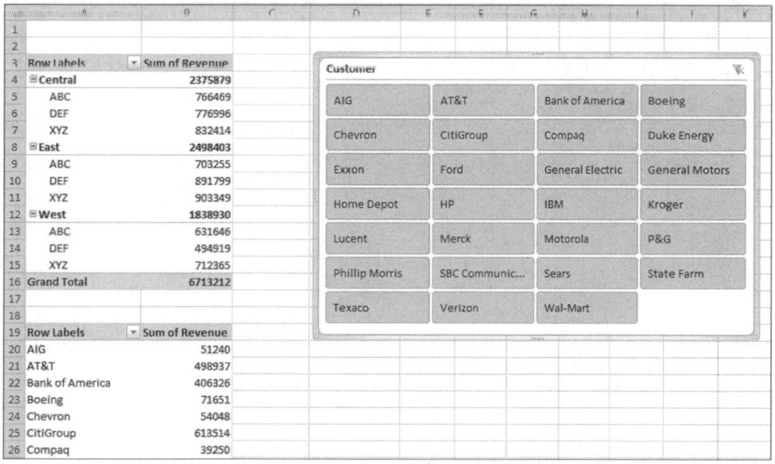

Figure 9.28
Pivot tables and a slicer built without using the PowerPivot layout.

Instead, I built two pivot tables with one slicer by following these general steps:

1. Use Insert Pivot Table to build the first pivot table based on external data.
2. Add a slicer to that pivot table using Insert Slicer on the PivotTable Tools Option tab.
3. Select the slicer and format the slicer however you want. As you see in Figure 9.28, I went with big tall buttons.
4. Use Insert Pivot Table to build the second pivot table. Place this pivot table below the first pivot table.
5. If desired, repeat step 4 additional times.
6. Select the slicer. On the Slicer Tools Options tab, select PivotTable Connections. Excel shows a list of all pivot tables in the workbook. Only the first pivot table is currently hooked up to the slicer, as shown in Figure 9.29.

Figure 9.29
After adding additional pivot tables, you can connect them to a slicer using this dialog.

7. Select all of the pivot tables and click OK.

You now have two pivot tables being driven by one slicer, as shown in Figure 9.30.

Figure 9.30
Two pivot tables driven by one slicer.

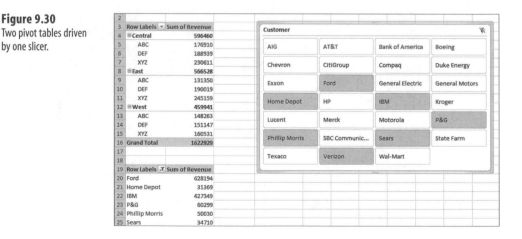

NOTE To be fair, you are not completely ignoring the PowerPivot add-in in this situation. The PowerPivot add-in still works as you build the pivot tables with the PowerPivot Field List. You are relying on the PowerPivot add-in to define measures for you as you drag fields into the Values drop zone of the field list.

Next Steps

In the next chapter, you will be introduced to massively powerful DAX measures you can add to your pivot tables.

9

Using DAX for Aggregate Functions

You really have to read this chapter. My plan is to show you some really simple examples of stuff that would be insanely hard in a regular pivot table but would be really easy thanks to something called a DAX measure.

But first, I have to tell you that I hate sentences where I don't understand a majority of the words. A long time ago, my fiancé was in nursing school and I knew how to type. I would stay up late typing her papers, and there would be entire sentences where I couldn't tell nouns from adverbs from adjectives. Then, back in 2005, someone in an airport said a sentence that was completely foreign to me: "Leo's TWiT podcast is number one at iTunes." I knew he was talking about Leo Laporte, and I knew what number one meant, but I had never heard of podcasting, I had never heard of iTunes, and I had never heard of TWiT. I didn't have a clue how to react to the sentence because not enough of the words had enough meaning to me.

So, if I am going to convince you to read this chapter, I feel like I need to get some vocabulary out of the way.

DAX is Data Analysis Expression, which is a new formula language in PowerPivot. 71 of the DAX functions came straight out of Excel's function library. But, DAX also has some things in common with another formula language called MDX (Multidimensional Extensions). So, there are parts of DAX that are very similar to what you already know in Excel.

Back in Chapter 6, "Using Data Sheet View," you used DAX to add new columns in the PowerPivot data sheet. This chapter and the next cover the other use for DAX.

Measure is the fancy term for any field that is dropped in the Values section of a pivot table.

So, when the PowerPivot people at Microsoft talk about DAX measures, they are really saying that they are using a new formula language called DAX to create a calculated field for use in the Values area of the pivot table.

You've seen calculated fields before. Maybe you even created one in a regular Excel pivot table. Calculated fields are a bit limited. DAX measures actually run circles around calculated fields.

DAX Measures Are Calculated Fields for the Values Area of a Pivot Table

Back in Chapter 6, you used the DAX formula language to create a new column called Year and another column called Month. If you have a 10 million row data set and you add a DAX calculated column, the PowerPivot engine must calculate that field for all 10 million rows.

DAX measures are better than calculated fields. A DAX measure is calculated just one time for each value cell in a pivot table.

Consider the pivot table shown in Figure 10.1. The Values area of that pivot table has 28 cells. If you define a new DAX measure, PowerPivot has to calculate that measure only 28 times.

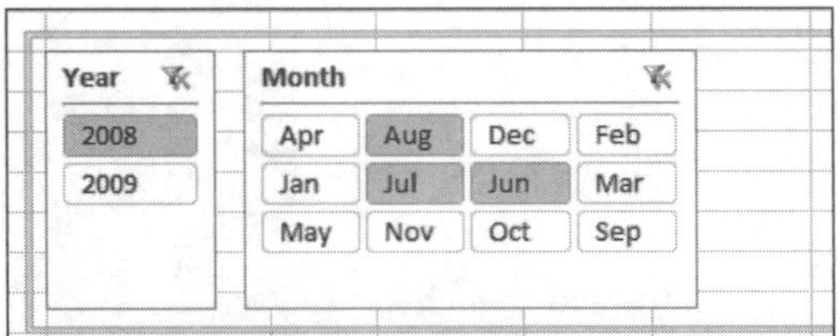

Figure 10.1

A DAX measure only has to get calculated for the 28 cells in the values area of this pivot table.

Year		Month			
2008		Apr	Aug	Dec	Feb
2009		Jan	Jul	Jun	Mar
		May	Nov	Oct	Sep

Sum of Revenue				
	Books	**Consulting**	**Seminars**	**Grand Total**
Communications	48,079	119,801	13,866	181,746
Energy	56,073	9,704	23,399	89,176
Financial	99,271	53,418	271,747	424,436
Manufacturing	39,265	106,917	39,592	185,774
Retail	0	26,980	73,213	100,193
Technology	34,137	12,135	48,341	94,613
Grand Total	**276,825**	**328,955**	**470,158**	**1,075,938**

> **NOTE** At the risk of confusing you, the PowerPivot add-in has secretly been creating a few DAX measures for you along the way. When you change from SUM to AVERAGE, the add-in writes a DAX measure formula for you.

Five of the Six Pivot Table Drop Zones Are Filter Fields!

Here is a quiz question for you. The active cell in Figure 10.1 contains 271,747. How many filters are applied to that cell?

The answer is four:

- The Year slicer filters to only records from 2008.
- The Month slicer filters only to records in June through August.
- The Seminars column heading filters to only records where the product is Seminars.
- The Financial row heading filters to only customers who are in the financial sector.

Four different filters are applied.

To further illustrate that there are four filters applied, I created a simple Excel worksheet with the PowerPivot data, turned on the AutoFilters, and applied filters to four of the columns. The resulting records add up to 271,747 just like that one cell in the pivot table (see Figure 10.2).

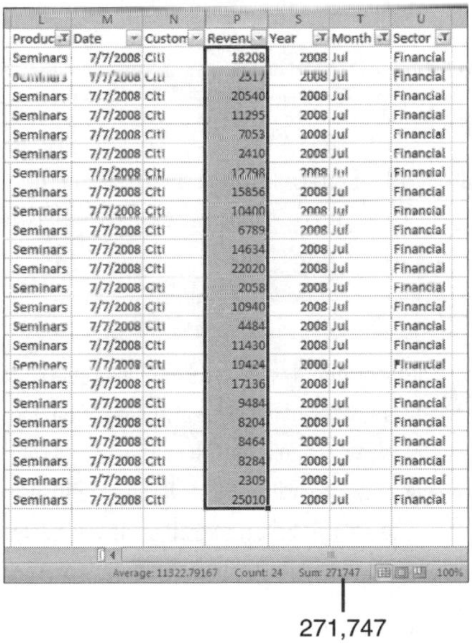

Figure 10.2

After applying four filters to a regular Excel worksheet, you get the same 271,747.

271,747

I never really thought about the row and column headers as being "filters" in a pivot table, but if you are trying to calculate that 1 cell that contains 271,747, there really are 4 filters applied to that 1 cell.

Out of the six drop zones in the PowerPivot Field List, five of those drop zones are really filters that get applied when calculating values in the Values drop zone.

DAX Measures Respect the Home Table Filters

One cool thing about DAX measures: If you don't specify otherwise, a DAX measure automatically respects all the filters that are otherwise applied to the cell.

When you are writing a DAX measure, you don't need to specify that you want the measure to follow the slicers, follow the row headings, follow the column headings. That all happens by default.

If you build a DAX measure and don't do anything to override the filters, the DAX measure will automatically respect all of those filters. For these first examples, having those filters work is perfect. (In the "Denominators Frequently Need to Ignore the Filters" section of this chapter, there will be cases where you want to override the filters.)

> **CAUTION**
>
> This rule applies only to fields in the home table. If a DAX measure references a field in the lookup table, you will always get 100% of the rows in the lookup table. To overcome this limitation, use the RELATED function to create a calculated column in the home table to bring the field from the lookup table into the home table.

Generate a Count Distinct

The count distinct has been a holy grail of pivot table enthusiasts since the beginning. It was always easy to get a count of records. Getting a count of the distinct number of products or customers or whatever was nearly impossible.

> **NOTE**
>
> "Nearly impossible"; People who were wizards with Excel formulas could write a formula in the original data set to count how many other records had the same attributes as this record. They would then divide that number into one and add up the column. Thus, if you had 3 records for the same customer, the formula would assign a value of 1/3 to each customer. If you have 10 records for the same customer, you would assign a value of 1/10 to each of those records. It made you feel really smart if you could figure this out, but it calculated slowly, and if the shape of the pivot table changed, you had to rewrite the formula.

Using the DISTINCT Function

The DISTINCT function in DAX has this syntax:

```
DISTINCT(<column>)
```

The preceding syntax returns a one-column table that contains the distinct values from the specified column.

So, you have to give the DISTINCT function a column to evaluate. For each cell in the values section of the pivot table, PowerPivot will apply all the other filters for that cell and then return the distinct list of cells for that column.

If you used a formula of DISTINCT(Sales[Customer]) and PowerPivot had to calculate that formula for 2008 June–August manufacturing customers who bought consulting, the filtered set would look like Figure 10.3.

Figure 10.3
To calculate the DISTINCT for one cell in the values area of the pivot table, PowerPivot has to apply four filters.

Product	Date	Customer	Revenue	Year	Month	Sector	
Consulting	7/14/2008	Ford	15876	2008	Jul	Manufacturing	
Consulting	7/1/2008	G.E.	21960	2008	Jul	Manufacturing	
Consulting	7/29/2008	G.E.	12984	2008	Jul	Manufacturing	
Consulting	8/6/2008	G.E.	2320	2008	Aug	Manufacturing	
Consulting	8/24/2008	G.E.	8744	2008	Aug	Manufacturing	
Consulting	7/4/2008	GM	7593	2008	Jul	Manufacturing	
Consulting	8/5/2008	GM	19584	2008	Aug	Manufacturing	
Consulting	8/24/2008	Motorola	17856	2008	Aug	Manufacturing	

You can scan through the Customer column of Figure 10.3 and see that although eight records match the filters, there are only four unique customer names in that list of eight records. Thus, the DAX DISTINCT function is going to return a one-column table with four values in it.

Using COUNTROWS as a Wrapper Function

For those of you who have written array formulas in regular Excel, you know that getting four answers for a single cell is bad. You need to use a wrapper function to add up those answers or count those answers or somehow consolidate those answers into a single answer. In Excel, you could use the COUNTA function. In an annoying twist, COUNTA doesn't work in this case, because COUNTA can't accept an entire table, it can only work with a column. (Yes, DISTINCT returns a one-column table, so any rational person would think that passing a one-column table to COUNTA would be the same as passing a column to COUNTA, but unfortunately, DAX doesn't work that way. Don't fret, as the DAX function COUNTROWS will happily count how many rows are in a table.)

The syntax of COUNTROWS is as follows:

```
COUNTROWS(<table>)
```

The COUNTROWS function counts the number of rows in the specified table, or in a table defined by an expression.

Therefore, to calculate the distinct number of customers, you combine the COUNTROWS and DISTINCT functions:

```
=COUNTROWS(DISTINCT(Sales[Customer]))
```

10

Entering a DAX Measure

There are two entry points for creating a DAX measure:

- You can click New Measure on the PowerPivot tab in Excel.
- You can right-click the table name in the PowerPivot Field List and select Add New Measure.

Figure 10.4 shows both methods.

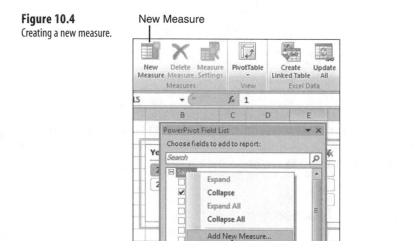

New Measure

Add New Measure

When you choose to create a new measure, Excel displays the Measure Settings dialog, as shown in Figure 10.5.

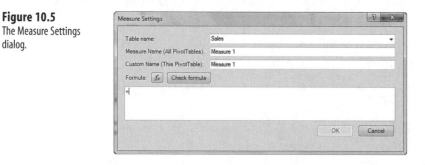

- Table Name is the name of the home table. This is almost always your main transaction table.

- Measure Name is the name that you want to use for this measure. When you type a new name for the measure name, the custom name will change to the same value.

- You can use the fx button to choose a function or simply type the formula in the formula box.

- When the formula is complete, click the Check Formula button to have the syntax checker see whether the formula will calculate.

Figure 10.6 shows the completed Measure Settings dialog for the Distinct Customers field.

Figure 10.6
Define a new DAX measure.

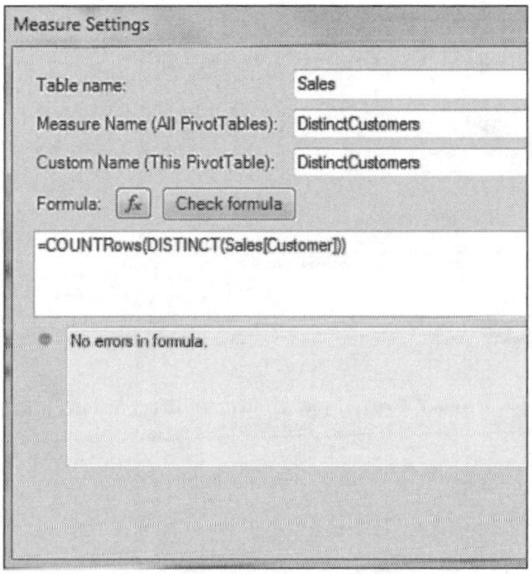

Measure Settings

Table name: Sales

Measure Name (All PivotTables): DistinctCustomers

Custom Name (This PivotTable): DistinctCustomers

Formula: [fx] [Check formula]

=COUNTRows(DISTINCT(Sales[Customer]))

No errors in formula.

When you click OK, the DAX measure is added to the PowerPivot Field List and the measure is added to the pivot table. In Figure 10.7, four manufacturing customers bought consulting in June–August 2008.

> **NOTE** You already knew this answer was going to be four from a quick glance through Figure 10.3. Realize that to calculate the 28 different cells in Figure 10.7, PowerPivot would have to do the calculation in Figure 10.3 another 27 times.

Filtering the DAX Measure

That DAX measure for distinct customers is cool. If you want to know how many unique customers you had in the spring of 2009, a few changes to the slicers provide the answer, as shown in Figure 10.8

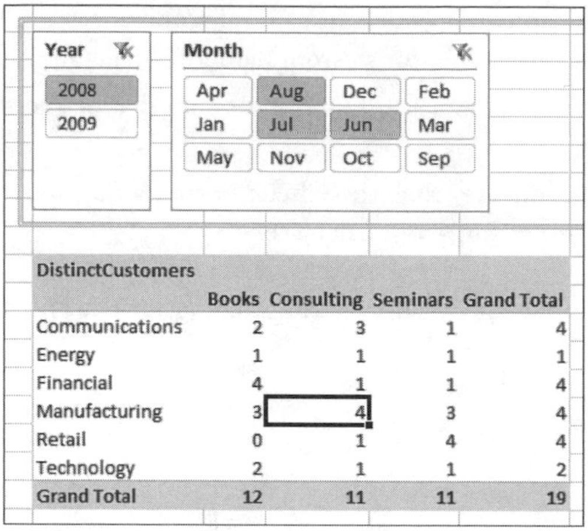

Figure 10.7
The 4 in the active cell isn't surprising. The fact that you get the other 27 numbers so quickly is surprising.

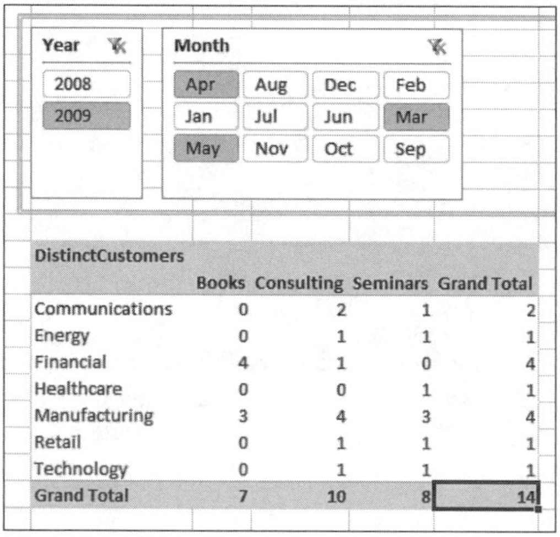

Year ⟨K⟩	Month ⟨K⟩			
2008	Apr	Aug	Dec	Feb
2009	Jan	Jul	Jun	Mar
	May	Nov	Oct	Sep

DistinctCustomers

	Books	Consulting	Seminars	Grand Total
Communications	2	3	1	4
Energy	1	1	1	1
Financial	4	1	1	4
Manufacturing	3	4	3	4
Retail	0	1	4	4
Technology	2	1	1	2
Grand Total	12	11	11	19

Figure 10.8
Change the slicers and the DAX measures recalculate.

Year ⟨K⟩	Month ⟨K⟩			
2008	Apr	Aug	Dec	Feb
2009	Jan	Jul	Jun	Mar
	May	Nov	Oct	Sep

DistinctCustomers

	Books	Consulting	Seminars	Grand Total
Communications	0	2	1	2
Energy	0	1	1	1
Financial	4	1	0	4
Healthcare	0	0	1	1
Manufacturing	3	4	3	4
Retail	0	1	1	1
Technology	0	1	1	1
Grand Total	7	10	8	14

If you change the pivot, there is no need to change this DAX measure. Remove Sector from the Row Labels and add Region, and you can then see the number of unique customers by region in the spring of 2009 (see Figure 10.9).

Note in Figure 10.9 that the Grand Total column is not just a total of the other columns. In the Central region, the five consulting customers must have been the same customers buying books and seminars, because the grand total of unique customers is five. In the East region, seven unique customers bought consulting. At least 4 of the books or seminar customers must not have bought consulting, because the grand total for the East region is 11.

Figure 10.9
Move fields around the
pivot table, and the DAX
measure recalculates
properly. This time, it had
to calculate 16 values.

Year		Month			
2008		Apr	Aug	Dec	Feb
2009		Jan	Jul	Jun	Mar
		May	Nov	Oct	Sep

DistinctCustomers				
	Books	Consulting	Seminars	Grand Total
Central	3	5	4	5
East	5	7	6	11
West	3	2	2	5
Grand Total	7	10	8	14

DAX Measures Are Calculated Only on Demand

If you define 50 DAX measures but don't put them in your pivot table, PowerPivot is not trying to calculate those at every change in the slicers. DAX measures are very efficient. They get calculated only when they are in the pivot table, and they calculate only the exact number of cells needed for the pivot table.

DAX Measures Can Reference Other DAX Measures

If you've been following along, you just defined your first DAX measure. Getting the distinct number of customers is a cool thing. But, now that you have this measure, which you've been waiting so long to be able to calculate, it brings up new questions.

For example, what was the average purchase for each of those distinct customers?

If you built a pivot table with both sum of revenue and distinct customers, it would be easy enough to add an Excel formula to divide total sales by the number of customers. But, maybe you only want to show the average customer size in the pivot table.

Create a measure to calculate the sum of revenue divided by the distinct customers column from the sales table. The formula would be as follows:

```
=Sum(Sales[Revenue])/Sales[DistinctCustomers]
```

Figure 10.10 shows the sum of revenue, the distinct customers, and then the average customer size. Grab a calculator (or a blank Excel worksheet) and plug in 329,329/5 and you will see that the average customer size calculation of 65,865.80 is correct.

But, you can also show only the Average Customer Size field and put another field in the column area. In Figure 10.11, PowerPivot is doing some pretty intense calculations for the 16 cells in the pivot table. Somehow, seminars in the Central region are seven times larger than seminars in the West region. That is an amazing statistic (see Figure 10.11).

10

Figure 10.10
Average customer size is
a calculation from two
other measures in the
pivot table.

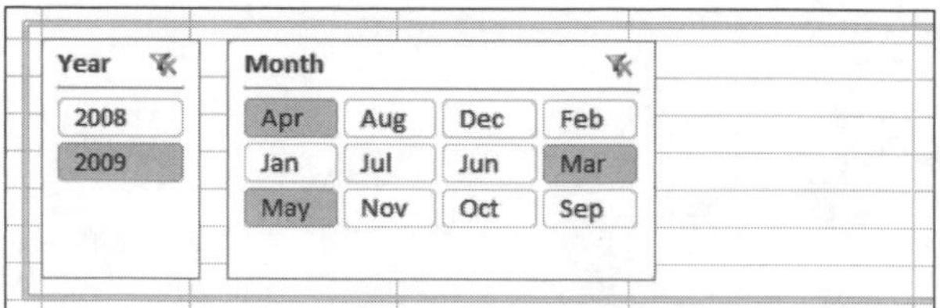

Figure 10.11
For each of the 16 cells
in the values area of the
pivot table, PowerPivot
is doing some intense
filtered calculations.

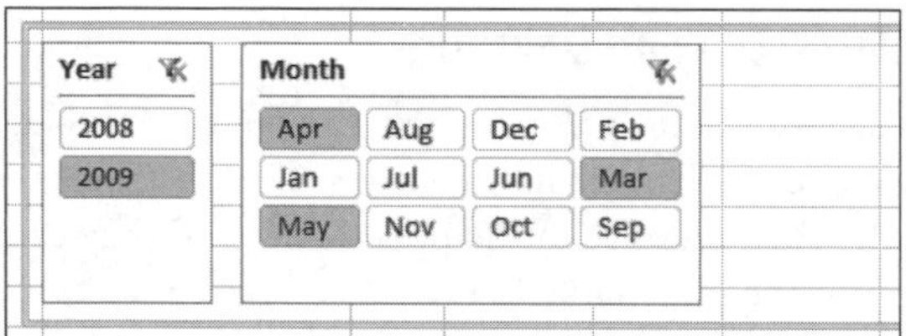

Using Other DAX Functions That Respect Filters

When you add a numeric field to the Values area in a PowerPivot pivot table, the
PowerPivot add-in will automatically generate a DAX measure that uses the SUM function.
Open the drop-down in the Values drop zone and select Summarize by to choose between
Average, Count, Max, Min, and Sum. PowerPivot will use one of these functions:

- AVERAGE(<column>) returns the average (arithmetic mean) of all the numbers in a
  column.

- COUNTA(<column>) counts the number of cells in a column that are not empty.

- MAX(<column>) returns the largest numeric value in a column.

- MIN(<column>) returns the smallest numeric value in a column. Ignores logical values
  and text.

- SUM(<column>) adds all the numbers in a column.

All five of those functions take a table column as an argument. All of them respect the other
filters that are in place on the result cell being calculated.

The AVERAGE, MAX, MIN, and SUM functions operate only on the numeric cells. COUNTA includes all text cells and logical cells.

There is a version of COUNT that only counts numbers:

COUNT(<column>) The COUNT function counts the number of cells in a column that contain numbers.

There is a version of COUNT that gets all of the blank records ignored by COUNTA:

COUNTBLANK(<column>) counts the number of blank cells in a column.

There are A versions of AVERAGE, MAX, and MIN, although they really only seem to work with logical values and not text values:

- AVERAGEA(<column>) returns the average (arithmetic mean) of the values in a column. Handles text and non-numeric values.

- MAXA(<column>) Returns the largest value in a column. Logical values and blanks are counted.

- MINA(<column>) returns the smallest value in a column, including any logical values and numbers represented as text.

In Figure 10.12, the AVERAGEA function is able to analyze a column of true/false data to find what percentage of the people answered true to each question. (True is calculated as 1, false as 0.)

Figure 10.12
The functions ending in A can deal with true/false values.

Row Labels	AverageAQ1	AverageAQ2	AverageAQ3	MinAQ1
Female	100%	20%	80%	1
Male	40%	50%	100%	0
Grand Total	70%	35%	90%	0

Respondent	Gender	Q1	Q2	Q3
R1	Female	TRUE	FALSE	TRUE
R2	Female	TRUE	FALSE	TRUE
R3	Male	FALSE	TRUE	TRUE
R4	Male	TRUE	FALSE	TRUE
R5	Male	FALSE	FALSE	TRUE
R6	Male	TRUE	FALSE	TRUE
R7	Male	FALSE	FALSE	TRUE
R8	Male	FALSE	TRUE	TRUE
R9	Male	FALSE	FALSE	TRUE
R10	Male	TRUE	TRUE	TRUE
R11	Male	TRUE	TRUE	TRUE
R12	Female	TRUE	FALSE	TRUE
R13	Male	FALSE	TRUE	TRUE
R14	Female	TRUE	FALSE	FALSE
R15	Female	TRUE	TRUE	TRUE
R16	Female	TRUE	TRUE	FALSE
R17	Female	TRUE	FALSE	TRUE
R18	Female	TRUE	FALSE	TRUE
R19	Female	TRUE	FALSE	TRUE
R20	Female	TRUE	FALSE	TRUE

10

It is a bit contrived, but you could use MINA and MAXA to see whether 100% of the respondents said true or false. In Figure 10.12, the 1 in cell F4 indicates that the minimum answer for Question 1 among female respondents was true.

Denominators Frequently Need to Ignore the Filters

It is great that by default a DAX function will respect the filters applied to the cell that is being calculated. This really simplifies the formulas that you create in DAX.

There is a class of calculations, though, where you don't want DAX to respect the filters. Suppose, for example, that you want to show this cell's sales divided by the total sales for all records.

This formula is a division formula:

> =Sales for This Cell / Sales for All Cells

The numerator of that expression is simple:

> =SUM(table[column])

By default, the SUM function will apply all the filters that are already applied to the cell in the pivot table.

To get the denominator, you need to use two new functions.

DAX Calculate Function Is Like the Excel SUMIFS Function

In Excel 2007, Microsoft introduced the plural conditional calculation functions of SUMIFS, COUNTIFS, and AVERAGEIFS. These functions could sum, count, or average a data set after applying several filters.

The CALCULATE function in DAX is similar, in that it can calculate an expression after applying several filters to the expression.

CALCULATE(<expression>,<filter1>,<filter2>...) evaluates an expression in a context that is modified by the specified filters.

This is a bit more powerful than the three Excel 2007 functions because you are not limited to SUM, COUNT, AVERAGE. The Expression could be MIN(table[column]) or any other expression that you might write.

Before you can finish the formula, let's talk about some filters.

Normally, applying a filter means that you end up with fewer rows.

Figure 10.13 shows a database of the fleet of vehicles in use at a small company. The total mileage reimbursement for the 22 records is $137,184.85

Say that you use the Filter drop-downs to find only the vehicles that are used by the Sales department. There are four records that total $49,084.75 (see Figure 10.14).

Figure 10.13
The total reimbursement for the whole database is $137,184.85.

Figure 10.14
The reimbursement for the sales department is $49,084.75.

In the pivot table in Figure 10.15, the DAX measure SUM(Fleet[Reimbursement]) for cell C6 does the exact same calculation shown in Figure 10.14 to get the $49,084.75.

Figure 10.15
When PowerPivot uses DAX to calculate cell C6, it is virtually performing the filter shown in Figure 10.14.

	Sum of Reimbursement	Pct of Reimbursement
Office	$26,680.50	19.4%
Repair	$61,419.60	44.8%
Sales	$49,084.75	35.8%
Grand Total	**$137,184.85**	**100.0%**

Think about how you would calculate the 35.8% shown over in cell D6. That is going to be the sum of reimbursement for the Sales department divided by the total of all sales for all departments.

Because the default state of DAX is to respect all the filters already applied to a cell, the DAX formula is going to be looking at only the four records that you can see in Figure 10.14. How the heck are you going to figure out the total of all the records when DAX has already virtually filtered the records to only Sales records?

To see a demo of a DAX Measure that uses different filters than the pivot table, search for MrExcel PowerPivot 10 at YouTube.

In DAX, a Filter Might Give You More Rows Than You Started With!

This concept caused my head to spin around.

In the SUMIFS function, you start with a big huge database and use the filters to narrow the rows down to a small subset of the rows.

With the CALCULATE function in DAX, we are unfortunately starting with a data set that has already been filtered down too far. The data set in Figure 10.14 has too few records for us to figure out the total reimbursement for all departments.

Normally a filter might say Color="red". In DAX, they support a wild kind of filter, as follows:

    ALL(Fleet)

When used as a filter, the ALL function tells DAX to temporarily unfilter the entire Fleet table in order to calculate the expression.

> **NOTE** I am really sorry to belabor this point. I think that I am still trying to completely wrap my head around this concept, and so while I am pretending to teach you about this concept, I am really trying to firm up my understanding. I think it will help you, too.

The formula to calculate the percentage of reimbursement is as follows:

    =SUM(Fleet[Reimbursement])/CALCULATE(SUM(Fleet[Reimbursement]),ALL(Fleet))

When that DAX measure is added to the pivot table shown in Figure 10.15, PowerPivot has to calculate four answers to populate cells D4:D7.

Here is the process for calculating cell D6, the value for the Sales department:

■ The first part of the formula says to sum the Reimbursement field. There is one filter that is inherently applied to all of row 6; the Dept field has to be Sales. So, the numerator of the calculation is the 49,084,75 shown in Figure 10.16.

Figure 10.16
The numerator of the calculation respects the filters inherent in row 6 of the pivot table, Dept=Sales.

	H24	▼		*fx*	=SUBTOTAL(109,Fleet[Reimbursement])		
	A	B	C	D	E	F	G	H
1	Name ▼	Make ▼	Type ▼	Color ▼	Dept ▼	Year ▼	Driven ▼	Reimbursement ▼
10	Jay	Ford	Car	White	Sales	2007	25468	$14,007.40
11	Kelly	GM	Car	Red	Sales	2008	21932	$12,062.60
17	Robin	Ford	Car	Red	Sales	2009	21083	$11,595.65
21	Wayne	Ford	Car	Silver	Sales	2010	20762	$11,419.10
24								$49,084.75

- The denominator of the DAX measure says to calculate the sum of reimbursement for a new filter. The filter says to select all records from the Fleet table.
- So, in the process of calculating the denominator of cell D6 in the pivot table, PowerPivot has to temporarily choose (Select All) from the filter drop-downs to calculate a total of $137,184.85.

The denominator calculation is going to look something like Figure 10.17.

Figure 10.17

The denominator of the calculation temporarily overrides the inherent filters with a filter of A11.

		f_x	=SUBTOTAL(109,Fleet[Reimbursement])		
D	E	F	G	H	
Color	Dept	Year	Driven	Reimbursement	
Copper	Office	2006	4607	$2,533.85	
Red	Office	2010	3364	$1,850.20	
Red	Office	2010	2412	$1,326.60	
Red	Office	2002	2733	$1,503.15	
Red	Office	2002	2458	$1,351.90	
Red	Office	2002	4367	$2,401.85	
Blue	Office	2001	4790	$2,634.50	
Blue	Office	2007	3336	$1,834.80	
White	Sales	2007	25468	$14,007.40	
Red	Sales	2008	21932	$12,062.60	
Red	Repair	2008	29437	$16,190.35	
Green	Office	2008	4354	$2,394.70	
Red	Office	2000	4870	$2,678.50	
Black	Office	2010	4260	$2,343.00	
Black	Office	2009	2647	$1,455.85	
Red	Sales	2009	21083	$11,595.65	
Black	Office	2001	2258	$1,241.90	
Yellow	Repair	2009	25434	$13,988.70	
Blue	Repair	2009	27196	$14,957.80	
Silver	Sales	2010	20762	$11,419.10	
Green	Repair	2009	29605	$16,282.75	
White	Office	2009	2054	$1,129.70	
				$137,184.85	

> **NOTE**
>
> Of course, Figures 10.16 and Figures 10.17 are a metaphor or an allegory of what PowerPivot is doing in memory. PowerPivot isn't actually using AutoFilter drop-downs and Excel functions to calculate the value.

ALL Function Says to Ignore All Existing Filters

In the first example, you had to calculate the percentage of a total. Thus, the filter portion of the CALCULATE function used the ALL function to temporarily ignore all filters already applied to the fleet table.

ALL(<table_or_column>) returns all the rows in a table, or all the values in a column, ignoring any filters that might have been applied.

Thanks for letting me explain the ALL function first. In real life, if you need to calculate the percentage of a total, you can use the Show Values As drop-down to select % of Total.

ALL is still a great way to demonstrate that the filter portion of the CALCULATE function might take a previously filtered data set and expand it to provide more rows than you started with.

CASE STUDY: SCENARIOS WHERE THE FILTER CHOOSES A DIFFERENT SET OF ROWS

I spent a few years at a company where the president of the company is a former sales guy. In his mind, the only activity worthwhile was the activity by the sales reps. I honestly think that he saw everyone else in the company as a drain on the sales team. I could imagine this guy going on a rant about the expenses being incurred by non-salespeople. He would ask to see the expenses of each department as a percentage of the expenses incurred by the Sales department. As I would head back to my desk to run the analysis, I knew that if the report revealed that any department was spending more than the Sales department that there would be an angry call from the president to the head of the offending department. In fact, when I handed the report to Ray, he would often dial the phone and start yelling at the department manager right there, right in front of me. I guess he considered it good entertainment for me.

In this case, the denominator needs to be all the rows in the data set that have a department of Sales.

In Figure 10.18, an intermediate result calculates the sales reimbursement for each row in the pivot table. Even though the department filter is limiting to only the office personnel in row 4, the explicit Dept=Sales filter overrides that and provides an answer of $49,084.75 for each row in the pivot table. This, of course, is the total value for the Sales department.

Figure 10.18
In this case, the filter in the CALCULATE formula is overriding the original formula and applying a different filter.

	Sum of Reimbursement	Pct of Reimbursement	Sales Reimbursement
Office	$26,680.50	19.4%	$49,084.75
Repair	$61,419.60	44.8%	$49,084.75
Sales	$49,084.75	35.8%	$49,084.75
Grand Total	$137,184.85	100.0%	$49,084.75

Measure Settings

Table name: Fleet

Measure Name (All PivotTables): Sales Reimbursement

Custom Name (This PivotTable): Sales Reimbursement

Formula: fx   Check formula

=Calculate(Sum(Fleet[Reimbursement]),Fleet[Dept]="Sales")

No errors in formula.

OK   Cancel

The same DAX formula will do something different if the pivot table changes. In Figure 10.18, the pivot table included a Dept field, so there was already a Dept filter applied to each row of the pivot table. In that case the Dept filter is overriding the filter in the pivot table.

Figure 10.19 shows the exact same calculation after changing the pivot table. In this figure, Dept is replaced in the Row Labels with Color. Cell C8 shows that the company paid $50,960.80 to reimburse red cars. In cell E8, the same formula as in Figure 10.18 is now further filtering the $50,960.80 to only cars used by the Sales department. Because this pivot table has no inherent filters for department, the FILTER clause of the calculation now applies a Dept filter and you end up with fewer rows.

Figure 10.19
Because this pivot table doesn't use the department field, the Dept filter becomes a limiting filter.

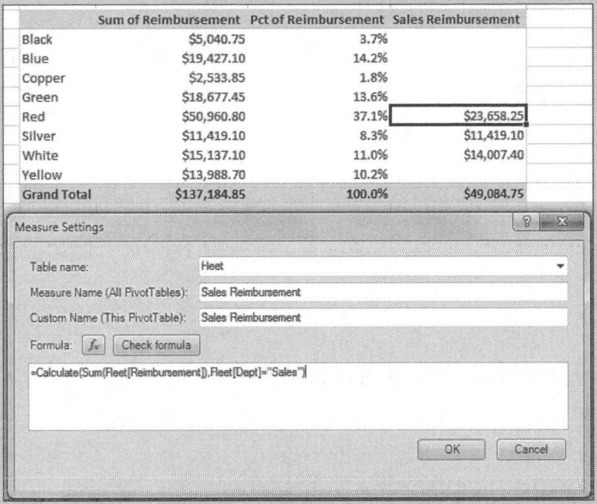

	Sum of Reimbursement	Pct of Reimbursement	Sales Reimbursement
Black	$5,040.75	3.7%	
Blue	$19,427.10	14.2%	
Copper	$2,533.85	1.8%	
Green	$18,677.45	13.6%	
Red	$50,960.80	37.1%	$23,658.25
Silver	$11,419.10	8.3%	$11,419.10
White	$15,137.10	11.0%	$14,007.40
Yellow	$13,988.70	10.2%	
Grand Total	$137,184.85	100.0%	$49,084.75

Measure Settings

Table name:	Fleet
Measure Name (All PivotTables):	Sales Reimbursement
Custom Name (This PivotTable):	Sales Reimbursement
Formula:	Check formula

=Calculate(Sum(Fleet[Reimbursement]),Fleet[Dept]="Sales")

OK   Cancel

Figure 10.20 attempts to conceptually show how C8 and E8 in the pivot table are calculated. First, the whole table is filtered to Color=Red. This leads to a total reimbursement calculation in H24 of $50,960.08.

Figure 10.20
The Calculate filter is now further filtering the results.

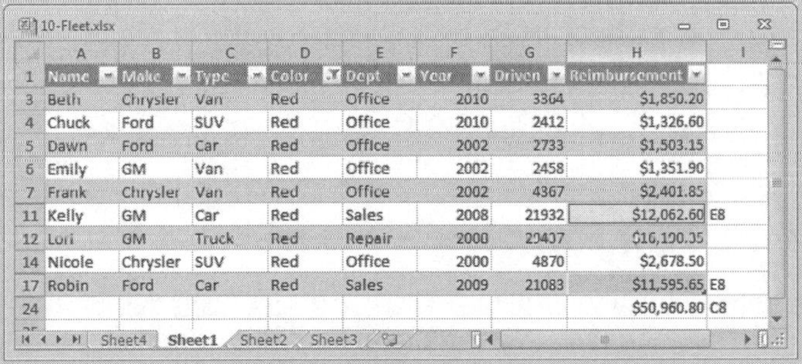

	A	B	C	D	E	F	G	H	I
1	Name	Make	Type	Color	Dept	Year	Driven	Reimbursement	
3	Beth	Chrysler	Van	Red	Office	2010	3364	$1,850.20	
4	Chuck	Ford	SUV	Red	Office	2010	2412	$1,326.60	
5	Dawn	Ford	Car	Red	Office	2002	2733	$1,503.15	
6	Emily	GM	Van	Red	Office	2002	2458	$1,351.90	
7	Frank	Chrysler	Van	Red	Office	2002	4367	$2,401.85	
11	Kelly	GM	Car	Red	Sales	2008	21932	$12,062.60	E8
12	Lori	GM	Truck	Red	Repair	2000	29437	$16,190.35	
14	Nicole	Chrysler	SUV	Red	Office	2000	4870	$2,678.50	
17	Robin	Ford	Car	Red	Sales	2009	21083	$11,595.65	E8
24								$50,960.80	C8

Sheet4 **Sheet1** Sheet2 Sheet3

The DAX CALCULATE function now applies an additional filter, further filtering the red cars to give you only the red cars used by the Sales department, leading to the total of cell H11 and H17.

To recap, the identical formula is as follows:

- Replacing a filter in Figure 10.18 because the pivot table includes the Department field as a filter
- Adding a new filter in Figure 10.20 because the pivot table does not include the Department field

To get back to the issue of calculating each department's expense as a percentage of what the Sales department spent, because of the intermediate formula in the Sales Reimbursement field, the new measure becomes a simple formula, as follows:

```
=Sum(Fleet[Reimbursement])/Fleet[Sales Reimbursement]
```

Figure 10.21 shows the calculation. The head of the Repair department is going to be getting a call demanding to know how it can be that his department is racking up 25% more miles than the Sales department.

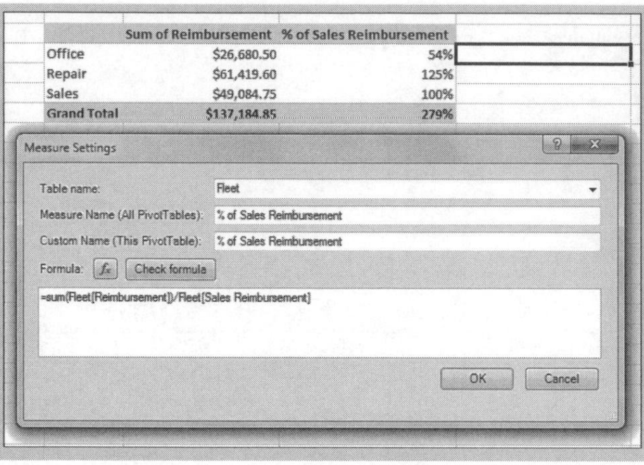

Figure 10.21
This % calculation uses an unusual denominator.

	Sum of Reimbursement	% of Sales Reimbursement
Office	$26,680.50	54%
Repair	$61,419.60	125%
Sales	$49,084.75	100%
Grand Total	$137,184.85	279%

Measure Settings

Table name: Fleet

Measure Name (All PivotTables):   % of Sales Reimbursement

Custom Name (This PivotTable):   % of Sales Reimbursement

Formula: *fx*   Check formula

=sum(Fleet[Reimbursement])/Fleet[Sales Reimbursement]

OK   Cancel

CALCULATE Is So Powerful, There Is a Shortcut

In the previous examples, the first parameter of the CALCULATE function was always Sum(Fleet[Reimbursement]).

If you define a measure such as Reimb as =Sum(Fleet[Reimbursement]), you can reuse that measure in future CALCULATE functions. Both of these become equivalent:

```
=Calculate(Sum(Fleet[Reimbursement]), All(Dept))
=Calculate([Reimb], All(Dept))
```

Although is the latter is shorter, it is not the real shortcut! In the second case above, you can use the measure name as if it were a function, listing the filters in parentheses:

```
=[Reimb](All(Dept))
```

Using the FILTER Function

The FILTER function will return a table that represents the subset of another table or function after applying both the context filters and additional filters.

FILTER is different from CALCULATE because the filters specified in the FILTER function do not overwrite the filters already in the context of the pivot table.

Figure 10.22 shows four examples of new DAX measures.

In Column C, the measure counts the unique number of colors in each department. There are six different colors in the Office department, four colors in the Repair department, and three colors in the Sales department. This measure is counting the unique number of colors, not the number of cars:

```
=COUNTROWS(Values(Fleet[Color]))
```

The VALUES function is similar to the DISTINCT function. It returns a table of unique values found in the current context. For cell C16, it returns a list of Black, Blue, Copper, Green, Red, White. The COUNTROWS counts how many colors there are.

Figure 10.22
Four DAX measures
show the FILTER and
VALUES functions.

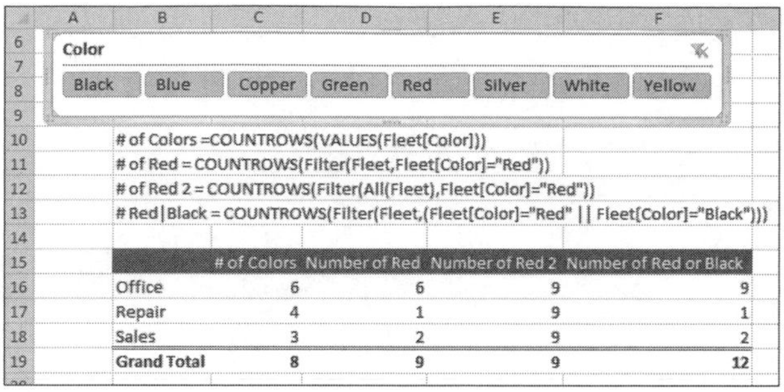

	# of Colors	Number of Red	Number of Red 2	Number of Red or Black
Office	6	6	9	9
Repair	4	1	9	1
Sales	3	2	9	2
Grand Total	8	9	9	12

# of Colors =COUNTROWS(VALUES(Fleet[Color]))
# of Red = COUNTROWS(Filter(Fleet,Fleet[Color]="Red"))
# of Red 2 = COUNTROWS(Filter(All(Fleet),Fleet[Color]="Red"))
Red | Black = COUNTROWS(Filter(Fleet,(Fleet[Color]="Red" || Fleet[Color]="Black")))

This would be easier to see if you add the Color as a row label, as shown in Figure 10.23. The six colors in the office are because there are six different colors. There are a total of 14 cars in the office, but only 6 unique colors.

Figure 10.23
After adding the Color
field, you can see how the
# of Colors is calculated.

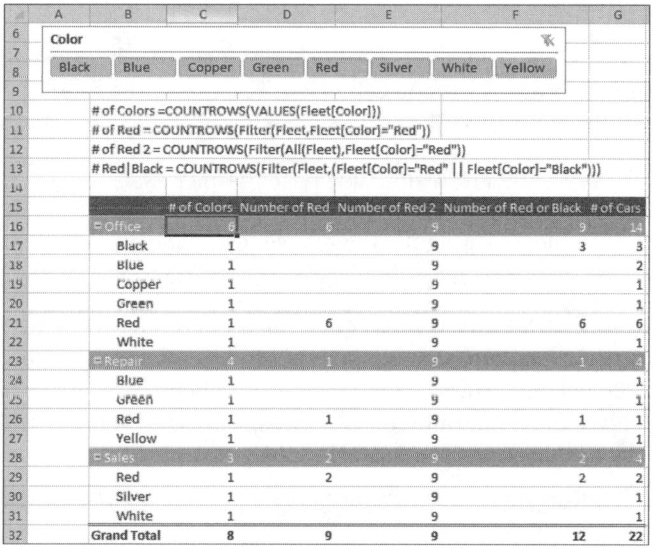

# of Colors =COUNTROWS(VALUES(Fleet[Color]))
# of Red = COUNTROWS(Filter(Fleet,Fleet[Color]="Red"))
# of Red 2 = COUNTROWS(Filter(All(Fleet),Fleet[Color]="Red"))
Red | Black = COUNTROWS(Filter(Fleet,(Fleet[Color]="Red" || Fleet[Color]="Black")))

	# of Colors	Number of Red	Number of Red 2	Number of Red or Black	# of Cars
Office	6	6	9	9	14
Black	1		9	3	3
Blue	1		9		2
Copper	1		9		1
Green	1		9		1
Red	1	6	9	6	6
White	1		9		1
Repair	4	1	9	1	4
Blue	1		9		1
Green	1		9		1
Red	1	1	9	1	1
Yellow	1		9		1
Sales	3	2	9	2	4
Red	1	2	9	2	2
Silver	1		9		1
White	1		9		1
Grand Total	8	9	9	12	22

The VALUES function respects the other filters in the context of the table. If you use the slicer to remove red and copper, the number of colors in the office is reduced to four (see Figure 10.24).

The FILTER function also returns a table.

FILTER(<table>,<filter>) returns a table that represents a subset of another table or expression.

Unlike VALUES, FILTER returns all the rows that match the filter.

The filter is additive to the existing filters in the context of the table.

In column D, the Number of Red measure uses the following:

```
=COUNTROWS(FILTER(Fleet,Fleet[Color]="Red"))
```

Figure 10.24
VALUES respects the filters applied to the pivot table.

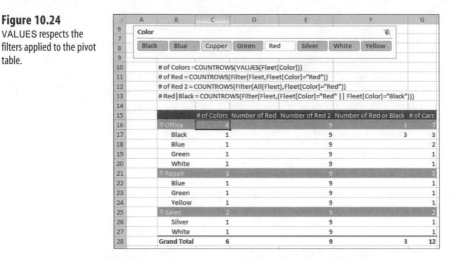

In cell D16, the number of red for the office is reported as six. This means that there are six red vehicles in the office. That 6 in cell D16 is respecting the filter of Dept=Office inherent for that cell in the pivot table. The Color=Red filter is additive to all existing filters.

If you want to ignore the pivot table filters, you have to use the ALL function on the Fleet table. The Number of Red 2 measure shows you the total number of red cars in the entire company for every single row, using the following:

```
=COUNTROWS(Filter(All(Fleet),Fleet[Color]="Red"))
```

Columns D and E operate very differently if the red color is removed from the slicer. Because the FILTER function respects the other filters applied to the pivot table, the Number of Red column returns empty values for the entire table. The Number of Red 2, because of the ALL function, still returns 9 for all rows (see Figure 10.25).

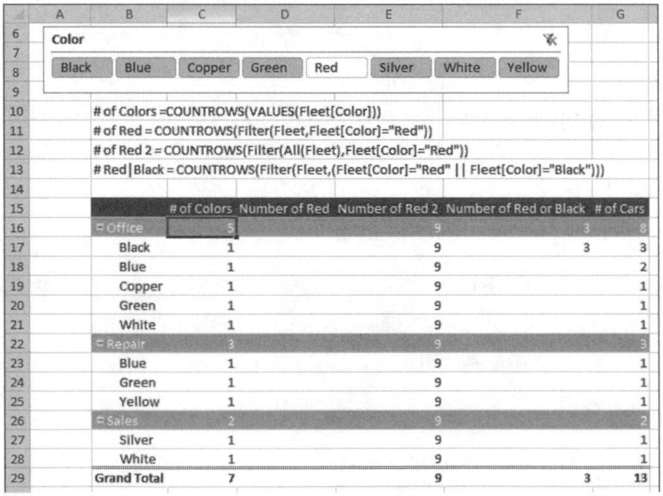

Figure 10.25
The ALL ( ) function in column E keeps reporting the total number of red cars, even if red is removed from the slicer.

Column F in these figures uses the double-pipe operator to filter to cars that are either red or black:

```
=COUNTROWS(Filter(Fleet,(Fleet[Color]="Red" ¦¦ Fleet[Color]="Black")))
```

The Double Negative of `AllExcept`

In the preceding example, one question that might come up is how many red cars are in each department.

When you used `ALL(Fleet)`, the calculation could tell you how many red cars are in the whole company, but not how many red cars are in a particular department.

The `ALL` function overrides all context filters.

The `ALLEXCEPT(<table>,column1>,<column2>,...)` function overrides all context filters in the table except filters that have been applied to the specified columns.

If that seems tough to understand, it is a double or triple negative.

■ By default, a DAX measure will respect all context filters and remove those rows from the table before performing the calculation.

■ The ALL function tells the DAX measure to ignore all context filters and to put those filtered rows back into the data set.

■ `AllExcept` says to ignore all context filters except for specific filters. Any filters applied to columns listed in the `AllExcept` function get reapplied to the table.

Figure 10.26 might make this a bit clearer.

Figure 10.26
Examples of
AllExcept.

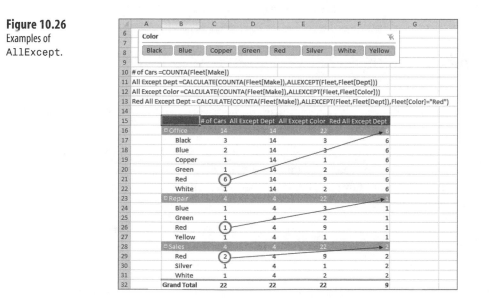

Per cell C16, there are 14 cars in the Office department.

Per cell C17, there are three black cars in the Office department. That cell has context filters of `Dept=Office` and `Color=Black`.

In column D, the formula uses `AllExcept Dept`. In cell D17, the count of cars ignores the `Color` filter, but respects the `Dept` filter. There are 14 totals cars in the Office department.

```
=CALCULATE(COUNTA(Fleet[Make]),ALLEXCEPT(Fleet,Fleet[Dept]))
```

In column E, the formula uses `AllExcept Color`. In cell E21, the 9 means that there are nine red cars in the entire company. The calculation is respecting the `Color=Red` filter, but ignoring the `Dept=Office` filter.

```
=CALCULATE(COUNTA(Fleet[Make]),ALLEXCEPT(Fleet,Fleet[Color]))
```

In Column F, two filters are passed to the `CALCULATE` function. The first filter says to use `AllExcept Dept`. The second filter says to override the color filter with a filter of `Color=Red`. This returns six red cars for all of the Office rows, one red car for all of the Repair rows, and two red cars for all of the Sales rows:

```
=CALCULATE(COUNTA(Fleet[Make]),ALLEXCEPT(Fleet,Fleet[Dept]),Fleet[Color]=
"Red")
```

In Figure 10.26, three arrows show where the Red All Except Dept value comes from.

> **CAUTION**
>
> I am still not comfortable with `ALLEXCEPT`. If someone later adds new slicers to your pivot table, your `ALLEXCEPT` is now going to start ignoring those slicers, which is going to lead to some unexpected results in the pivot table. Now, if you know that you won't be adding more slicers to the pivot table, `ALLEXCEPT` is fine. This is just one of those things that someone is going to forget about 6 months from now, add a slicer, and things will look wrong.

Other DAX Functions

There are a few other DAX functions.

`ALLNONBLANKROW(<table_or_column>)` returns all the rows, except for blank rows, in a table or column, and disregards any context filters that might exist.

If you have a table that has empty cells, or a calculated table that returns the `BLANK()` function in some cells, you can count the total of the nonblank values in a column using this function. Be very careful, however, because as the description says, the function ignores all context filters.

`FIRSTNONBLANK(<column>,<expression>)` returns the first nonblank values in column, filtered by expression. This returns a column of values, but the column generally only contains a single value.

→ The time intelligence functions are covered in Chapter 11, "Using DAX for Date Magic."

Table 10.1 summarizes in alphabetic order the DAX measure functions covered in this chapter.

Table 10.1   Summary of DAX Measure Functions

Function	Description
ALL(<table_or_column>)	Returns all the rows in a table, or all the values in a column, ignoring any filters that might have been applied.
ALLEXCEPT(<table>,column1>, <column2>,...)	Overrides all context filters in the table except filters that have been applied to the specified columns.
ALLNONBLANKROW(<table_or_column>)	Returns all the rows, except for blank rows, in a table or column, and disregards any context filters that might exist.
AVERAGE(<column>)	Returns the average (arithmetic mean) of all the numbers in a column.
AVERAGEA(<column>)	Returns the average (arithmetic mean) of the values in a column. Handles text and non-numeric values.
CALCULATE(<expression>, <filter1>,<filter2>...)	Evaluates an expression in a context that is modified by the specified filters.
COUNT(<column>)	The COUNT function counts the number of cells in a column that contain numbers.
COUNTA(<column>)	The COUNTA function counts the number of cells in a column that are not empty.
COUNTBLANK(<column>)	Counts the number of blank cells in a column.
COUNTROWS(<table>)	The COUNTROWS function counts the number of rows in the specified table, or in a table defined by an expression.
DISTINCT(<column>)	Returns a one-column table that contains the distinct values from the specified column.
FILTER(<table>,<filter>)	Returns a table that represents a subset of another table or expression.
FIRSTNONBLANK(<column>, <expression>)	Returns the first nonblank values in column, filtered by expression.
MAX(<column>)	Returns the largest numeric value in a column.
MAXA(<column>)	Returns the largest value in a column. Logical values and blanks are counted.
MIN(<column>)	Returns the smallest numeric value in a column. Ignores logical values and text.
MINA(<column>)	Returns the smallest value in a column, including any logical values and numbers represented as text.
SUM(<column>)	Adds all the numbers in a column.
VALUES(<column>)	Returns a one-column table that contains the distinct values from the specified column. This function is similar to DISTINCT function, but VALUES function can also return Unknown member.

10

Next Steps

In the next chapter, you will learn how to use the time intelligence functions when calculating DAX measures.Case studies are set off in boxes such as this one:

Case studies walk you through the steps to complete a task.

Using DAX for Date Magic

11

Be honest. Did you really read Chapter 10, "Using DAX for Aggregate Functions," or did you skip it?

If you skipped it, let me offer a recap for you:

```
=CALCULATE(Sum(Sls[Sales]), Filter 1, Filter
2, ...)
```

This calculated field will calculate the total sales for all rows that match the filters specified. If one of the filters specified in the CALCULATE function is for a dimension already in the pivot table, the filter in CALCULATE will override the filter in the pivot table.

Most of the time intelligence functions are designed to be used as the filter in the CALCULATE function.

Figure 11.1 will give you a taste of what is possible using CALCULATE in conjunction with a time intelligence function in the filter.

Figure 11.1 has daily dates in the row labels field. In row 785, you have the date for March 26, 2008.

The DATESMTD(Sls[Date]) function will return a table of dates from March 1, 2008 through March 26, 2008.

The CALCULATE function overrides the dates used to calculate the pivot table. So, cell C785 is not a total of just March 26, 2008, but a total of all of the dates from March 1 through March 26, 2008.

Figure 11.1
Column B is a regular column. Everything else is a DAX measure using time intelligence.

	A	B	C	D	E	F	G	H	I
1	Date	Sum of Sales	MTD Sales	QTD Sales	YTDSales	EndOfMonth	Sales This Day Last Year	Sales This Weekday Last Year	FullMonthSales
785	3/26/2008	$3,405	$115,599	$298,018	$685,017	3/31/2008	3717	3551	137598
786	3/27/2008	$5,045	$120,644	$303,063	$690,062	3/31/2008	3568	2711	137598
787	3/28/2008	$4,047	$124,691	$307,110	$694,109	3/31/2008	3551	3053	137598
788	3/29/2008	$4,475	$129,166	$311,585	$698,584	3/31/2008	2711	5307	137598
789	3/30/2008	$5,170	$134,336	$316,755	$703,754	3/31/2008	3053	5085	137598
790	3/31/2008	$3,262	$137,598	$320,017	$707,016	3/31/2008	5307	3735	137598
791	4/1/2008	$3,276	$3,276	$3,276	$710,292	4/30/2008	5085		97773
792	4/2/2008	$3,608	$6,884	$6,884	$713,900	4/30/2008	3735	1996	97773
793	4/3/2008	$4,562	$11,446	$11,446	$718,462	4/30/2008		4049	97773
794	4/4/2008	$4,290	$15,736	$15,736	$722,752	4/30/2008	1996	4188	97773
795	4/5/2008	$4,028	$19,764	$19,764	$726,780	4/30/2008	4049	4313	97773
796	4/6/2008	$3,209	$22,973	$22,973	$729,989	4/30/2008	4188	4184	97773
797	4/7/2008	$3,417	$26,390	$26,390	$733,406	4/30/2008	4313	2476	97773
798	4/8/2008	$3,141	$29,531	$29,531	$736,547	4/30/2008	4184	1899	97773

Using Time Intelligence Functions

Table 11.1 provides an alphabetic list of the 35 time intelligence functions.

Table 11.1 Summary of Time Intelligence Functions in DAX	
Function	**Description**
CLOSINGBALANCEMONTH(<expression>, <dates>,<filter>)	Evaluates the specified expression at the calendar end of the given month. The given month is calculated as the month of the latest date in the dates argument, after applying all filters.
CLOSINGBALANCEQUARTER(<expression>, <dates>,<filter>)	Evaluates the specified expression at the calendar end of the given quarter. The given quarter is calculated as the quarter of the latest date in the dates argument, after applying all filters.
CLOSINGBALANCEYEAR(<expression>, <dates>,<filter>)	Evaluates the specified expression at the calendar end of the given year. The given year is calculated as the year of the latest date in the dates argument, after applying all filters.
DATEADD(<date_column>, <number_of_intervals>,<interval>)	Returns a table that contains a column of dates, shifted either forward in time or back in time from the dates in the specified date column.
DATESBETWEEN(<column>, <start_date>,<end_date>	Returns a table of dates that can be found in the specified date column beginning with the start date and ending with the end date.
DATESINPERIOD(<date_column>, <start_date>,<number_of_intervals>, <intervals>)	Returns a table of dates that can be found in the specified date column beginning with the start date and continuing for the specified number of intervals.
DATESMTD(<date_column>)	Returns the subset of dates, from date_column, for the interval that starts at the first day of the month and ends at the latest date in the specified dates column for the month that is the corresponding month of the latest date.
DATESQTD (<date_column>)	Returns the subset of dates, from date_column, for the interval that starts at the first day of the quarter and ends at the latest date in the specified dates column for the quarter that is the corresponding quarter of the latest date.

Function	Description
DATESYTD (<date_column> [,<YE_date>])	Returns the subset of dates, from date_column, for the interval that starts the first day of the year and ends at the latest date in the specified dates column for the quarter that is the corresponding quarter of the latest date.
ENDOFMONTH(<date_column>)	Returns the last day of the month in the specified date column.
ENDOFQUARTER(<date_column>)	Returns the last day of the quarter in the specified date column.
ENDOFYEAR(<date_column>,<YE_Date>)	Returns the last day of the year in the specified date column.
FIRSTDATE (<date_column>)	Returns the first date in the current context for the specified date_column.
FIRSTNONBLANK (<date_column> <Expression>)	Returns the first date in the current context for the specified date_column. When the optional argument, expression, is supplied, the function returns the last date where the conditions in the expression return a non-blank value.
LASTDATE (<date_column>)	Returns the last date in the current context for the specified date_column.
LASTNONBLANK (<date_column>,<expression>)	Returns the last date in the current context for the specified date_column. When the optional argument, expression, is supplied, the function returns the last date where the conditions in the expression return a non-blank value.
NEXTDAY(<date_column>)	Returns the next day date from date_column.
NEXTMONTH(<date_column>)	Returns the set of dates in the next month from date_column.
NEXTQUARTER (<date_column>)	Returns the set of dates for the next quarter from date_column.
NEXTYEAR(<date_column>[,<YE_date>])	Returns the set of dates for the next year from date_column.
OPENINGBALANCEMONTH(<expression>, <dates>,<filter>)	Evaluates the specified expression at the calendar end of the month prior the given month. The given month is calculated as the month of the latest date in the dates argument, after applying all filters.
OPENINGBALANCEQUARTER(<expression>, <dates>,<filter>)	Evaluates the specified expression at the calendar end of the quarter prior to the given quarter. The given quarter is calculated as the quarter of the latest date in the dates argument, after applying all filters.
OPENINGBALANCEYEAR(<expression>, <dates>,<filter>)	Evaluates the specified expression at the calendar end of the year prior to the given year. The given year is calculated as the year of the latest date in the dates argument, after applying all filters.

11

continues

Table 11.1	Continued

Function	Description
PARALLELPERIOD(<date_column>, <number_of_intervals>,<intervals>)	This function moves the specified number of intervals and then returns all contiguous full months which contain any values after that shift. Gaps between the first and last dates are filled in, and months are also filled in.
PREVIOUSDAY(<date_column>)	Returns the previous day date from date_column.
PREVIOUSMONTH(<date_column>)	Returns the set of dates in the previous month from date_column.
PREVIOUSQUARTER(<date_column>)	Returns the set of dates in the previous quarter from date_column.
PREVIOUSYEAR(<date_column>[, <YE_Date>])	Returns the set of dates in the previous year from date_column.
SAMEPERIODLASTYEAR(<date column>)	Returns the date from 1 year ago.
STARTOFMONTH (<date_column>)	Returns the first day of the month in the specified date column.
STARTOFQUARTER (<date_column>)	Returns the first day of the quarter in the specified date column.
STARTOFYEAR(<date_column>[, <YE_date>])	Returns the first day of the year in the specified date column.
TotalMTD(<expression>,<dates>, <filter>)	Evaluates the specified expression for the interval that starts at the first day of the month and ends at the latest date in the specified dates column, after applying all filters.
TotalQTD(<expression>,<dates>, <filter>)	Evaluates the specified expression for the interval that starts at the first day of the quarter and ends at the latest date in the specified dates column, after applying all filters.
TotalYTD(<expression>,<dates>, <filter>)	Evaluates the specified expression for the interval that starts at the first day of the year and ends at the latest date in the specified dates column, after applying all filters.

Fiscal Quarters and Calendar Quarters

Microsoft did the brilliant move of allowing DAX to calculate dates for fiscal years that end on dates other than December 31. If your fiscal year ends on January 31, you could specify a value of 1/31 for the optional <YE_Date> argument in some of the date functions.

However, they must have thought that those fiscal years would be ending on March 31, June 30, or September 30.

When they implemented logic for quarters, they did not allow you to specify a year ending date. This means that the quarter ending date for January 23 will always be March 31.

The most popular fiscal-year ending date is December 31. But the second most popular date is January 31. This means that you have a way to report on fiscal years, but not fiscal quarters. I sent a note to the PowerPivot team documenting this oversight on February 9, 2010. I am hoping that there is time that they can change it by the time this book is in your hands.

Using Period-to-Date Calculations

The previous figure showed how to calculate month-to-date sales:

```
=CALCULATE(Sum(Sls[Sales]),DATESMTD(Sls[Date]))
```

A similar function will calculate calendar quarter-to-date sales:

```
=CALCULATE(Sum(Sls[Sales]),DATESQTD(Sls[Date]))
```

When you calculate dates in year-to-date, you can specify an optional year-ending date. The screen shot shows a calculation assuming a June 30 fiscal year end:

```
=CALCULATE(Sum(Sls[Sales]),DATESYTD(Sls[Date],"6/30"))
```

Comparing Today's Sales to Yesterday

To find sales for the day before the date in the pivot table, use the following:

```
=CALCULATE(Sum(Sls[Sales]),PREVIOUSDAY(Sls[Date]))
```

To find the sales for the day after the date in the pivot table, use this:

```
=CALCULATE(Sum(Sls[Sales]),NEXTDAY(Sls[Date]))
```

Comparing Today's Sales to One Year Ago

If the current row of the pivot table contains sales for a single day, this function will return the sales for the same day 1 year ago:

```
=CALCULATE(Sum(Sls[Sales]),SAMEPERIODLASTYEAR(Sls[Date]))
```

Say that you have 3 years of daily dates. The SamePeriodLastYear calculation for the 365 days will return a blank because there is not history for that date.

Leap years are somewhat handled. If you ask for sales from one year ago from February 29, 2008, the report will give you sales for February 28, 2007. This means that the sales from February 28, 2007 will be repeated twice, showing as the previous year sales for both February 28 and 29, 2008 (see Figure 11.2).

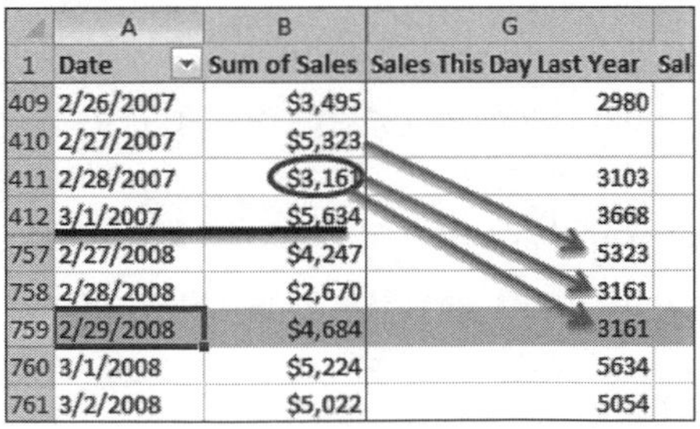

Figure 11.2
PowerPivot attempts to be intelligent about leap years.

	A	B	G	
1	Date	Sum of Sales	Sales This Day Last Year	Sal
409	2/26/2007	$3,495	2980	
410	2/27/2007	$5,323		
411	2/28/2007	$3,16	3103	
412	3/1/2007	$5,634	3668	
757	2/27/2008	$4,247	5323	
758	2/28/2008	$2,670	3161	
759	2/29/2008	$4,684	3161	
760	3/1/2008	$5,224	5634	
761	3/2/2008	$5,022	5054	

Here is the bigger problem with this calculation. If today is a Friday, 1 year ago is a Thursday. (It might be a Wednesday if last year was a leap year and it is March or later). If you are a retail business where sales follow a cyclical weekday pattern, comparing sales on a Friday to sales on a Thursday is pointless.

A better solution is to look at sales from 364 days ago. This will ensure that you are always comparing Friday to Friday. The DateAdd function will calculate a date that is 364 days ago:

```
=CALCULATE(Sum(Sls[Sales]),DateAdd(Sls[Date],-364,day))
```

> **NOTE** Note that the final argument in DateAdd is day,month,quarter,or year.

 To see a demo of calculating sales from 364 days ago, search for MrExcel PowerPivot 11 at YouTube.

Reporting Sales for the Full Month

The function to report sales for a full month is a little bit harder because you have to use three new functions.

```
=DatesBetween(<date column>,<start date>,<end date>)
```

This function returns all the daily dates between a start date and an end date.

To calculate the beginning of the month, use the following:

```
StartOfMonth(Sls[Date])
```

To calculate the end of the month, use this:

```
EndOfMonth(Sls[Date])
```

Therefore, to calculate all sales for the full month, use the following:

```
CALCULATE(Sum(Sls[Sales]),DatesBetween(Sls[Date],StartOfMonth(Sls[Date]),
EndOfMonth(Sls[Date])))
```

To calculate sales for the full quarter, use this:

```
CALCULATE(Sum(Sls[Sales]),DatesBetween(Sls[Date],StartOfQuarter(Sls[Date]),
EndOfQuarter(Sls[Date])))
```

To calculate sales for a full calendar year, use the following:

```
CALCULATE(Sum(Sls[Sales]),DatesBetween(Sls[Date],StartOfYear(Sls[Date]),
EndOfYear(Sls[Date])))
```

To calculate sales for a full fiscal year that ends on January 31, use this:

```
CALCULATE(Sum(Sls[Sales]),DatesBetween(Sls[Date],StartOfYear(Sls
[Date],"1/31"),
EndOfYear(Sls[Date],"1/31")))
```

Calculating Sales for the Previous or Next Month, Quarter, Year

To find sales for the previous month, use this:

```
=CALCULATE(Sum(Sls[Sales]),PreviousMonth(Sls[Date]))
```

If the date for this row in the pivot table contains May 5, 2011, the `PreviousMonth` will return the dates of April 1 through April 30.

To find sales for the next month, use the following:

```
=CALCULATE(Sum(Sls[Sales]),NextMonth(Sls[Date]))
```

Similar functions are available for the previous and next quarter:

```
=CALCULATE(Sum(Sls[Sales]),PreviousQuarter(Sls[Date]))
=CALCULATE(Sum(Sls[Sales]),NextQuarter(Sls[Date]))
```

To get sales for the entire previous calendar year, use this:

```
=CALCULATE(Sum(Sls[Sales]),PreviousYear(Sls[Date]))
=CALCULATE(Sum(Sls[Sales]),NextYear(Sls[Date]))
```

To get sales for the previous or next fiscal year, use the following:

```
=CALCULATE(Sum(Sls[Sales]),PreviousYear(Sls[Date],"1/31"))
=CALCULATE(Sum(Sls[Sales]),NextYear(Sls[Date] ,"1/31"))
```

Sales for the Last 30 Days

The `DatesInPeriod` function will go from a start date and extend some number of periods. This function is incredibly versatile:

```
DATESINPERIOD(<date_column>,<start_date>,<number_of_intervals>,<intervals>)
```

Suppose you have a pivot table with daily dates running down the first column.

The `date_column` would be `Sls[Date]`.

The `start_date` would be `FirstDate(Sls[Date])`.

The number of intervals would be `-30`.

The interval would be `day` without the quotes.

This will refer to a 30-day period ending on the current day.

You could use this to show running 30-day periods.

One problem is that the first 29 days in the data set will not be reporting full 30-day periods.

The full formula is as follows:

```
=CALCULATE(Sum(Sls[Sales]),DatesInPeriod(Sls[Date]),-30,Day)
```

Other valid values for interval are `month`, `quarter`, `year`.

Using Date Functions for Data Reported at a Monthly Level

In Figure 11.3, the daily dates have been rolled up to months through a calculated column in the PowerPivot window:

```
=Format([Date],"YYYY-MM")
```

Figure 11.3
LastDate and
FirstDate can return
dates that you can use in
the DatesBetween
function.

	A	B	C	D
1		Sum of Sales	PeriodStart	PeriodEnd
24	2007-11	$76,328	11/1/2007	11/30/2007
25	2007-12	$77,275	12/1/2007	12/31/2007
26	2008-01	$82,155	1/1/2008	1/31/2008
27	2008-02	$100,264	2/1/2008	2/29/2008
28	2008-03	$137,598	3/1/2008	3/31/2008
29	2008-04	$97,773	4/1/2008	4/30/2008
30	2008-05	$73,737	5/1/2008	5/31/2008
31	2008-06	$49,954	6/1/2008	6/30/2008
32	2008-07	$53,995	7/1/2008	7/31/2008
33	2008-08	$43,202	8/1/2008	8/31/2008
34	2008-09	$40,514	9/1/2008	9/30/2008
35	2008-10	$65,112	10/1/2008	10/31/2008
36	2008-11	$74,739	11/1/2008	11/30/2008
37	2008-12	$72,959	12/1/2008	12/30/2008
38	Grand Total	$2,790,407	1/1/2006	12/30/2008

The resulting pivot table reports 1 month at a time. If you need to find the first and last day of each period, use the following:

```
=FirstDate(Sls[Date])
=LastDate(Sls[Date])
```

Use Care with ParallelPeriod

For some reason, ParallelPeriod does not overwrite the date filter. This one function is acting as if it is additive to the existing date filter in the pivot table. That never works out well.

Say that you have January 2011 in the pivot table. You try to calculate ParallelPeriod(Sls[Date],-12,Months). That returns all the dates in January 2010.

Because the filter is additive, you are looking for all sales that happened to fall in January 2010 and also at the same time to fall in January 2011. That results in an empty set.

> **NOTE** One person in the blogosphere claims that this is a pre-release bug and that it will be fixed in the final product. Give it a try.

If your calculation returns an empty set

```
=CALCULATE(Sum(Sls[Sales]),ParallelPeriod(Sls[Date],-12,Months))
```

Then modify the calculation by adding All(Sls) as an additional filter:

```
=CALCULATE(Sum(Sls[Sales]),ParallelPeriod(Sls[Date],-12,Months),All(Sls))
```

> ┌ **CAUTION** ───
> Unfortunately, this modification will cause your calculation to ignore all filters in the pivot table.

Opening and Closing Balances

These six functions can be somewhat helpful for reporting accounts receivable balances and the like:

- =OpeningBalanceMonth() will look at the date and return a value from the end of the previous month. If you are reporting on A/R balances for March 2011, this calculation will show you the A/R balance from February 28, 2011:

  ```
  =OpeningBalanceMonth(sum(AR[ARBalance]),AR[Date])
  ```

- The ClosingBalanceMonth would return the balance for the last day of the month:

  ```
  =ClosingBalanceMonth(sum(AR[ARBalance]),AR[Date])
  ```

- Similar functions return the balance from the beginning or end of the quarter or year:

  ```
  =OpeningBalanceQuarter(sum(AR[ARBalance]),AR[Date])
  =OpeningBalanceYear(sum(AR[ARBalance]),AR[Date])
  =ClosingBalanceQuarter(sum(AR[ARBalance]),AR[Date])
  =ClosingBalanceYear(sum(AR[ARBalance]),AR[Date])
  ```

Skip the CALCULATE Function in Three Cases

Almost all the time intelligence functions are returning a series of dates that are then passed as a filter to the CALCULATE function.

For some reason, three functions do not require you to use the CALCULATE function:

- =TotalMTD(Sls[Sales],Sls[Date])
- =TotalQTD(Sls[Sales],Sls[Date])
- =TotalYTD(Sls[Sales],Sls[Date])

These three functions are easier to use than CALCULATE, but strangely, the YTD function supports only calendar years and not fiscal years.

As with CALCULATE, you can specify additional filters after the date column.

Next Steps

In the next chapter, you will learn three advanced concepts: named sets, cube functions, and GetPivotData.

Named Sets, GetPivotData, and Cube Formulas

12

These techniques are not unique to PowerPivot.

For people who usually use regular PivotCache pivot tables, you will be encountering named sets and cube formulas for the first time.

GetPivotData is a function that is mostly reviled, but it has a very cool use that is documented in the "Preserving Report Formatting Using GetPivotData" section of this chapter.

Defining Territories with Named Sets

Suppose that you are responsible for 20 stores in 1 region of the country. Your IT department provides a database that contains data for all 150 stores in the chain.

There is no field in the table to define which 20 stores are your stores.

As you can imagine, it would be a pain to repeatedly go through the filter, unselect All, and then reselect the 20 stores that you are responsible for.

A named set is a new feature in Excel 2010 online analytical processing (OLAP) pivot tables. You can define a named set once and reuse it each month after importing new data to your table.

Figure 12.1 shows a report with all 150 stores.

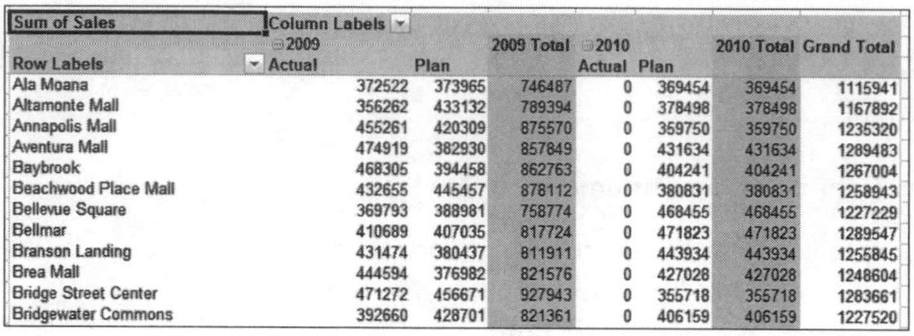

Figure 12.1
You repeatedly have to filter out your 20 stores.

Sum of Sales	Column Labels							
	2009			2009 Total	2010		2010 Total	Grand Total
Row Labels	Actual		Plan		Actual	Plan		
Ala Moana	372522	373965		746487	0	369454	369454	1115941
Altamonte Mall	356262	433132		789394	0	378498	378498	1167892
Annapolis Mall	455261	420309		875570	0	359750	359750	1235320
Aventura Mall	474919	382930		857849	0	431634	431634	1289483
Baybrook	468305	394458		862763	0	404241	404241	1267004
Beachwood Place Mall	432655	445457		878112	0	380831	380831	1258943
Bellevue Square	369793	388981		758774	0	468455	468455	1227229
Bellmar	410689	407035		817724	0	471823	471823	1289547
Branson Landing	431474	380437		811911	0	443934	443934	1255845
Brea Mall	444594	376982		821576	0	427028	427028	1248604
Bridge Street Center	471272	456671		927943	0	355718	355718	1283661
Bridgewater Commons	392660	428701		821361	0	406159	406159	1227520

To define a named set of your stores, follow these steps:

1. Select one cell inside the pivot table so that the PivotTable Tools tabs appear.
2. On the Options tab, open the new Fields, Items, and Sets drop-down.
3. Select Create Set Based on Row Items (see Figure 12.2).

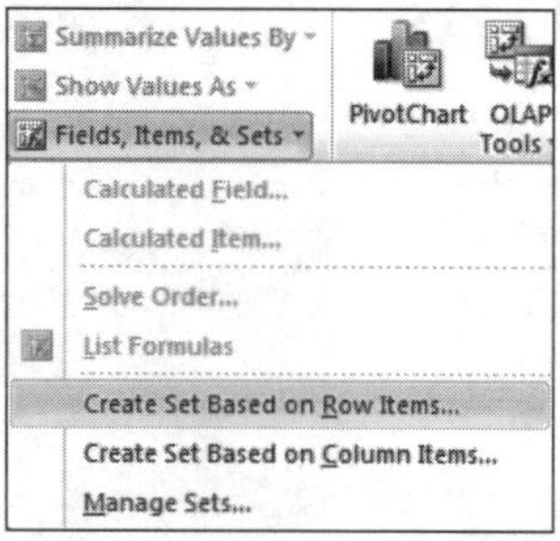

Figure 12.2
Named sets are new in Excel 2010 and valid only for OLAP or PowerPivot databases.

4. Type a name for your set in the New Set dialog, something along the lines of TexasStores or Texas Stores or My Stores.
5. All 150 rows are presented in the dialog. The first row is selected, as shown in Figure 12.3. If that store is not one of your stores, click the Delete button.

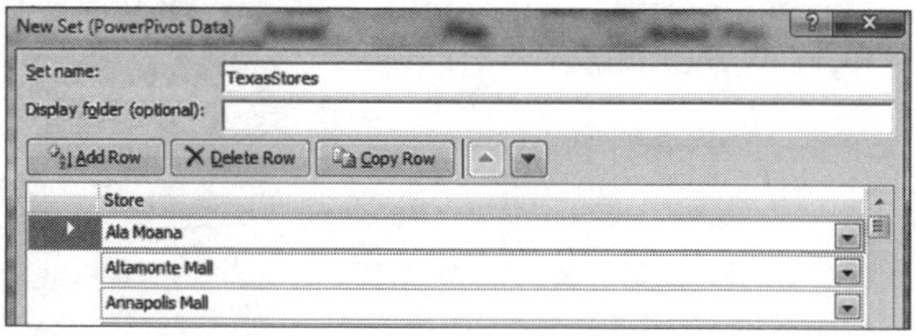

Figure 12.3
Select a store and click Delete.

6. Continue deleting stores. This is a quick process as focus moves to the next store after you delete a store. When you get to a store that you want to keep, use the mouse to click the next store.

T I P You will inevitably click Delete one too many times and delete a store that you wanted to keep. Click Add Row, and then use the drop-down in that row to bring your store back.

7. The last item in the list is All. Keep this, as it is the grand total.

N O T E When you have finished deleting stores, you might find that the stores are in the wrong sequence. In Figure 12.4, three stores have "The" in their name, which causes them to be alphabetically in the wrong place.

Because there is a city whose name is actually "The Woodlands," then maybe "The Woodlands Mall" really belongs in the T's instead of the W's.

8. Choose a store and click the up- or down-arrow buttons to reorder the list.

Figure 12.4
Use the up and down arrows to reorder an item.

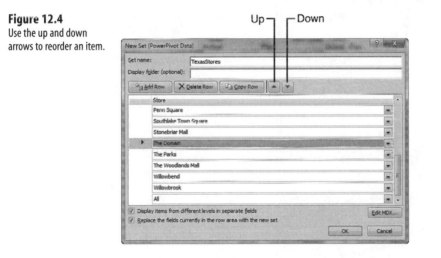

9. Figure 12.5 shows the final list of stores. Click OK to create the set.

Interesting things happen in your PowerPivot Field List. There is a new field called TexasStores. The TexasStores field has automatically replaced the Stores field in the Row Labels area (see Figure 12.6).

12

Figure 12.5
When the set is in the proper order, click OK.

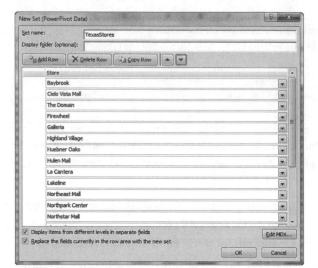

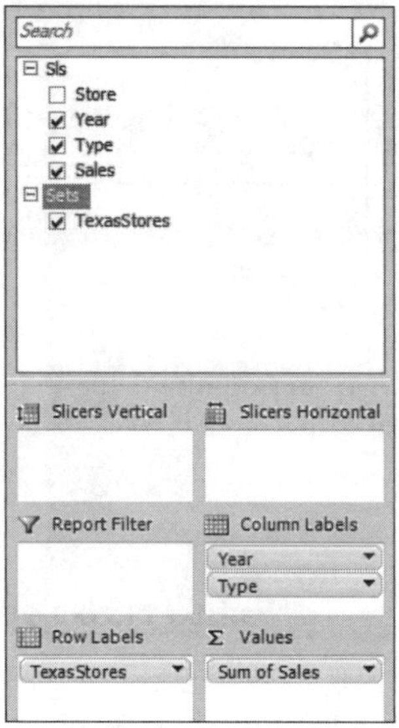

Figure 12.6
The named set automatically replaces the original field in the Row Labels area.

Correcting the Grand Total Row in Named Sets

Your pivot table now only shows the 20 stores in your territory, plus a grand total of all 150 stores. This probably is not what you want. In Figure 12.7, a regular Excel formula in C28 confirms that the total of your stores should be $8.5 million, not $60 million.

To correct the grand total row, follow these steps:

1. Select a cell inside the pivot table.
2. Click the Options icon on the left side of the Options tab.

Figure 12.7
The Grand Total row for a named set is initially wrong.

Sum of Sales	Column Labels ▼	
	= 2009	
Row Labels	Actual	
Baybrook	468,305	
Cielo Vista Mall	454,032	
The Domain	400,636	
Firewheel	467,897	
Galleria	448,173	
Highland Village	453,150	
Huebner Oaks	410,386	
Hulen Mall	401,353	
La Cantera	434,695	
Lakeline	352,230	
Northeast Mall	409,465	
Northpark Center	435,066	
Northstar Mall	419,682	
The Parks	379,006	
Penn Square	438,881	
Southlake Town Square	471,883	
Stonebriar Mall	463,203	
Willowbend	415,347	
Willowbrook	457,833	
The Woodlands Mall	352,022	
Grand Total	60,112,104	
	8,533,245	

fx =SUM(C6:C25)

3. Go to the Totals & Filters tab in the PivotTable Options dialog.

4. There is a new setting called Include Filtered Items in Set Totals. This setting is selected by default. Clear the check box for this setting (see Figure 12.8).

5. Click OK.

Figure 12.8
By default, items filtered out of a set are still included in the total.

Include filtered items

PivotTable Options					
Name: PivotTable6					

Layout & Format | **Totals & Filters** | Display | Printing | Data | Alt Text

Grand Totals
☑ Show grand totals for rows
☑ Show grand totals for columns

Filters
☐ Include filtered items in totals
　☑ Mark totals with *
☐ Include filtered items in set totals
☑ Subtotal filtered page items
☐ Allow multiple filters per field
☑ Evaluate calculated members from OLAP server in filters

Sorting
☑ Use Custom Lists when sorting

OK　Cancel

12

The result is a refreshable report that includes only your 20 stores and a total of those stores (see Figure 12.9).

Figure 12.9
The row labels now look good in this report. The columns are another matter.

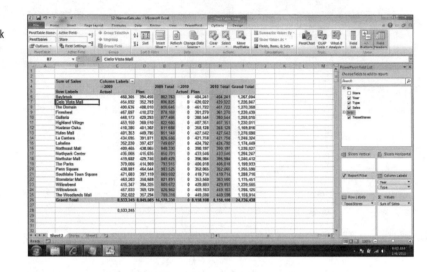

Using Named Sets for Asymmetric Reporting

That pivot table columns back in Figure 12.9 are horrible. Adding Plan + Actual in columns E & H makes no sense. The Grand Total in column I makes no sense. Showing 2010 actuals of 0 makes no sense.

Ideally, you might want to display only 2009 Actual and 2010 Plan.

This was tough to do in regular pivot tables. You could turn off the subtotals for the Year field and you could suppress the Grand Total column, but unless you started hiding columns, there was no way to hide 2010 actuals without also hiding 2009 actuals.

Named sets come to the rescue when you are trying to produce asymmetric reports. Follow these steps to create an asymmetric report:

1. Select a cell inside the pivot table.
2. On the Options tab, select, Fields, Items & Sets, Create Set Based on Column Items. Excel displays the New Set dialog with each combination of Year and Type field (see Figure 12.10).
3. Give the set a name, such as ActPlan.
4. Use the Delete Row button to delete all the columns except for 2009 Actual and 2010 Plan (see Figure 12.11).
5. Click OK to create the set.

Figure 12.10
You can delete columns from the report.

Figure 12.11
Delete the total columns and the 2010 Actuals.

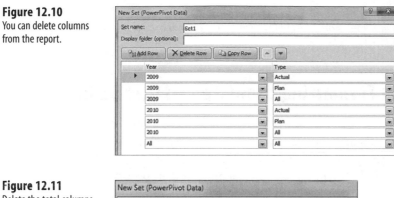

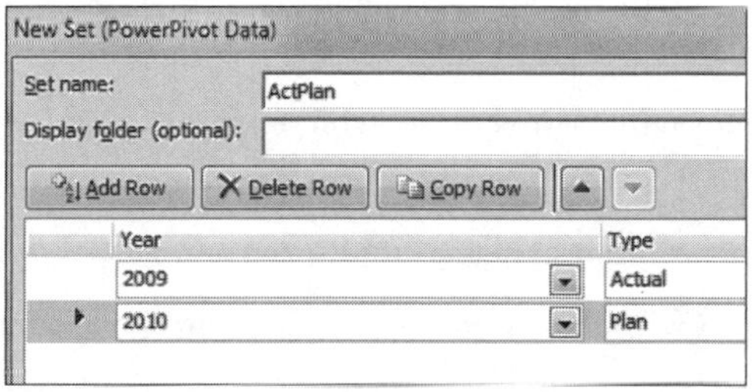

The new ActPlan set appears in the PowerPivot Field List and is moved to the Column Labels area.

In Figure 12.12, the pivot table includes only the columns in the set.

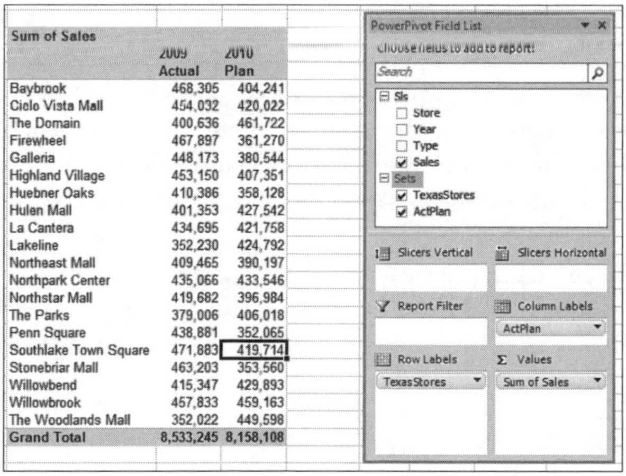

Figure 12.12
The named set allows asymmetric reporting.

If you have to change a set later, you can use the Manage Sets command in the Fields, Items, & Sets drop-down in the PivotTable Tools Options tab.

To see a demo of using Named Sets for Asymmetric Reporting, search for MrExcel PowerPivot 12 at YouTube.

Preserving Report Formatting Using `GetPivotData`

I love pivot tables.

However, a few things about pivot tables drive me crazy. It is really hard to format a pivot table to make it look really good. If you start to overwrite some of the built-in formats, you can lose those on a refresh. Column widths have a mind of their own. You certainly can never insert blank rows between groups of row labels.

So, I frequently create a pivot table, convert the table to values, and then do the formatting that I need to do.

This means that when the next month rolls around, I have to restart with a new pivot table.

The technique in this section will prevent you from having to go through that hassle.

It makes use of a feature that 99% of the pivot table fans absolutely hate. If you are ever outside of a pivot table and write a formula that points inside the pivot table, you end up with a bizarre `GetPivotData` formula that returns an absolute reference that can not be copied.

> **NOTE** In fact, I usually teach people in my Excel seminars how to turn *off* the annoying `GetPivotData` feature. It is a bit ironic that `GetPivotData` is actually the secret to ending all of the frustrations with pivot tables.

Figure 12.13 shows an ugly pivot table: 150 stores stretch down the left side, and 12 months of actuals and 12 months of plan stretch across the top. The months are appearing in alphabetic order because PowerPivot can't seem to respect the custom lists.

Figure 12.13
This is one ugly pivot table.

Sum of Sales	Column Labels														Actual Total	Plan
	Actual															Plan
Row Labels	Apr	Aug	Dec	Feb	Jan	Jul	Jun	Mar	May	Nov	Oct	Sep				Apr
Ala Moana	23727	0	0	16105	11739	0	0	19816	24038	0	0	0			95425	22200
Altamonte Mall	22918	0	0	14854	11421	0	0	20510	23188	0	0	0			92891	22700
Annapolis Mall	23134	0	0	14675	11689	0	0	17641	23271	0	0	0			90410	21600
Aventura Mall	25647	0	0	17473	13646	0	0	21214	25256	0	0	0			103236	25900
Baybrook	24822	0	0	16625	12366	0	0	21584	23518	0	0	0			98915	24300
Beachwood Place Mall	22929	0	0	16370	10833	0	0	18120	22780	0	0	0			91032	22800
Bellevue Square	26851	0	0	17821	13684	0	0	24520	26948	0	0	0			109824	28100

Each month, you would have to reformat this report. Some of the many steps include the following:

- Copying the pivot table and pasting as values
- Deleting the stores in which you are not interested

- Keeping the actual sales for months that have completed
- Adding planned sales for future months
- Sorting the stores into the proper sequence
- Adding subtotals and grand totals
- Applying formatting to the subtotal rows
- Following the actual accounting rules such as currency symbols on the first row and subtotal rows, single underlines before the subtotals and a double underline under the grand total

Producing a Perfectly Formatted Shell Report

Figure 12.14 shows a Report worksheet. This worksheet has all the labels and formatting that you usually report each month. A date in cell P1 is referenced by a formula in row 4 to put either Actual or Budget in each cell.

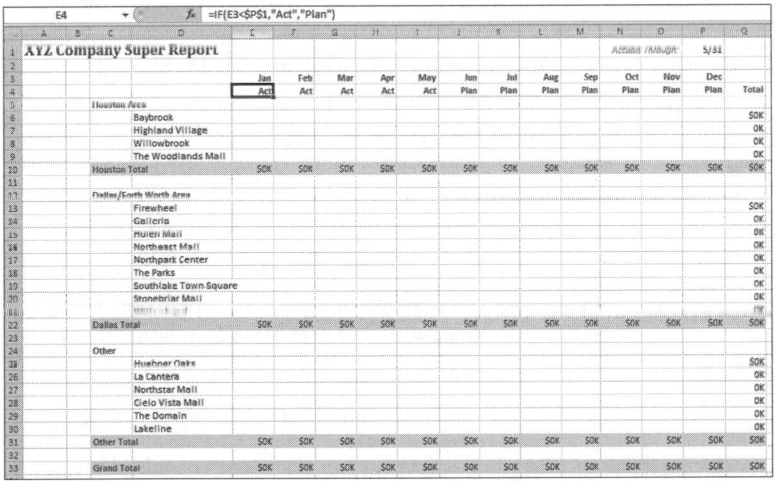

Figure 12.14
This report shell shows the structure that you would like to use each month.

The technique that follows will keep that ugly pivot table as a live pivot table. Each month, you will have to use Update All to refresh the linked table in PowerPivot, and then Refresh on the PivotTable Options tab to get new data into the pivot table. No one ever has to see the ugly pivot table. And live formulas will populate the Report worksheet with numbers from the pivot table.

After you paste new data to your table each month, it will take just two mouse clicks to produce a perfectly formatted report with new data.

Follow these steps to populate the shell report:

1. You need to make sure that the GetPivotData feature is selected. To do this, select one cell in your pivot table. Go to the Options tab.

2. Look carefully at the Options icon on the left side of the ribbon. There is a drop-down arrow next to the Options icon. Open that drop-down arrow and make sure the Generate GetPivotData check box is selected (see Figure 12.15).

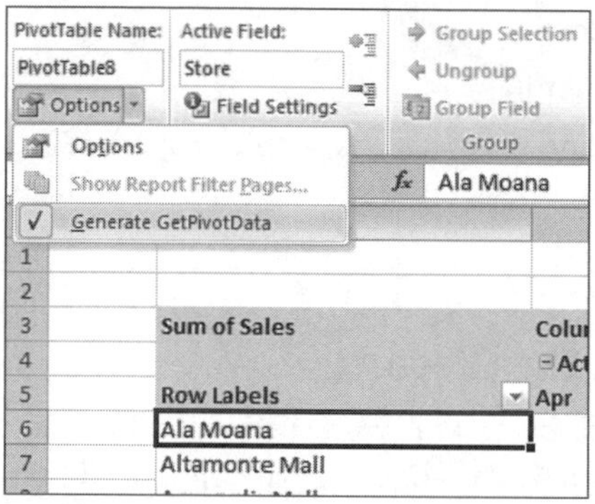

Figure 12.15
If you've turned the feature off, turn it back on for a few minutes.

3. Go back to the first value cell in your report. Make a mental note that this cell is for Baybrook, January, Actuals.

4. Type an equal sign in that cell (see Figure 12.16).

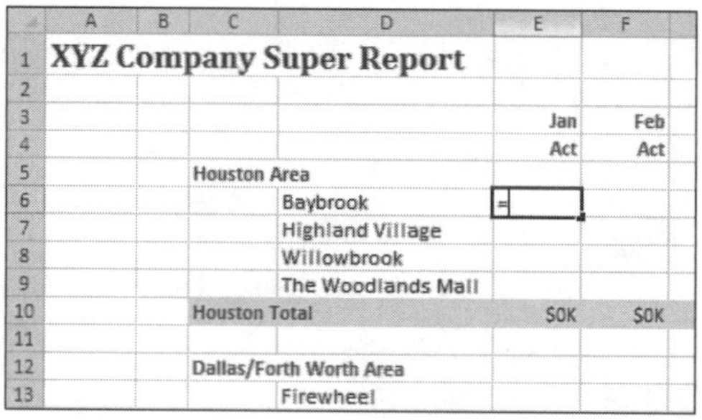

Figure 12.16
Start by typing an equal sign in your report work-sheet.

5. Using your mouse, click the sheet tab for the pivot table. Find the cell in the pivot table that gives you Baybrook, January, Actuals. Click that cell.

6. Press Enter. Excel will build a horribly complex formula, as shown in Figure 12.17.

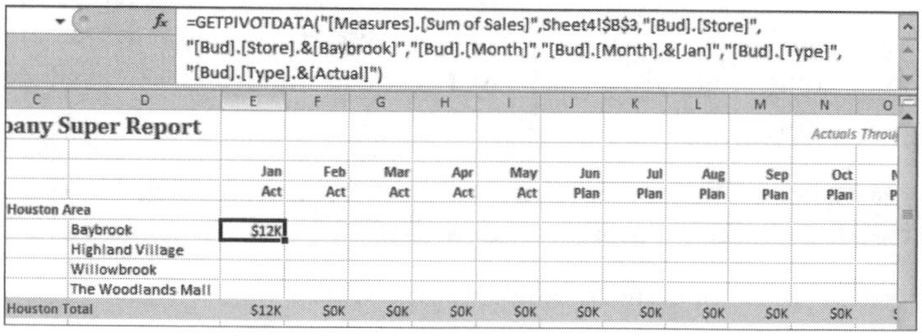

Figure 12.17
Excel builds a GetPivotData formula.

Let's step back and analyze that formula.

Here is the basic syntax of GetPivotData:

```
=GetPivotData(
   The name of a numeric field,
   Any one cell inside the pivot table,
   A field name, the value for that field,
   A field name, the value for that field,
   A field name, the value for that field,
   And so on
```

> **NOTE** The reason why people hate GetPivotData is that the formula that is automatically built by Excel is hard-coded to grab one specific value. This is nearly useless. Microsoft expects you to edit that formula and to replace the hard-coded values with cell references.

Evaluating the Formula Built by Excel

Let's take a look at the formula built by Excel. I'll add some line breaks to improve the readability. I will also bold the hard-coded pieces that need to be changed:

```
=GETPIVOTDATA(
"[Measures].[Sum of Sales]",
Sheet4!$B$3,
"[Bud].[Store]","[Bud].[Store].&[Baybrook]",
"[Bud].[Month]","[Bud].[Month].&[Jan]",
"[Bud].[Type]","[Bud].[Type].&[Actual]")
```

It is always a bit of a surprise to see the format that GetPivotData uses for the date fields. If you have real dates rather than month names, you might need to put a 1 for January. Once you see the GetPivotData formula, you can make tweaks to your reporting worksheet to match the parameters required in the GetPivotData formula. For example, my formula in row 4 needed to return Actual rather than Act.

For the argument that specifies the store name, the new syntax would have to be this:

```
"[Bud].[Store].&["&$D6&"]"
```

The dollar sign before the D in D6 ensures that the formula always gets the store name from column D. The lack of a dollar sign before the 6 allows the formula to be copied to other rows and get the store name from those rows.

For the argument that specifies the month, you have to be a little creative. The values in row 3 are actually dates that used a MMM format. I did this to make the formula in row 4 work:

```
=IF(E3<$P$1,"Actual","Plan")
```

To convert those dates to a three-character month, you use the following:

```
"[Bud].[Month].&["&TEXT(E$3,"MMM")&"]"
```

12

Again, note the careful placement of one dollar sign in E$3. This allows you to always point to the month in row 3, but the column is allowed to change as the formula is copied.

The argument that specifies Plan or Actual would be as follows:

```
"[Bud].[Type].&["&E$4&"]"
```

Here is the complete formula, after editing. Again, line breaks are added, and the changed elements highlighted in bold:

```
=GETPIVOTDATA(
"[Measures].[Sum of Sales]",
Pivot!$B$3,"[Bud].[Store]",
"[Bud].[Store].&["&$D6&"]",
"[Bud].[Month]","[Bud].[Month].&["&TEXT(E$3,"MMM")&"]",
"[Bud].[Type]","[Bud].[Type].&["&E$4&"]")
```

> **NOTE**
> I admit that changing the formula is a pain in the neck. But just realize this: You have to change this formula once and then not have to touch it again for years.

Now you want to parameterize the GetPivotData formula generated by Excel. Picking up with our steps:

1. Edit the GetPivotData formula to be =GETPIVOTDATA("[Measures].[Sum of Sales]",Pivot!$B$3,"[Bud].[Store]","[Bud].[Store].&["&$D6&"]","[Bud].[Month]","[Bud].[Month].&["&TEXT(E$3,"MMM")&"]","[Bud].[Type]","[Bud].[Type].&["&E$4&"]") (see Figure 12.18).

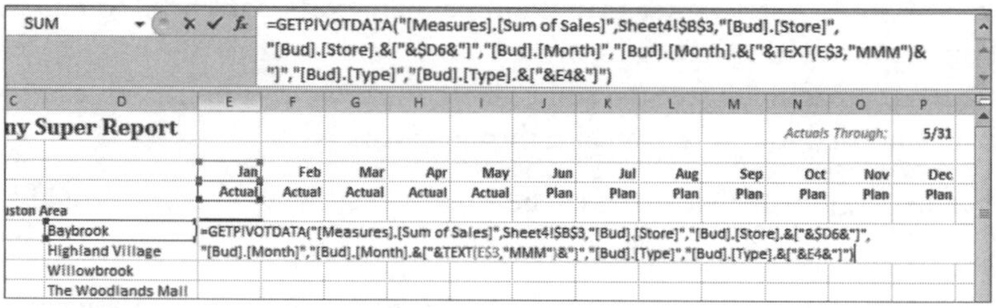

Figure 12.18
Edit the formula to make it use labels in the report instead of being hard-coded.

2. Copy the cell with the edited formula.

3. Choose a contiguous block of values cells in the report. Use Home, Paste, Paste Special. In the Paste Special dialog, select Formulas, as shown in Figure 12.19. Click OK.

4. Continue using the Paste Special dialog to paste the formulas to the other sections of the report.

Figure 12.20 shows the final report.

Figure 12.19
I still like the words in the Paste Special dialog rather than the icons in the new Paste flyout menu.

Figure 12.20
Change the date in P1 and the report updates.

	Jan	Feb	Mar	Apr	May	Jun	Jul	Aug	Sep	Oct	Nov	Dec	
	Actual	Actual	Actual	Actual	Plan	Plan	Plan	Plan	Plan	Plan	Plan	Plan	Total
XYZ Company Super Report										Actuals Through:		4/30	
Houston Area													
Baybrook	$12K	$17K	$22K	$25K	$24K	$32K	$28K	$24K	$20K	$32K	$49K	$121K	$407K
Highland Village	13K	17K	20K	24K	24K	33K	29K	24K	20K	33K	49K	122K	407K
Willowbrook	15K	19K	24K	30K	28K	37K	32K	28K	23K	37K	55K	138K	465K
The Woodlands Mall	14K	19K	24K	28K	27K	36K	32K	27K	23K	36K	54K	135K	453K
Houston Total	$54K	$71K	$90K	$106K	$103K	$138K	$120K	$103K	$86K	$138K	$207K	$516K	$1,732K
Dallas/Forth Worth Area													
Firewheel	$11K	$15K	$18K	$23K	$22K	$29K	$25K	$22K	$18K	$29K	$43K	$108K	$363K
Galleria	11K	15K	19K	25K	23K	30K	27K	23K	19K	30K	46K	114K	382K
Hulen Mall	13K	17K	23K	26K	26K	34K	30K	26K	21K	34K	51K	128K	429K
Northeast Mall	11K	15K	19K	23K	23K	31K	27K	23K	20K	31K	47K	117K	389K
Northpark Center	12K	18K	22K	27K	26K	35K	30K	26K	22K	35K	52K	130K	435K
The Parks	13K	17K	20K	26K	24K	33K	28K	24K	20K	33K	49K	133K	108K
Southlake Town Square	14K	17K	22K	25K	25K	34K	29K	25K	21K	34K	50K	126K	422K
Stonebriar Mall	11K	14K	19K	22K	21K	28K	25K	21K	18K	28K	42K	106K	356K
Willowbend	13K	17K	23K	28K	26K	34K	30K	26K	22K	34K	52K	129K	434K
Dallas Total	$109K	$144K	$186K	$225K	$216K	$288K	$252K	$216K	$180K	$288K	$432K	$1,081K	$3,618K
Other													
Huebner Oaks	$11K	$15K	$18K	$23K	$22K	$29K	$25K	$22K	$18K	$29K	$43K	$107K	$361K
La Cantera	13K	18K	22K	26K	25K	34K	30K	25K	21K	34K	51K	127K	425K
Northstar Mall	13K	16K	21K	24K	24K	32K	28K	24K	20K	32K	48K	119K	400K
Cielo Vista Mall	12K	18K	22K	26K	25K	34K	29K	25K	21K	34K	50K	120K	422K
The Domain	15K	19K	24K	29K	28K	37K	32K	28K	23K	37K	55K	139K	466K
Lakeline	13K	17K	23K	27K	26K	34K	30K	26K	21K	34K	51K	127K	428K
Other Total	$76K	$107K	$133K	$165K	$149K	$199K	$174K	$149K	$124K	$199K	$298K	$745K	$2,502K
Grand Total	$239K	$318K	$409K	$488K	$468K	$625K	$546K	$468K	$390K	$625K	$937K	$2,342K	$7,852K

When you have data for a new month, complete these steps:

1. Paste the actuals for the new month in the row below the table on the Table worksheet.
2. On the PowerPivot tab, select Update All.
3. Select one cell in the Pivot Table. Click Refresh on the Options tab.
4. Change the date in cell P1 of the report worksheet.

Although it is a bit of a hassle to edit the GetPivotData formulas, the benefit in future months of not having to re-create the pivot table and formatting makes it worthwhile.

Converting Live Pivot Table to Cube Formulas

The GetPivotData trick would work for PowerPivot pivot tables and for regular pivot tables.

Because the PowerPivot table is also an OLAP table, you have a different option that will save you one extra layer of work.

In Figure 12.21, I've fixed up the ugly pivot table just a bit. I used the More Sort options to actually get the months to sort into sequence. I removed the subtotals that were adding Plan+Actual. I got rid of the grand total for rows.

Figure 12.21
A less-ugly pivot table.

	B	C	D	E	F	G
3	Sum of Sales	Month ▼	Type ▼			
4		⊟ Jan		⊟ Feb		⊟ Mar
5	Store ▼	Actual	Plan	Actual	Plan	Actual
6	Ala Moana	11739	11100	16105	14800	19816
7	Altamonte Mall	11421	11400	14854	15100	20510
8	Annapolis Mall	11689	10800	14675	14400	17641
9	Aventura Mall	13646	12900	17473	17300	21214
10	Baybrook	12366	12100	16625	16200	21584

To convert the table to formulas, select a cell in the pivot table. Go to PivotTable Tools Options, open the OLAP Tools drop-down, and select Convert to Formulas (see Figure 12.22).

Figure 12.22
Convert to formulas.

> ⌐ C A U T I O N ────────────────────────────
>
> Do not panic at what happens next. Your whole report changes to ###### signs. This lasts for a good 15 seconds. Then, the report comes back.

Each value pivot table has now been replaced with a `CubeValue` function. As you can see in Figure 12.23, the formula specifies a data connection of PowerPivot Data, and then refers to three other cells: $B$3, $B6, C$5. Do you see that? They were smart enough to make the formula copyable this time.

Figure 12.23
The `CubeValue` function automatically uses the right mix of relative and absolute references.

	B	C	D	E	F	G
3	Sum of Sales	Month	Type			
4		Jan		Feb		Mar
5	Store	Actual	Plan	Actual	Plan	Actual
6	Ala Moana	=CUBEVALUE("PowerPivot Data",$B$3,$B6,C$5)				
7	Altamonte Mall	11421	11400	14854	15100	20510
8	Annapolis Mall	11689	10800	14675	14400	17641

Because I am new to cube formulas, I wondered why they never pointed to the word *Jan* in C4. It turns out that the word *Actual* that appears in C5 is pretty important. It is not a single value of Actual. It is actually returning an array of both Actual and Jan by way of a `CubeMember` formula (see Figure 12.24).

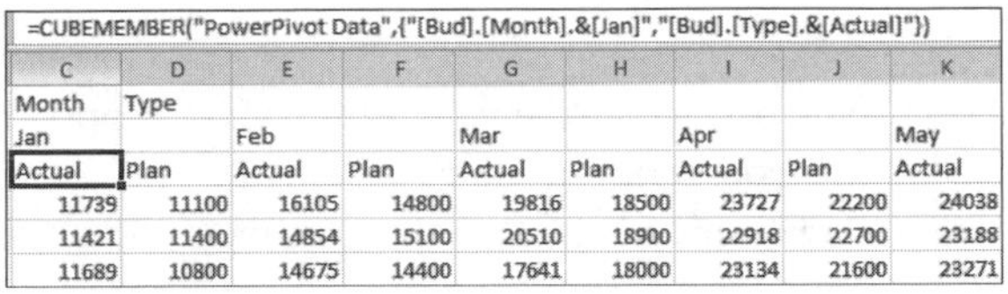

Figure 12.24

This heading displays Actual but also contains Jan in the array returned by the function.

Customizing the Formatted Report

At this point, you can start sorting rows, deleting rows, inserting rows, adding formatting, and so on. I deleted the plan columns for months where there are already actuals and hid the future months' actual columns that are zero.

Figure 12.25 shows the formatted report. Most of those values are coming from the underlying PowerPivot data.

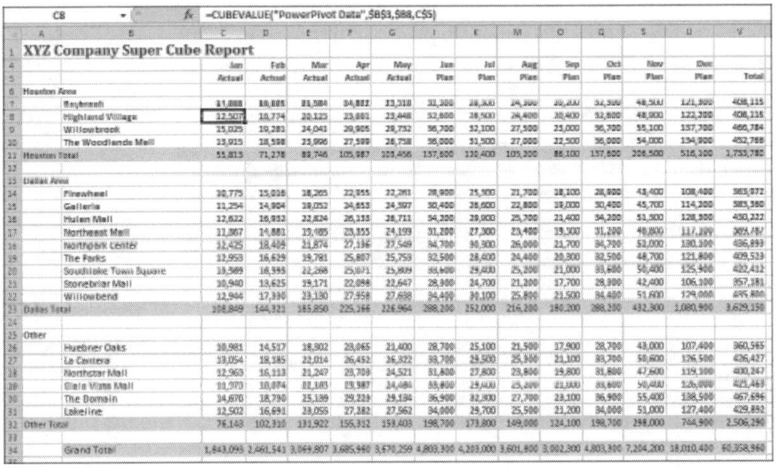

Figure 12.25

By converting the pivot table to cube formulas, you can format it as you want.

When you get data for a new month, follow these steps:

1. Paste the data in the first blank row below your table.
2. On the PowerPivot tab, select Update All.
3. On the Data tab, use the Refresh All button in the External data group.

Your report will then update. In my report, I would have to unhide the June Actual column in H and delete the June Plan column from I.

> **TIP**
> Cube formulas are a great trick, but they only work with OLAP and PowerPivot pivot tables. They will not work with ordinary pivot cache pivot tables.

Next Steps

The next chapter covers some tricks to make your PowerPivot reports look excellent. Whether you are sharing the workbooks in the Excel client or publishing the workbooks to SharePoint, you can take a few steps to make the reports look different from Excel worksheets.

Final Formatting: Making the Report Not Look Like Excel

13

It is easy to create powerful reporting structures with PowerPivot. You can have one set of slicers that are driving multiple charts. As an Excel data analyst, you can appreciate the analytical power that PowerPivot brings to the table.

There is a good chance that your PowerPivot models are going to make it to the boardroom, either as a standalone model or as a SharePoint report.

This chapter focuses on some final formatting that you can do to make the report not look like Excel. Whereas you and I live in Excel all day and are comfortable with the environs of Excel, it might be completely foreign to the people who will be consuming the model that you created.

Figure 13.1 shows a PowerPivot model in Excel. Six slicers are driving four pivot charts.

Charts Should Have Less Ink, More Information

You can't see Figure 13.1 in color, but PowerPivot did manage to draw the first chart in blue, the second chart in green, the third chart in red, and the fourth chart in purple. I do appreciate that variety.

But that is where the variety ends and many similarities begin:

- The title on each chart is Total. Horrible.
- The legend on a one-series chart is always unnecessary.
- Having four column charts is boring.

■ You are wasting a lot of ink with gridlines, zeros along the vertical axis.

■ The on-chart pivot controls are redundant now that you've added slicers.

Figure 13.1
Four pivot charts all controlled by five slicers make a nice dashboard.

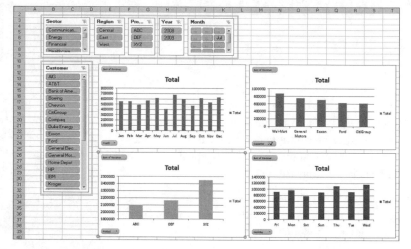

Component Charts Make Great Pie Charts

The lower left chart with sales by product shows how the products add up to 100%. This is the perfect data to show in a pie chart. Follow these steps to change that chart to a pie:

1. Click the lower-left chart. A group of four PivotChart Tools should appear in the ribbon. Select the Design tab in that group.

2. Click the Change Chart Type icon on the left side of the ribbon.

3. Select Pie in the left navigation bar.

4. Select the first pie chart, which is the 2D pie shown in Figure 13.2.

> **NOTE**
> In step 4, avoid selecting the 3D pie charts since they distort the items in the front of the chart.

5. Click OK to close the Change Chart Type dialog.

Time Series Charts Should Be Columns or Lines

If you have charts with time along the primary axis, those charts should be column charts or line charts. Twelve points or less make great column charts. More than 12 points and you should consider going to a line chart.

The top-left and bottom-right charts both are showing time, so they should stay as column charts.

Figure 13.2
You can change the chart
type for each chart.

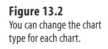

Category Charts Make Great Bar Charts

When your chart has non-time-related information, consider using that as a bar chart. The
nature of the bar chart means that there is more room for long labels to stretch out to the
left of the chart.

Figure 13.3 shows the Top Five Customers chart as a bar chart.

Figure 13.3
When there is no time
component, consider a
bar chart.

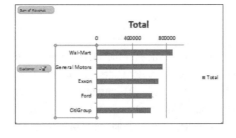

 Bar charts in Excel have the annoying property that the first category appears closest to the bottom of
the chart. This means that your number one customer will be last in the list.

To move the number one customer to the top of the list, double-click the customer names in the chart.
In the Format dialog box, look for a setting called Categories in Reverse Order in the middle of the dialog. Select that setting to move the first customer to the top of the chart.

Use Descriptive Titles

All Excel charts start out with stupid titles. They don't have to stay that way. There are two
ways to change the titles, and the default method tends to trip people up.

13

When you click a chart title to select it, the title will be surrounded by a solid box, as shown in the lower-right chart in Figure 13.4. When the title is in this state, you can type a new title. The confusing issue is that the letters you are typing do not appear in the title. You will feel like you are typing without seeing what you are typing. The trick is that you have to look in the formula bar, just above the Excel grid. You can see the new title being typed there. When you press Enter, Excel takes the words from the title bar, sizes them appropriately, and redraws the chart.

Figure 13.4
Click the title and watch your typed words appear in the formula bar.

Formula Bar

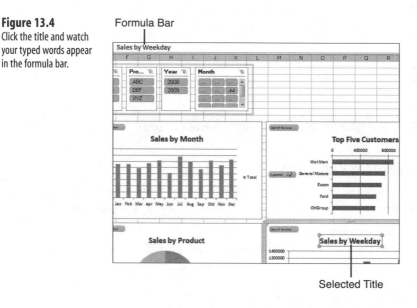

Selected Title

> **NOTE** Now that I understand why Excel doesn't show you the title as you type, it actually makes sense to me. Excel shows short titles in a large font and long titles in a smaller font. Think about when you are typing the tile Sales by Weekday. As you start to type that title and you've types S-a-l, the title looks really short and Excel would render it in a large font. Every time that you type a character, the title gets longer, and Excel recalculates the proper font. It would be annoying to watch the title constantly resize and dance around as you are typing. So, in the default state, you watch the words that you are typing in the formula bar, and then let Excel do all the sizing and rendering logic once after you press Enter.

There is a second way to change the title. In this method, you click once on the title to get the solid box, and then click a second time inside the title to get a dashed box. This is edit mode. You can now type letters right inside the title, but be aware that you are going to have to Backspace and press the Delete key a bunch of times to get rid of the characters in the existing title. If you triple-click the title, you will be edit mode and the entire title will be selected so you can simply begin typing to replace the current title.

Single-Series Column and Bar Charts Do Not Need Legends!

This is already Chapter 13, and I don't think that I've used an exclamation point in a section heading anywhere else in the book. This one clearly bugs the heck out of me, and it is on the super-short-list of things that I wish Microsoft would fix in their charting engine.

A bar or column chart with a single series absolutely never benefits from having a legend. The legend adds no information to the chart. The legend takes up a lot of space.

The official way to remove a legend is this:

1. Select the chart
2. Go to the PivotChart Tools Layout tab in the ribbon.
3. Open the Legend drop-down.
4. Select None.

The faster way to remove the legend is as follows:

1. Click the legend. It will get selected like in the lower-right chart in Figure 13.5
2. Press the Delete key.

> **NOTE** It if it makes you feel better, in step 2, press the Delete key really forcefully while making an annoyed look in the direction of Redmond, Washington.

Figure 13.5
Remove the legends for bar and column charts.

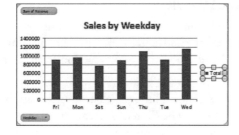

Reduce the Number of Zeros on the Values Axis

This dashboard is for a company who is selling about half a million dollars each month. The larger a company gets, the more annoying this problem becomes.

In the charts in Figure 13.5, the labels along the values axis have numbers like 100000, 200000, 300000, 400000, and so on. The five zeros in every chart are hard to read and add little to the chart.

If you are working for a company who does 90 million every month, your charts will be even worse, with 90000000 in really small font next to each gridline.

13

This is an easy fix. Double-click the numbers next to the axis in the chart. There is a setting in the Format Axis dialog called Display Units. Open that drop-down and choose an appropriate scale.

In Figure 13.6, the dialog sets a scale in thousands. The units label will say Thousands right on the chart. If your audience would understand that these are in thousands, you can clear the Show Display Units Label on the Chart in the dialog box.

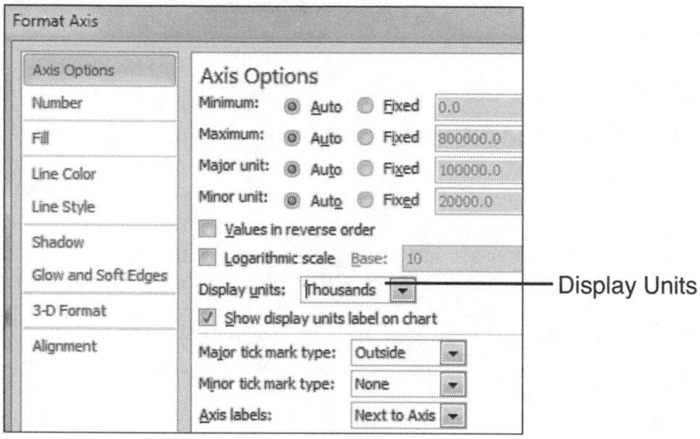

Figure 13.6
Simplify the numbers along the scale. You don't need zeros repeated at every gridline.

The drop-down offers a choice for hundred thousands. However, the label appears as x100000 and is as hard to make out as the original labels. It is your call. Try a few different label scales and see what is the easiest to read.

Slicers Make the On-Chart Controls Obsolete

Pivot charts in Excel 2003 were ugly things. Their appearance improved in Excel 2007 as Microsoft improved the charting engine and moved the on-chart filtering labels to an external dialog box. That apparently did not receive a great reaction from people who actually use pivot charts.

In Excel 2010, the external dialog is gone and the on-chart controls are back, although in a scaled-down version. I still hate them. The Sum of Revenue field uses a strange way of saying Total Revenue, and you've already communicated that information in the title. The Filter drop-down is taking up space and is redundant with the slicers that you've added to the worksheet.

To remove the on-chart controls, select each of the four pivot charts one at a time. On the PivotChart Tools Analyze tab, open the Field Buttons drop-down and select Hide All, as shown in Figure 13.7.

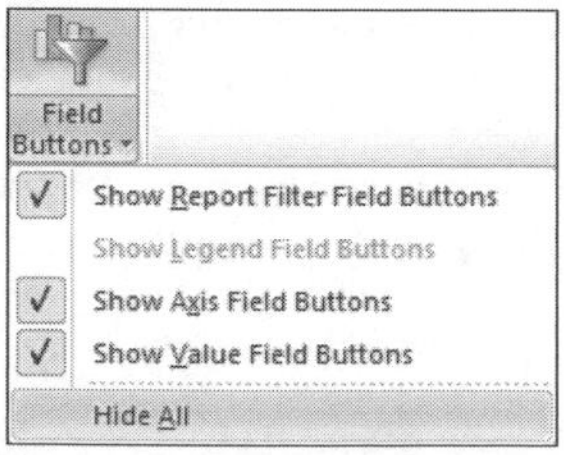

Figure 13.7
Hide the Field Buttons on each pivot chart.

Replace Pie Chart Legends with Labels

The legend on a pie chart is too far removed from the pie chart to be useful. People have to move their eyes from the chart to the legend to the chart to the legend. Instead, it is better to put the labels for each pie slice right on the pie.

Excel has choices for this, but you will not find them in the ribbon.

Follow these steps to add data labels to the pie chart:

1. Click the pie chart to activate it and bring back the PivotChart Tools tabs.
2. Select the Layout tab in the ribbon. This tab offers the most popular settings for 13 chart elements. Unfortunately, most popular does not mean "most useful."
3. Open the drop-down for Data Labels. Select More Data Label Options. Excel displays the Format Data Labels dialog.
4. Select to show Category Name and Value. Clear the Value box. This provides a short label on each pie slice, as shown in Figure 13.8.

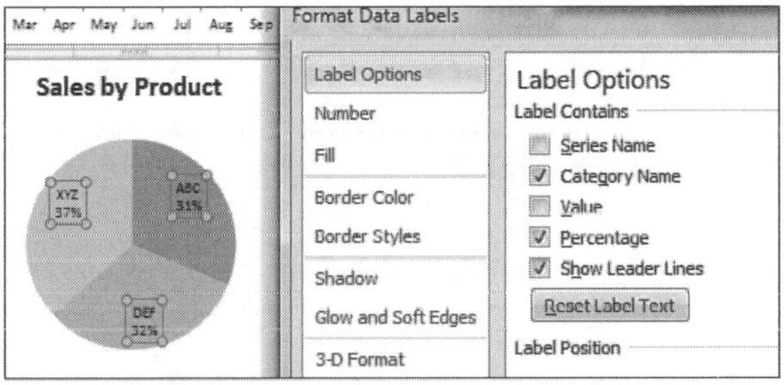

Figure 13.8
Replace the pie chart legend with labels.

5. Click OK to close the dialog.
6. Click the now-redundant legend in the chart. Press the Delete key.

Gridlines, Tick Marks, Axis, and Column Widths

Charting guru Kathy Viella from PowerFrameworks.com says that every bit of ink on the chart should be necessary for understanding the chart. If there is ink on the chart that is not necessary, you should get rid of it.

Delete Gridlines

Gridlines really clutter up a chart.

Are gridlines necessary? Gridlines might be necessary to allow the reader's eye to follow across the chart to the numbers along the left axis. In Figure 13.9, look at the top left chart. Can you tell whether November is above $500,000?

One great way to avoid the need for gridlines is to remove the values axis and add a data label to each bar or column. In the right charts of Figure 13.9, the gridlines and values axis are gone completely. Because each column has a data label, there is no need for a values axis and hence no need for gridlines.

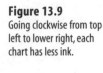

Figure 13.9
Going clockwise from top left to lower right, each chart has less ink.

There are two methods to delete the gridlines. You can select PivotChart Tools Layout, Gridlines, Horizontal Gridlines, None. Or, you can click one gridline to select all the gridlines and press Delete.

Add Data Labels

If you get rid of the gridlines, you should add data labels, as follows:

1. Select the chart.
2. Right-click a bar or column and select Add Data Labels.
3. Double-click the Data Labels to open the Format Data Labels dialog.
4. In the left navigation, select Number.
5. In the category, select Number, Zero Decimal Places, and Use 1000 Separator. Don't close the dialog yet; you still have some decisions to make.

Take a look at the chart to see how the labels look.

If you've been following along and changed the Display Units of the values axis to thousands, your labels are already showing thousands. This may or may not be confusing to your reader. You might want to add a K abbreviation after the number.

In the Format Data Labels dialog, there is a Format Code box. Right now, it is showing #,##0. To simply add a K after the number, type a **K** after the zero and click Add. Your new format will be added to the Custom category and be selected.

If you had not previously changed the display units to thousands, you might have numbers showing as 123456. In this case, you need to both scale the number and add an abbreviation. Use a format code of #,##0,K. This is a subtle difference. The comma after the final zero indicates that the number should be divided by a thousand before it is displayed as a label on the chart.

The K abbreviation is one of the few letters that you can type in the formatting code without being in quotes. If your numbers are in millions, you need to surround the "M" abbreviation in quotes.

Table 13.1 shows examples of format codes to use in various situations.

Table 13.1	Selected Format Codes			
Data Value	Display Units Setting	Default Display	Custom Format	Final Display
546789	None	546789	#,##0,K	547K
546789	None	546789	$#,##0,K	$547K
546789	Thousands	547	#,##0K	547K
546789000	None	546789000	#,##0,,"M"	547M
546789000	Millions	547	#,##0"M"	547M

Tick Marks

Take a close look at the horizontal axis of the top-left chart in Figure 13.9. Do you notice those tiny vertical marks between each month? Those are called tick marks. They are added to Excel charts by default.

The top-right chart does away with the tick marks. You don't need the tick marks. They really add nothing to the chart.

To get rid of the tick marks along an axis, double-click the labels along that axis. Excel displays the Format Axis dialog box. In the center of the dialog box, there is a drop-down for Major Tick Mark Type. Open that drop-down and select None.

Delete the Values Axis

In the top-right chart of Figure 13.9, the values axis is gone completely. It is not missed, because the data labels show the size of each bar.

To delete the values axis, click the labels in that axis to select the axis. Press the Delete key. The axis disappears.

Is the Line Along the Axis Needed?

The top right chart in Figure 13.9 still has a line between the customer names and the bars. In the bottom-right chart, the line between the weekday names and the columns is gone. If your chart doesn't include negative numbers, you really don't need the axis line.

If you delete the axis as above, you would lose the axis labels and those are important. Instead, follow these steps to remove the axis line:

13

1. Double-click the words along the category axis to open the Format Axis dialog box.
2. In the left navigation, select Line Color.
3. In the Line color section, select No Line.
4. Click OK.

Make the Bars or Columns Thicker

After you delete all the extra chart junk, you will realize just how much white space is left between the columns.

In Figure 13.9, I made all the columns and bars wider. This reduces the white space and makes the columns the focus of the chart. It also provides a wider platform to support the column labels.

You might think to look for a setting called Column Width. In a strange twist, you actually make the columns wider by making the gaps between the columns narrower!

Follow these steps to change the column widths:

1. Double-click a column or bar in the chart to open the Format Data Series dialog.
2. There is a Gap Width slider that starts at 150%. The range in the slider is from 0% for No Gap to 500% for Large Gap. Drag the slider down to about 65%. Tweak the slider until you get something that looks good to you.
3. Click OK to close the dialog box.

Trying to Tame the Slicers

The PowerPivot really tried to improve the slicer experience.

Adding drop zones to the PowerPivot Field List for Vertical Slicer and Horizontal Slicer prevents the slicers from being stacked on top of each other and on top of the chart or pivot table.

The PowerPivot add-in will take an intelligent stab at changing the number of columns in each slicer. That is an improvement.

The problem is that PowerPivot keeps trying to auto-adjust the slicers. If you try to move a slicer, there is a good chance that PowerPivot will move it back!

Here is the key to having any hope of taming the slicers. There is a rectangle that surrounds the horizontal slicers and another rectangle that surrounds the vertical slicers.

To move the group of slicers, you need to access this shape, resize the shape, and move the shape.

The big problem is that the shape loves to hide itself.

Once you click away from the pivot table or pivot chart, the shape is supposed to hide itself.

Once the shape become hidden, it is hard to coax it back.

You definitely have to click inside of a pivot chart or a pivot table.

You definitely have to click in the slicer area but not on a slicer.

> **TIP**
>
> Don't try to use Home, Find & Select, Selection Pane. The shapes show up there, but as soon as you select those check boxes to make them visible, PowerPivot clears the boxes to hide them.

> **NOTE**
>
> By the time you are reading this book, I am sure that the elusive behavior of the rectangle will be fixed. Or maybe not. Maybe you should resize the slicer before you start to adjust the chart. I've had luck coaxing the box back by moving to a sheet that contains the pivot table for the chart, selecting the pivot table, and then moving back. I've had luck in coaxing the box back by saving the file.

Figure 13.10 shows the rectangle when it is finally selected.

You want to do several things:

1. Use the resize handle on the right side to stretch the box to be as wide as both charts on the screen. As you make the box longer, the PowerPivot auto-layout will resize and change the number of columns in each individual slicer.

2. You want to move the box so that it is safely outside of row 1. You are going to be using row 1 later for a title or a decorative element. Make sure that the top edge of the rectangle is not inside of row 1.

Figure 13.10
Resize and position the rectangle around the slicers.

13

If the slicer resizing becomes to annoying, try dragging the slicer completely outside of the bounding box. You will now have control over the slicer. You should make the bounding box small and move it out of the way. If you ever move the slicer back near the bounding box, the slicer will snap back into place in the bounding box.

Change the Slicer Color

A slicer styles gallery on the Slicer Tools Options tab offers various color schemes for the slicers.

To access that tab, you have to click inside one of the slicers. Clicking on the box surrounding the slicers is not enough. Instead, you need to click inside the slicers.

All the slicers start out as the same color. You can choose to either leave them monochromatic or change the color for each slicer.

> **TIP**
>
> I prefer having each slicer be a different color so that the person using the application understands that each slicer is separate.

Here is a proposal. Earlier in the chapter, I noted that the four charts each have a different color. These colors should be the first four theme colors in your theme. If you have a slicer that includes the same information as one of the charts, try making that slicer the same color as the chart.

It will not show up in Figure 13.11, but the Product pie chart is green. Change the Product slicer to be green. The Top Five Customers chart is dark red. Change the Customer slicer to be red. The Sales by Month chart is blue. Change the Month slicer to be blue. Change the color of the other slicers to be different colors from the gallery.

Figure 13.11
Change the slicer color.

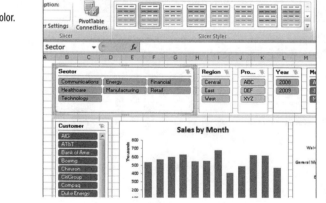

Remove Excel Interface Elements

To someone who is new to Excel, the gridlines are a lot of noise. There are a lot of other distractions in the Excel window: the PowerPivot Field List; the sheet tabs that people don't need to navigate to; the A, B, C column headings and the 1, 2, 3 row headings. If you make your model fits in one screen of data, you can get rid of the scrollbars.

Hide the Gridlines

It used to be pretty tough to hide the gridlines in Excel 2003. Now, it is just a couple of clicks. Go to the Page Layout tab. To the right of the center of the ribbon, two check boxes control whether you can view or print gridlines. Clear the View check box.

This will give you a less-cluttered look in the worksheet, as shown in Figure 13.12.

Figure 13.12
Hide the worksheet gridlines.

Hide Other Interface Elements

To create a less-cluttered report, consider hiding certain elements of the Excel interface. Complete the following steps:

1. Open the File menu and select Options.

2. In the Excel Options dialog, select the Advanced category in the left navigation.

3. Scroll down to Display Options for this Workbook, as shown in Figure 13.13.

Figure 13.13
Hide various elements of the Excel interface.

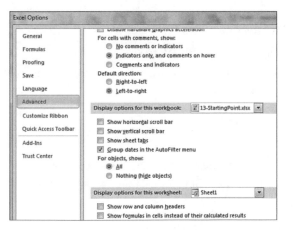

13

   4. Clear the Show Horizontal Scroll Bar check box.

   5. Clear the Show Vertical Scroll Bar check box.

   6. Clear the Show Sheet Tabs check box.

   7. Scroll down to the next section, Display Options for this Worksheet:

   8. Clear the Show Row and Column Headers check box.

> **TIP**
>
> After you've hidden those worksheet elements, you might feel like you cannot navigate through the workbook. Use these cool navigation secrets:
>
> PgDn, PgUp will scroll down and up your worksheet.
>
> Ctrl+PgDn will move jump to the next worksheet.
>
> Ctrl+PgUp will jump to the previous worksheet.
>
> Ctrl+A will select all cells in the worksheet.
>
> Ctrl+Spacebar selects the entire current column.
>
> Shift+Spacebar selects the entire current row.

Hide the PowerPivot Field List

Click one of the pivot charts. The PowerPivot Field List will come back. Go to the PowerPivot tab in the ribbon and toggle off the Field List.

Making a Report Look Like a Dashboard

You can take a few final steps to make your report look like a dashboard.

Change the Background Color

   1. Select all cells in the worksheet using Ctrl+A.

   2. On the Home tab, open the fill color drop-down and choose a color other than white for the worksheet background.

Contrast Color and Title in Row 1

   1. Scroll to the top of the worksheet.

   2. Select cell A1. Select the whole row by using Shift+Spacebar.

   3. Open the fill color drop-down and choose a contrasting color for row 1.

   4. Type a title in cell A1.

   5. With A1 selected, select Home, Styles, Title.

   6. If necessary, use the Increase Font icon to make the title larger.

7. If necessary, increase the row height of row 1 by using Home, Format, Row Height. (Or, press Alt+O+R+E).

Minimize the Ribbon

Your goal is to get as much of the worksheet on the screen as possible. The people using your dashboard will not need anything on the Excel Ribbon, so minimize it. There is a new "minimize" icon on the right side of the Excel screen. It is a white carat symbol (^) and should be to the left of the Help question mark. Click this to minimize the ribbon.

It is your call if you want to hide the formula bar. To hide it, clear the Formula Bar check box on the View tab.

> **CAUTION**
>
> Hiding the Formula Bar is a global setting. If you hide it, it will be hidden for every workbook.

Micro-Adjust the Zoom Slider

Make sure that your cell pointer is in cell A1 before you start adjusting the zoom slider. This will keep A1 in view as you adjust the zoom.

Do not use the + or – buttons at the ends of the zoom slider, because these cause the slider to jump in increments of 10%. That is too much. Drag the actual slider itself. You want to be able to see all four charts plus one additional blank row below the charts.

In my workbook, on my screen, 84% was too big, 83% worked fine.

Add a Row of Color at the Bottom of the Dashboard

Select the blank row below the bottom chart. You can select one cell and then use Shift+Spacebar to select the entire row.

Use Home, Fill Color and select the same fill color as you used for the title row.

This final swath of color sends a message to the person using the worksheet that they are seeing the bottom of the spreadsheet.

If you want to claim credit for the model, put small text there with "For Questions, call Joe Smith at extension 1234."

Figure 13.14 shows the completed dashboard.

Hide the Cell Pointer Behind a Slicer

The active cell is a bit of a distraction in the dashboard. One cool trick is to use the arrow keys to move the active cell to directly behind one of the large slicers. This will prevent the active cell from being seen.

13

Figure 13.14
The formatted dashboard.

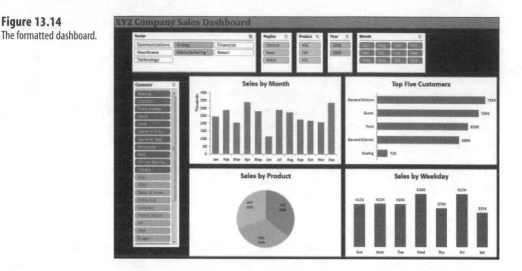

Adding a Picture as a Top Banner

If you look at any PowerPivot demos done by Microsoft, they always have a graphic at the top of the dashboard.

When I first saw this, I could not figure out how they managed to move the pivot charts and the slicers down several rows to make room for the graphic. Although you can achieve this through several clicks, there is an easier way.

Those graphics are nearly always jammed into a very tall row 1.

1. Select row 1. Use Home, Format, Row Height and increase the row height to 300.

2. Use Insert, Picture and navigate to a company logo.

> **TIP**
>
> Your company website probably already has a nice graphic across the top of it. You can open the browser, use Insert, Screenshot, and grab the banner from across the top of your website!

3. Stretch the picture to fit across your screen.

4. Adjust the row height of row 1 to just fit the picture. This is easiest if you add the Row & Column Headers back momentarily.

13

NOTE

If you ever swing by the Jelen household on a Saturday morning, you will most likely find my wife Mary Ellen watching HGTV to get ideas for ways to redecorate the house. I would not call myself a fan of these shows, but I've been around them enough to know that the final 5 minutes of the Drastic Rejuvenate genre of shows is a bunch of before and after shots that fade back and forth. In the spirit of those HGTV shows, Figure 13.16 is a repeat of the first screenshot from this chapter so that you can compare the Before and After of the dashboard.

Figure 13.15
A PowerPivot dashboard complete with the Microsoft-standard graphic in row 1.

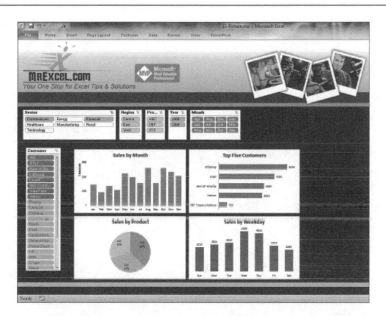

Figure 13.16
Before...

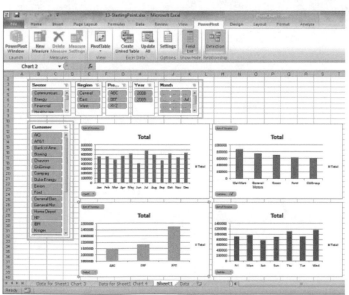

To see a demo of using formatting a report, search for MrExcel PowerPivot 13 at YouTube.

Next Steps

The next chapter shows you how to publish your reports to the server version of PowerPivot.

13

Upgrading to PowerPivot Server

This book is about the PowerPivot add-in—the free client-side add-in that lets you do incredibly powerful things with Microsoft Excel.

Microsoft is giving this add-in away with the hopes that some percentage of the people using the client add-in will be drawn to the server version of PowerPivot.

Requirements to Run the Server Version of PowerPivot

To run PowerPivot for your department, you are going to need a pretty serious server. They recommend 64GB of RAM, 8 processors. This single box will be running the following:

- SharePoint
- SQL Server
- Internet Information Services (IIS)
- Excel Services
- PowerPivot System Services
- Analysis Services IMBI

To run PowerPivot for an enterprise, you will need a server farm with one server each running Excel Services, PowerPivot, and SQL Server.

I think that I've previously mentioned that PowerPivot brings together the confluence of Excel experts, SQL Server experts, and SharePoint experts. The people writing the instructions for setting up a server are mostly SQL Server experts. Frankly, they speak a different language. I don't mean to scare you away. I was able to successfully walk into Best Buy, buy a serious machine, wipe the hard drive, install Windows Server 2008 SP2, install SQL Server, install SharePoint Server, and install

PowerPivot for Office. It all pretty much works. It took the better part of a morning and following step-by-step guidelines from Vidas Matelis, published at: http://powerpivot-info. com/post/66-step-by-step-guide-on-installing-powerpivot-for-sharepoint.

Still, even though Vidas's instructions are the best that I have found, they make huge assumptions about what we understand about servers and SharePoint administration. For example, if you are getting x error, then "add your SharePoint administrator account to the Active Directory user group Domain Admins and restart your machine." This assumes that I know what an Active Directory user group is or that I can figure out where to make this change. I am sure that this statement seems as easy to the server people as "change your Excel calculation mode to Automatic (except tables)" would seem to us. But, you will find yourself gritting your teeth often and trying the guess what the heck they are talking about. Look around, you can usually find it.

If you work for a company that already has SharePoint, there is a fairly good chance that your company already has a SharePoint administrator who can configure SharePoint to do this for you.

If you are at a small company without deep IT support, you are going to have some issues getting the server set up.

Benefits of the PowerPivot Server

Here are some of the benefits of using PowerPivot Server:

- **Easier to share reports:** You can publish the report directly from the Excel File menu. Or, use the Upload button from your SharePoint site.

- **Security:** You are sharing the report but not the underlying data. No one can change formulas in the workbook. No one can drill down to the underlying data and accidentally delete 40 rows from the data set.

- **Fewer versions of the truth:** I hate when vendors talk about "one version of the truth." There is never one version of the truth. When they ask me to upload a report to the SharePoint library, it is just one more version of the truth than what existed before I uploaded the data to the SharePoint library. Now, I will admit that if you used to send a workbook to 40 people and you can now get 40 people going out to the SharePoint site, you will have fewer versions of the truth floating around.

- **Easy deployment of fixes:** If you discover an error in the data, you can change it in your version of the truth, upload it to the SharePoint site, and then everyone will have the new version after a refresh.

- **Beautiful Report gallery:** The gallery generated by SharePoint has amazing thumbnails. You will think someone spent a fortune to build the gallery.

- **You can go on vacation:** I think this is where they've got you. I think this is the hook. Microsoft provided this amazing client-side add-in that lets you create all sorts of amazing reports. Do you want to know the really, really, really bad downside? You have to show up to work to click the Refresh All button every day. Now, can you train a co-worker to do this while you spend a week at the beach? Sure. But, then you will be on the hook to run reports for that person when he or she is at the beach. The PowerPivot server is the only way to get AutoRefresh.

■ **The IT department will like PowerPivot:** There is a IT dashboard that will let them see which reports are popular and popular with whom. The IT department hates to be blindsided to find that a critical report has gone down, especially when they didn't even know that the critical report existed. With PowerPivot, your models are actually prototypes of future systems. The popular PowerPivot reports are items that the IT department may choose to formalize.

How the Report Looks in the Server

Figure 14.1 shows a PowerPivot model in Excel. As described in Chapter 13, "Final Formatting: Making The Report Not Look Like Excel," most of the Excel interface has been hidden.

Figure 14.1
Two pivot elements all controlled by four slicers make a nice dashboard.

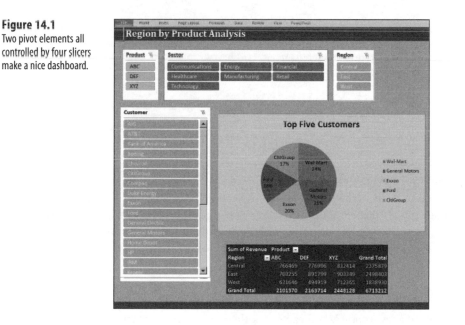

To get this file in your SharePoint gallery, you can either use File, Share, Publish to SharePoint, or upload from SharePoint. Follow these steps to upload the report:

1. Browse to your SharePoint site. Sign in.
2. In the left navigation bar, select your PowerPivot Gallery.
3. In the top navigation, select Library Tools, Documents.
4. Select Upload Document (see Figure 14.2).

14

Figure 14.2
Select Upload.

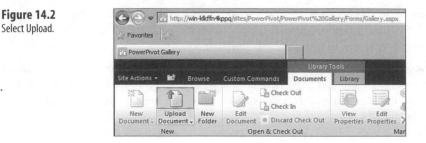

5. Browse for a file. After the file is uploaded, you can type a title for the file (see Figure 14.3).

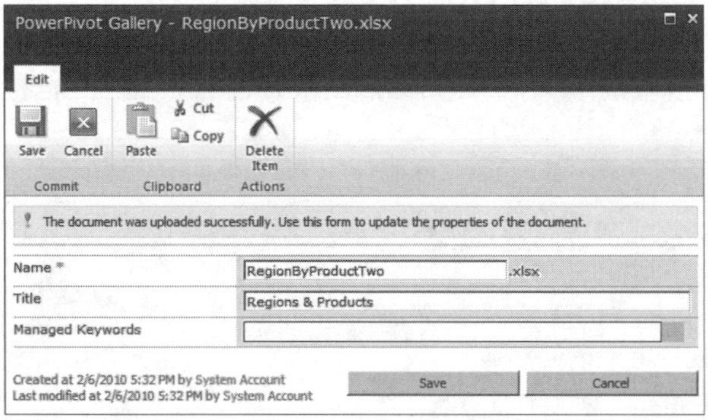

Figure 14.3
Type a title for the report.

When you open this report in SharePoint, it looks almost exactly like the report in Excel. (See Figure 14.4)

You can interact with the report by using the slicers. When you choose something from a slicer, the bottom-right corner of the screen indicates that SharePoint is working. During the "working" phase, SharePoint uses the external connection to the original database, changes the filters, gets the new numbers, and brings them back. The charts update, the pivot tables update. It is all pretty cool. (See Figure 14.5)

The Report Gallery Is Slick

After you upload a few reports, you can check them out in the Report gallery. The gallery uses Silverlight to actually generate thumbnails of the worksheet.

Figure 14.6 shows the default gallery view.

14

Figure 14.4
This isn't Excel. It is the
Excel workbook rendered
in a browser.

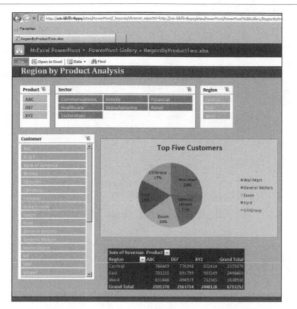

Figure 14.5
Change a slicer and the
worksheet updates.

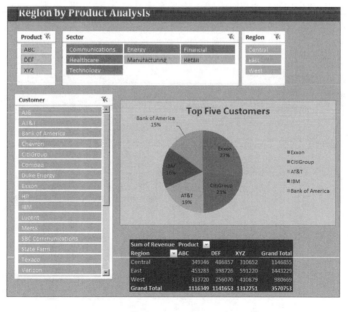

Figure 14.6
Even the boring gallery view is cool.

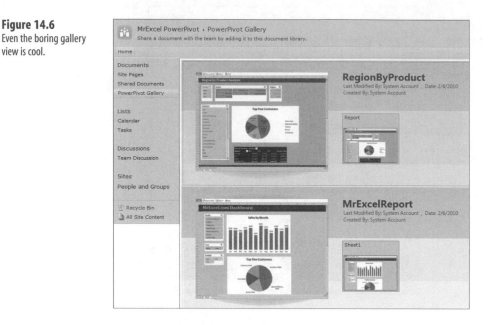

Figure 14.7 shows the theater view. In this view, thumbnails across the bottom show each report that has been uploaded. As you click the arrows to scroll through, you get a really large view of the data.

Figure 14.7
This is the theater view.

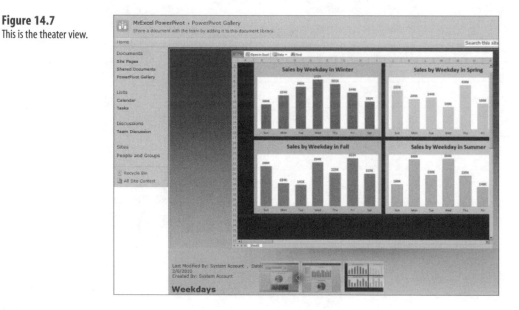

By far, though, the coolest view is called the carousel view. This reminds me of the iTunes Cover Flow, except instead of scrolling through classic albums like Born to Run and Foreigner IV, I am scrolling through Excel workbooks (workbooks that I created). It makes me feel like a rock star.

To give you a feel for how cool this is, Figure 14.8 and Figure 14.9 attempt to show you how the screen animates when you move from scroll through the reports.

Figure 14.8
Carousel view, before scrolling.

Figure 14.9
Carousel view, after scrolling.

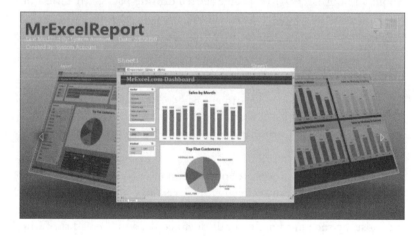

Why the IT Department Will Embrace PowerPivot

There is a love-hate relationship between the people in IT and the data analyst. As data analysts, we need to get our data from the IT department. Once we get that data, we tend to start producing our own reports.

> **NOTE** Frankly, working in Excel, data analysts can often develop useful reports much more quickly than our counterparts in the IT department. Usually, the IT department wants a complete specification before they start coding. As data analysts, we can start developing a report without a complete specification. We can start putting stuff together and run it past our manager for his feedback.

As my manager always says, "I don't need you to hit a home run, just get me to first base." And, the fact is that once we get that first report and we are at first base, new ideas always come up. The view of the field from first base always looks different. You might have some insights from the first phase of the report that makes you want to do something for the next phase of the report. This iterative process doesn't work at all when you are required to give the entire specification to the IT department before they start coding.

The PowerPivot reports published to the server are safer. People cannot get to the underlying data sets. There is less chance for someone to accidentally sort half the data and not all of the data.

One Microsoft guy loves to tell a story about a client visit. They were sitting around a conference table when every pager in the room started buzzing. All the IT people in the room stood up and left.

About an hour later, the IT people started drifting back in. It turns out that the company shipping system had gone down, causing everyone to panic. When IT had moved a server, the application was pointed at the wrong place, bringing the shipping system down.

The funniest line, though, came from one of the IT guys who said, "The strangest thing, is that we didn't even *know* that we had a company shipping system!"

So, someone out in some department had created a home-grown system that had been running fine, undetected, for who knows how long. It took the IT department moving the server for anyone to learn that there was a mission-critical shipping system running in the company.

The administrator of the SharePoint system has access to some amazing reports about PowerPivot. If they turn on logging, they can access reports that show them which are the most popular reports over the past 52 weeks. They can sort by which reports were accessed the most, by the most number of distinct people, and even a list of who is accessing which reports. If you manage to create a dashboard that is being accessed eight times a day by the company CEO, then the IT department can know that this report needs to keep running. They might actually consult with you before they move servers the next time.

Mistakes to Avoid When Publishing Reports to SharePoint

The following sections provide a few things I've learned through experience when publishing reports to the PowerPivot server.

Always Add Interactivity

People love to interact with the slicers. I have one report that I created without any slicers, and every time that I open it in SharePoint, it seems incredibly unsatisfying.

Always Select Cell A1 Before Saving a Workbook

The thumbnail in the Report gallery starts from the cell pointer and extends down and to the right. Although your view of the worksheet may look amazing, if you happen to leave the cell pointer in the lower-right corner of the screen, you are going to get a preview in the report gallery that looks like Figure 14.10.

Figure 14.10
If your cell pointer is not in cell A1, the thumbnail will not be what you expect.

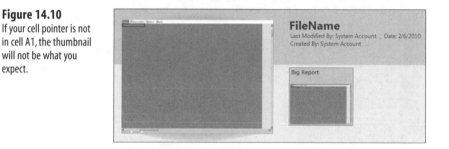

Further, when the report opens in SharePoint, the top-left corner of the report will be at the active cell pointer. You can always navigate up with PgUp and left with Shift+Tab.

Pictures Will Not Render on the Server

In Chapter 13, I showed two dashboards at the end. One had a title in row 1, and one had a banner and logo in A1. The banner is great when you are using the chart in the Excel client. If you are publishing to the server, go with the words rather than the banner. You get a red X and a message that this element is not supported if you go with the picture.

Hide All but the Main Worksheet

If you start with a data worksheet and add a four-chart pivot layout, you are going to have six worksheets in the workbook. If you publish that report to the server, thumbnails for all six worksheets will show up in the gallery. This just looks stupid (see Figure 14.11).

Figure 14.11
If you don't hide the extra worksheets, they appear as thumbnails.

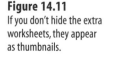

Whatever Is Not Hidden in Excel Shows Up in SharePoint

Take a look at the SharePoint report in Figure 14.12. This was a report that I put together quickly and published without paying attention. Because I forgot to hide the scrollbars and the row and column headers, they show up in the SharePoint report. It's not the end of the world, but it doesn't look as clean at the other reports.

Figure 14.12
If you forget to hide the row and column headers, they show up in SharePoint.

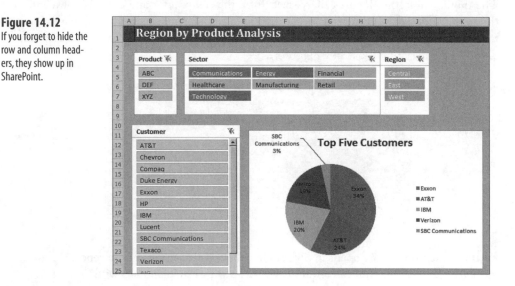

Next Steps

The appendix lists a variety of additional resources for PowerPivot.

More Resources

The information included in this appendix provides you with a variety of additional resources for PowerPivot. As with any new technology, early adopters are constantly discovering new ways to utilize the program. The blogs listed here will undoubtedly serve as a source of inspiration and troubleshooting as people test the limits of PowerPivot.

More PowerPivot Resources

Three different types of people are interested in PowerPivot:

- The Excel people. As one of those people, I wrote this book from the perspective of the 500 million Excel data analysts.
- The SQL Server people. I have to apologize. I can't even spell SQL.
- The SharePoint people looking for content.

These three disparate groups of people all are coming together to marvel over the wonders of PowerPivot.

> **NOTE**
> Although this book focuses on the Excel side of the equation, many blogs have sprung up that cover the other points of view.

Resources from Inside Microsoft

Many blogs and websites have been created by people who are on the PowerPivot team at Microsoft.

PowerPivot Team Blog

The official PowerPivot team blog focuses more on the server version of PowerPivot. Read insight from the PowerPivot team at http://blogs.msdn.com/powerpivot.

Rob Collie's PowerPivotPro.com

Rob spent some years as a project manager on the Excel team and worked as a project manager on PowerPivot. Rob has several great examples of using PowerPivot at http://www. PowerPivotPro.com. Rob has instructional videos, as well as sample data sets that you can download.

Donald Farmer's Twitter Feed

Donald Farmer is the Microsoft voice of PowerPivot. It was his demo at the 2008 MVP Summit when I realized this book had to become a reality. Watch his twitter stream at http://twitter.com/donalddotfarmer.

Dave Wickert Is the PowerPivot Geek

Dave, who works at Microsoft, has spent a lot of time on the SQL Server Analysis Services team. His blog is focused on the server side of PowerPivot. Check out his blog at http:// powerpivotgeek.com.

PowerPivot Twins Write About PowerPivot Best Practices

This blog name is clever when you consider that PowerPivot was originally codenamed Gemini. Dave Wickert and Denny Lee write about Excel best practices from the SQL Server point of view at http://powerpivottwins.com.

Resources from Outside Microsoft

With all due respect to the folks at Microsoft, they don't quite work in the real world. People outside of Microsoft frequently have to use Microsoft technologies to get their jobs done, and these folks have been testing PowerPivot as a means to improve their real-life reporting requirements. You will find these resources to be candid with any problems in PowerPivot and also with suggested workarounds.

The Great PowerPivot FAQ

Rob Collie started it, but many early adopters built it (including me). Visit the Great Power Pivot FAQ at http://powerpivotpro.com/the-faq.

Kasper de Jonge's Business Intelligence Blog

Kasper takes a look at PowerPivot from the point of view of a business intelligence consultant: http://business-intelligence.kdejonge.net.

Articles and a Forum at PowerPivot-Info

More great articles about the server side of PowerPivot. When I was first trying to install a SharePoint Server so that I could test out the server benefits of PowerPivot, the post by Vidas Matelis was invaluable. Vidas is a regular contributor at http://www.powerpivot-info.com.

Add-Ins for PowerPivot

While writing this book, I realized that the one thing that is sorely missing is a visual database map of your table structure. The MrExcel PowerPivot Data Visualizer add-in will be on the market by the time you are reading this book. To see details about this add-in, visit http://www.mrexcel.com/powerpivotaddin.html.

INDEX

informIT.com
THE TRUSTED TECHNOLOGY LEARNING SOURCE

PEARSON

InformIT is a brand of Pearson and the online presence for the world's leading technology publishers. It's your source for reliable and qualified content and knowledge, providing access to the top brands, authors, and contributors from the tech community.

Addison-Wesley | Cisco Press | EXAM/CRAM | IBM Press. | QUE | PRENTICE HALL | SAMS | Safari Books Online

LearnIT at InformIT

Looking for a book, eBook, or training video on a new technology? Seeking timely and relevant information and tutorials? Looking for expert opinions, advice, and tips? **InformIT has the solution.**

- Learn about new releases and special promotions by subscribing to a wide variety of newsletters.
  Visit **informit.com/newsletters**.

- Access FREE podcasts from experts at **informit.com/podcasts**.

- Read the latest author articles and sample chapters at **informit.com/articles**.

- Access thousands of books and videos in the Safari Books Online digital library at **safari.informit.com**.

- Get tips from expert blogs at **informit.com/blogs**.

Visit **informit.com/learn** to discover all the ways you can access the hottest technology content.

Are You Part of the IT Crowd?

Connect with Pearson authors and editors via RSS feeds, Facebook, Twitter, YouTube, and more! Visit **informit.com/socialconnect**.

informIT.com
THE TRUSTED TECHNOLOGY LEARNING SOURCE

PEARSON

Addison-Wesley | Cisco Press | EXAM/CRAM | IBM Press. | QUE | PRENTICE HALL | SAMS | Safari Books Online

FREE Online Edition

Your purchase of **Power Pivot for the Data Analyst: Microsoft® Excel 2010** includes access to a free online edition for 45 days through the Safari Books Online subscription service. Nearly every Que book is available online through Safari Books Online, along with more than 5,000 other technical books and videos from publishers such as Addison-Wesley Professional, Cisco Press, Exam Cram, IBM Press, O'Reilly, Prentice Hall, and Sams.

SAFARI BOOKS ONLINE allows you to search for a specific answer, cut and paste code, download chapters, and stay current with emerging technologies.

Activate your FREE Online Edition at www.informit.com/safarifree

> **STEP 1:** Enter the coupon code: WRJYYBI.

> **STEP 2:** New Safari users, complete the brief registration form.
> Safari subscribers, just log in.

Safari
Books Online